LAUREN RABINOVITZ AND

ABRAHAM GEIL, EDITORS

MEMORY BYTES

History, Technology, and Digital Culture

DUKE UNIVERSITY PRESS

DURHAM AND LONDON   2004

D1439723

Excerpt from "Burnt Norton" in *Four

Quartets* by T. S. Eliot, copyright 1936 by

Harcourt, Inc., and renewed 1964 by T. S.

Eliot, reprinted by permission of the pub-

lisher.

CONTENTS

Lauren Rabinovitz and Abraham Geil

INTRODUCTION

Discussions on the advent of digital culture now occur in most disciplines in the sciences and humanities. Literary critics address digital culture's radical challenge to book culture and print literacy. Sociologists query the quality of community and the structure and shape of newly forming institutions in cyberspace. Feminists ponder whether disembodied identities will result in a liberation from the asymmetries of gender relations or in the calcified lines of privilege and power. Anthropologists and human geographers consider the dynamics of computerized civilization. Communications and media specialists discuss both an ecology and political economy of a world organized around the dissemination and reception of information; and computer scientists, medical professionals, and philosophers alike worry about the ethical consequences of digital culture. All of these discussions share a larger, common concern for understanding recent consequences of social and physical change. Yet, they all too often displace what they have in common onto a duplicated language of revolution: talk about digital culture has been invested in throwing off the past and emphasizing what is unique, radical, revolutionary.

Discussions about digital culture assume that new computerized technologies provide such fundamental rupture from the past that there are no continuities or, worse, that they willfully obliterate the past in creating new models. Such ahistoricism is problematic because it tends to reproduce at the level of scholarship what is one of the hallmarks of digital culture—its rhetoric of newness. It is painfully obvious that this is neither the first technological revolution in human history nor an event independent from its cultural heritages and historical roots, and so a rhetoric of newness is at best a myopic one.

Current discussions fail to take into account how digital culture has come into its own. Over the course of the nineteenth century, capitalist industrialization drove a wide range of new technologies —telegraphic, telephonic, phonographic, and photographic—that remade society through tremendous social, political, and economic change and through radically reorganizing people's perceptions of time and space. These changes provided the cultural and technological basis for the twentieth century—for mass production, for modern and postmodern industrialization, and for the societies of consumption that have prevailed in the West during the twentieth century. To understand the current consequences of social and physical change—to understand digital culture—requires a philosophical and historical framework for a duration longer than the last twenty years.

The rhetoric of amnesia that surrounds current discussions of digital culture facilitates utopic as well as dystopic visions of the role of computer technologies in the twenty-first century. It provides a vision of the future that relieves anxiety over any imagined loss of control; in the celebration of revolution and uniqueness, it promises a new future rife with limitless possibilities. In its dystopian guise, the rhetoric of amnesia removes all agency from social subjects: a new technologically deterministic course of history takes the future out of our hands. In either case, the rhetoric of amnesia erases the complex interplay among the institutions—economic, juridical, and political—that selected, authorized, and deployed specific technologies over other possibilities and secured their development in highly specific ways for explicit purpose over time. The rhetoric of amnesia erases all that—the multiple relationships between culture and *techne* that have always been grounded in purpose and specific social interests. By obscuring the relationship of computer technologies to older modes of capitalist production and distribution, the status quo becomes naturalized and the material base of technology in history assumes transparency.

This is not to say that all discussions of digital culture are neglectful of history. But among the discussions that are growing at a tremendous rate of production—more than a dozen anthologies on digital culture have appeared in only the last five years—very few *think* historically or foreground the relationship of historical perspective to the current discussion. Most often, "history" stands apart and is represented by intellectuals of previous generations for their role as prophets or architects of what is to come (e.g., Marshall McLuhan's *Understanding Media* [1964] and *The Medium Is the Massage* [1967], Vannevar Bush's "As We May Think" [1945], Alan Turing's "Computing Machinery and Intelligence" [1950]). McLuhan forecasts the information society of the "global village"; Bush provides a prophecy of hypertextuality; Turing's discussion of artificial intelligence celebrates the future of disembodiment. One of the things that distinguishes these self-proclaimed visionaries from twentieth-century philosophers concerned with technology is that by popularizing the very concepts they proclaim, they changed social attitudes and values about the new technologies they were describing. In this regard, they are something of self-fulfilling prophets because they make popular the vision of society that they claim will result from new technological interventions. The history of prognostication omits dead ends and vain predictions and is ultimately history as teleology.

Another way that history often comes into play in discussions of digital culture is through the idea of remediation. That is, that new technologies, media in particular, always reinscribe what was already present in previous technologies. This works best in a history of media technologies as technics of representation with little regard to their material and institutional bases, and it has resulted in a linear history of transitions from cinema to television to hypermedia, the World Wide Web, and virtual reality. Such historical modeling suffers from two important narrowings of the field: it first reduces digitality to communications media and then reduces media technologies to their instantiation as *visual* representational forms. The latter especially ignores the status of movies, video, and the like as audio-visual representations so as to distance them from their intersection with telephonic, radio, and other communications technology industries. The result is digital culture merely as a linear history of technological representation and of visual signification. Using a teleological history of the media to understand digital culture is no corrective to the original problem of a rhetoric of amnesia—it is merely another form of amnesia.

What we need is to adopt a reflexive historical lens that attends to the dynamic of erasure itself in history writing as well as to who benefits from it. Through this approach, we may preserve a certain tension that serves both historical specificity and the relevance of the past to the present. Therefore, this volume foregrounds the very problem of how to draw historical comparisons across different technological and cultural moments. In this regard, *memory* is not cast as a simple antidote to forgetting but is a form of historical perspective in the truest sense of memory as in its Latin root *memor* or "mindful." The historical attitude of this volume accommodates multiple lines of inquiry into the social integration of new technologies by describing material and economic circumstances and by particularizing the interrelationship between machines and the formation of human subjectivity.

What Is Digital Culture?

Everyone uses the term digital culture, but no one defines it. It is one of those key terms that in its simplest usage merely designates a society saturated by telecommunications and information networks, electronic products, and computational systems based on binary data using electronic or electromagnetic signals. Depending on where the stress falls, *digital* culture can simply designate a discrete technological preoccupation. In this sense, the term simply describes one among a plurality of subcultures (e.g., car culture, music culture, gun culture)—with its own set of enthusiasts. In its broadest usage, however, digital *culture* becomes a trope for the ethos of contemporary life. In this sense, the essential qualities of Western culture in late modernity are described in terms of the salient features of digital technology: its speed, interchangeability, mutability, and so on. The *digital* then becomes the master sign for culture of the last decade, the years since 1970, or even the span of time since World War II.

Whatever the intention of its meaning, the ubiquitous usage of the term digital culture has two important underlying assumptions: (1) community revolves around distributed communication; and

(2) efforts to increase community take the form of new devices, systems, and technologies for abetting telecommunication. Many collections about digital culture are thus really about communication and the chain of new technologies that intensify speed, efficiency, and the symbolic systems themselves through which we communicate. Timothy Druckrey's *Electronic Culture: Technology and Visual Representation* defines digital culture through the transitions from cinema, television, and video to hypermedia, virtual reality, and cyberspace; he charts a course that demonstrates how communications systems increasingly technologize human experience.[1] John Caldwell's *Electronic Media and Technoculture* purposefully wrests definitions, terms, and discussions of digital culture away from the computer and software industries and popular journalism and makes media theorists the legitimate authorities for how modern society works.[2] Likewise, Peter Lunenfeld's *The Digital Dialectic: New Essays on New Media* tries to find a way for the practice and critical theory of new media to energize each other.[3] An array of essays, but especially those in Andrew Herman and Thomas Swiss's *The World Wide Web and Contemporary Cultural Theory* and Timothy Druckrey's two collections *Ars Electronica: Facing the Future* and *Electronic Culture: Technology and Visual Representation*, look to aesthetic strategies of new media forms as the means for producing an ontological map of digital culture.[4]

The contributors to this volume sanguinely accept such orientations and organizations of digital culture but go further than media-centric approaches. The essays herein are more concerned with what is at stake socially, politically, and ethically in the effects of digital culture. Toward this end, the definition of digital culture must also presume that digital culture is transformative of the individual and of the group. Most importantly, as a means of framing cultural experience it serves as a conduit for the confluence of power that technology, the government, and the corporation intertwine in the modern state.

In this sense, Martin Heidegger's 1949 essay, "The Question Concerning Technology," serves as an animus to the contributors' points of view.[5] Heidegger's interest in technology was neither utopic nor dystopic. He believed that technology's essence was not so much technical as instrumental in producing a mode of human existence. His concern at the time for the dangers of technology was for the ways that machines could alter social existence. Written immediately after the horrors of World War II and at the onset of what we think of as the computer age, Heidegger's essay serves as a conceptual bridge connecting the concerns of the history of technology and culture to the specifics of the digital.

The perceived threats of digital culture—from the eradication of book and print culture to the disappearance of community— often prevail in discussions that are more socially and politically committed. Volumes like *Digital Democracy: Discourse and Decision Making in the Information Age*; *On the Internet: Thinking in Action*; *Prometheus Wired: The Hope for Democracy in the Age of Network Technology*; and *Reading Digital Culture* worry about whether or not cybersociety opens or closes possibilities for a more democratic society.[6] As representatives of these approaches, influential critical theorists Mark Poster and Avital Ronell are concerned about the Internet's effects of disengagement from public life, its consequent eradication of community, and its undermining of a public sphere of informed-citizen discussion.[7] It is important to remember, however, that these issues did not simply arise in the late 1990s after the Internet became a widespread part of Western culture, but were in fact historically bound up with the Internet's origins in the cold war era.

Authors also regularly express concern about continuing oppression in digital culture, especially the ways that new technologies are used to reinscribe class disparities and exploit labor. In *Reading Digital Culture*, for example, Stanley Aronowitz's "Technology and the Future of Work" and Arthur Kroker and Michael A. Weinstein's "The Theory of the Virtual Class" are both important critical analyses of the material conditions of living in an immaterial world.[8] They move well beyond technologically deterministic narratives by grounding their histories in social, economic, and political contexts. Nevertheless, as Roy Rosenzweig's survey of recent scholarship on the history of the Internet suggests, such contexts themselves often constitute highly conflicted arenas.[9]

This volume on the one hand builds on the best of these earlier works while, on the other, seeks not to engage further polemics about digital culture's reifying and totalizing effects. Rather, the historical orientation of this volume enables a consideration of how and why technology, the government, and the corporation converged to the extent that their interconnections produce such cause for alarm.

Digital culture needs to be understood as at once an outgrowth of Enlightenment thought and an agent of its steady erosion. Western assumptions originating in the eighteenth century about the relationship between the liberal subject, technology, and the modern state continue to set the terms for talk about technology's capacity to change society. The Industrial Revolution is the technological and social upheaval against which the digital revolution is measured. In discussions of digital culture, the Enlightenment *stands* as a kind of "structuring absence."

Promises of self-determination made in the name of digital culture are implicit invocations of the Enlightenment view that individual identity is rooted in rational thought. The liberal humanist subject, conceived as a self-possessing autonomous individual capable of entering into voluntary market relations under the regulation of a social contract, represents the Enlightenment ideal of human emancipation and agency. Hence, whatever new technologies enhance the individual's rational exercise of economic and political capacities are liberatory within the terms of Enlightenment thought. By the same terms, new technologies that appear to suppress those capacities threaten the freedom of the liberal subject. Criticism about new technologies often gets expressed in the fear that the liberal subject will be forced to submit to antidemocratic corporate control.

At the same time, N. Katherine Hayles holds out a third position that does not make agency contingent on the continuity of the liberal subject. While the liberal subject has already been critiqued as something that never really existed historically but masqueraded as a universal ideal in order to serve specific political projects of domination and oppression, Hayles crystallizes a new model of subjectivity in the "posthuman."[10] Since the Enlightenment, the continuous integration of man and machine has led to a steady erosion of the notion of the "human" as a distinct individual thinking subject. Because this process blurs the line between bodily existence and intelligent machines, human identity is no longer exclusively located in individual people as such but rather is distributed across biological and technological systems.

Hayles, even in revising the categories for human subjectivity, still defines the posthuman as a historical development in relation to the legacy of the Enlightenment. She writes: "The historical processes leading to this [transformation from 'human' to 'posthuman'] . . . were never complete transformations or sharp breaks; without exception, they reinscribed traditional ideas and assumptions even as they articulated something new. . . . 'Human' and 'posthuman' coexist in shifting configurations that vary with historically specific contexts."[11] Following Hayles's reasoning, we claim that digital culture is neither simply a rupture from Enlightenment thinking nor Enlightenment's final flowering.

By assuming the origins of digital culture in the Enlightenment, we are setting up a self-consciously Western history. More narrowly, this volume is an inquiry into the relationship between culture and technology from the point of view of the United States and, although we encompass historical connections from the Enlightenment to the present, our definition of digital culture is also contingent on a history of post–World War II computing in the United States. After World War II, three strains stemming from the Enlightenment—*techne*, the subject, and the state—converge in a new way with the development of computing. The history of computing cannot simply be made to stand in for a definition of digital culture, but it is necessary to that definition.

The origins of modern computing are to be found in the techno-military context of World War II. The new strategic demands of the war drove massive government investment in computer technology in Germany, Britain, and the United States. With the end of the war, the buildup of apparatus, expertise, and investment for airplane and missile technology, code breaking, and other military applications extended to industrial and civilian government uses. Many of these technologies did not have to remain secret any longer.

A key figure in this transformation from wartime computer research to civilian and corporate application is Vannevar Bush. Bush, a former professor of electrical engineering at MIT and participant in the Manhattan Project, was a top advisor to President Franklin Roosevelt during the war. Even during the war, in 1944, Roosevelt was already thinking about how to apply the lessons from World War II to civilian, peacetime activities, and he asked Bush to study the problem. Six years later, Bush's recommendations led to the formation of the National Science Foundation, with Bush as its first director. By 1945, however, Bush had already popularized these concerns when he asked in the *Atlantic Monthly* what social role scientists should play in the wake of their wartime involvement.[12]

Bush's *Atlantic Monthly* article, "As We May Think," specifically addresses the problem of how American scientists who had put aside institutional and other rivalries for the war effort might continue to share information. For him, the chief obstacle that lay ahead was not competition but the surfeit of information and the acceleration of scientific specialization in the wake of World War II. He offers a technological antidote in his conception of the memex, a device he had already been thinking and writing about for over a decade. As a kind of dream tool of the information age, the memex would be "a device in which an individual stores all his books, records, and communications, and which is mechanized so that it may be consulted with exceeding speed and flexibility."[13] The memex, in other words, would contain no less than "the record of the race," and moreover it would preserve and organize that record with a kind of "associative" architecture that mimicked the structure of human memory.[14] Bush's thinking about the memex depends on an analogical relationship between the individual mind and larger structures, which means between organic memory and networked systems.

While Bush focused on how to optimize the technology of information storage and retrieval by modeling it on memory, the field of cybernetics simultaneously generalized the analogy between organism and machine and extended it to the widest possible range of fields of knowledge. The term *cybernetics* describes the study of communication and control in living organisms or machines, and it comes from the title of Norbert Wiener's pathbreaking 1948 book on theories of feedback control processes.[15] Wiener originally developed his ideas through their application to antiaircraft artillery control during World War II.

Under the auspices of the Josiah Macy Jr. Foundation, ten conferences on cybernetics were held between 1946 and 1953. Organized and chaired by the neurophysiologist Warren McCulloch, the Macy conferences were dedicated to a radically interdisciplinary exploration of cybernetics. Participants included the mathematicians John von Neumann, Walter Pitts, Norbert Wiener; engineers Heinz von Foerster, Claude Shannon; anthropologists Margaret Mead and Gregory Bateson; social psychologist Alex Babelas; and scholars from the fields of philosophy, semantics, and literature. Indeed, as

N. Katherine Hayles has shown, the very ability of the conference participants to communicate with one another across disciplinary boundaries depended largely on the use of metaphor: a specialist in one field could adopt a mechanism from another by associating it metaphorically with a mechanism familiar to her or his own work.[16] This form of interdisciplinary communication replicates the logic of feedback that is fundamental to cybernetics. The Macy conferences initiated the logic by which digitality could be understood as cultural.

This is not to say that the U.S. military assumed anything less than a central role in the post–World War II development of computing. Although private industries and government civilian agencies carried out important research and development, they often did so under Defense Department contracts or with an eye to the military as a reliable market. As historian Roy Rosenzweig notes, "in 1950, for example, the federal government—overwhelmingly, its military agencies—provided 75 to 80 percent of computer development funds."[17] Although companies like UNIVAC (Universal Automatic Computer) and IBM (International Business Machines) built supercomputers that were used by entities such as the U.S. Census Bureau and General Electric, they worked for a market dominated by cold war military priorities. As writer Frank Rose points out, "the computerization of society has essentially been a side effect of the computerization of war."[18]

Even the Internet, one of today's most culturally ubiquitous applications of computer technology, has its origins in U.S. cold war military defense strategies. In the 1950s the U.S. Department of Defense faced a concern about how to maintain a command-and-control network of communication in the event of a nuclear strike. Because any central authority would be an immediate enemy target, the department sought the means to establish a decentralized communications network that would be invulnerable to attack because it would be disbursed and able to continue operation even if any point it was disabled. Throughout the 1960s, government-sponsored research into such a "blast-proof" network for maintaining national security occurred at the Rand Corporation and at MIT and UCLA.[19] In 1969, ARPANET (Advanced Research Project Agency Network) began operation at UCLA: it was an infant high-speed network for transmitting data over long distances. As the federal government's ARPANET grew and expanded in the 1970s, the researchers who had access to it used it for a purpose additional to its original intention. Rather than using it to transmit computing data, they treated it as a personal communications medium by sending long-distance personal and informational messages to their fellow researchers. Soon these workers had developed "mailing lists" for sending batches of communications to those who shared the same hobbies, side interests, and personal pastimes. The network grew rapidly because it was unlike standard corporate computer networks that depended on having similar machines. The very means that made ARPANET decentralized—that it did not depend on any one type of computer—meant that so long as any individual computer could speak the packet-switching language of the network it could become linked to the system.

At the same time, some of the university researchers who had access to ARPANET began to question and resist the government-authorized projects in which they were involved that were connected, even indirectly, to U.S. war operations. While the decentralized communication of ARPANET was designed to preserve the central authority (the "command and control") of the government in the event of nuclear war, many of ARPANET's first generation of users saw its promise for just the opposite: the dissolution of central authority in a nonhierarchical organization of society. In the climate of the Vietnam antiwar movement of the late 1960s and early 1970s and the formation of a counterculture centered at university campuses across the United States, ARPANET users began to take command of the network as a means for more grassroots, democratic participation among their peers.

By the 1980s, ARPANET became linked to other government networks at NASA, the National Science Foundation, the Department of Energy, the National Institutes of Health, and others. As the single network became a network of networks, technical advances occurred regularly so that speed, efficiency, and a conventional infrastructure all expanded into the Internet configuration that is familiar today. In 1989, ARPANET expired—a victim of its own success and seriously outdated and overpowered by its heirs. What is important here is that what rapidly became in the 1990s a cultural institution, a high-speed and high-tech communications medium, and a symbol of digital culture cannot be separated from the social, material, and economic conditions that gave rise to it and shaped its applications. Indeed, the origins of the Internet still inevitably shape today's discussions about its political valence as a communications medium. Does the Internet open up possibilities for democratic participation or further shut them down? Is it a medium of the people or an engine of corporate and governmental dominance? Although we do not mean to suggest that the only way to take up these questions is in such simple binary terms, it is important to focus on the fact that these issues did not arise only in the 1990s after the Internet had become a widespread, integral part of Western culture, but rather were always structurally part of its development.

It may have been too easy to forget that the development of computer technologies has a material and political base once leisure and entertainment, education and the workplace, and health and medicine all became dependent on digital technologies in order to function successfully. By the 1990s, digitality and the computerized technologies that employ this process were no longer a matter of augmentation or luxury but an essential infrastructure of modern society. Their widespread development and application for a home-consumer market resulted in everything from the consumption of music to the automobile to the kitchen oven as commodified products of digital technologies. Such a move was neither predetermined nor an unexpected byproduct of scientific and government research but instead a complex consequence of three decades of technological progress in miniaturization, the importation from non-Western countries of new technological advances as well as the cheap manufacturing labor that they offered, and the important U.S. "engine" of market-driven profits from the sales of consumer goods. Such political and economic conditions make one's music CD (and its player), one's car, and one's kitchen microwave more than wonders, achievements unavailable to our grandparents, and conveniences of modern everyday life in the twenty-first century. They are all steeped in the politics of their production, material bases, and technological intersection with larger cultural issues. When one goes for a ride, relaxes with a tune, or heats up a fast-food snack, one also represses the politics of the history of the relationships between machines and human subjectivity that have resulted in the present moment. This volume seeks to undo that repression: it asks what we can learn from the past that provides a philosophical and historical framework for the sets of issues being framed for the way we live today in contemporary digital culture.

The collection of essays in this book stresses four broad themes: (1) it defines digital culture in relationship to the information age but also as a political and cultural phenomenon larger and older than the information age; (2) it historicizes the digital and its antecedents in terms of multisensory effects and as somatic experience; (3) it attends to the integral interrelationship between machines and how human subjectivity has been historically formed; and (4) it particularizes technologies as dependent on their material and economic circumstances. The essays may individually bridge different disciplines from the social sciences and humanities, but they collectively have common concerns. Most of the volume's contributors wrote their essays while participants in the University of Iowa Obermann Center for Advanced Studies Summer 2000 Interdisciplinary Research Seminar. This three-week seminar, directed by Lauren Rabinovitz, brought together ten scholars from different disciplines, universities, and regions in order to study, read about, and write on the themes in this volume in an intensive learning atmosphere. Seminar fellows developed their ideas through lively exchanges with each other and through shared readings and lectures that cut across disciplinary boundaries. The result was not only a transdisciplinary approach to the subject but also a truly synthetic one that regardless of each individual topic maintains a vision of a larger coherent whole.

To assist the reader in preserving the larger, more synthetic claims and issues that motivated, animated, and linked together these discussions, the separate studies that comprise this volume have been grouped into four thematic sections or categories, including "Intellectual Histories of the Information Age," "Visual Culture, Subjectivity, and the Education of the Senses," "Materiality, Time, and the Reproduction of Sound and Motion," and "Digital Aesthetics, Social Texts, and Art Objects."

In the first section, the authors provide three case studies of the relationship between intellectuals' formative work on technology and their ideological underpinnings. They offer a snapshot intellectual history that encompasses the Enlightenment, the Romantic era, and Modernism in the first half of the twentieth century, and they lay the groundwork for the intellectual orientation of the information age that follows World War II. In the first of these studies, Laura

Rigal calls for a critical history of electricity from the Enlightenment to the present that accounts for the way that theories of electricity are embedded in the ideological and economic foundations of the state. Through a reading of Benjamin Franklin's widely circulated 1751 pamphlet, Rigal demonstrates that Franklin's model of electrical charges and discharges was not merely technical, it also was an elastic, efficient ideological mechanism for elaborating the dynamics of economic expansion and social control within the emerging federalist state. David Depew traces a history of the scientific rhetoric of the body from the Victorian era to the mid-twentieth century to show how the body as figured as a thermodynamic heat engine became replaced by an image of a kind of printout from a hydrocarbon-based computer display. He shows conclusively how the recent reception of the Human Genome Project is tied to a picture of the body as digital that is both a product of self-conscious rhetoric and a matter for concern insofar as it screens out energetic, ecologically embedded views of the body. In the third essay in this section, Ronald E. Day argues that the positivist logic of the information age has worked to erase its own history. He looks at the careers of two forgotten but important advocates for the positivist organization of information in the mid-twentieth century: Paul Otlet and Suzanne Briet. At the same time, he reexamines two famous theorists of modernity—Martin Heidegger and Walter Benjamin—as important critics of that emerging information age. By recovering both the advocates and critics of earlier information ages, we may learn how current meanings of information, knowledge, and language have a highly conflicted, less than inevitable history.

The second section, "Visual Culture, Subjectivity, and the Education of the Senses," deals exclusively with the ongoing historical relationship between technological applications in audio-visual or highly somatic experiences (often linked in the twentieth century to "entertainment") and the production of ideological states of consciousness. Using examples both from very early and very recent cinema, Lauren Rabinovitz shows how technologically futuristic movies have only addressed a *fantasy* of disembodiment while they actually emphasize physical presence and the delirium of multiple senses. They have played a regular, crucial historical role in preserving knowledge grounded in the body when radical technological transformation has prompted a crisis in visually ascertaining truth. The second essay in the section also treats the relationship of disembodied and embodied viewing practices with the discovery of knowledge. Judith Babbits describes how at the turn of the twentieth century progressive educators adapted stereographs in an attempt to standardize teaching techniques and to inculcate an American national culture across an increasingly diverse population. The proliferation of stereographs and the rhetorical strategies of the stereograph industry were central both to the construction of a paradigm of visual knowledge and to a modern theory of vision.

In a sly move, the last essay in the second section brings home the message that even in the world of leisure and entertainment, the relationship between the U.S. military and the postwar world of the development of computing remains integral. Sharon Ghamari-Tabrizi analyzes the curious convergence of the Pentagon and Hollywood when, in 1999, the U.S. Army gave $45 million to the University of Southern California in order to establish the Institute of Creative Technologies, a center for developing cutting-edge virtual reality military training simulations that would deliver the emotional impact of Hollywood movies. Using government documentation and defense industry publications, Ghamari-Tabrizi shows how the Pentagon became convinced that the way to improve "realism" in military simulation was to incorporate methods of "good storytelling" practiced by entertainment professionals. The Pentagon's aim was to produce an emotionally immersive experience to match the somatic immersion provided by the newest virtual reality technology.

The third section, "Materiality, Time, and the Reproduction of Sound and Motion," opens with an essay by John Durham Peters that probes the intimate connection between the study of physiology and the explosion of media technologies in the nineteenth century. Although Marshall McLuhan linked media and physiology some time ago, he neglected to pursue the connection with the historical research this essay provides—research that shows how media were fashioned precisely as "artificial portals" to the human nervous system. Through the work of the German scientist Hermann von Helmholtz and the American inventor-entrepreneur Thomas Edison, Peters examines the foundational moments in the history of sound recording. More than just an intellectual and technological history of the phonograph, this essay is also a meditation on the ways media retroactively redefine previously accepted standards of human capacity as fragile and flawed.

In the next essay, Lisa Gitelman argues for how the material meanings of any new technology centrally contribute to the history of its social integration. Too often, materiality disappears behind the mutually reinforcing auras of transparency and inevitability. To counter this tendency, Gitelman focuses on a specific material—paper—and the historical case of the cultural and legal conflicts over the status of player piano rolls. She traces the ways that the emergence of listening habits, technical standards, new corporate structures, copyright strictures, and the like instituted a cultural hierarchy among mechanized player pianos (the hardware) and their paper rolls (the software). The "matter of piano rolls" is a precedent for the confusion over the intellectual property status occasioned by digital technologies such as eBook, e-paper, and MP3 files.

The third essay in this section shifts from a shared set of concerns regarding the materialist bases of media technologies as such to the application of those same technologies within the institution of medicine—specifically analyzing such digital medical imaging techniques as computed tomography (CT) and magnetic resonance imaging (MRI). Scott Curtis argues that while such new technologies of medical motion pictures have seemingly revolutionized the way physicians "read" the human body, the interpretation of the human body relies on a dialectic steeped in the material basis of the image—between stillness (the corpse, the medical illustration) and movement (the living human body). He illuminates the philosophical relationship between cinema and medicine by tracing its historical echo to digital medical imaging.

The final section of the book, "Digital Aesthetics, Social Texts, and Art Objects," concludes with a series of essays that examine *new* art objects that are the result of recent digital technologies. The essays consider the historical dimensions that impinge on the entire domain of any aesthetics of digital culture; they take into account the longstanding relationships among books, painting, and sculpture—art writ large—and bodies as the means to stand in for one another in a metaphorical connection between word and flesh or picture and flesh. Do these "metaphoric networks" between bodies and art texts undergo any reconfiguration once texts cease to take material form and manifest instead in the electronic forms of digital media? Do the bodies represented within them undergo a corresponding transformation in embodiment? To directly address these concerns, N. Katherine Hayles closely examines two pairs of works in digital media and shows how gender as a central category of embodiment is transfigured in the creation of these new textual bodies.

In the next essay, which shifts the focus from new media art objects themselves to the discourses surrounding them from the late-1980s through the 1990s, Thomas Swiss argues that the debates on the status of electronic literature reveal a deep cultural anxiety over digitization. He illustrates how in the early years an avant-garde community of hypertext artist/authors resembled earlier modernist literary avant-gardes. The passing of this "golden age" followed the same path as many historical avant-gardes: digital literature lost its disruptive function of opposing dominant institutions of American literary culture and achieved a more central status within those institutions.

The last essay seeks to preserve an artifact of digital technology — the QuickTime movie — by isolating it from the "quickening" flow of a cinematic art that aims for the seamless reproduction of reality. Vivian Sobchack compares the phenomenological experience of QuickTime movies and Joseph Cornell's "boxed relics" sculptures from the 1930s and 1940s. By putting these objects in relation to one another, Sobchack shows how the very qualities that technicians wish to remove from QuickTime movies — their stuttering transmission, fragmentation, and miniature framing — have the aesthetic power to evoke the experience of memory and desire through an "aesthetics of absence."

The contributors to this volume propose a change in approach to current concerns about digital culture by examining historical models for the social integration of new technologies. While some of the authors emphasize those past practices that inform or provide the foundations for the present, and others explore more fully present practices (especially facets of the World Wide Web) that borrow from the past, they all treat digital culture itself as a historical phenomenon. The authors make history writing and the dynamic of erasure itself in history writing central preoccupations throughout this volume, yet they do not naively regard the elucidating effects of history here as a panacea. Rather, they focus on — and thus the volume highlights — the thorny dilemma of how to draw historical comparisons across different technological and cultural moments.

1 Timothy Druckrey, *Electronic Culture: Technology and Visual Represen-tation* (New York: Aperture, 1996).
2 John Thornton Caldwell, ed., *Electronic Media and Technoculture* (New Brunswick: Rutgers University Press, 2000).
3 Peter Lunenfeld, *The Digital Dialectic: New Essays on New Media* (Cambridge: MIT Press, 1999).
4 Andrew Herman and Thomas Swiss, eds., *The World Wide Web and Contemporary Cultural Theory* (New York: Routledge, 2000); Timothy Druckery, ed., *Ars Electronica: Facing the Future: A Survey of Two Decades* (Cambridge: MIT Press, 1999); Druckrey, *Electronic Culture.*
5 Martin Heidegger, "The Question Concerning Technology," in *Basic Writings*, ed. David Farrell Krell (San Francisco: Harper Collins, 1977).
6 Barry N. Hague and Brian Loader eds., *Digital Democracy: Discourse and Decision Making in the Information Age* (New York: Routledge, 1999); Hubert L. Dreyfus, *On the Internet, Thinking in Action* (New York: Routledge, 2001); Darin Barney, *Prometheus Wired: The Hope for Democracy in the Age of Network Technology* (Chicago: University of Chicago Press, 2000); David Trend, ed., *Reading Digital Culture* (Malden, Eng.: Blackwell Publishers, 2001).
7 Mark Poster, *What's the Matter with the Internet?* (Minneapolis: University of Minnesota Press, 2001); Avital Ronell, *The Telephone Book: Technology—Schizophrenia—Electric Speech* (Lincoln: University of Nebraska Press, 1989).
8 Stanley Aronowitz, "Technology and the Future of Work," in Trend, ed., *Reading Digital Culture*, 133–43; Arthur Kroker and Michael A. Weinstein, "The Theory of the Virtual Class," in Trend, ed., *Reading Digital Culture*, 144–53.
9 Roy Rosenzweig, "Wizards, Bureaucrats, Warriors, and Hackers: Writing the History of the Internet," *American Historical Review* 103, no. 5 (December 1998): 1530–52.
10 N. Katherine Hayles, *How We Became Posthuman: Virtual Bodies in Cybernetics, Literature, and Informatics* (Chicago: University of Chicago Press, 1999).
11 Ibid., 6.
12 Vannevar Bush, "As We May Think," *Atlantic Monthly* (July 1945): 101–8.
13 Ibid., 106–7.
14 The ways that the memex is in fact prophetic of contemporary modes of producing, storing, and disseminating information facilitated by personal computers, hypertext, and the Internet is a point that has not been lost on numerous scholars of digital culture.

15 Norbert Wiener, *Cybernetics; or, Control and Communication in the Animal and the Machine* (Cambridge: Technology Press, 1948).

16 Hayles, *How We Became Posthuman*, 51.

17 Rosenzweig, "Wizards, Bureaucrats, Warriors, and Hackers," 1538.

18 Quoted in Paul N. Edwards, *The Closed World: Computers and the Politics of Discourse in Cold War America* (Cambridge: MIT Press, 1996), 65.

19 "Blast-proof" is Bruce Sterling's term. See his "Short History of the Internet," available on the Web at: http://www.library.yale.edu/ div/instruct/internet/history.htm.

PART I

INTELLECTUAL HISTORIES

OF THE INFORMATION AGE

Laura Rigal

IMPERIAL ATTRACTIONS

Benjamin Franklin's *New Experiments* of 1751

If any one should doubt whether the electrical matter passes through the substance of bodies, or only over and along their surfaces, a shock from an electrified large glass jar, taken through his own body, will probably convince him.

Thus common matter is a kind of spunge [*sic*] to the electrical fluid. — BENJAMIN FRANKLIN, *New Experiments and Observations on Electricity*

American cultural historians have typically focused upon Benjamin Franklin's lightning rod and kite experiments as the most meaningful of his electrical innovations of the 1740s and 1750s. The folk mythology of Franklin's kite-flying adventure, for example, has become a byword for a democratic, do-it-yourself "American" scientific culture, in which ordinary people using ordinary materials produce extraordinary results. Franklin's invention of the lightning rod has made him similarly accessible to Whig allegory as a "modern Prometheus" bringing fire from heaven and stealing thunder from kings and gods. Franklin's most significant contribution to electrical science as cultural practice was not his lightning rod, however, but his single-fluid model of electricity and the "discovery" and naming of "positive" versus "negative" electrical charges.[1] Indeed, Franklin could not have imagined performing experiments with lightning without having first articulated his model of a single electrical fluid operating according to the principle of bipolar charges, a fluid that could then be "drained" from the clouds by means of a pointed rod or wire.[2]

Elaborated throughout his *New Experiments and Observations on Electricity, made at Philadelphia in America* (1751, 1753, 1769, 1774), Franklin's single-fluid model and his theory of charges were demonstrated in comparatively mundane performances such as "the electric kiss," the "electric party," or "the electric book."[3] Unlike his famous kite experiment, these were not particularly original in form but rather closely mimicked electrical entertainments already being performed in European courts and philosophical circles.[4] Unlike the lightning rod, moreover, experiments like "the electric kiss" did not pretend to shield organic beings from electrical power; on the contrary, they inserted human bodies directly into Franklin's electrical system as conduits of the electrical fluid and witness to its effects.

When Franklin first began to perform experiments in Philadelphia in 1745, he entered a highly politicized world of European electrical investigation in which British, French, Dutch, and German experimenters played a leading role. Many of the parameters of electrical experiment had already been marked out by British exhibitors (such as William Watson, Benjamin Rackstrow, and Benjamin Martin), when in 1751 Watson read a paper before the Royal Society summarizing Franklin's contributions. Like Franklin, Watson had spent the late 1740s sending electricity across rivers, igniting alcoholic "spirits," and directing electric shocks through the bodies of variously connected ladies and gentlemen.[5] And, like Watson, Franklin would exploit the Newtonian doctrine of active fluids (sometimes called "electrical *aether*") elaborated in Newton's texts as well as in those by Homberg and Boerhaave.[6]

Franklin used numerous metaphors to describe the Newtonian flows of his electricity, calling it variously a "fluid," a "fire," or an "aether," consisting of "particles extremely subtile [*sic*] that can permeate common matter, even the densest metals, with . . . ease and freedom."[7] But Franklin's electrical matter was, above all, a single, unitary substance and his *New Experiments* are, therefore, an extended demonstration of the conservation of charges, whereby "any production of a positive charge in one body (a net gain in electrical fluid) is always accompanied by an equal and opposite negative charge (a net loss in electrical fluid) in one or more other bodies."[8] The shocking or entertaining effects of plus (+) and minus (−) charges remain embedded in the underlying "sameness" of a fluid that "is equally diffused in our walls, floors, earth, and the whole mass of common matter." Thus, Franklin writes, friction "will produce electrical fire, not by creating, but collecting it."[9] The terms plus (+) and minus (−) mathematize the accumulations (+) or evacuations (−) of an electrical fluid that could be collected or subtracted via conduction or, conversely, contained or blocked by nonconducting materials. When set in motion by the electrician the fluid simply circulates, creating remarkable effects (and affects) in the process of "electrising" or "de-electrising" the bodies brought into contact with the system—until it reaches equilibrium or again finds "its original equality."[10]

Historian of science Otto Mayr has argued that the eighteenth-century origins of cybernetic systems must be traced to pneumatic and steam technologies, and especially to James Watt's centrifugal "governor" of 1788, a mechanical feedback device that automatically controlled the intake of steam in relation to engine load.[11] By contrast, Franklin's electrical experiments of the 1740s and 1750s do not describe any such automatic, self-governing device capable of feeding information—about results, or output—back into a dynamic system. Yet while they do not technically anticipate closed-circuit feedback systems, Franklin's New Experiments are indispensable to narrating the history of the adoption or assimilation of such systems by other (social, political, and cultural) systems. This examination of Franklin's New Experiments argues that the origin of cybernetics must be traced not only to a collection of mechanical or intellectual devices but also to the emergence of a remarkably simple code. Stated as a mathematical relation, Franklin's +/− installed the principle of dynamic balance as a universal inscription device. A sign system so simple and insistent that it outstripped (while integrating) all signifieds, Franklin's device preceded, and then accompanied, the development of early industrial technologies such as Watt's steam engine. Franklin's +/− was a "metacode" that put into circulation the binary structure of systematicity itself. Readily suturing to the dynamic binaries that constituted other systems and macrosystems, it revealed their structures to be parallel and thus accessible to integration. Even today, any "open" (yet closed) dynamic system that is marked by speed and universal penetration is often denominated "electric."

As a result +/– was also, however, a management device that promised control over unruly energies that threatened (even while they were becoming vital resources for) an imperial, early industrial nation-state. This is why Franklin's articulation of electrical "flows" helps to explain the dynamics of digital assimilation today, particularly the mixture of conflict and (ultimately) consensus that structures the way in which Americans absorb and adapt to new technologies. In this essay I focus on those experiments in which Franklin's sign system +/– functions to integrate an array of objects and bodies while working at the same time to suture larger institutional, political, social, and even economic systems into a virtually integrated whole. Because Franklin's electrical ideas were put into circulation in the form of published letters and papers (in books, pamphlets, or magazines) it is necessary to begin with his medium, the printed text of his *New Experiments*, and, within it, his predilection for experimenting on the physical bodies of books themselves.

Franklin's *New Experiments* of 1751 circulated in the form of a scientific pamphlet. The first edition consisted of twelve letters and papers addressed primarily to Peter Collinson, a Fellow of the British Royal Society and a London merchant. While the *New Experiments* eventually went through five London editions between 1751 and 1774, the papers of the first edition were, for the most part, reprinted in each of the subsequent editions.[12] The genre and style of the writings collected in the *New Experiments* are closely adapted from the "good-humoured" prose of eighteenth-century magazines or periodical essays, such as the London *Gentleman's Magazine*, the *Tatler*, the *Spectator*, and the straightforward style of essays in the *Transactions of the British Royal Society*. In fact, excerpts of Franklin's experiments eventually appeared in both the *Gentleman's Magazine* and the Royal Society's *Transactions*, and it was editor Edmund Cave of the *Gentleman's Magazine* who published the first edition of the *New Experiments*.

Performed in response to, and for, publication, Franklin's *New Experiments* constitute a form of what Bruno Latour calls "paperwork," or science performed inseparably from the writing and the publishing of texts.[13] But while the *New Experiments* operated as paperwork at the level of London publishing, they also operated as paperwork at a more mathematized level of inscription because they put into circulation the marks of (+) and (−) that are still used to indicate positive versus negative electrical charges.[14] Historian of science Simon Schaffer observes that Franklinian electricity eventually won out over numerous French and British competitors, most of whom had been in the field long before Franklin. Shaffer argues that Franklin's success was due to the fact that Franklin managed to avoid the kind of political and social controversy that inhibited the reception and advancement of European experiments.[15] Other historians have suggested that Franklin's originality was due to his comparative isolation in Philadelphia where he could think more independently or with a kind of freshness, so that his theory suddenly gave "a single unified account of all the data of the subject and thereby for the first time congealed a miscellaneous collection of knowledge into the rigid form of a single unified scientific discipline."[16] However, Franklin's bipolar electrical fluid was not merely "American," it was Anglo-American. And its most original features must be attributed to the fact that his single-fluid model of charges was an economic model that primarily replayed—albeit in a more efficient, streamlined form—the structural dynamics of an expanding British industrial state.

Written in an accessible, plain style, Franklin's *New Experiments* read like electrical recipes or do-it-yourself magic tricks that almost anyone might see and imitate. Like his later autobiography (1790), they appear to be "good-humoured" guides to the generation of power by any ordinary or "common" person who is able to read. Despite their emphasis on ultimate equality and equilibrium, however, the *New Experiments* are not only about the liberation of physical, affective, and economic energies but also are equally about their control. Franklin was committed to the Enlightenment ideal of the diffusion of information, and he believed that republican political power was rooted in and diffused through the collective body of what he called "the People."[17] Yet, like an Enlightenment-era Prospero, Franklin believed that this body must, finally, be controlled by its head. It was to be managed (or rather, self-managed) by a knowing bourgeois managerial class of engineers: the owners of books, schooled in the flows of energy. As an electrical engineer of the British imperial state, Franklin was deeply invested in print pedagogy as a way of stimulating and embodying his heady dreams of union and expansion.

In the 1740s and 1750s, Franklin was a colonial Loyalist and a Whig expansionist who admired the English Constitution, especially the House of Commons, and he hoped to see the more liberal elements of Britain's political and economic system expand across North America, if not the globe.[18] He published the first edition of his *New Experiments* in the years immediately preceding the Seven Years' (or "French and Indian") War, the war of empire that the British won in 1763. As his autobiography points out, he actively aided the British military operation of the Seven Years' War even while his fame as an electrician was growing in Europe.[19] Indeed, Franklin often employed military materials like guns and shot in his *New Experiments*, not only because they were made of metal but because (like books and bookbinding materials) they came conveniently to hand in Philadelphia.

Certainly, as Shaffer and others have suggested, Franklin's scientific success can be traced to his evasion of open personal and political conflict and to his skill at silently turning conflict to his own advantage.[20] Yet, these personal and political forms of success cannot be neatly separated from his elaboration of the +/– denotation of electrical bipolarity, the inscription device he deployed as a way of summarizing and proliferating electricity. Nor can Franklin's summation of dynamic balance (or connection *via* separation) be fully understood apart from the array of institutional, socioeconomic, and political transformations through which he emerged as printer and author and which he helped to integrate.

Instead of his legendary kite experiment, then, the key to Franklinian science lies in those experiments in which Franklin charged, discharged, and recharged comparatively ordinary bodies and objects in the process of performing his *New Experiments*. Franklin's electrical wizardry consists in conversion of powerful physical and/or affective "energies" (including sexual desire and lust for power) into the +/– of "electricity." In American cultural history, the ideology of affect and the emergence of sensationalism are usually traced to the eighteenth-century Gothic and sentimental novel, or to eighteenth-century oratory and theater and the epistemological or psychological theories that informed them.[21] The texts of eighteenth-century electrical science are less often included in the history of the emergence of affective and physiological "feeling." Experiments such as the "electric kiss" or "electrocuted turkey," however, reveal that Franklin's writings on electricity not only occupy a central position in the history of eighteenth-century electrical science, but also articulate an array of bipolar feeling states, such as pleasure and pain, fear and laughter, attraction and repulsion. Even while they are evoked and displayed, the energies (and historical valence) of powerful feelings are always ultimately under the electrician's control—rendered chaste, "good-humoured," and mathematically balanced even while the industrious generation of charges remains intertwined with entertainment and erotica.

From Bodies Erotic to the Body Electric

Franklin began to experiment with electricity in 1745, when Collinson sent him a glass tube for creating static electricity and the Pennsylvania proprietor Thomas Penn sent him a more elaborate apparatus—the Leyden jar, or "phial." A Leyden jar is a lead-covered glass jar filled with water or metal, with a wire passed into the interior and protruding from the cork at the top. When this wire is charged positively the lead exterior of the jar is charged negatively, and vice versa.[22] Franklin experimented extensively with the Leyden jar, and in one instance he demonstrates its function by suspending a cork between two wires; the first wire is attached to the lead at the bottom of the jar, and the second extends from the cork at the top. The inequality of charges in the two wires is evidenced by the motion of the cork, which must perform the labor of "fetching and carrying" the electrical charge until "equilibrium is restored": "If a cork suspended by a silk thread (*f*) hang between these two wires, it will play incessantly from one to the other, 'till the bottle is no longer electrised; that is, it fetches and carries fire from the top to the bottom of the bottle, 'till the equilibrium is restored."[23] In a closely related experiment, the labor of fetching and carrying becomes the principle of both animation and entertainment when the Leyden jar is used to electrify a "spider" made of thread. Here the +/− of Franklinian electricity equates the life energy of organic systems with the fluid mechanics of motion to produce a "life-form": "Made of a small piece of burnt cork, with legs of linnen [*sic*] thread, and a grain or two of lead stuck in him, to give him more weight [the spider is suspended by a thread between two wires, set at about eight inches apart]. . . . Then, we animate him [by applying the Leyden jar to one of the wires] . . . He will immediately fly to the wire of the phial, bend his legs in touching it; then spring off, and fly to the wire in the table: thence again to the wire of the phial, playing with his legs against both, in a very entertaining manner [and appearing] perfectly alive to persons unacquainted."[24] Here the +/- code of electricity sutures a mechanical system to "animated" nature—making nature seem to operate by mechanical laws—while displaying, in the body of the leaping spider, the back-and-forth act of the suturing itself.

Franklin also generated charges with the glass tube sent to him by Collinson, which he "electrised" by "rubbing" it up and down, or "exciting" it, with a cloth.[25] Along with the tube, Collinson had enclosed a copy of London *Gentleman's Magazine* of April 1745, which contained an essay by Albrecht von Haller describing recent German experiments with electricity. Haller's essay emphasized electrical performances involving human bodies and alcoholic "spirits," and it declared that tricks with static electricity had "taken the place of quadrille" in "the fashionable world."[26] His account offers moderately erotic, slighty sadistic and titillating, experiments that involve clothing, human bodies, and metaphors linking the "electrical fire" to the energy of sexual desire. Haller narrates, for example, the evocation of sparks from "electrised petticoats" or from a man's button. He also recounts an experiment called "a hanging boy," in which a small boy was "strung up" and sparks of fire evoked from his face and hands "by only rubbing a Glass Tube at his Feet," in order to prove "that Fire is diffus'd through all Space, and may be produc'd from all Bodies."[27] Unlike Franklin's mathematized plus (+) and minus (–), Haller's essay distinguishes "sparks" from "luminous emanations" by sexing them as "male" versus "female" fire: "If any other person not electrised puts his finger near one who is so, no matter where it be to his naked skin or his clothes, there issues thence a fire, with a painful sensation . . . of which both parties are but too sensible."[28] This line of entertainment is concluded in the *Venus electrificata*, "whose caress was so painful that a gallant 'dur'st not renew his kisses more than three times.' "[29]

On receiving a copy of Haller's essay, Franklin immediately began to imitate the German experiments. And in his first substantive letter to Collinson four months later he details a chaste, Philadelphia version of the *Venus electrificata* in which Franklin (and fellow experimenters Ebenezar Kinnersley and Thomas Hopkinson) claim to have been able to "encrease vastly the force of the electrical kiss"

"Let A and B stand on wax; or A on wax and B on the floor; give one of them the electrised phial in hand; let the other take hold of the wire; there will be a small spark; but when their lips approach, they will be struck and shock'd. . . . [The same effect is produced when] another gentleman and lady, C and D approach and 'shake hands' with those who have performed the 'kiss.' " [30]

In the Philadelphia experiment, the bodies of Franklin's "gentlemen" and "lady" are denominated by letters rather than names, and the experiment is called "the electric kiss" rather than "Venus electrificata." Unlike many European electrical pamphlets of the same period, furthermore, Franklin's *New Experiments* are not illustrated —although the edition of 1774 includes a frontispiece.[31] Despite the changes made in the German experiment, in fact, the channeling of the European flows of imperial, social, political, and economic power through Philadelphia and Franklin's electrical (and print) shop ultimately wrought little change in the social and class elements of the "Venus electrificata."[32] As wittily recounted anecdote and visually flashy performance, Franklin's experiment is easy to categorize as entertainment. Yet, the chaste, plain-style (markedly *un*illustrated) letters and papers of the *New Experiments* are also works of erotica insofar as they invoke an illicit, adjacent universe of licentious "energies" that includes both sexual desire (*eros*) and undisguised socioeconomic ambition ("vanity").

After the success of his lightning rod experiment in France, Franklin linked sexuality and ambition in a humorous anecdote in which the violent and dangerous affect of his own pride is coyly half-repressed. When Franklin received a note of thanks from the king of France following a performance of his experiments in Paris, he claims to have a hard time managing his vanity. In order to get a grip on his pride, he tells a little story about a girl and her garters. In the process, the nonproductive quality of his vanity is gendered, sexualized, and equated with the position of "the girl" in the story. "The *Tatler* tells us," he writes,

of a Girl, who was observed to grow suddenly proud, and none cou'd guess the Reason, till it came to be known she had got on a new Pair of Garters. Lest you should be puzzled to guess the Cause, when you observe any Thing of the kind in me, I think I will not hide my new Garters under my Petticoats, but take the Freedom to show them to you, in a Paragraph [from] our friend Collinson's Letter, vis—But I ought to mortify, and not indulge, this Vanity: I will not transcribe the Paragraph, yet I cannot forbear. . . . [to tell you that] the Grand Monarch of France strictly commands the Abbe Mazeas to write a Letter [returning] the King's Thanks and Compliments in an express Manner to Mr. Franklin of Pennsylvania.[33]

There are countless such examples in Franklin's autobiography and elsewhere of his rhetorically profitable struggle with vanity in which he forces his own (feminized) vanity and desire down and re-"channels" it into a dynamic connection through print with his male correspondents. In doing so, of course, he converts "useless" affect or feeling back into a profitable and productive circulation of himself in print. Both revealing and repressing (as "natural") the energies of his own desires, Franklin therefore maintains a productive equilibrium in the wake of any social, economic, or psychological conflict. On the one hand, Franklin always stands somewhat above his materials (as their conductor), while, on the other, he is equally careful never to appear to rise too high above his audience— or above the bodies he employs. In more than one instance, he even interpellates his own body into the current—appearing on the stage of his *New Experiments* as the object (a conductor) of his own electrical science.

One such dangerous moment occurs when he and Ebenezer Kinnersley use large Leyden jars to electrocute chickens and turkeys. Half-pint jars, Franklin recalls, "were sufficient to kill common Hens outright." But the case was different with turkeys, who "tho' thrown into violent Convulsions, and then lying as dead for some minutes, would recover." Eventually by using five jars Franklin and Kinnersley were able to kill one ten-pound turkey. "I conceit," Franklin observes, "that the Birds kill'd in this Manner eat uncommonly tender." But, while making the attempt, the electrician "inadvertently took the Stroke of two of those Jars, when they were very near full charg'd. . . . [The effect was that of a] universal Blow from head to foot throughout the Body, followed by a violent quick Trembling in the Trunk [and] a Swelling [on my Hand] about the bigness of half a Swan Shot or pistol Bullet." As the inadvertent object of his own science, Franklin discovers that "a man can bear a much greater Electrical Shock than I imagined."[34] Indeed, repeated observations of electrical shocks to human bodies convince him that electrocution "would certainly . . . be the easiest of all deaths."[35]

Franklin is known for his humor rather than for emotional expressiveness or sentimental discourse. He repeatedly converts disaster, death, and simple failure into new opportunity—for jokes, entertainment, or further experiment—rather than occasion for grief or anxiety. "Chagrined," writes Franklin, for instance, at the end of a frustratingly inconclusive experiment, "that we have been hitherto able to produce nothing in this way of use to mankind," it is proposed "to put an end to [electrical experiments] for this season, somewhat humorously, in a party of pleasure on the banks of *Skuylkil*." Frustration is defused in an evening's entertainment that opens with the "firing of spirits [glasses of wine] by means of a spark sent [from one side of the river to the other] without any other conductor than the water. [Next] a turkey [is] killed for our dinner by the electrical shock, and roasted by the electrical jack, before a fire kindled by the electrified bottle: when the healths of all the famous electricians in England, Holland, France, and Germany [are drunk] in electrified bumpers, under the discharge of guns from the electrical battery."[36] Accompanied by a humorous discharge of imperial weaponry and an evocation of "spirits," this party of pleasure would have made Franklin entirely recognizable to his scientific counterparts in the imperial states of "England, Holland, France, and Germany." Although quaintly performed on the banks of the Philadelphia river "*Skuylkil*," Franklin's party remains class-coded as a European imperial attraction.

Indeed, entertaining anecdotes such as his "electrical party" made Franklin's *Experiments* as much a literary as a scientific success, and the Franklin who floated himself so successfully in European circles did so primarily through his letters on electricity. As Joseph Priestly comments in 1767, the form and "simple and modest" style of Franklin's electrical letters were as much admired as their content, and "nothing was ever written upon the subject of electricity which was more generally read and admired in all parts of Europe, than these letters."[37] Ultimately, Franklin's access to political power in the 1750s and 1760s would be due as much to his literary celebrity as to his genius for conducting diplomacy.

So great a degree of electricity was excited [by the Leyden jar]
that, when discharged the spark made an hole thro' a quire of paper,
which is thought to be pistol proof.—Advertisement for Franklin's
New Experiments in the *Gentleman's Magazine*

In Franklin's *New Experiments*, the management of power is a matter of both physiology and of literacy. As if to illustrate the electric
connection of bodies and letters in his *New Experiments*, Franklin
repeatedly electrifies whole books, or the parts of books, as if to attack (even while celebrating) the privileged medium of the scientific
Enlightenment: reading, writing, and print circulation. Franklin di-
rects: "Lay two books back towards back [on two wine glasses, at
two or three inches distant.] Set an electrifed [Leyden jar] upon one
of the books, and touch the wire. This book will be electrified *minus*.
Then, use the Leyden jar to electrify the second book *plus*. A suspended small cork-ball will play between these books till the equilibrium is restored." Take off the bottle, and holding it in your hand,
touch the other with the wire; that book will be electrified *plus*; the
fire passing into it from the wire, and the bottle at the same time
supplied from your hand.[38] Likewise, Franklin experiments with
sending electrical shocks through thick "quires of paper" in order
to demonstrate that "electricity . . . will kill without a Wound, and
pass through every thing."[39] He electrifies the gilt covers of books
to create glowing lines "in the dark," and he uses leather itself either
to create charges by "rubbing" other objects or, in the case of book
covers, to serve as a nonconductor.

In each of these experiments, books and book parts are seemingly random objects that have come to the electrician's hand—
the equivalents of cork, wire, wood, or glass—to demonstrate the
principles of conduction versus nonconduction, of +/− charges and
equilibrium restored. Franklin himself was a bookbinder as well as
a printer, and he often supplied printers in distant colonies with
the materials needed for binding and gilding books.[40] Like the bookbinding vises he used to electrify panes of glass and strips of metal,
book gilt and leather were available in Franklin's own print shop. As
a material for construction and experiment, whether as a whole or
in part, the book as an object of experiment within the *New Experi-*

ments is *not* simply analogous to the "pamphlet" (or the individual letters, papers, and other electrical transactions) that constitute the *New Experiments* themselves. If Franklin experiments, for example, on a whole book, its title is never given and its contents are ignored. If he experiments on its parts, whether paper, gilt, or leather binding, the book becomes virtually random material, serving the further conduction of knowledge. At the same time, nevertheless, the books used as objects of experimentation do implicitly reference the physical medium of the *New Experiments* themselves. Of course, the reduction of books within the *New Experiments* to the status of materials suggests Franklin's willingness to submit any object, including himself and his own book, to his electrical and economic purposes. At the same time, however, just like the tick-tock of the Enlightenment world clock (forged by some artisan deity or "clockmaker" god), the +/– principle of electrical bipolarity also transcends the universe of material objects in which it is briefly instantiated.

Within the text of the *New Experiments*, then, the employment of a leather-bound book as object reveals a number of fluid gaps within Franklin's electrical science: between science as an artifact of print versus science as spectacle; between linguistic and visual representational forms; and between the book as object or "common matter" equal to any other versus the book as a privileged repository of value, memory, and status. Franklin himself raises these gaps and tensions in the fourth edition of his *New Experiments* when, in the (turkey electrocution) letter dated 18 March 1755, he complains of the difficulties of being an "inventor" in a highly competitive environment assailed on the one side by the "Envy, Jealousy, and Vanity" of his "competitors for Fame" and, on the other, by ignorance and hatred directed at him by people who are "totally destitute of any inventive faculty themselves." Because of these corrosive conditions, Franklin continues, "the origin of many of the most extraordinary inventions, though produced within but a few centuries past, is involved in doubt and uncertainty. We scarce know to whom we are indebted for the *compass*, and for *spectacles*, nor have even *paper* and *printing*, that record every thing else, been able to preserve with certainty the name and reputation of their inventors."[41]

Franklin's complaint here with the fragility of knowledge and power stands in marked contrast to his usual lack of concern about the potential costs of his electrical system or about its more explosive, destructive aspect as a force for dissolution, transformation, and globalization. The ethic of the eighteenth-century Enlightenment itself depended on opening and controlling flows of information. In Franklin's book experiments, acts of experimental violence against a privileged object of Enlightenment knowledge (its production and circulation) reveal the degree to which a bound or unbound book could stand in for the vulnerable, yet powerful, preservative force of the human body. Acts of electrical violence against books and their parts also reveal the degree to which books (bound in animal hide) as conductors of knowledge were sutured to human and animal bodies via Franklinian electricity—as the site and source of new forms of power that could be generated through and on the skin.

Like other eighteenth-century books, the books in Franklin's *Experiments* are bound in animal hide, but they are also often gilt with gold. Like other materials involved in bookbinding, gold is one more material in the world of electrical conductors; however, when "electrified" a gilt book could be made to glow magically, temporarily revealing its value and even its transcendent status as a sign of social status, as a theatrical prop, and as a privileged, even sacred site of Enlightenment.

Franklin was preoccupied with the conducting powers of gold in general. Electricity could not be seen in its passage through dense metals or wires, but gold was a porous medium through which the electric fire was visible. When passing through gilt, the small sheets of hammered gold, its "motion" was clearly visible. The electrical fluid flowing through gold leaf could be seen, Franklin writes, "leaping from body to body, or from particle to particle through the air. [F]or the leaf-gold is full of pore; hold a leaf to the light and it appears like a net, and the fire is seen in its leaping over the vacancies."[42] When the gilt lines on a book cover were electrified with a Leyden jar, the light passed along the book's edges, like "sharpest lightening":

> Take a book whose covering is filletted [*sic*] with gold. Then, bend a wire some ten inches long in the form of the letter "m" and slip it over one end of the book so that one shoulder of the "m" presses upon one end of the gold line, with the other end of the wire leaning up toward the other end of the book. Lay the book on a glass or wax. [Then, posi-

tioning the Leyden jar on the gold line at the other end of the book,] bend the springing wire toward the bottle electrised [i.e., the Leyden jar], by pressing [the wire] with a stick of wax till its ring approaches the ring of the bottle wire. Instantly there is a strong spark and stroke, and the whole line of gold, which completes the communication, between the top and bottom of the bottle, will appear a vivid flame, like the sharpest lightning. . . . The room should be darkened.[43]

As this passage demonstrates, a leather-bound book gilt with gold lines worked as a kind of luminous lightning rod. But such books combined a nonconducting element (leather made of animal skin) with a highly conductive one (gold). As Franklin notes of book gold and imperial leather in the first substantive letter of his *New Experiments*: "[If] we electrify, upon wax in the dark, a book that has a double line of gold round upon the covers, and then apply a knuckle to the gilding[,] the fire appears every where upon the gold like a flash of lightning: [but] not upon the leather, nor, if you touch the leather instead of the gold." Furthermore, he continues, shifting subjects abruptly: "We rub our tubes with buckskin, and observe always to keep the same side [of the buckskin] to the tube, and never to sully the tube by handling; thus [our tubes] work readily and easily without the least fatigue . . . This I mention, because the *European* papers on Electricity frequently speak of rubbing the tube as a fatiguing exercise."[44]

Franklin's preoccupation with the uses of leather, whether for bookbinding, "rubbing tubes," or generating electrical energies, illuminates the systematic deployment of skins more generally in his *New Experiments*. Eighteenth-century books were usually made of calfskin, goatskin, and, sometimes in the colonies, of deerskin. While deerskin could still be harvested in British woods and forests, by the mid-eighteenth century it was imported primarily from North America where it had become a native export crucial in various ways to the colonies' economies. Franklin's pointed, rather humorous reference to "buckskin" exploits this Enlightenment and market association of America with natural or native materials because the thirteen colonies were a prime source of "buckskin." Procured primarily by American Indian hunters from New York to Georgia and shipped to Britain via middlemen in East Coast seaport towns, deerskin had innumerable craft uses. And, by the mid-eighteenth century, Europe was dependent on North America for large shipments of deerskin. Americans were, in turn, dependent on Europe for many manufactured goods, including books unavailable in the colonies.

Throughout his *New Experiments*, Franklin systematically plays on the transatlantic exchange of American "raw materials" for European manufactures. It was this transatlantic, imperial network of transactions, exchanges, and correspondence that made his electricity possible. The *New Experiments* opens, for example, with a brief introductory letter, where Franklin simply thanks his patron for sending him the invaluable Leyden jar, or "capacitor," with which Franklin made a majority of his discoveries.[45] Franklin also thanks Collinson for the many magazines and books that Collinson had generously sent "from Time to Time."[46] Franklin would reciprocate, of course, with his own electrical writings, bound (eventually) in a book that would constitute a form of "buckskin" in the Euro-American literary market. In other words, tube, Leyden jar, and gentlemen's magazines are reciprocated with buckskin in the form of a book from America, which will circulate, advertise, and memorialize the name of Franklin and of his British supplier. Like Franklin's legendary "coon-skin" cap in the court of Louis XVIII, the allusion to buckskin at the end of the second letter exploits the distinction between American raw goods and British manufactures, together with the simple, semifictional class opposition, so often made by artisan republicans like Franklin, between British "aristocrats" and nature's "democrats."

The allusion to rubbing with buckskin further highlights the role of efficiency, portability, and a peculiarly ragged "smoothness" of style that would make the +/− solution of Franklin's electrical *New Experiments* the most successful—because the most economical and universal—of eighteenth-century electrical theories. Europeans are "fatigued," Franklin suggests, because they don't keep their rubbing cloths "clean," they sully their "tubes," and they irrationally, stupidly impair their productive "power" through lack of attention to work efficiency. The generative power at issue here is the power of British imperial industrial expansion and bourgeois class construction. But it also includes both a negativized world of erotic sexuality and the generative power of the "skin trade," the trade in those bodies submitted to productive purposes globally—through factory labor, domestic labor, or slave labor—in the colonies of the British empire, in the British or French Caribbean, or through the production of staple crops and industrial goods for an increasingly global market. In other words, the skin trade illuminated in Franklin's electrification of "bound" books also references enslaved and laboring human bodies as well as the other countless diverse, organic materials employed to generate and integrate +/– values (and their associated value systems) across internationalizing industrial and commercial contexts. The skin-bound books used for electrical experiments in Franklin's *New Experiments* were not books for reading. In this regard, the unopened book experimented on by the electrical engineer stands in close relation to the role of the unread, unopened book as a supercharged fetish in the collection of the genuinely obsessed bibliophile.

Conclusion

J. L. Heilbron notes that Franklin's theory of plus (+) and minus (–) charges bears a remarkable resemblance to account bookkeeping.[47] But Franklin's theory of an endlessly accumulative and dischargeable natural "fund" of electricity is clearly more than merely analogous to market dynamics. Channeling electrical flows through various bodies, Franklin experimented with inserting—if not identifying—human and animal bodies with the dynamic flow of his electrical "currency." In fact, as outlined in his *New Experiments*, the oscillating flows of plus (+) and minus (–) constitute a universal "suture" linking the account-book world of market transactions to the dynamic binary oppositions that would one day structure federalist political theory—of power divided and "balanced" and of local or state "bodies" united under a national "head." With its dramatic visual effects of attraction and repulsion, the fluid dynamics of plus (+) and minus (–) articulated flows of commercial exchange and consumer desire as well as the many kinds of "bonds" that in federalist political theory would unite demographically and territorially extended social groups while bridging the differences within such groups. Already in the mid-eighteenth century, then, Franklin's +/– denotation of electrical charges had put into circulation a bipolar interface that sutured a globally expansionist, imperial marketplace with a nationally constitutive principle of conflict harmonized in union.

Franklin's electrical work helps to explain the mixed global and national dynamic of the spread of digital technologies today both inside and outside the United States. It also helps to explain the recurrent debate over the "elite" versus "democratic" nature of digital communication devices; the place of sexuality and pornography as a feared materialization within digital media; and, above all, the continuing absence of debate about the proliferation of digital technologies. Digital technology follows longstanding bipolar pathways. The "age of information" and the "new" economy it implies are not only profoundly electrical but profoundly Enlightenment in structure. And, if Franklin's *New Experiments* displays the fluid dynamics and integrated systems that continue to constitute (post)Enlightenment knowledge, it also raises the question of whether knowledge is even possible—without electricity.

Notes

I am indebted to Kim Marra, Leslie Schwalm, Lisa Gitelman, Corey Creekmur, Kathleen Diffley, and Harry Stecopoulous for their substantive comments on various drafts of this essay, and for the research assistance of Bill Bryant and Patrick Naick.

1 I. Bernard Cohen, "Introduction," in *Benjamin Franklin's Experiments* (Cambridge: Harvard University Press, 1941), 68–91, 76–77, 92. Cohen writes, "Franklin not only propounded the single fluid theory of electricity, but also invented the language of its expression" (73).

2 As Cohen summarizes: "Franklin's theoretical and experimental *discoveries*, upon which he based his *invention* of the lightning rod, were recognized as highly significant in the days before the confirmation of the lightning hypothesis made him famous" (Cohen, *Experiments*, 73). Carl Van Doren surveys the records of the kite experiment and notes: "The episode of the kite, so firm and fixed in legend, turns out to be dim and mystifying in fact" (Van Doren, *Benjamin Franklin* [New York: Viking Press, 1938]). In Franklin's own view, the purpose of the kite experiment was to prove that lightning was identical in substance to the sparks of static electricity that could be produced by simply rubbing a glass tube with a cloth: Once "electric fire has been obtained [from the threads of a kite string], spirits may be kindled, and all other electrical experiments be performed, which are usually done by the help of a rubbed glass globe or tube, and thereby the sameness of the electric matter with that of lighting completely demonstrated" (Benjamin Franklin to Peter Collinson, 19 October 1752, in Cohen, *Experiments*, 266).

3 All references to Franklin's *New Experiments and Observations on Electricity, made at Philadelphia in America* (London: E. Cave, 1751, 1753; D. Henry and R. Cave, 1754, 1760; D. Henry, 1769, 1774) are from Cohen's edition of the *Experiments*, unless otherwise noted. The complex publishing history of the text is narrated in Cohen, *Experiments*, 141–61.

4 And, to a lesser extent by itinerants in the colonies such as Benjamin Spence, mentioned in Franklin's autobiography and other writings, ed. Kenneth Silverman (London: Penguin 1986), 133, and the mysterious traveling electrician who disappeared in South America, one "Domian of Transylvania" mentioned in Franklin's letter to Dr. Lining in 1755, Benjamin Franklin to Dr. [John] Lining, 18 March 1755, in Cohen, *Experiments*, 331–32.

5 In arguing that the conflicts over knowledge must be understood within the expanding world of goods that included instruments and scientific materials, Simon Schaffer surveys the settings and spaces in which mid-century European electrical culture was performed; see his "The Consuming Flame: Electrical Showmen and Tory Mysticism in the World of Goods," in *Consumption and the World of Goods*, ed. John Brewer and Roy Porter (London: Routledge, 1993), 488–526.

6 Ibid., 496.

7 Franklin, in Cohen, *Experiments*, 171.

8 I. Bernard Cohen, *Benjamin Franklin's Science* (Cambridge: Harvard University Press, 1990), 22.

9 Franklin, in Cohen, *Experiments*, 202.

10 Ibid., 175.

11 Otto Mayr, *The Origins of Feedback Control* (Cambridge: MIT Press, 1970), 2, 7. In the words of Norbert Wiener, "feedback is a method of controlling a system by reinserting into it the results of its past performance" (7). The concept of feedback, used in mechanical, pneumatic, hydraulic, or electrical systems alike, gave cybernetics its name. In 1947, Norbert Wiener christened the newly founded discipline (he had not known that in 1834, A.-M. Ampere had proposed "cybernetique" as a term for the science of government) by using the Greek word for steersman, *kubernetes*. He had come upon the name through the etymology of the word governor (English, to govern; Latin *gubernare*; Greek *kubernan*), the familiar term for the first popular feedback device: "[A feedback] system has the task of automatically maintaining some given variable equal to a desired value in spite of external disturbances . . . This is done *by comparing functions of these variables* (i.e. command and controlled variable) *and using the difference as a means of control*" (7). See also Otto Mayr, "The Feedback Concept in Economic Thought and Technology in Eighteenth-Century Britain," *Technology and Culture* 12, no. 1 (1971): 1–22.

12 Cohen surveys the publishing history of *New Experiments* in his introduction, "The Editions of Franklin's Book," in *Experiments*, 139–61.

13 Bruno Latour, "Drawing Things Together," in *Representation in Scientific Practice*, ed. Michael Lynch and Steve Woolgar (Cambridge: MIT Press, 1990), 21–24.

14 Cohen points out that Franklin's analogy of a single fluid, and of +/– charges, remains central to the understanding and application of electricity, because most people "still analyze electric circuits in terms of a 'fictitious' (Franklinian) current" (*Benjamin Franklin's Science*, 9–10). While Franklin's electricity does not reflect the present-day model of electrons and molecules, in the end it doesn't much matter. In 1936, J. J. Thompson, the discoverer of the electron, observed that scientists still account for the major facts of "electrostatics" much as Franklin had proposed: "The central elements of Franklin's 'fictions' continue to structure research. The service the one fluid theory has rendered to electricity can hardly be overestimated. It is still used by many of us when working in the laboratory. If we move a piece of brass and want to know whether that will increase or decrease the effect we are observing, we do not fly to the higher mathematics, but use the simple conception of the electric fluid which would tell us as much as we wanted to know in a few seconds" (Thomson, *Recollections and Reflections* [London: Bell, 1936], 252–53, quoted in Cohen, *Benjamin Franklin's Science*, 9–10). Van Doren lists the electrical terminology coined by Franklin, including "battery, charged, charging, condense, conductor, discharge . . . electrical shock, electrician, electrified, electrify . . . nonconducting" (*Benjamin Franklin*, 173).

15 Franklinian electricity was widely popularized and circulated in Joseph Priestley's *History and Present State of Electricity* (London: J. Dodsley, 1769). See Schaffer, "The Consuming Flame," 497, 513, 525 n.496.

16 Cohen, "Introduction," in *Experiments*, 73.

17 Franklin, "The Way to Wealth" (1757), in *Autobiography and Other Writings*, 216.

18 Francis Jennings uses the term "imperialist Whig" to describe Franklin's politics at mid-century: "He was an imperialist Whig, believing in the simultaneous expansion of empire and liberty" (Jennings, *Empire of Fortune, Crowns, Colonies, and Tribes in the Seven Years War in America* [New York: Norton, 1988], 87–90).

19 Many pages of Franklin's autobiography are, in fact, devoted to his activities during the Seven Years' War; see *Autobiography and Other Writings*, 138–69.

20 Robert A. Ferguson is especially illuminating on the meaning of silence in Franklin's texts and diplomatic strategy: "Agreement often

requires the second of the thirteen virtues enumerated in his auto-biography: silence. The major source of evil in Franklin's autobiography is disputation . . . Silence is the vital interstice in a consensual literature; what is spoken or written is peculiarly a function of what *cannot* be spoken or written *there*" (Ferguson, "Finding the Revolution," in *The American Enlightenment, 1750-1820* [Cambridge: Harvard University Press, 1997], 16).

21 See, for example, Bruce Burgett, *Sentimental Bodies, Sex, Gender, and Citizenship in the Early Republic* (Princeton: Princeton University Press, 1998); Jay Fliegelman, "Soft Compulsion," in *Declaring Independence: Jefferson, Natural Language, and the Culture of Performance* (Stanford: Stanford University Press, 1995); and Colin Campbell, *The Romantic Ethic and the Spirit of Modern Consumerism* (London: Blackwell, 1985).

22 Cohen, *Experiments*, 178n; Franklin to Collinson, 1 September 1747, in Cohen, *Experiments*, 183.

23 Ibid.

24 Franklin to Collinson, 27 March 1747, in Cohen, *Experiments*, 177.

25 Ibid.

26 Quoted in J. L. Heilbron, *Electricity in the Seventeenth and Eighteenth Centuries: A Study of Early Modern Physics* (Berkeley: University of California Press, 1979), 326.

27 Ibid., 324.

28 Ibid., 325-26.

29 In a first, short letter to Collinson, which opens his *New Experiments*, Franklin is also careful to note: "For what with making experiments when I can be alone, and repeating them to my Friends and Acquaintance, who, from the novelty of the thing, come continually in crouds [*sic*] to see them, I have, during some months past, had little leisure for anything else" (28 March 1747, in Cohen, *Experiments*, 170).

30 "The same [thing happens] if another gentleman and lady, C and D, standing also on wax, and joining hands with A and B, salute or shake hands" (Franklin To Collinson, 11 July 1747, in Cohen, *Experiments*, 177).

31 In a related experiment, Franklin uses a simple glass tube to distribute charges among persons designated by letter. In this experiment, each person begins with "his equal share" of "the common element," the electrical fire: A and B stand on wax. A first rubs the tube, which collects electricity from him, leaving A with a negative charge. Then A hands the same tube to B, who, upon receiving it, finds himself with an excess of charge, delivered to his body from the charged tube. Because the wax cuts off his body's "communication" with "the common stock" of electricity in the earth, he retains the collected charge. "To C," then, "standing on the floor, both A and

B appear to be electrised, and C will receive a shock from both . . . For he having only the middle quantity of electrical fire, receives a spark upon approaching B, who has an over quantity; but [C] gives [a shock] to A, who has an under quantity." From this arrangement, Franklin concludes, "have arisen some new terms among us." "We say B is electrised positively; A, negatively. Or rather, B is electrised plus; A, minus. And we daily in our experiments electrise bodies plus or minus, as we think proper" (cited in Cohen, *Experiments*, 175).

32   The suggestion made by the word "channeling" of a connection be-
     tween Franklin's electricity and the occult channeling of "spirits"
     has been pursued by Werner Sollers in the case of the connection
     between the telegraph and spirit-rapping in the nineteenth century.
     See Werner Sollers, "Dr. Benjamin Franklin's Celestial Telegraph,
     or Indian Blessings to Gas-Lit American Drawing Rooms," *American
     Quarterly* 35, no. 5 (winter 1983): 459–80.

33   Franklin to Eliot, 12 April 1753, quoted in Cohen, "Introduction," in
     Experiments, 104.

34   Benjamin Franklin to Peter Collinson, 4 February 1750, quoted in
     Cohen, "Introduction," in *Experiments*, 93–94.

35   Benjamin Franklin to Dr. John Lining, 18 March 1755, in Cohen, *Ex-
     periments*, 336. Electricity was used medically to attempt cures for
     physical ailments such as arthritis, gout, and paralysis. As Franklin
     recounts of one such "cure": "I had seen a young woman that was
     about to be electrified through the feet, (for some indisposition) re-
     ceive a greater charge through the head, by inadvertently stopping
     forward to look at the placing of her feet, till her forehead . . . came
     too near my prime-conductor: She dropt, but instantly got up again"
     (336) For a discussion of John Lining's work on human metabolism
     and the maintenance of body temperature, see Cohen, "Introduc-
     tion," in *Experiments*, 73n.

36   Benjamin Franklin to Peter Collinson, "Farther Experiments and
     Observations" 29 April 1749, in Cohen, *Experiments*, 199–200.

37   Jared Sparks, "Introduction to Letters and Papers on Electricity," in
     The Works of Benjamin Franklin, vol. 5 (Boston: Tappan, Whittemore,
     and Mason, 1837), 179.

38   Quoted in Cohen, *Experiments*, 184–85.

39   John Freke, *An Essay to Shew the Cause of Electricity, and why some
     things are non-electricable*, 2nd ed. (London, 1746), 29, quoted in
     Cohen, "Introduction," in *Experiments*, 107.

40   Franklin's own binding of Cicero's *Cato Major*, or *de Senectute*, in
     1747 is discussed by Hannah Dustin French in her "Early American
     Bookbinding by Hand," in *Bookbinding in America: Three Essays*, ed.
     Hellmut Lehmann-Haupt (New York: R. R. Bowker Company, 1967),
     18–39. This discussion includes a black-and-white photograph of the
     cover of Franklin's *Cato*. For a discussion of the English panel style

of gilt decoration, known as the "Cambridge style" used by colonial binders throughout the seventeenth century and part of the eighteenth century, see Edith Diehl, *Bookbinding: Its Background and Technique*, vol. 1 (Port Washington, N.Y.: Kennikat Press, 1946), 155. In this volume Diehl offers a detailed description of the specialized process used by goldbeaters for pounding gold into leaf for use by bookbinders (188–89). For an overview of orders for bookbinding that Franklin received between 1728 and 1737, see G. S. Eddy, *Account Books Kept By Benjamin Franklin*, 2 vols. (New York: Columbia University Press, 1928–1929); these volumes also document Franklin's role in supplying far-flung colonial bookbinders with gold leaf and other materials. C. Clement Samford surveys the numerous kinds of account books ("blank books," "legers," "alphabets," "journals," "account books," "day books," "wastebooks") bound and gilt by a contemporary Virginia printer in his *The Bookbinder in Eighteenth-Century Williamsburg, and Account of His Life and Times and of His Craft* (Williamsburg, Va.: Colonial Williamsburg, 1964), 17.

41 Franklin to Lining, in Cohen, *Experiments*, 338.

42 Indeed, Franklin used this image of the network-like passing of electrical fire through particles of gold to explain the aurora borealis as a phenomenon of electricity "discharged" somewhere thousands of miles to the south, but then visible, "leaping through a presumably porous and particulate atmosphere in the polar regions to the North —as from a canal suddenly opened." Piling analogy on analogy or, rather, leaping himself from analogy to analogy, Franklin's line of gilt in this passage is explicitly compared to both a canal and to the "particles" surrounding the North Pole, "as when a long canal filled with still water is opened at one end . . . the motion of the water begins first near the opened end, and proceeds towards the close end, though the water itself moves from the close towards the opened end: so the electrical fire discharged into the polar regions, perhaps from a thousand leagues length of vaporized air, appears first where it is first in motion" (quoted in Cohen, *Experiments*, 208–9). The pole would be surrounded by an "atmosphere"; this description of the aurora presumably is a product of Franklin's now discounted theory of "atmospheres" (rather than electrical "fields"). See Roderick W. Home, "Franklin's Electrical Atmospheres," *British Journal for the History of Science* 6, no. 22 (1972): 131–51.

43 Quoted in Cohen, *Experiments*, 185–86.

44 Ibid., 177.

45 Franklin to Collinson, 28 March 1747, in Cohen, *Experiments*, 169–70. See also "Additional Papers to Peter Collinson," 29 July 1750, in Cohen, *Experiments*, 212.

46 "I must . . . leave myself Time to Answer your Favour of March last, which came to Hand by Dowers, with the Magazines & Le Blank's

Letters, Martin's Electricity & Watson's first Part and Sequel. We are, as we always have been, extreamly [*sic*] obliged to you for your kind Care in sending us from Time to Time, what is new and curious, tho' not wrote for" (from the Bowdoin Ms., quoted in Cohen, *Experiments*, 178n).

47 J. L. Heilbron, "From Horsehair to Lightening Rods," *Nature* 401 (23 September 1999): 329.

David Depew

FROM HEAT ENGINES

TO DIGITAL PRINTOUTS

Machine Models of the Body from the Victorian Era

to the Human Genome Project

The Human Genome Project and the Digital Image of the Body

It is not news to say that our insight into ourselves, into other sorts of living things, and indeed into nature as a whole penetrates no further and no deeper than what our current technologies can afford us by way of models. *Verum et factum convertuntur*, the eighteenth-century rhetorician Giambattista Vico famously wrote: our ideas can be said to be true only when we have used art to produce the made objects to which these ideas primarily refer. Nor was Vico alone in thinking that we can only understand things we have put together ourselves. Several decades after Vico published *The New Science*, Immanuel Kant proclaimed: "Reason has insight only into what it produces after a plan of its own."

By this standard at least, our knowledge of biology has lagged well behind our knowledge of physics and chemistry. Physics found its first exploitable technological models in the seventeenth century.

While it is true that theoretical physics contributed much to the perfection of the art of ballistics, it was the art of ballistics—the technological practices that sprang up around siege and artillery warfare—that in no small measure gave rise to modern physics in the first place. Many early modern "natural philosophers" worked as part-time defense contractors. Chemistry, for its part, acquired its theoretical basis hand-in-hand with the development of chemical engineering in the second half of the nineteenth century. Nor was the connection with the art of war any less marked in this case than in mechanics. Bismarck's Germany was as aware as its bellicose successors that its ability to project its power was limited by access to natural resources. It sought to make up some of the difference through industrial chemistry. Arguably, however, it has only been in the last several decades that humans have begun to acquire abilities to manipulate living systems in ways that are quantitatively and qualitatively analogous to our skills in manipulating physical, chemical, and even biochemical systems. This quite recent transition has been accompanied, as all such sudden changes are, by extravagantly utopian hopes and equally extravagant fears. Talk about genetically engineered plants evokes visions of the end of hunger (a claim advanced by Archer Daniels Midland [ADM] in its television advertising) as well as of "frankenfoods." Talk about genetically engineered humans—"designer babies"—features paeans to reproductive choice as well as tirades against "backdoor eugenics."

What technologies, we may ask, and what discourses centered around sites of technological innovation, have constituted the condition of the possibility of the biogenetic revolution in the sense that ballistics once constituted the condition of the possibility of physics? Certainly, the massive expansion of techniques for making the body visible, and intervening by microsurgery in its workings, has had a lot to do with it. In this essay, however, my attention will be focused on biogenetic engineering proper, an array of technologies that goes no further back than the development of restriction enzyme techniques in the 1970s. Restriction enzymes are complex molecules found in bacterial cells. They have the ability to cut up pieces of foreign DNA and RNA at specific, recognizable sites. Because bacteria multiply very fast, this technique provides experimental platforms by means of which genes can be sequenced and the effects of different genetic combinations, which can be inserted into the genomes of the same or different species between the points where restriction enzymes cut, can be rigorously explored. Of particular interest are restriction fragment length polymorphisms (RFLPs), which cut the DNA of conspecific organisms at slightly different points. These differences, or polymorphisms, can be identified by using (automated versions of) the well-established technique of gel electrophoresis. Because the DNA polymorphisms that reside in each individual, including humans, underlie much of their diversity, RFLPs can be used to find genetic markers within a population, including variant alleles that fail to guide the correct development and proper functioning of a normal, healthy organism. It is hoped, even presumed, that the same recombinant DNA techniques that reveal defective genes can be used to cure inherited genetic diseases by introducing nondefective pieces of DNA into the somatic cells, indeed even into the sex cells and hence lineages, of malfunctioning organisms. It is imagined that biotechnology of this sort has initiated a revolution in medicine no less staggering in its implications than the germ theory of disease, which got underway in the nineteenth century and has dominated medical science ever since.

To date, the industrial uses of transgenic technology have been most vividly felt in agriculture, where they sometimes meet a somewhat dystopic reception. In view of the potential of genetic biotechnology for meddling with the human reproductive system, however, and so of disturbing the numinous set of values with which every culture has surrounded its regulation and expression, it is odd that the dominant tone of the discourse about genetic medicine has been surprisingly, though far from uniformly, upbeat. To the extent that this is so, I suspect it is because the topic of genetic medicine has from the outset been framed by promises that advocates of the Human Genome Project put into circulation when they first went searching for funding in the mid-1980s.

In their joint announcement of the earlier-than-expected completion of the primary, mapping phase of the Human Genome Project in summer 2000, Bill Clinton and Tony Blair did little more than repeat promises that had first been made in 1992 in a largely promotional anthology for the Human Genome Project called *The Code of Codes*.[1] In his contribution to this book, Walter Gilbert, a pioneer in the techniques of gene sequencing, spoke of the proposed project as a "search for the Holy Grail." He looked forward to the day when "one can pull a CD out of one's pocket and say, 'Here's a human being; it's me.'" "Over the next ten years," Gilbert continued, "we will understand how we are assembled in accord with dictation by our genetic information."[2] It is noteworthy that eight years later, in a newspaper article reporting the earlier-than-predicted completion of the mapping phase of the project in June 2000, Elizabeth Neus of Gannett News Service duly reported, "By the end of June, scientists hope to have reached a biological Holy Grail."[3]

Seldom, I suspect, has rhetoric designed to acquire funding flowed so smoothly down a single channel from senders to receivers over such a protracted period of time. If anything, the puffery has been enhanced by casual misinterpretations of what authors like Gilbert actually said. Gilbert thought of the Holy Grail as a distant prospect in which medicine would have transformed the human condition, not as the outcome of the mapping phase of the Human Genome Project itself. This remarkable rhetorical success leads to the first assertion I will put forward in this essay. The rhetoric of the Human Genome Project, I claim, could not have been as successfully deployed as it has been (and probably will continue to be) if the lived body had not already come widely to be seen as a computational system running on a genetic program. The mere fact that transgenics is generally thought of as a matter of uploading and downloading information from one hard drive to another, thereby construing genes as discrete packets of information, testifies to the truth of this judgment. (A recent cartoon features a young boy saying to his mother, "I know how I was downloaded, but I don't understand how I was uploaded.")

The relevance of computation to the rise of genetic biotechnology is not limited, accordingly, to the relatively trivial fact that high-powered computers and programs are needed to keep track of the information about where variant genes are in the chromosome, and how they differ from individual to individual, population to population, species to species. The Viconian themes announced above support a more contentious and more interesting claim: if computational machines had not been used to interpret organisms as print-out from a genetic program, the swift transformation of transgenic technology from an experimental aid to abstruse theoretical inquiry into a growing plethora of biotechnological industries might not have occurred so quickly or effortlessly. Nor, I suspect, would the diffusion of the rhetoric of the Human Genome Project have been put in such a positive light. Nothing like this, as I have already mentioned, has happened in the field of agricultural biogenetics. It is hard to resist the conclusion that a conception of the human body (indeed of the mind, too)[4] as printout from a digital program running on a hydrocarbon-based rather a silicon-based computer has not only preceded and to some extent guided the reception of the Human Genome Project, but has more or less silently justified it as well.

How, we may go on to ask, did this figuration of the body arise? The digital tropology of the body that now shills for the Human Genome Project is quite recent; in its full-blown form, it extends no further back than the enthusiasm for computer programs that characterized the personal computer revolution of the 1980s. At the same time, however, this rhetoric is clearly the culmination of a series of rhetorical framings of the body that first began to take shape when scientists in the late 1950s and early 1960s tried to determine the relationship between DNA and protein. Scientific mythology suggests that the "coding problem," as the effort to link ribonucleic acids to protein assembly was known to those working on it, was solved almost as soon as Francis Crick and James Watson discovered the structure of the DNA molecule in 1953. The fact is, however, that this effort was characterized by many false starts; a decade and a half passed before it was definitively worked out.[5] Eventually, it was determined that a redundant code transcribes the four bases of DNA into RNA and then translates RNA into the twenty amino acids out of which proteins are made. This "code of codes" was worked out by what historian of science Lily Kay has presented in her 2000 book *Who Wrote the Book of Life?* as a somewhat fortuitous conjuncture of three overlapping but nonetheless distinct discourses: molecular genetics, which was busy attempting to supplant classical genetics during this mid-century period; cybernetics, or the study of devices, whether analog or digital, for assuring that systems, both artificial and living, homeostatically maintain themselves in their environment by way of feedback, generally negative; and information or computer science, which emerged from the wartime experience of a group of talented mathematicians and electrical engineers who had been commandeered to crack codes (and solve problems connected with nuclear fission) by building, programming, and using first analog, then digital, computers.[6]

According to Kay, the trope of the Book of Life was deployed to allow this array of heterogeneous discourses to coalesce into a single, seemingly integrated tropological system.[7] This has been achieved by recycling an old metaphor: Galileo's and Descartes's idea that scientists read the Book of Nature in the same way that sacred Scripture has, by a gift of God, allowed us to read the Book of History. This trope reached an early peak in Newton's heady idea that in discovering the calculus he had stumbled on the language in which God had written the Book of Nature, by which he meant inanimate astrophysical nature. It was to be several centuries before the same image was brought to bear on living systems. When at last that came to pass, however, it gave new resonance to the Old Testament notion that our deeds, and our fate, are written in a Book of Life. Only at the end of the 1950s, Kay argues, did biochemists begin to recast their chemical representations of heredity as "scriptural," thereby bringing the "age-old metaphor" of the Book of Life to bear on a historically specific and culturally contingent problem: how to state the relation between genes and proteins.

Francis Crick was a continuously important source for the coding-decoding conception of the relationship between DNA, RNA, and protein. Throughout the 1960s, he and other influential scientific middlemen—James Watson, George Gamow, Robert Sinsheimer, Jacques Monod, and others—used the language of communication and information theory as a sort of pidgin in order to forge links between disciplines such as molecular biology, protein biochemistry, and immunology, all of which had important roles in the experimental work on which success in solving the coding problem depended, but whose native tongues were mutually unintelligible. The problem of communication among research communities was perhaps more responsible for the construction of a common object of inquiry in terms of the language of information theory than has been acknowledged. However that may be, by the time Sinsheimer reported the solution of the coding problem to the public in his widely disseminated 1967 work, *The Book of Life*, the DNA-RNA-protein link was presented unambiguously as an informational, indeed a linguistic, bond.[8] According to Kay, Sinsheimer's book did more than any other to turn what had been a facultative and pragmatic lingo, designed to facilitate communication between different research communities, into the obligatory "scriptural" image of DNA that has prevailed ever since. Writing in the *New Yorker* in the week preceding Clinton's and Blair's announcement in summer 2000, Robert Preston was doing little more than recycling Sinsheimer's title when he wrote, "The Book of Life is now opening, and we hold it in our hands."[9]

The connection between Sinsheimer's book and the Human Genome Project, it should also be noted, was far from merely journalistic. When Sinsheimer became chancellor of the University of California at Santa Cruz, he sought consciously to reverse his new university's persistently nonscientific image by teaming up with Charles DeLisi, an administrator at the Department of Energy and a former official at Los Alamos National Laboratory, to propose the Human Genome Project to an at first skeptical biological and medical community. For his part, DeLisi was betting that the genetic information that had been collected and stored at Los Alamos ever since the survey of the results of the Hiroshima bombing might help the laboratory negotiate its way into a future in which there might be less call for atomic weapons design.[10] In view of Sinsheimer's earlier exercises in figuration, it should not be surprising that he and DiLisi pitched their project as one in which the genetic structure for a human being was figured as "The Code of Codes." In using this phrase as the title of their 1992 anthology, Daniel Kevles and Leroy Hood (the latter of whom is a molecular geneticist who took a hand in the highly profitable work of developing automated gene sequencers) were merely following Sinsheimer's lead.[11] The phrase has circulated more or less uncritically ever since in both expert and lay communities.

Having reported on the role of scriptural tropology in articulating the notion of the lived body as printout from a code, in this essay I will as the first order of business project Kay's excellent historical work somewhat further back in time than the mid-twentieth century world on which she so diligently reports. Kay is fully aware that there was a time when it was still possible to talk about the relationship between genes, proteins, and traits without invoking scriptural imagery about this relationship, or indeed without invoking the notion of information transfer that this imagery was designed to capture. She declines to note, however, something that *has* been noticed by N. Katherine Hayles, who in her 1999 book *How We Became Posthuman* recognizes that the cybernetic-informational-scriptural image of the body that emerged in the last quarter of the twentieth century was not created out of whole cloth, but rather supervened on an older conception of the body as a thermodynamic engine or heat machine.[12] Thus my next order of business, after pushing the tropological history of the body as far back as the Victorian era where this thermodynamic image has its roots, will be to project the story Kay tells about the mid-century origins of the scriptural figuration of the body into the 1980s and 1990s, where this imagery began for the first time to be interpreted in explicitly digital ways. I will argue that the conception of the lived body as printout from a digital computer program arose from a technical, indeed philosophical, question about what biological information means rather than from any new empirical knowledge, and the central effect, if not the function, of its dissemination is to give ideological cover to the biotechnological revolution that is now upon us. The digitalization of the body, I wish to suggest, has pushed out of sight, by way of what rhetoricians (following Kenneth Burke) call "terministic screening," aspects of living things that are no less well established and important to our understanding than genetics, and no less relevant to the prospective successes and limitations of genetic medicine. I will argue that this result has been achieved by a series of slippages, silencings, and screenings that occurred precisely at the historical juncture when the discourse of a feedback-controlled or cybernetic body was recast, for quasi-theoretical reasons, in terms of digital information.

Seen in this light, Kay's implication that the cybernetic and digital conceptions of the body form a coherent line of development stands in need of qualification and disruption. There is little, I suggest below, that is biologically realistic or theoretically perspicuous about the notion of a digital body. By contrast, the older notion of a cybernetic body, which guided mid-century efforts to solve "the coding problem," is realistic enough. But, as Hayles has suggested, the notion of the body as a negative feedback system is realistic only to the extent that it was still tied by its mid-twentieth-century advocates to the energetic model of the body that had its roots in the mid-nineteenth-century technology of steam engines. The rhetoric of digitalization has cast this older image adrift. By attracting the cybernetic image of the body into its orbit, that is to say, the digital image of genetics has expunged the energetic, and ecologically embedded, view of the body on which cybernetics is actually based. The reasons for this erasure remain to be seen—and, if truth be told, its practical consequences deserve to be worried about.

In the middle of the nineteenth century, modern physics, which had for some time been organized in terms of the notion of force, was busy rearticulating itself in terms of the new architectonic concept of energy. It was in this context that a tropology of the body as an energy-using and entropy-dissipating system—a heat engine—began to displace earlier mechanistic conceptions. The most accessible technological model for this purpose was the water wheel, but only insofar as the water wheel was used to understand the workings of the steam engine. "We get mechanical effect," James Thompson wrote to his soon-to-be-more famous brother William, who became Lord Kelvin, "when we let water fall from one level to another, as well as when we let heat fall from one degree of intensity to another, lower intensity."[13] In both cases, and indeed in all cases where work is produced, energy itself is conserved, as Rudolf Clausius had stipulated in the first law of thermodynamics. Because of statistical considerations, however—disorder is more probable, *ceteris paribus*, than order—there is always at least some energy that cannot be captured into work: some waste, some dissipation, or, when it was given a mathematical measure by Boltzmann, some entropy. So says the second law of thermodynamics. As M. Norton Wise and Crosbie Smith have argued, Kelvin's primary interest in this law, which was to minimize dissipation and maximize efficient work in steam engines, was also of help to him in expressing his moral indignation at the dissipation of the lower classes, which had not yet been efficiently integrated into the industrial order. By the same token, however, it is likely that the latter concern, and the language associated with it, entered into the social construction of thermodynamics itself.[14]

In view of these technological tropings, it soon became obvious to biochemists, biologists, and medical scientists that the equilibrium or homeostasis of the lived body is not the result of a balance between four bodily secretions, or humors, as the Hippocratic and Galenic tradition had it, or between opposed centrifugal and centripetal forces, as Newtonians saw it, but between phases of a cycle in which the body takes in energy at one level, breaks it apart to do work, exports it in a degraded state to the environment, and begins over again by taking in more energy-containing matter. The constancy of this anabolic and catabolic cycle, which is itself modeled on the phases of a steam engine, is measured by temperature. By reiteratively asking how the organism staves off, however temporarily, the inevitable consequences of the second law, and how it manages to maintain itself in such a remarkably steady state, the energetic conception of the body frames much of what we now know about medicine. It undergirds, for example, the insistence of physicians that before they do anything else they must take a patient's temperature. It also marks the contested boundary between traditional anatomy, with its stress on inert morphology, and the more process-based physiology that is focused on the cell, which is conceived as a miniature factory for the efficient creation and dissemination of matter and energy.

The control of energy flows is as essential in the body as it is in industry, for without control it can be very violent and very inefficient indeed. The cell would incinerate itself unless its energetic work were not distributed over millions of very small reactions, each of which releases only a minuscule amount of heat. Although evolution has solved this problem for the cell, solutions to the analogous problem in industrial applications are hampered by the fact that control cannot be achieved by direct human intervention alone. Our visual and other sensory monitors, and indeed our brain itself, cannot quickly enough, precisely enough, or safely enough observe the process of energy release and direct its transmission.[15] Thus automatic control systems are required.[16]

In the case of external combustion or steam engines, this need was met by means of flywheels and mechanical governors. Governors are, quite literally, steering devices; the term comes from the Greek word *gubernetes*, steersman. The little flywheel governor invented by the Scotsman James Watt is paradigmatic of the mechanism. One can see the tropological application of this conception to the body in such phrases as "blowing one's top." A more fruitful application of this energy-and-control conception to the specific case of organisms did not occur, however, until external combustion or steam engines evolved into internal combustion engines. This development imported electricity into the energetic image of the body, both as a form of energy and as a means of control. In an internal combustion engine, electricity is used to release energy in the cylinders by sparking off an explosion of pressurized gas. Electricity is also used to control this energy release, transmitting it by means of on-off switches in the distributor. This model can be, and has been, readily superimposed onto the thermodynamical conception of the body that I have sketched above. For the form of energy on which organisms run is largely electrical energy generated by chemical gradients, for which nerves serve as conduits and switches. On this view, the brain can be portrayed as a sort of central switchboard that receives and sends on messages and, in order to maintain the body's characteristic homeostasis, distributes the overall load appropriately at peak times and down times, as in an electrical grid. Before the identification of DNA as hereditary material within the cell nucleus, it was even imagined that life itself might have begun when bolts of electricity "galvanized" the presumably undifferentiated protoplasm of the protocell into life. (Many a quaint feature film provides fevered images of this Promethean idea, which mirrors the role of energy release and control in the "lifelike" images afforded by the technology of moving pictures themselves.)[17]

An electrified body using chemical gradients emerges, accordingly, from the assimilation of organisms to heat engines. Yet as Erwin Schrödinger recognized in his influential 1944 essay *What Is Life?*, living things do more than merely exchange matter. They do even more than exchange energy. For unlike physical and chemical systems, which do both of these things, organisms have a remarkable ability to avoid the precipitous fall toward thermodynamic equilibrium that we call death by maintaining themselves in a homeostatic state far away from thermodynamic equilibrium. An ascription of agency to living things in expressing this sort of goal orientation is well-nigh unavoidable. In addition, unlike merely physical and chemical systems, organisms have a capacity actively to reduce the entropy production within their boundaries, which would otherwise take its toll far more quickly than we observe. "The essential thing in metabolism," Schrödinger wrote, "is that the organism succeeds in freeing itself from all the entropy it cannot help producing while alive."[18] Animals can do this without offending the second law by actively increasing the entropy of their surroundings, degrading it faster than would otherwise happen, by identifying prey, moving through space to get them, and using other organs to extract their energy by destroying and ingesting them. Plants, for their part, do this when they extract energy from soils that they deplete. In this sense, all organisms "suck order," as Schrödinger memorably phrased it, or "positive entropy," or what he called "negentropy" from their surroundings, especially from high-energy, organic components of their surroundings.

The conception of an organism as a peculiar sort of energy-using and entropy-dissipating system that can maintain itself far from thermodynamic equilibrium by means of internal feedback and external coupling to its environment informed the discourse of cybernetics that self-consciously emerged in the 1940s in the now famous Josiah Macy conferences.[19] The term "cybernetics" is merely a variant on the Greek word for a steersman, *gubernetes*, which we have already encountered. According to early cybernetic theorists like Norbert Wiener, whose 1948 book *Cybernetics: Control and Communication in the Animal and the Machine* was an influential development of Schrödinger's ideas of a few years earlier, cybernetics is a way of automating the task of determining, and in this sense knowing, when and in what quantities energy should be released or acquired in order to restore imbalances that would otherwise disturb the homeostatic end point that any goal-seeking system, by its very nature, is intended to attain and maintain, but which is constantly being threatened by the thermodynamic activities of the system itself.

For their parts, however, Schrödinger and Wiener could not imagine how organisms could stave off the disordering tendencies of the second law unless their ordering tendencies came from something that was already ordered. This is so because both men, trained as classical physicists, were still haunted by the Victorian image of the prospective heat death of the universe, which notoriously troubled such turn-of-the-century amateurs as Henry Adams. Thus, even physicists as advanced as Schrödinger and Wiener failed to recognize that organisms, like other complex systems that maintain themselves far away from thermodynamical equilibrium, have self-organizing or "autopoietic" properties that rely as much on positive as on negative feedback and, more importantly, do not depend for their functioning on a central control system.[20] It is these self-organizing properties that are more important than anything else, including allegedly coded information, in maintaining a living system far from thermodynamic equilibrium.

The first inklings of this thought emerged in the 1950s in the work of Nobel laureate Ilya Prigogine. His insights have been developed by the so-called second-order cybernetics of Humberto Maturana and Francisco Varela.[21] Even now, however, this alternative paradigm is highly contested—largely, I suspect, because many (techno)scientists, with their eye on both theoretical and technological control, are loath to give up the analogy between organisms and centrally controlled (and highly decomposable) industrial systems and machines. It is both true and interesting that Wiener himself was inclined to think of cybernetic machines as like organisms rather than the reverse; he was, as Hayles has argued, an anxious humanist.[22] It is no less true, however, that the digitalization of cybernetics (which began with the "numerical control" of machine tools but reached the figuration of genetic mechanisms only quite recently) has done more than anything else to reverse the direction of this analogy. We now commonly think of organisms and persons as like machines, carrying out instructions that are coded either in genes or neurons, and not the other way around. In view of the steady drift of both popular and expert thought in this direction, the so-called second-order cybernetics expressed in the work of Prigogine's followers, including Maturana and Varela, has taken upon itself the difficult task of making plain precisely the *disanalogies* between organisms and machines.[23]

To follow this body of thought toward the more ecologically embedded and interpretive framework in which living things are placed, however, lies well beyond the scope of this essay. Here I can merely note that, although an alternative path lay open, the assumption of (and demand for) central control of systems that are regarded more as assemblies of replaceable parts than as organic totalities passed, by way of the idea of a coded program, from the cyberneticists of the 1950s to today's theorists, technologists, and propagandists of the Human Genome Project. Even if its medical successes eventually prove to be more limited than anticipated, it should be recognized that digital discourse about the body has already succeeded, perhaps irreversibly, in publicly legitimating the idea that the body is a complex machine made of subassemblies that can in principle be taken apart and put back together again. The risks and difficulties of genetic medicine are played down by the circulation of this system of imagery. Changing one's genes can appear in its light as no more difficult than replacing the logic board of one's computer. Unfortunately, however, the blithe dissemination of this very imagery may create or exacerbate some of the problems for which this tropology envisions a metaphorical, and to that extent fantasized, solution.

How, we may now ask, did the digitalization of the cybernetically construed body come about? Again, we must begin with Schrödinger. In *What Is Life?*, Schrödinger, unable as we have seen to break with classical thermodynamics, predicted that "the nucleus of the fertilized egg would contain an elaborate code-script involving all the future development of the organism."[24] This code-script was to provide a source of "order from order" that would guide the development of organisms and direct their ongoing attempts to beat the second law. Memorably, Schrödinger also predicted that this code-script would be inscribed in an "aperiodic crystal" that would serve as a template for organic reproduction in the same way that ordinary crystals, working on much simpler algorithms, serve as templates for new ones.

The search for the genetic material, which was first imagined as a contest between the two basic materials of the cell nucleus—proteins and ribonucleic acids—was explicitly and actively guided by a reading of this prediction; Crick and Watson, when they finally showed how DNA could do the job, literally thought that they had found Schrödinger's "aperiodic crystal." I say that this research program was guided by a *reading* of Schrödinger's speculation, however, because, while Crick and Watson blithely used the notion of *coded* information, Schrödinger himself was merely thinking of a template copying mechanism, albeit one more mathematically complex than that of a periodic crystal.[25] Nonetheless, this reading stood. It guided the efforts that went on throughout the 1960s to link the four bases of DNA and RNA (adenine, guanine, thymine, and cytosine) to the twenty amino acids out of which protein is made. Until the amino acid sequences of particular proteins were known, this problem was well-nigh impossible to solve. For in the absence of sequence information about proteins, the problem, as one researcher noted, would be a little like trying to decode the Rosetta Stone without knowing anything about any of the languages, Greek, Egyptian, and Hebrew, that were interrelated by the stone.[26] Things got a lot better, accordingly, when the amino acid sequence of the tobacco mosaic virus was fully analyzed. That was in 1960. In the following year, Marshall Nirenberg and Walter Matthaei, working at the National Institutes for Health, established by very clever experimentation how three RNA bases specify a particular amino acid, phenylalanine, in the bacteria *e coli*. On the one hand, this result confirmed the speculation of George Gamov and other "code crackers" that amino acids would be specified by a nonoverlapping code of triplet bases, or codons, such as AAT or GGC. On the other hand, it set off a race to verify the larger hypothesis about the role of DNA in protein assembly by completing the correlation between codons and all twenty amino acids. This took some years.

During this time, the project of decoding "the code of codes" was universally framed by those participating in it as matter of communication—of sending a coded message down a channel in such a way that the message sent would be accurately picked up by the receiver. There can be little doubt that the most important consideration in fixing this representational matrix was the fact, also established in the early 1960s, that DNA specifies proteins by way of one form of RNA, "messenger" RNA, which carries information to a ribosomal site where protein is manufactured. The notion that a message had to be sent from place to place by way of an intermediary in turn reinforced the notion that this message had to be written in some sort of code. This link was readily forged in large part because throughout the 1960s the DNA-RNA-protein relationship was explicitly guided by Claude Shannon and Warren Weaver's 1949 book *The Mathematical Theory of Communication*, which promulgated the conception of communication as quantifiable bits of information moving down a channel by way of more or less efficient codes (such as Morse Code). It was during this period that the four bases of DNA first came to be thought of as letters: A, C, G, T. They are, of course, not letters at all, any more than amino acids are words or proteins are sentences. They are merely chemicals with a certain specificities for bonding with other chemicals.

It is of great importance to notice at this point that the wellnigh universal acceptance of mathematical communication theory as a guide to unraveling the DNA-RNA-protein relationship was not yet equivalent to the notion that an organism is a readout from something like a computer program. During the period in question, in fact, computers and computer programs were not yet widely known. As a gesture toward explaining why this further transformation took place, I will point to four crucial, if insufficient, moments in this process. At each of these moments the energetic view of the body on which the coherence of the cybernetic image is based was thrown deeper and deeper into the shadows.

The first consideration takes us back once more to the cybernetic pioneers of the late 1940s. All of them, as we have seen, viewed information as a matter of feedback control of energetic processes, whether natural or artifactual. Precisely because they presupposed this energetic framework, they were all impressed by how *little* energy is needed to run an organic control mechanism. Wiener clearly acknowledges in *Cybernetics: Control and Communication in Animal and Machine* that "the living organism is above all a heat engine." He quickly goes on to note, however, that "the bookkeeping which is most essential to describe organic function is not one of energy." The books are kept, Wiener says, in informational terms: "The information fed into the central control system [of the body] very often contains information concerning the functioning of the effectors themselves."[27]

In retrospect it is easy to see in this text Shannon and Weaver's claim, put forward the following year, that information can be quantified into discrete bits. It is no less easy to see in it an acknowledgment of the work of the code crackers and engineers who were beginning to build computers based on digital programs. It is even easy to see in it an anticipation of the molecular geneticists' notion, in the wake of Crick and Watson's triumph in 1953, that organic information is "encoded" into pieces of DNA. When one looks directly at Wiener's text, however, there is no mention, or even inkling, of any of these things. Information is not quantified or localized in the genes. It is guided, admittedly, by some sort of "aperiodic crystal." Yet just how this happens is never made at all clear; if anything is certain, in fact, it is that Wiener's picture of this control mechanism is not that of digital printout but rather of the control of energetic flow by feedback cycles that are distributed over the entire system rather than metonymically compressed into one of its parts. Wiener is still imagining the control of the body, construed as a heat engine, as being like the control of a home furnace by a thermostat—an analogue device, even when it has a digital readout; or like a ship stabilized by gyrocompasses and automatic steering systems; or, even more appropriate, like the newer military technologies that had been set afoot in the final years of the World War II, such as "self-propelled missiles and anti-aircraft fire-control systems," which are explicitly mentioned in the text and in whose development Wiener himself had a hand. On this view, information, whatever it is, comes into the system from an external environment. Once there, it is distributed throughout a system and the environment to which it is linked. It is not read out from a magic molecule that is sealed off from the outside within a machine or an organism.

This reading of Wiener's text leads to a second crucial moment in the emergence of the digital image of the body. The solution of the coding problem in biology—the use of the paired bases of DNA to specify the twenty amino acids from which protein is assembled—was put in place by means of what came to be called the "central dogma" of molecular biology, which forbade the reinscription of amino acid sequences, and hence the information in proteins, into RNA and DNA sequences. It was Crick who formulated the central dogma.[28] It conveys, as we now know, a decidedly inadequate sense of what goes on in the cell nucleus. Our coevolution with viruses, for example, depends on their wicked ability to insert their DNA sequences into our cellular machinery by means of what is called reverse transcription; as much as 40 percent of the genome, it is currently estimated, may consist of mechanisms for blocking, containing, or otherwise controlling this sort of invasion. In taking up genetic biotechnology, we are, from this perspective, doing nothing other than aping nature's profound ability to plug the DNA of one organism into another. The extent of which this process goes on in a competively coevolving world is only becoming clear to us now that we are acquiring mastery of the techniques of gene transfer that mimic it; such is the power of the Viconian epistemology evoked at the outset of this essay.

At the time, however, there were good reasons for insisting on the central dogma. Failure to abide by it would, in the first instance, open up living systems to the inheritance of acquired characteristics. This leakage from "nurture" into "nature" would not only bring down the wrath of decidedly anti-Lamarckian evolutionary biologists on the new community of molecular geneticists but would undermine their own markedly reductionist ideology, which aimed explicitly at absorbing the anti-Lamarckian genetical theory of natural selection into molecular biology rather than at contesting it. (Watson has acknowledged that his personal motives for working on the structure of DNA, in addition to the glory of winning the Nobel Prize, included a burning desire to prove that life is nothing but chemistry; other pioneers of molecular biology, such as Jacques Monod, held similarly reductionistic views.)[29] There were, moreover, practical reasons for insisting on the central dogma in addition to theoretical ones. Without the central dogma in place, it would be difficult to maintain the boundaries of a research program that was single-mindedly focused on the coding problem, and in consequence studiously indifferent to (and in some cases ignorant of) many other phenomena going on in the cell, even in its nucleus. In many of these processes, there is indeed massive feedback between the environment, the organism, the cells, and the nucleus. Even if they cannot inscribe the information they bring directly into the genome, environmental signals tell cells when to turn genes on and off. It is just here that the practical demands of sealing off a research program from complexities and disturbances resulted in something more dubious—an erasure of complex cellular and environmental processes by exclusive concentration on the one-way "transcription" and "translation" of allegedly information-containing genes into proteins. From this perspective, the multidirectional flow encoded in the energetic-cybernetic image of the body projected by Schrödinger and Wiener was, in spite of its limitations, far more biologically realistic than the unidirectional image that emerged among molecular biologists, which continues implicitly to dominate the rhetoric of the Human Genome Project.[30]

I come now to a third moment in the emergence of a digitalized version of the cybernetic body. It was pointed out by many people in the 1960s, including Shannon and Weaver themselves, that, if mathematical communication theory has anything at all to do with it, genes and genetic programs can be said to store, call up, and transmit information only in a formal sense.[31] Quantified information does not, literally, make *sense*. It contains merely a syntax, not a semantics. To be afforded a more biologically realistic interpretation, genetic information had to be given a semantics, and indeed something analogous to a pragmatics, that would determine its uses. What did the job was the evolutionary concept that variant genes or alleles code for slightly variant forms of proteins in organisms, families, and populations *just because* variation within the amino acid sequences of proteins is the very stuff out of which adaptive traits have been made by natural selection. In other words, genetic "information" came to be regarded as meaningful in a semantic sense because, from a pragmatic point of view, it was adaptively functional in the same way that a machine's construction is adapted to uses to which it is put. Molecular biologists and evolutionary biologists all signed on to this interpretation. It was by means of this evolutionary interpretation, in fact, that the central dogma of molecular biology was converted from a heuristic tool for policing the boundaries of a particular research program into what, by the mid-1960s, was taken to be a fundamental law of nature.

The selectionist interpretation of the *meaning* of genetic information certainly gave substance to the evolutionary biologist Theodosius Dobzhansky's famous maxim that "nothing in biology makes sense except in the light of evolution." Nonetheless, there arose throughout the 1960s and 1970s considerable anxiety among many evolutionary biologists about the prospective assimilation of genetic Darwinism, whose fundamental principles had already been worked out in the 1930s, to molecular biology. For one thing, in spite of their common agreement on the central dogma, there was no love lost between these disciplinary communities. During the entire period we are studying, molecularists were busy taking over biology departments at universities by calling into question the scientific credentials of "whole organism" biologists, including ecologists and evolutionary biologists. Even E. O. Wilson, whose proposal for a gene-based sociobiology would later cause him to be painted as highly reductionistic by the standards of many other evolutionary biologists, was heard to refer to James Watson, his colleague at Harvard during the 1960s, as "Caligula." (Wilson claimed that Watson was the most unpleasant human being he had ever met.)[32] Evolutionary biologists, moreover, seconded by many philosophers of science who came to their defense, were doubtful that the Mendelian notion of genes on which genetic Darwinism was founded could ever be reduced to the molecular gene. Certainly there is a tie between protein and adaptations. But that tie is complicated, indirect, and many-to-many. There are so many levels to go through that, except in cases where variation in one codon of a particular amino acid leads directly to physiological failure, as in the case of phenylketonuria, it is well-nigh impossible to infer any direct and exclusive route between a given gene and a given adapted trait.[33] Many well-informed genetic Darwinians would agree with Richard Lewontin, an eminent population geneticist who is no friend either to the selfish gene theory or to the overblown medical promises associated with the Human Genome Project, that it is impossible to "compute the organism" from its DNA sequences: "Even the *organism* does not compute itself from its DNA. A living organism is at any moment in its life the unique consequence of a developmental history that results from the interaction of and determination by internal and external forces; and the external forces, what we usually think of as the 'environment,' are themselves partly a consequence of the activities of the organism itself as it produces and consumes the conditions of its own existence."[34]

Nevertheless, by the 1980s a growing number of influential Darwinians began to be converted to the view that the Mendelian gene, on which genetic Darwinism had hitherto been predicated, is identical to the molecular gene, and to a presumption that the tie between DNA, protein, and adaptive traits—including behavioral traits—is more straightforward and potentially unravelable than had been assumed. The most influential theorist in leading this *volte face* has been Richard Dawkins of Oxford University. Dawkins's conception of "the selfish gene" was designed to reformulate genetic Darwinism in such as way that adapted traits come into existence just because they are the means whereby coding sectors of DNA get replicants of themselves represented in greater numbers in successive generations. Those chunks of DNA—genes, by Dawkins's lights—that succeed best in building the adapted traits that fight their battles with other organisms become, to the extent of this success, "immortal replicators." In spite of the loud, but largely ineffective, protests of figures such as Lewontin, this DNA-centered conception of natural selection, in which organisms and their traits serve as mere "vehicles" for the self-perpetuation of self-replicating DNA, had become, under the influence of the sociobiological and evolutionary-psychological research programs that have been framed in its terms, so dominant by the last decade of the twentieth century that it had monopolized the name "Darwinism."

I come by this route to the fourth and final moment in the process by which genetic programs, already scripturalized in the way described by Kay and rendered linear by the central dogma, began to be construed as digital printout. Until recently at least, organism-centered (as distinct from gene-centered) Darwinians have not been opposed to construing the genome as containing a genetic program. Ernst Mayr, for example, professor at Harvard's Museum of Comparative Zoology and a founding father of the Modern Evolutionary Synthesis, has long spoken of genomes as containing "genetic programs." Eager to burnish the credentials of genetic Darwinism by extruding from it any lingering elements of Lamarckism, Mayr's assent to the central dogma has been sealed by his construction of the genome as guiding the development of an embryo by means of such programs.[35] In saying this, however, Mayr was not thinking either about a linear, one-to-one relationship between genes and adapted traits, or about a digital program running on computers. The latter had barely been developed when Mayr first started using the phrase "genetic program." Instead, Mayr was thinking of the genome in good mid-century cybernetic terms as a goal-oriented, feedback-driven "teleonomic" (rather than the more suspiciously Lamarckian "teleological") process. In this cybernetic conception of the relationship between genes and organisms Mayr was at one with the cybernetically oriented researchers at the Institut Pasteur—Monod, Francois Jacob, and Andre Lwoff—who first discovered how structural genes are turned on and off in the process of development by regulatory sectors of the genome.[36] Mayr's thinking also accorded, in this respect at least, with the work of developmentalist Darwinians such as C. H. Waddington, who since the 1940s had been appropriating cybernetic conceptions of feedback to explain the way in which embryos, as they slide down "epigenetic landscapes," can push a restart button to compensate for the many contingencies, some induced by insults, others due merely to chance, that a fertilized egg must encounter as it differentiates. Waddington went out of his way to insist that "the traffic is certainly two way."[37] Mayr would have agreed.

It is precisely *not* this conception of "genetic program," however, that has been projected by Dawkins in books such as *The Blind Watchmaker* (1986) and *Climbing Mount Improbable* (1998), which followed *The Selfish Gene* (first edition, 1976). In these works the assimilation of genetic programs to computer programs—and in particular to so-called genetic algorithms that mimic the sheep-and-goats process of natural selection, in which only adapted combinations of genes are allowed to "reproduce"—is presented as a way of adumbrating, protecting, and even empirically confirming the selfish gene hypothesis, which was first put forward without any analogy to computational software or hardware. In this approach, Dawkins has been seconded by the philosopher Daniel Dennett, who in his 1995 monograph *Darwin's Dangerous Idea* construes natural selection itself as an "algorithm" in which various genetic combinations or "macros"—stable, even immortal, units of genetic structure and phenotypic function that can be recycled into new combinations whenever adaptive utility requires—are submitted to a process in which inefficient combinations are programmatically weeded out by a recursive decision procedure.[38] This "algorithmic" construction of natural selection inscribes computer imagery into the very process of natural selection itself. "The capacity of computers to run algorithms with tremendous speed and reliability," writes Dennett, "is now permitting theoreticians to explore Darwin's dangerous idea in ways heretofore impossible, with fascinating results."[39]

Fascinating as it may be, this "algorithmic" conception of natural selection—Darwin's "dangerous idea"—is foreign to anything in the earlier history of Darwinism. In its disturbance of the delicate balance between the chancy and the necessitated aspects of the process of natural selection, this tropology gives the impression that the evolutionary process is more orderly, more programmatic, more oriented toward adaptive efficiency than the main line of Darwinism has hitherto assumed. This effect is rhetorically enforced by the projection of the language of engineering design onto the statistical process of natural process. Dennett even speaks of natural selection as a designer, whereas Darwin, and the majority of Darwinians after him, have merely claimed that selection achieves what design produces without a designer.[40] This rhetorical performance is underwritten by the belief that we have finally built the right kinds of machines to make sense out of living nature, and to show that natural selection is, as Dennett puts it, "the best idea anyone ever had."[41]

The assimilation of the notion of a genetic program to a digital readout is, no doubt, largely the product of a pretheoretical public enthusiasm for seeing the world through the eyes of a new technology. For journalists, computer programs provide an inviting source of metaphors useful in translating technical results into terms that various publics can readily understand. Taking this system of imagery seriously, however, is a different matter. Dennett's reasons for using it to make a theoretical case are, from one point of view at least, innocent enough. He wishes to give aid and comfort to Dawkins's conception of natural selection, to back up the central dogma, and implicitly, at least, to extend the scriptural imagery that, as Kay has shown, has come to constitute genetic discourse. At the same time, when it is disseminated into the wider public sphere in which genetic and other forms of biotechnology are being harnessed to capitalist production, Dawkins's and Dennett's digital tropology gives a tacit blessing to biogenetic engineering by conceiving of natural selection as a machinelike process with an efficient testing and management system, as ruthless in its decision making as any downsizing post-Reagan capitalist enterprise. This rhetoric celebrates the cyborgian notion that there is no distinction in principle between organisms and machines that can be programmed to perform various tasks. It supports the view that, in a reversal of the words of the Nicene Creed, organisms are made, not born, *factum, non genitum*. It thereby pushes into the background the populational, statistical, and chance aspects of Darwinism that have enabled it during the twentieth century to become a mature science.[42]

As widespread as digital imagery of the gene now is among both expert and popular audiences, it is nonetheless a markedly imprecise representation of the relationship between genes and traits. Even if we insist on seeing the relationship between nucleic acids and protein as a coded and programmed one, still there is no "machine language"—no binary system of zeros and ones—lurking beneath the correlation between the base pairs of nucleic acids and proteins. To be sure, a tropology that construes genes as "macros," which are recycled by both evolution and human ingenuity when occasion demands, has been useful in recording and expressing one of the most salient discoveries that has arisen from sequence data generated by the various "model organism" programs—mouse, fruit fly, flatworm, bacterium—that have gone on concurrently with the Human Genome Project. Genes, it seems, are highly conserved across very distant lineages. Nonetheless, it is by no means clear that the genes that are conserved across distant lineages make sufficient contact with the conception of genes that figures in Darwinian population genetics, with its stress on quite subtle differences among the alleles that are distributed statistically in populations, to contribute to the further development of evolutionary theory.

Precisely this suspicion has been voiced by Darwinians and philosophers who, like Lewontin, tend to see in the Human Genome Project, with its inflated and utopian rhetoric about curing diseases, enhancing reproductive choice, and intervening benevolently in social policy by identifying genes for "homelessness" and a "propensity for violence," a worrisome underestimation of genetic diversity and epigenetic complexity, and a revival of quasi-eugenic political and social fantasies that are deeply, if sometimes unwittingly, embedded within the checkered history of the Darwinian tradition.[43] Even when advocates of the Human Genome Project insist that the sequence data they put down as "the gene for X" are no more than a point of reference for comparison among individuals and populations, population geneticists like Lewontin suspect that the very idea of calling a single sequence *the* gene for some species-specific trait serves as a terministic screen behind which the natural diversity that exists within populations—which, in its struggle to overcome its eugenic past, the Darwinian tradition recognized only with great difficulty—disappears from view and is replaced by the homogenizing "quality control" tendencies on which genetic engineering depends and at which it is explicitly aimed at producing. Digitalized rhetorics of the gene have the effect of minimizing this conceptual dissonance, at the expense of the gene concept that is built into evolutionary population genetics. If properly diagnosed, however, this conceptual dissonance may in the end serve to show that genetic variation and selection cannot be reduced to molecular machinery, and that Dawkins's selfish gene, which was designed to hybridize the Mendelian gene with the molecular gene, subtracts more from good science than it adds.

Whatever its relation to the larger contours of the Darwinian tradition, the moral of *this* essay is that the digital tropology of the body has obscured ecological and energetic facts that, in spite of its limitations, had been brought to light by cybernetics with its link to the heat machine. When considered as a formal algorithmic process analogous to the reiterated running of a computer program, natural selection must be presented as "substrate neutral"; that is, as indifferent to the kinds of material on which it operates—carbon based, silicon based, and so forth—and to the unique sorts of processes, structures, and properties that may inhere in particular materials. Dennett is explicit on this very point: "Darwin's dangerous idea is reductionism incarnate . . . Its being the idea of an algorithmic process makes it all the more powerful, since the substrate neutrality it thereby possesses permits us to consider its applicability to just about anything."[44] This formalized conception has obscured, however, not only the statistical nature of population genetics, but the complex physiology of the cell and the organism as energy processing, cybernetically controlled, goal-seeking, homeostasis-maintaining systems that are coupled deeply to energy flows in their environment through the specificities of the materials on which they are based. What has replaced this notion is the idea that genes specify functional modules that can be taken out of and inserted into the organism in the same way they are taken out of and into machines.

To be sure, few contemporary biologists or biochemists will deny that bodies use genetic information precisely in order to efficiently process energy so that it does work. Even a newspaper report in May 2000 about progress in the Human Genome Project concedes that "proteins, not genes, do the work. They build tissues, digest food, store memories, process waste, and tell cells when to die."[45] Enthusiasts for treating the organism as a collection of "macros," moreover, continue to speak of the ways in which living things "beat," as Dennett puts it, the second law.[46] Nonetheless, one almost never hears that, far from genes giving instructions to everything else in the cell, it takes all of the complex energy-and-matter cycling processes that are distributed through the cell to tell genes when to build tissue, digest food, store memories, process waste, or die. Nor in casual contemporary talk about how organisms "beat" or "stave off" the second law is any distinction registered between closed and isolated thermodynamic systems, such as those whose "heat deaths" Lord Kelvin and Henry Adams worried about, and the open, far-from-equilibrium systems that are actually presupposed by a robust and realistic cybernetic discourse of living systems. As a result, the current apotheosis of the digital body, by tending to drop out the cybernetic middle term, has led to conceptions of biogenetic engineering that minimize and misconstrue the structuring and constraining roles that energetics actually plays in living things. Digital imagery also assigns a far greater degree of agency to genes, which after all are relatively inert molecules, than they can possibly exercise in a complex system in which nothing happens without feedback, both positive and negative. This exaggerated sense of the agency of the genes is an effect of the erasure of everything that stands between a gene and the organisms in which it is, after all, only a minute part. This erasure, which began with the scripturalization of DNA, has been considerably enhanced by the recent digitalization of the gene.[47]

A digitalized image of the body is probably necessary if a conception of the organism favorable to unrestricted biotechnology and utopian medical technoscience is to be legitimated. Industrial genetics demands a body that is a manipulable collection of genetic-physiological-behavioral modules that can be taken apart and reassembled like so many "macros." Anything more holistic would be technically intractable and morally suspect. Nonetheless, the systematic erasure of the distinction between the natural and the artifactual that is implied by the digital image of the gene-protein-trait-organism relationship cannot help but create a discursive framework within which unrestricted genetic technology and overly optimistic genetic medicine can flourish without a just appreciation of the difficulties, both physiological and ecological, that these new technologies, however useful and inevitable they may be, must encounter. The dissemination of the digital image can, accordingly, lead to misperceptions on the part of the public, and perhaps on the part of professionals themselves, about just how complicated and messy genetic medicine and genetic agriculture are likely to be. Precisely because we will be, and even should be, engaging in these practices and techniques, it is desirable to have an accurate, and ideologically uncontaminated, conception of what we are and will be doing.

Notes

1 Daniel Kevles and Leroy Hood, eds., *The Code of Codes: Scientific and Social Issues in the Human Genome Project* (Cambridge: Harvard University Press, 1992).

2 Walter Gilbert, "A Vision of the Grail," in Kevles and Hood, eds., *The Code of Codes*, 96.

3 Elizabeth Neus, "Genetics 'Man on the Moon' Moment Nears," *Iowa City Daily Press Citizen* (19 June 2000): 1.

4 In this essay I leave out of consideration a parallel development in which the coalescence of various disciplinary strands into "cognitive science" has been predicated on a conception of the mind as printout from software that runs on the hardware of the brain. Key to this idea is the so-called functionalist interpretation of the mind-body relationship, which was initially set forth by Hilary Putnam, according to which mental functions are distinct from, but not independent of, bodily states because, although every mental function must be realized in some material or another, the same function can be realized in different materials. This doctrine, which skirts both traditional materialism and Cartesianism, is built on

and gives added support to the notion that the relationship between mind and brain is like the difference between computer software and hardware. It thus illustrates clearly the marked dependence of our conceptions on our technologies that is the leitmotif of this essay.

5 A standard history is Horace Freeland Judson, *The Eighth Day of Creation* (New York: Simon and Schuster, 1979).

6 Lily E. Kay, *Who Wrote the Book of Life? A History of the Genetic Code* (Stanford: Stanford University Press, 2000).

7 A similar thesis has been defended in a different idiom in Richard Doyle, *On Beyond Living: Rhetorical Transformations of the Life Sciences* (Stanford: Stanford University Press, 1997).

8 Robert L. Sinsheimer, *The Book of Life* (Reading, Mass.: Addison-Wesley, 1967).

9 Robert Preston, "The Genome Warrior," *New Yorker* (12 June 2000): 66.

10 On the atomic bomb and the origins of the Human Genome Project, see John Beatty, "Origins of the U.S. Human Genome Project: The Changing Relationship of Genetics to National Security," in *Controlling Our Destiny: Historical, Philosophical, Social, and Ethical Perspectives on the Human Genome Project*, ed. Phillip Sloan (Notre Dame, Ind.: University of Notre Dame Press, 1999).

11 Kevles and Hood, eds., *The Code of Codes*.

12 N. Katherine Hayles, *How We Became Posthuman: Virtual Bodies in Cybernetics, Literature, and Informatics* (Chicago: University of Chicago Press, 1999), 100-108. The theme is more fully developed in Hayles's earlier work, *Chaos Bound: Orderly Disorder in Contemporary Literature and Science* (Ithaca: Cornell University Press, 1990).

13 Quoted in M. Norton Wise and Crosbie Smith, "Work and Waste: Political Economy and Natural Philosophy in Nineteenth Century Britain (III)," *History of Science* 28 (1990): 345.

14 M. Norton Wise and Crosbie Smith, *Energy and Empire: A Biographical Study of Lord Kelvin* (Cambridge: Cambridge University Press, 1989).

15 Maxwell's demon, who pushes molecules one way or another by inspecting them, affords an image of the problem of control by inspection. Maxwell's conclusion is that there is no such demon in nature. The process of the distribution of energy states in molecules is purely statistical, random, and chancy.

16 See also James R. Beniger, *The Control Revolution: Technological and Economic Origins of the Information Society* (Cambridge: Harvard University Press, 1986).

17 For deeper reflections on how film, as a modernist medium, inscribes the conditions of its own production, see Garrett Stewart, *Between Film and Screen* (Chicago: University of Chicago Press, 1999).

18 Erwin Schrödinger, *What Is Life? The Physical Aspect of the Living Cell* (Cambridge: Cambridge University Press, 1946), 76.

19 For a detailed account of the history and proceedings of the Macy conferences, see Hayles, *How We Became Posthuman*, 50–83.

20 On these concepts, see David Depew and Bruce H. Weber, "Self-Organization," in *The MIT Encyclopedia of the Cognitive Sciences*, ed. Robert Wilson and Frank Kiel (Cambridge: MIT Press / Bradford Books, 1999), 737–38.

21 Humberto Maturana and Francisco J. Varela, *Autopoeisis and Cognition: The Realization of the Living* (Dordrecht: Reidel, 1980).

22 Hayles, *How We Became Posthuman*, 84–100.

23 See also the journal *Cybernetics and Human Knowing: A Journal of Second-Order Cybernetics, Autopoeisis, and Cyber-Semiotics*, edited by Soren Brier.

24 Schrödinger, *What Is Life?* 61.

25 Kay makes this point in *Who Wrote the Book of Life?*

26 As Kay shows, the Rosetta Stone image was common among researchers during the 1950s; it adumbrates the Book of Life metaphor.

27 Wiener, *Cybernetics*, 41–42.

28 Francis Crick, "On Protein Synthesis," *Symposia of the Society for Experimental Biology* 12 (1958): 138–67, and "The Central Dogma of Molecular Biology," *Nature* 227 (1970): 561–63.

29 James D. Watson, "A Personal View of the [Human Genome Project]," in Kevles and Hood, eds., *The Code of Codes*, 164. The materialist reductionism of the molecular biology community was a marked part of its internal culture. See Watson's memoir, *The Double Helix* (New York: Atheneum, 1980), and Jacques Monod, *Chance and Necessity* (New York: Vintage, 1972).

30 A full inventory of the complexities of cellular replication is presented by Eve Jablonka and Marion J. Lamb in *Epigenetic Inheritance and Evolution: The Lamarckian Dimension* (Oxford: Oxford University Press, 1995). Jablonka and Lamb characterize their project as "Lamarckian" because they wish to ferret out aspects of this process that defy the central dogma. This rhetorical choice, which can easily backfire, testifies implicitly to the hegemony of the central dogma over contemporary Darwinians, who have signed on the central dogma with few reservations, and who in consequence have given the impression that to defy the central dogma is to make oneself over as a non-Darwinian.

31 Kay, *Who Wrote the Book of Life?* 303–4.

32 See U. Segerstrale, *Defenders of the Truth: The Battle for Science in the Sociobiology Debate and Beyond* (Oxford: Oxford University Press, 2000), 291–92.

33 For a recent summary and defense of the antireductionist consensus among philosophers of biology, see Kim Sterelny and Paul Griffiths,

Sex and Death: An Introduction to the Philosophy of Biology (Chicago: University of Chicago Press, 2000).

34 Richard Lewontin, "The Dream of the Human Genome," *New York Review of Books* 39 (1992); reprinted in Richard Lewontin, *Biology as Ideology* (New York: Harper-Perennial, 1992), 61–83. The passage quoted can be found on page 63 of *Biology as Ideology*.

35 Ernst Mayr, *Toward a New Philosophy of Biology* (Cambridge: Harvard University Press, 1988).

36 For an account of the French school of molecular biology, see Kay, *Who Wrote the Book of Life?* chapter 5.

37 C. H. Waddington, "Architecture and Information in Cellular Differentiation," in *The Cell and the Organism*, ed. J. A. Ramsay and V. B. Wigglesworth (Cambridge: Cambridge University Press, 1961), 121; as cited in Keller, *Refiguring Life*, 100 n.16.

38 Daniel C. Dennett, *Darwin's Dangerous Idea* (New York: Simon and Schuster, 1995).

39 Ibid., 51.

40 Ibid., 69–71.

41 Ibid., 21.

42 On the history of Darwinism as becoming a mature science by harnessing itself to the statistical revolution in science, see Jean Gayon, *Darwinism's Struggle for Survival* (Chicago: University of Chicago Press, 1998), and David J. Depew and Bruce H. Weber, *Darwinism Evolving: Systems Dynamics and the Genealogy of Natural Selection* (Cambridge: MIT Press, 1994).

43 For a vivid summary of these objections, see Lewontin, "Dream of the Human Genome."

44 Dennett, *Darwin's Dangerous Idea*, 82. For the defense of the contrary view that natural selection, properly so called, arises only from the properties and processes associated with certain materials, see Bruce H. Weber and David J. Depew, "Developmental Systems, Darwinian Evolution, and the Unity of Science," in *Cycles of Contingency: Developmental Systems and Evolution*, ed. Susan Oyama, Paul E. Griffiths, and Russell D. Gray (Cambridge: MIT Press, 2001), 239–54.

45 M. Crenson, "Genome Race Already Having Profound Effects," *Iowa City Press Citizen* (29 May 2000): 7A.

46 Dennett, *Darwin's Dangerous Idea*.

47 On the claim that the selfish gene and the digitalization of genetics has ascribed to genes much more agency than they can conceivably exercise, see Evelyn Fox Keller, *Refiguring Life: Changing Metaphors in Twentieth-Century Biology* (New York: Columbia University Press, 1995); Ruth Hubbard, *Exploding the Gene Myth* (Boston: Beacon, 1997); and Lewontin, *Biology as Ideology*.

Ronald E. Day

THE ERASURE AND

CONSTRUCTION OF HISTORY

FOR THE INFORMATION AGE

Positivism and Its Critics

The true history of information and communication in the twentieth century may be understood as a series of struggles around the
reification and commodification of knowledge. Indeed, the common picture or image of "information" today as a commodity value,
as well as a historical value of progress in modernism in general,
and capitalist modernism in particular (e.g., "the information age"),
may be understood in terms of the dominance of modernist and
capitalist modes of production. One symptom of the historical and
social success of the common picture of information may be the historical loss of critiques of it, as can be found in Martin Heidegger's
and Walter Benjamin's writings. Ironically, another symptom may
be the loss of early positivist models of information, as in the work
of the European documentalists Paul Otlet and Suzanne Briet—lost
to that same amnesia that positivism has to historical differences
in general. The same mechanisms of historical canceling that have
buried Heidegger's critiques of information and have diluted the

critical Marxist power of Benjamin's texts have reduced Otlet's and Briet's historical presence to that of being mere "forerunners" to more successful instrumentalizations of language, human agency, and culture along the lines of theories and ideologies of information, as found, for example, in information theory and post–World War II cybernetics. One might propose that such historical erasures of contrary views and "forerunners," as well as the unwillingness of information historians to see the history of information in anything other than American and English language enterprises and texts, contributes to the problem of forming a critique of the ideology of information in late modernity. By recovering such erasures, however, we can see that the "information age" has previously occurred and that its global destiny was neither innately assured nor without substantial critiques. We can also see that our own "information age" has a history, one that has been produced and one that valorizes, as well as negates, certain meanings for "information," knowledge, and language today.

We must recall that historical erasure has both intellectual and practical effects. Intellectually, it has led to a difficulty in finding vocabulary and critical tools to counter the utopian ideologies of information and communication that are manifest in such terms as "the information age" and "the information society."[1] Both Heidegger's and Benjamin's works, although rooted in different intellectual traditions, share a critique of positivist historiography. They also share a central concern with the way in which mass information and communication technologies reinforce positivist historiography and, subsequently, work to create actual history by shaping the historical resources at hand for social agents. Putting aside truisms about the differences between Heidegger's work and the work generated by the Frankfurt school, Heidegger's and Benjamin's works both share a common concern with the technically formed *image* of reproduction in information and the power of that image to cancel out the very powers of design that construct and organize that image in society and culture.

Both Heidegger and Benjamin were concerned with the relationship between informational or communicational hegemony and the political canceling out of the potentials of human historicity. The reason for this common concern is that both share a skepticism toward the representational image understood as information—or in other words, as fact or "presence"—and both saw that history, when understood essentially as a representational phenomenon, leads to a vast scaling down of human possibilities. To attempt a historical and philosophical recovery of information during the twentieth century therefore requires that we reenter Heidegger's and Benjamin's discourses from the aspect of their critiques of the aesthetic form of social production, representation, and history.

Although the intellectual effects of historical erasure mushroom with the passage of time, there are also the individual, practical effects of historical erasure that now need to be recounted. As both Heidegger and Benjamin's work teaches us, "history" is not just an intellectual category but one of politics and of existence itself. Before continuing further with an intellectual history, let us pause in memoriam to paint a picture of some of the issues of the informationally and communicationally governed administrative state and its national and transnational ideologies that affected a set of individuals who shared a common time and space. Certain historical trajectories can be seen in microcosm in this narrative, and the narrative will also serve to introduce the analysis that will follow.

For his Arcades project, Walter Benjamin utilized both graphic and written artifacts at the Bibliothèque Nationale. There he also utilized as a resource George Bataille, who was active in his own battles against fascism through his critical and literary writings and through the Paris-based College of Sociology and who, as a librarian at the Bibliothèque Nationale, would save through the war years much of what we now have of Benjamin's writings. As a researcher, Benjamin would most certainly have frequented the Salle des Catalogues et des Bibliographies (i.e., the reference room) in order to find information for his project. At the Salle des Catalogues et des Bibliographies was a librarian, a little bit younger than Benjamin, named Madame Suzanne Briet. Briet had founded the Salle des Catalogues et des Bibliographies, and she later carried on some of the ideas of the father of European documentation, Paul Otlet, as vice president of the Fédération Internationale de Documentation. In time, she acquired the nickname "Madame Documentation."[2] (Later, in her autobiography, Briet acknowledges Bataille's presence at the Bibliothèque Nationale only by describing his "blue eyes and burning heart," and adding what an English reader at the library once said about him: "Good-looking boys know nothing" [English in the original]).[3]

After the war, Briet advocated in her manifesto *Qu'est-ce que la documentation?* such ideas as the cyborg integration of human beings and machine technologies and the technical and cultural necessity of "scientific" information management, systematicity, and standards (because, for Briet, documentation is a "cultural technique" and "our" culture is one of "science" that needs to be spread globally to impoverished nations).[4] Briet's social-political resurrection of a culture of information from its submersion in the militarism of World War II was only partially successful on a historical scale: a more total theoretical integration of human agency within mechanical and social engineering was occurring at this time across the Atlantic with the Josiah Macy Jr. cybernetics conferences. Against this success, Briet and, indeed, the history of European documentation was largely forgotten. Benjamin, on the other hand, did not live to see any of these events, because his image disappeared off the map in 1940 as he apparently committed suicide after being blocked from crossing the border into Spain as part of an attempt to flee to the United States.

The lesson to be learned here is that both advocates and critics of the information age tend to disappear from the historical record with the development of that age. Why the information age, as both a subject of historiography and as an ideological praxis, increasingly erases its predecessors and its critics so that it tends to ahistorically reappear, as the "new" of modernity itself, is a curious problem. I would suggest that this problem involves the very concept of information, which is a product of a series of cultural positions and actions that I will trace in the pages following.[5]

Paul Otlet

Paul Otlet is generally considered to be the founder of European documentation. The active history of European documentation spans the years from the founding of the International Institute of Bibliography in Brussels in 1895 by Paul Otlet and Henri La Fontaine (winner of the Nobel Peace prize in 1913) to its eclipse by information science after World War II.[6] Although European documentation still exists in the form of such organizations as the Fédération Internationale de Documentation, the period just before and after World War II saw the publication of several defining texts by leading figures in documentation: the *Traité de documentation* (1934) and

Monde (1935)[7] by Paul Otlet, and the small but important manifesto by Suzanne Briet, *Qu'est-ce que la documentation?* (1951). The distinguishing characteristic of European documentation, in contrast to both librarianship in Europe and to what would subsequently become information science in the United States, was the systems approach through which European documentation understood the relationship between information technology and social systems. For European documentation, the technical retrieval of materials was linked to their social and institutional use and goals for documentary production. In contrast to the (particularly European) tradition of libraries and librarians, which defined themselves in terms of the historical collection and preservation of books, European documentalists emphasized the integration of technology and technique toward specific social goals.

The founders and leaders of European documentation advocated documentation as an upcoming profession, distinct from librarianship, both serving and leading the development of "science" in modernity. As an organized system of information techniques and technologies, documentation was presented as a central player in the historical development of global modernity. Within the context of a global "scientific" culture of modernity, documentation was understood as not simply bibliographical technique but, in the words of Suzanne Briet, as "a cultural technique for our time."[8]

Otlet was a prolific writer. With his global vision, Otlet in his writings tended toward not only large treatises on documentation but also on such topics as the creation of world universities and the creation of a world monetary fund. The late nineteenth century in western Europe was a period of industrialization, aided by the development of national and international standards and the formation of associations to assist in their development.[9] Otlet's bibliographic and organizational works were part of these trends, driven by his passion on the issue of world peace.

For Otlet, world peace was obtainable through international knowledge and communication. To further this goal, La Fontaine and Otlet began in 1895 to build a world bibliography, the Répetoire Bioliographique Universel (RBU), that would eventually find its home in what Otlet called the Palais Mondial, or Mundaneum, in Brussels, an institution that he hoped would be the foundation for a world center for knowledge and culture. By the time that the right-wing Belgian government forced its closure in 1934, the RBU had collected eighteen million items, organized by the universal decimal classification (UDC), a scheme that Otlet had constructed based on Melvil Dewey's decimal classification.[10]

As W. Boyd Rayward has suggested, the basis for Otlet's philosophy and collection practice lies in his notion of the "monographic principle."[11] For Otlet, knowledge was essentially positivistic or "factual." For example, the monographic principle operated in the RBU by the process of cutting up texts into "atomic" units and then linking them together through the UDC. For Otlet, the construction of such atomic, linked chunks of knowledge aided world peace because elementary, factual, "scientific" knowledge could thus be collected and made available to all the leaders of the world, and eventually—through new information and communication technology—to all the world's people. This sharing of factual knowledge would prevent wars because all facts would be available and known by all people and, consequently, there could be no disagreement that could not be settled by an appeal to documented facts. The monographic principle was thus part of the world encyclopedia movement that included such luminaries as H. G. Wells.[12]

The apotheosis of this movement occurred at the World Congress on Universal Documentation, which was associated with the 1937 World Exhibition in Paris. Otlet, Briet, and Wells all attended the congress.[13] For Otlet, as for Wells, peace rested in the creation of a "world mind" or "world brain" constructed through documentary collection and transmission.[14] History, for Otlet, was the progressive development of ever-accumulating knowledge and clarity. For Otlet, all that was lacking at the time was the storage, retrieval, and communication of this progressive store.

Otlet, as other European documentalists, understood the term "document" to refer to signifying materials of all sorts: paper-based texts, physical artifacts, images, newsreels, radio, and the emerging medium of television.[15] In his book *Monde*, Otlet proposes that the world would best be served by the collection and distribution of "facts" through machines that resemble today's personal computers. He believed that the "ultimate problem of documentation" was that of creating a documentary process and a mechanical device that would present to each person, in the comfort of his or her own armchair, an omniscient, yet personal, vision of the world. At one stroke, this device would solve the problem of positivist science (to form a representational knowledge of all things in the world);

the problem of documentary technique (to organize all the knowledge of the world); and the problem of international society (to make available to each person all the knowledge of the world).[16] To these lofty ends, Otlet envisioned a multimedia device that, "acting at a distance . . . would combine the radio, the television [*les rayons Rontgen*], cinema, and microscopic photography," projecting the information of the world onto an "individual screen" (390–91). Such a device would provide for each person a true and complete picture of all knowledge in a manner that would best be understood by each person, thus eliminating conflicts over differing interpretations and providing the grounds for true and complete communication. Indeed, such a device "would become the liberator of each person, its operation being controlled by each person himself, and the things [in their representations] being placed in a convenient order for each person" (390–91).

Otlet's optimism about the global dissemination of truth is based on two elements: first, his belief that knowledge is composed of atomic units of indisputable facts that merely need to be technically distributed to be completely understood, and, second, that the dissemination of this knowledge would be done by "honest men," because propaganda is based not on persuasion or ideology but on "errors and falsehoods" (389–90) that are refuted by bringing them up against reality.

Ironically, of course, it was the production of a sense of "factual" or "commonsense" beliefs that brought about the possibility of total war in 1937. The reduction of the world to "facts" merely means the acceptance of prejudice and the denial of interpretation; the realm of scientific facts becomes confused with easily manipulated "common sense." Otlet's grandiose later works such as *Traité de documentation* and *Monde* display elements of overkill in their arguments and examples, and they take on the rhetorical form of pleading in an attempt at political engagement. By 1937 it was difficult to distinguish mass information and communication from hegemonic forms of government control and from military operations. Otlet's positivist epistemology of knowledge had been transformed, through mass technology and social organization, from a populist utopia to a military machine. Of course, the weakness of Otlet's argument did not lie just in an empirical absence of "honest men" but in his naive understanding of the nature of language, knowledge, truth, and science. For totality was indeed made present for masses of people through information and communication technology, and that totality had the smell of death. Language and knowledge as absolute truth was formed by the repetition of the same message across the hermeneutic differences of space and time. The very success of technical reproduction, from the stabilization of meaning at the level of the signifier to the control of meaning's effects in social space and history, resulted in leveling the problem of interpretation in language and canceling the generation of meaning *by* temporal and spatial differences. It was this leveling of interpretation and this canceling of the importance of spatial and temporal differences for the generation of meaning that Martin Heidegger criticized in the name of truth. On the other hand, it would be these social effects that Suzanne Briet would valorize in the name of "science."

Martin Heidegger

Heidegger's first explicit engagement with knowledge as a process of technical / technological reproduction occurs in his 1938 public lecture, "The Age of the World Picture."[17] Although the roots of Heidegger's critique reaches back to *Being and Time*'s construction of the phenomenological grounds for the destruction of metaphysics, "The Age of the World Picture" raises the problem of positivist thought as a social and cultural problematic on a global scale. Seen within the context of fascist totalitarianism, Stalinist totalitarianism, and the military alliance of democratic capitalist countries in Europe and in America, Heidegger's essay engaged national and global subjectivity at the point "not of random world views, but only of those that have already taken up the fundamental position of man that is most extreme, and have done so with utmost resoluteness."[18] Likewise, Heidegger's critiques of "science," reaching from "The Age of the World Picture" through "The Question Concerning Technology" (1951) up until at least "The End of Philosophy and the Task of Thinking" (1966), must be understood as critiques that not only address technical and institutional senses of the term "science" but also "science" as a cultural phenomenon, denoting the organization of both technical and technological agents according to predetermined objectives and logical processes.

For Heidegger in "The Age of the World Picture" and throughout his later critique of systems analysis and cybernetics, modern industrial science follows a procedure of representation wherein the object is understood solely in terms of instrumental reason, and representation is itself erased by a methodological framing that defines the object in terms of presence alone. In modern science, the being, as object (*Gegenstand*), is torn or sketched out (*reissen*) of a phenomenological context, and is then treated managerially, as a resource (*Bestand*) that is ready at hand (*vorhanden*) for further use. Modern industrial research, whose culture Heidegger sees as shaping intellectuals and the university, is characterized as a network of exploitative intellectual and practical activities performed on beings in the name of initial representations of them as resources.[19] The "busyness" of the research process easily merges into the business of research, and "thinking" becomes appropriated as a partner with modern industrialism. For Heidegger, modern research is the self-involved production of concepts and further research, even, and especially, in the absence of critical or self-reflexive thought on the grounds or validity of the initial *reissen*. What is lost in this modern method of human existence is the consideration of the nature of beings themselves in critical relation to human understanding and judgments. For Heidegger, modern research stresses the causal production and reproduction of ideas and products from initial representational frames (*Gestell*), rather than the creation and critical deployment of concepts for the happening of the event of truth in the world.

In poststructural terms, this shift from *reading* to *information* in terms of *Gestell* and the process of enframing (*gestellen*) involves a shift in educational values (the shift from philosophy's emphasis on primary textual engagement to secondary readings and technique acquisition), as well as a shift in temporal and historical values. The temporal shift that Heidegger sees in modernity's understanding of time as duration and causal effect involves the loss of human "ekstatic" senses of time (as identified in *Being and Time*). For Heidegger, the "scientific" method of modern industrial production stands in opposition to human existence as *Dasein*, and it defines freedom in terms of the "free time" given by historical determinants to *Dasein* in exchange for *Dasein*'s labor, rather than as an historical potentiality or as a potentiality for creating history. Modern research, as a method of time management, manages time in terms of industrial production, not in terms of the "ek-static" freedom that Heidegger claims is the very root of *Dasein*'s historicity and of the event of truth.

It is important to note that for Heidegger the process of enframing is not simply a repressive logic of the industrial age but rather an exploitation of *Dasein*'s essential mode of being in the world. As Heidegger explains in "The Question Concerning Technology," enframing (*gestellen*) is the manner by which human beings appear in the world, a manner that is as originary as the way that mountains jut forth as a mountain chain ("*Gebirg*"). The danger that Heidegger points to is not that of the frame (*Gestell*) of representational understanding itself, but of the blindness that humans have to the grounds for that framing, namely that of being itself. In other words, for Heidegger the problem is the forgetfulness of the fact that this mode of appropriating the world is something already *given* to human beings, not something that is the fruit of their domination over nature. This insight is important because it situates technological thinking within a broader ontological and historical condition of truth than its own production, and thus it marks an excess to technology and man on which technology and man are dependent and cannot control or exceed.

Of course, this attempt to think a more primordial condition to metaphysical subjectivity is a theme that runs throughout Heidegger's oeuvre. In "The Question Concerning Technology" it occurs most forthrightly in the very important but often overlooked beginning of that essay where Heidegger grounds human creative activity in what cannot be called other than a metaphysically grounded materialist critique of production. By returning to Aristotle's four causes (*aiton*; formal, material, efficient, and final), Heidegger argues that this concept is mistranslated by the Latin *causa*. In the Latin and subsequent Western metaphysical tradition, Aristotle's four *aiton* are no longer aspects of the object to which the object is indebted (*Vershulden*) for its creation, but rather such *aiton* are now causes for the production of the object. Heidegger chooses the example of a silver chalice to illustrate his argument, where the chalice can be spoken of according to the four *aiton* as four aspects (*eidos, Aussehen*): the chalice is indebted to silver for its appearance as substance or matter (*Stoff*); it is indebted to the idea of what a chalice is for its formal aspect; it is indebted to a cultural context of ritual for its final aspect; and it is indebted to the silversmith for bringing together the other three ways of indebtedness in order to bring it forth as an object. For Heidegger, the object comes forth as presence according to these four ways of being coresponsible (*Verschulden*): "The four ways of being responsible bring something into appearance. They let it come forth into presencing (*An-Wesen*)."[20] In contrast, in the Latin-influenced Western metaphysical tradition, the final cause dominates the other causes in terms of being a goal or an end (*telos*) for production, to which all the other causes contribute (foremost, the efficient cause). For metaphysically defined production, the historical indebtedness of the object is only relevant in order to predict the uses that a thing should have for a given end. The four aspects of a thing are no longer responsible for a thing but are now used up as resources for an instrumental production that may or may not have anything to do with historical debt or cultural placement. Material, culture, history, and effective agency are mere means to an envisioned end.

The importance of Heidegger's critique of the Latin interpretation of *aiton* is that it reasserts a mutual social, historical, natural, and intellectual indebtedness to the concept of production. In Heidegger's works such as his 1959 "The Way to Language," language is understood as the exemplary instance of indebtedness. Consequently, modern forgetfulness is characterized as the instrumental understanding and production of language, so that "information theory conceives of the natural aspect of language as a lack of formalization" (Die Informationstheorie begreift das Natüraliche als den Mangel an Formalisierung).[21] Against systemic and cybernetic understanding of beings and language in terms of *Gestell*, modern industry, and modern research production, Heidegger's understanding of the nature of being and truth takes refuge in the hermeneutic difficulties and the temporal and spatial horizons of poetry as a still-evident hinge that joins being and production. By the 1960s in "The End of Philosophy and the Task of Thinking," however, Heidegger expresses the fear that the arts, too, are becoming transformed into information-producing mechanisms:

> No prophecy is necessary to recognize that the sciences now establishing themselves will soon be determined and steered by the new fundamental science which is called cybernetics.
> This science corresponds to the determination of man as an acting social being. For it is the theory of the steering of the possible plan-

ning and arrangement of human labor. Cybernetics transforms language into an exchange of news. The arts become regulated-regulating instruments of information.[22]

Heidegger's work is noteworthy in relation to the history and historiography of information because it attempts to counter a metaphysics of presence, understood in terms of information, by a critique grounded in material production and the hermeneutic properties of being, history, and language. Its political failure, though, may be that as a discourse grounded in a philosophical critique of subjectivity it refuses a vocabulary that would be necessary for fully engaging the *productive* grounds for information in terms of the differences and antagonisms intrinsic to those grounds. Although it is useful to point to the material grounds for the production of information, and it is useful to counter Otlet's type of information utopia that is based on a grand sense of subjectivity (i.e., the "world-brain"), Heidegger's critical discourse is so primordially grounded that it can only be oppositional, not antagonistic, to the equally primordial claims of information positivism, and thus it seems to occupy the position of being a countermetaphysics to positivism. Politically speaking, this counterworld picture thus remains within the confines of the speculative because it lacks the very engagement that might break apart those productive mechanisms that are the basis for positivism's own speculative vision. Although Heidegger's critique loses none of its philosophical power by its method of critique, it does lose much of its social power, and it would be hard to deny, particularly in regard to the public lectures, that Heidegger's critique was, indeed, socially intended. In contrast, Benjamin's critique, examined below, takes up a materialist and antagonistic criticism of the ideology of information, remaining concerned with issues of historicism and historicity but without isolating these values in a countermetaphysics.

Before preceding to Benjamin's work, let us return to European documentation immediately following World War II in the form of Suzanne Briet's work. In examining Briet we can see how Otlet's atomic understanding of documents and documentation was transformed into a type of cultural systems theory, which was the very understanding of information that Heidegger most feared would occur.

Suzanne Briet (1894–1989) was one of the foremost leaders in early documentation just before and after World War II. Her publications range from *Qu'est-ce que la documentation?* (1951) to biographical work on the nineteenth-century poet Arthur Rimbaud (to whom she was related) to an autobiography formally composed in an avant-garde manner according to alphabetical entries. She created and was in charge of the Salle des Catalogues et des Bibliographies at the Bibliothèque Nationale from 1934 to 1954, and she was active in international circles, including serving as vice president of the Fédération Internationale de Documentation and holding assignments with UNESCO. Toward the end of her career as a librarian, she took a Fulbright-supported tour of libraries in the United States. Briet was one of the first women librarians at the Bibliothèque Nationale, and she was president of the Union of European Women.[23]

Briet's work represents an attempt to understand global information from the viewpoint of networked technological and social production. For Briet, Otlet's dream of universal bibliography was simply that, a dream. According to Briet, "*Documentology* lost nothing in alleviating itself of a Universal Bibliographic Catalog which everyone had treated as a dream and which did not offer a comparable attraction to the most localized of collective catalogs."[24]

While casting aside Otlet's desire for a universal bibliographical reflection of mankind, Briet's vision did not, however, discard the dream of global information. For Briet, documentation was a movement at the forefront of what she termed "science." For Briet, the documentalist must not only be deeply involved in the exchange of materials within "scientific" cultural production but, further, he or she must lead the individual scientist "like the dog on the hunt— totally before [the researcher], guided, guiding."[25] Science, for Briet, was not only a term for industrial, technical knowledge, but more generally it was a term for knowledge as a modern cultural phenomenon. Hence, as Briet repeats throughout *Qu'est que la documentation?*, documentation is a "cultural technique" for our time. In *Qu'est-ce que la documentation?* in particular Briet states that documentation is a exemplary symbol for science, even as science is the dominant cultural event in modernity, which documentation both occurs within and leads. Science and documentation are terms that are metonymically linked to one another by the shared attributes of "rapidity" and "precision" in Briet's texts. Her texts link rhetoric, history, culture, and technology by these common tropes for modernist progress.[26]

For Briet, the practice of documentation is also characterized by the integration of technically defined human agents and mechanical technology at a systems level. In *Qu'est-ce que la documentation?* the French term *technique* covers both human and mechanical technique and the integration of human and mechanical agency. In this manner, Briet praises the work done on cybernetics at the Massachusetts Institute of Technology, and she states that future man, as a *homo documentator*, must be prepared to assimilate machines so as not to be overtaken by them.[27] The human assimilation of technical machines requires that humans adapt themselves to the relatively narrow, reduced terms of mutual and interlinking standards that are native to machines. Briet's remarks suggest that the necessity for such standardization lies in the necessity for smooth communication between humans and machines within the historical progress and growth of science. Documentation advances at the forefront of science at both cultural and technical levels, demanding that documentalists advance like "new types of missionaries . . . in the wake of the driving force of the exploration vessel flying the United Nations flag" (41).

As Heidegger's critique of modernity suggests, however, the phenomenon of language remains a hurdle to global standardization. Unlike Otlet's vision being embodied in a world city, Briet's vision is network based, and thus it relies to a much greater degree on formal levels of standardization in order to join heterogeneous agencies because there is no one geographical and cultural space within which all materials can be centrally valued. For this reason, Briet engages as a central issue in the advancement of science the problem of language. She solves the problem of multiple languages by explaining that certain European-based languages (English, French, and Spanish) are the basis for the spread of science. Because German has "retreated," Russian is no longer in the forefront, and "the Orientals always speak their language and another language." Thus "the major languages, that is to say, English, French, and Spanish tend to spread and to become the indispensable interpreters of civilized people."[28] Briet's science therefore advances on the heels of documentation, which in turn advances on the heels of a linguistic colonialism led by the dominant nineteenth-century colonial powers and the victorious postwar capitalist nations.[29]

Briet's work is historically important as an advance over Otlet's understanding of documentation and information in that it attempts to give documentation and the notion of "information" a cultural definition rooted in political economy. By grounding her vision for information in an industrially based technical-cultural system, Briet's international vision matched the scale of Otlet's greatest dreams and some of Heidegger's greatest fears about information. At the same time, Briet's texts also embedded the global information age in a technology of networks and in a micropolitics of power.

Walter Benjamin

A good starting point for entering Benjamin's project of critically engaging the "information age" of the late 1920s and the 1930s occurs through the problematic of experience in his work of that period. "Experience" in Benjamin's work is expressed by two German terms: *Erlebnis* and *Erfahrung*.[30] As Hans-Georg Gadamer has pointed out, the term *Erlebnis* is of recent origin, only becoming common by the 1870s.[31] Gadamer claims that its origins in German writings lie in Goethe's poetic texts, where the term emphasizes both the factual unit of experience and the manner by which units of experience metonymically symbolize the subject's life as a whole.[32] By the end of the nineteenth century, Gadamer argues, both the term and concept of *Erlebnis* thoroughly permutated both Dilthey's life philosophy and his attempts to reintroduce the subject back into "scientific" modes of historiography.[33] Gadamer ultimately claims that the concept of *Erlebnis* may, perhaps, lie in Rousseau's writings, particularly in his *Confessions*.

The importance of this genealogy is that it establishes, especially in light of Theodor Adorno's charge that Benjamin had aestheticized and ahistoricized the role of fetishism in capitalism,[34] the likelihood that, at least in terms of the concept of *Erlebnis*, Benjamin's Arcades project was not amiss in critiquing capital's cultural and historical production through an examination of Baudelaire's poetics and the conception of experience and time that are expressed therein.

Benjamin sees Baudelaire's narratives of his life experiences (*Erleb-*

nis) in the midst of industrialized nineteenth-century Paris as reactions to the trauma inflicted on traditional, precapitalist societies and the subject's relatively assigned location within those societies.[35] Likewise, but in an opposing scale of values to Baudelaire's expressions of alienation, mass media and public information serve the dual function of distancing the reader or viewer from the violence of industrialization by generalizing its conditions and suggesting that such modern industrial rhythms are but moments within society's progressive march toward utopia.[36] The "self" here is both a refuge and a product of industrial capitalist production. By combining Marxism's explanation of alienation in terms of commodity fetishism with Freud's explanation of trauma, Benjamin arrives at a theory of the cultural commodity as dream, part of a larger process of subsumption and acculturation. And by understanding the experience of the fetishized object as commodity in terms of the ideological construction of historical experience,[37] Benjamin arrives at a conception of bourgeois historical production as located in particular symbols or "images" of industrial production. The role of mass communication and information, then, is to mediate between material production and historical form via the attribution of meaning to objects and signs. In other words, the historical role of communication and information technologies in capitalism is that of ideological production.

Benjamin's Arcades project concentrates on the remainder that is left out of, and left after, bourgeois dreams of history and cultural meaning. In modernity, experience in the sense of *Erfahrung* constitutes a point of excess in modern production, lying in the areas of the now supposedly private and inexpressible. Benjamin returned to this *Abfall* (trash or remainder) of history through decaying symbols of industrialism (the arcades) and the complex and contradictory experiences of workers. Benjamin's critical undertaking was to destroy the productive grounds for this division of experience wrought by capitalism's destruction of tradition, while also recognizing those values that are denied by the logic of modern progress.

In "The Work of Art in the Age of Mechanical Reproduction" (1935), Benjamin asserts that the violence of technical reproduction can be turned against itself by exploiting the difference between technological reproduction and its commoditization in culture. Benjamin's optimism regarding the revolutionary potential of communication and information technology lies with *newer* technologies. In "On Some Motifs in Baudelaire," [38] as well as in footnote 19 of "The Work of Art in the Age of Mechanical Reproduction," for example, Benjamin makes clear that the revolutionary value of cinema in his time was that of harnessing the rhythm of industrial life for purposes other than that of perpetuating the dream of progress. New technologies had the potential of exploiting the difference between material and idea, between industrialization and utopian ideology. In this way, the fundamental antagonism of workers and capitalists would find a mass form in technological reproduction, and this would essentially be seen at the level of social construction.

In contrast to Briet's utopian picture of a seamless flow of "scientific" industrially produced "information," Benjamin envisioned a picture of progress shattered by the rhythms of industrialization posed against itself. By exploiting the possibility for a temporal form of montage and defamiliarization in film, the linear narrative of bourgeois historical progress could be strained to the breaking point. In this way, the dialectical image of progress that is founded on the subsumption of matter by ideology could not only be held at a "standstill" but could be reversed, so that technological production outstripped its own subsumption by ideological narrative. For Benjamin, the promise of new media technologies was not that of linking the world into supposedly seamless networks or systems of information and communication that would give the illusion of global efficiency but, rather, of politicizing and artistically shattering the ideological goal of the illusion of a positive global totality. As Benjamin wrote in relation to the fascist project of nationalist subsumption: in response to politics' reorganization of life according to an aesthetics of representation and positive totality, "communism responds by politicizing art." [39] Benjamin understood that new information and communication technologies can play a role in this politicization of art because their new speeds and rhythms exist, at least for a while, in tension with old social forms of media and aesthetic meaning. Benjamin's observations in this regard and his hesitancy in applying such antagonistic potential to information and communication technologies without regard to their historical and cultural specificity may be instructive to us when we attempt to analyze the mass deployment and use of new information and communication technologies today.

I have presented here several dialectics of positions around the social meaning and use of new information and communication technologies during the first half of the twentieth century in western Europe. Through a historical recovery of the European documentalists we gain a better understanding that not only have the dreams and tropes of the "information age" occurred previous to this digital "information age," but we come to better understand the critical position of such writers as Heidegger and Benjamin against the types of technological utopianism that is reflected in the documentalists' writings. In reflection on our own time, we may be struck by both the prevalence of tried-and-true modernism in our own age and the striking disappearance of those critical positions espoused by Heidegger and Benjamin.

The question remains, then, how does the repetition of "the information age" continue the dream of modernity, and what is the role of historical erasure in that continuance? How is it that the European documentalists were forgotten within a history that repeated their claims? And how is it that academic research has largely ignored or mystified social critiques on the information age, even within the inherited presence of Heidegger and Benjamin?

How is it that amidst an information explosion the very historical foundations and critical commentary on that explosion are lost to time? Or is it the case, as Heidegger and Benjamin propose, that within that very explosion time itself has been lost through a certain type of construction of history?

Notes

All translations are mine unless indicated otherwise.

1 For two collections of historical studies on information science, see Michael K. Buckland and Trudi Bellardo Hahn, eds., *Historical Studies in Information Science* (Medford, N.J.: Information Today, 1988); and Mary Ellen Bowden, Trudi Bellardo Hahn, and Robert V. Williams, eds., *Proceedings of the 1988 Conference on the History and Heritage of Science and Information Systems* (Medford, N.J.: Information Today, 1989).

2 Michael K. Buckland, "The Centenary of 'Madame Documentation':

Suzanne Briet, 1894–1989," *Journal of the American Society for Information Science* 46, no. 4 (1995): 235–37.

3 Suzanne Briet, *Entre Aisne et Meuse . . . et au-delà: Souvenires* (Charleville-Mézières: Société des Écrivains Ardennais, 1976).

4 Suzanne Briet, *Qu'est-ce que la documentation?* (Paris: EDIT, 1951).

5 In my *The Modern Invention of Information: Discourse, History, and Power* (Carbondale: Southern Illinois University Press, 2001) I have engaged many of the themes of this paper in a more extended format.

6 Serge Cacaly, "Paul Otlet (1868–1944)," in *Dictionnaire encyclopédique de l'information et de la documentation* (Paris: Éditions Nathan, 1997), 446–47.

7 Paul Otlet, *Traité de documentation: Le livre sur le livre: Théorie et pratique* (Brussels: Éditiones Mundaneum, 1934), and *Monde: Essai d'universalisme: Connaissance du monde, sentiment du monde, action organisée et plan du monde* (Brussels: Éditiones Mundaneum, 1935).

8 Briet, *Qu'est-ce que la documentation?* 2.

9 See, for example, Armand Mattelart, *The Invention of Communication* (Minneapolis: University of Minnesota Press, 1996). On Otlet and international associations, see Isabelle Rieusset-Lemarié, "P. Otlet's Mundaneum and the International Perspective in the History of Documentation and Information Science," in Buckland and Hahn, eds., *Historical Studies in Information Science*, 34–42.

10 Cacaly, "Paul Otlet," 446–47; W. Boyd Rayward, "The Origins of Information Science and the International Institute of Bibliography / International Federation for Information and Documentation (FID)," in Buckland and Hahn, eds., *Historical Studies in Information Science*, 22–33. See also W. Boyd Rayward's biography of Otlet, *The Universe of Information: The Work of Paul Otlet for Documentation and International Organisation* (Moscow: VINITI, 1975).

11 W. Boyd Rayward, "Visions of Xanadu: Paul Otlet (1868–1944) and Hypertext," *Journal of the American Society for Information Science* 45, no. 4 (1994): 235–50.

12 See W. Boyd Rayward, "H. G. Wells's Idea of a World Brain: A Critical Reassessment," *Journal of the American Society for Information Science* 50, no. 7 (1999): 557–73.

13 W. Boyd Rayward, "The International Exposition and the World Documentation Congress, Paris, 1937," *Library Quarterly* 53 (1983): 254–68.

14 See Rayward, "H. G. Wells's Idea of a World Brain."

15 See Michael K. Buckland, "What Is a 'Document'?" in Buckland and Hahn, eds. *Historical Studies in Information Science*, 215–20.

16 Otlet, *Monde*, 390.

17 Martin Heidegger's thought is, of course, complex, not only intertextually but in terms of social and philosophical origins. It is not

my purpose in this section to delve into it deeply, especially in terms of its philosophical context, but rather to point out certain explicit social engagements that it makes with Otlet's type of positivism and with the development of information culture in the twentieth century.

18 Martin Heidegger, "The Age of the World Picture," in *The Question Concerning Technology and Other Essays* (New York: Harper and Row, 1977), 134–35.

19 It is interesting to note that Heidegger partly marks the transition from what he sees as scholarship to research work with the advent of public document collections, particularly in the form of publishers' series and sets: "The research man no longer needs a library at home. Moreover, he is constantly on the move. He negotiates at meetings and collects information at congresses. He contracts for commissions with publishers. The latter now determine along with him which books must be written" (Heidegger, "The Age of the World Picture," 125). See also Heidegger's comments in appendix 3 to "The Age of the World Picture" where he continues this train of thought, accusing the publishing industry of creating a commercially defined public space of knowledge through selective publishing strategies and the establishment of canons.

20 Heidegger, "The Question Concerning Technology," in *The Question Regarding Technology and Other Essays*, 9.

21 Martin Heidegger, "The Way to Language," in *On the Way to Language* (New York: Harper and Row, 1977), 111–36.

22 Martin Heidegger, "The End of Philosophy and the Task of Thinking," in *Martin Heidegger: Basic Writings* (New York: Harper and Row, 1977), 376.

23 Buckland, "The Centenary of 'Madame Documentation,' " 235–37.

24 Briet, *Qu'est-ce que la documentation?* 9.

25 Suzanne Briet, "Bibliothécaires et Documentalistes," *Revue de la documentation* 21 (1954): 43.

26 On the ethics and politics of Briet's rhetoric of "science," see my "Tropes, History, and Ethics in Professional Discourse and Information Science," *Journal of the American Society for Information Science* 51, no. 5 (2000): 469–75.

27 Briet, *Qu'est-ce que la documentation?* 29.

28 Ibid., 43.

29 For an exemplary analysis of capitalism understood as a process of semiotic encoding, see Félix Guattari and Eric Alliez, "Capitalist Systems, Structures, and Processes," in *The Guattari Reader* (Cambridge, Mass.: Blackwell Publishers, 1996), 233–47.

30 See, particularly, Walter Benjamin, "On Some Motifs in Baudelaire," in *Illuminations*, ed. Hannah Arendt, trans. Harry Zohn (New York: Schocken Books, 1968), 155–200.

31 Hans-Georg Gadamer, *Truth and Method* (New York: Crossroads, 1985), 55.

32 Ibid., 55–63.

33 Ibid. Gadamer's explanation helps elucidate Heidegger's disparaging remarks regarding Dilthey's tendencies to reduce knowledge to "life-experiences" (*Erlebnis*), in the latter's "The Age of the World Picture" (see, for example, pp. 134 and 142), and it also illuminates Heidegger's critique of life philosophy in *Being and Time*.

34 See, especially, Theodor Adorno's letter to Benjamin of 2–4 August 1935 in *Theodor Adorno and Walter Benjamin, The Complete Correspondence: 1928–1940* (Cambridge, Mass.: Harvard University Press, 1999), 104–16.

35 Benjamin, "On Some Motifs in Baudelaire."

36 See, for example, Benjamin's analysis of the function of newspapers in modernity in "On Some Motifs in Baudelaire," 158–59.

37 See Benjamin's discussion of time in section 9 of "On Some Motifs in Baudelaire."

38 Ibid., 175.

39 Walter Benjamin, "The Work of Art in the Age of Mechanical Reproduction," in *Illuminations*, 242.

PART II

VISUAL CULTURE, SUBJECTIVITY, AND

THE EDUCATION OF THE SENSES

Lauren Rabinovitz

MORE THAN THE MOVIES

A History of Somatic Visual Culture through *Hale's*

Tours, Imax, and Motion Simulation Rides

If my nightmare is a culture inhabited by posthumans who regard their bodies as fashion accessories rather than the ground of being, my dream is a version of the posthuman that embraces the possibilities of information technologies without being seduced by fantasies of unlimited power and disembodied immortality, that recognizes and celebrates finitude as a condition of human being, and that understands human life is embedded in a material world of great complexity, one on which we depend for our continued survival.
—N. KATHERINE HAYLES, *How We Became Posthuman*

Modernity is hence conceptualized in terms—shock, trauma—which suggest a penetration or breach of an otherwise seamless body. . . . The threats associated with shock and trauma, with modernity's assault on the body and its perceptual powers, can be ameliorated through a certain logic of the spectacle supported by a vast technology. . . . This is in effect accomplished in the cinema through the progressive despatialization and disembodiment of the spectatorial position. [The body of the spectator is deimplicated], producing it as a pure de-spatialized gaze.—MARY ANN DOANE, "Technology's Body"

I just call it immersive entertainment. By that I mean experiencing a total sense of being inside the movie. —DOUGLAS TRUMBULL, Imax Corporation

The history of cinema has always assumed that moviegoing affords a means for achieving a blissful state of disembodiment. Classical models of movie spectatorship presume that cinema produces modernist subjectivity through *being* a giant, disembodied set of eyes. Even when alternative views have surfaced, dominant film theories have perpetuated a belief in a single, unitary viewing position—centered, distant, objectifying—that makes the spectator an effect of a linear technological evolution from the camera obscura to photography to cinema. Involvement in the cinema has always meant the fantasy of a despatialized, dematerialized self. Psychoanalytic and feminist theories, arguably the most powerful developments in the last twenty-five years, may critique and even vilify the ideology of the spectator position that promises an illusory power and coherence in subjugation to vision itself. But they do not challenge the assumption that the spectatorial process is essentially a disavowal of corporeal presence (embodiment) and an absorption into the distant world of image and sound. Cinema, whose purpose is to articulate the frontiers of audio-visual technologies, contradicts this model of subjective experience. Since the inception of cinema, movies that claim to reveal the future of cinema have regularly depended not on fantasies of disembodiment and absorption into virtual worlds but on the reflexivity of embodied spectatorship.

Cinema was arguably the single most important new communication technology at the outset of the twentieth century and the best one for prefiguring the digital technologies that promise virtual worlds and simulated realities. By 1900, cinema was already touting its future in an extravagant, multimedia spectacle at the 1900 Paris International Exposition[1] and, a few short years later, at lavish disaster shows (e.g., *Trip to the Moon*; *Fighting the Flames*) at Coney Island and other urban amusement parks. The culmination of this trend in early cinema was *Hale's Tours and Scenes of the World* (1904–1911), a railroad car featuring travel films from the point of view of a moving train where the image is coordinated with sensory and atmospheric effects such as motion and train whistles. Contrary to our received notion of moviegoing, these first "ridefilms" simulated railroad travel in order to foreground the body itself as a site for sensory experience. *Hale's Tours* articulated a seemingly contradictory process: it attempted to dematerialize the subject's body through its extension into the cinematic field while it repeatedly emphasized physical presence and the delirium of the senses.

Although *Hale's Tours* disappeared soon after the U.S. film industry became systematized, ridefilms and related cinematic phenomena reappeared after World War II, the years that represented a downward economic turn for a Hollywood that seemed to require new technical gimmicks in order to boost movie attendance. Experiments in 3-D, their cyborgian implications in bespectacled audiences, and their shock effects of objects "coming at you" foregrounded bodily orientation to the screen and identification. New widescreen products like *This Is Cinerama* (Mike Todd, 1952) and *Cinerama Holiday* (Louis de Rochemont, 1955) relied on exaggerated uses of forward motion and objects flashing by at the margins, as well as publicity rhetoric, to argue for the spectator's increased immersion in the spectacle. But, like *Hale's Tours*, Cinerama provided an enlarged sense of corporeal involvement that made immersion an imaginary effect of reflexive spectatorship.

Experiments in 3-D, widescreen processes, new sound technologies, and the reappearance of new ridefilms like *Trip to the Moon* (Disneyland, 1955) and *Impressions of Speed* (Brussels's World's Fair, 1958) were all most successful not at suburban cinemas trying to outdo television and other forms of leisure entertainment but at amusement parks and expositions. It is tempting to align their appearance in such showcases of utopic technological determinism with the foundational era of the information age and an acceleration of disembodiment rhetoric in relationship to the erosion of the liberal subject. (At the same time, the development of flight training simulators in World War II, the postwar continuation of this technology and its extension to automobile driving simulators, and the rise of video games—all offshoots of technologies developed for military application—are central to my history.[2] Their histories, however, are beyond the scope of this essay.)

It was in the 1970s that this alternative cinema became more fully systematic, when Imax Corporation introduced a giant film image several stories high (approximately ten times the size of a 35mm movie). At first, Imax projected only at world's fairs—Expo 67 in Montreal and Expo 70 in Osaka. But then the company equipped special theaters at a variety of exceptional sites—museums, zoos, tourist centers—thereby developing a circuit of tourist cinema. In the 1990s, new systems and competing companies complemented Imax's initial project—Omnimax or movie domes, ridefilms, 3-D interactive movies, and 360-degree circular films. By relying on a vocabulary of high camera angles and movements that create vertiginous body orientations, these movies regularly utilize computer-generated imagery in order to manifest themselves as cinematic virtual voyages—digital updates of an old technology that resuscitate a complex machine for phantasmagoric pleasures and reveling in the physicality of one's own body.

Contemporary movies at the frontiers of cinema, now available worldwide in more than five hundred locations—amusement parks, shopping malls, theaters, museums, and hotel entertainment complexes—reproduce *Hale's Tours*'s original purpose. They develop a triangulated relationship among a compressed version of travel, heightened, and intensified relations between the body and the machine, and the cinematic rhetoric of hyperrealism. They do so by appealing to multiple senses through experiences featuring forward movement, wraparound screens, objects or lights flashing in the viewer's peripheral vision, subjective camera angles, semisync realistic sound, seat or floor movement, and narratives that alternate danger and command. They foreground the bodily pleasures of the cinematic experience, pleasures already inherent in cinema itself and important in such "body-oriented genres" as pornography, action adventure, horror, and melodrama. But *Hale's Tours* carefully coordinate the spectator's physical and cognitive sensations, whereas one might argue that the standard Hollywood approach involves substantial conflict between various cognitive cues.

These movies challenge our prevailing ideas about cinema in four ways. First, they regularly return movies to the fairgrounds, as it were, and uphold the "cinema of attractions" as an alternative tradition throughout the history of cinema.[3] Second, they engage multiple senses: they define the cinematic experience not as a pure visual relationship to a screen but as the pleasurable, physical self-awareness of coordinated perceptions within an architectonic space. Third, by grounding experience in the audience's bodily awareness, they demand a different kind of film spectator and produce an alternative spectatorial pleasure to the monolithic, ahistorical model of "distracted" spectatorship that shapes our understanding of the history of cinema. And, fourth, they preserve haptic knowledge grounded in the body in relationship to vision at moments of radical technological transformation when there is a crisis in visually ascertaining truth.

Theorizing Cinema as Sensory Spectacle

Admitting this alternative cinema into the discussion is important because cinema may be understood as the paradigmatic modernist experience of the twentieth century and as a significant model (both historical and theoretical) for knowledge of digital culture. But in order for cinema to occupy fully this role it must be contextualized within *more than* cinema. Thinking about how spectators experience cinema requires larger interdisciplinary frameworks that theorize perception and social subjectivity, and that historicize them beyond the confines of twentieth-century modernism and postmodernism. When N. Katherine Hayles asserts that postmodernism's erasure of embodiment is also a feature of liberal humanist subjectivity originating in the Enlightenment, she provides an important basis from which we can also understand cinema's origins not as the mechanical inventions of the apparatus but as the historically conditioned subjectivity of the movie audience.[4] Hayles receives unlikely support from art historian Jonathan Crary, who initially seems to contradict her: he argues that modernism does signal a historical break. But because he suggests that modernism as we understand it is not so much a radical affront to the past as it is a consequence of shifting regimes of vision and perception put into place in Enlightenment liberalism, he actually concurs with Hayles's historical justification.[5]

Crary amplifies Hayles's assertion in important ways because her definition of subjectivity is based on a Lacanian model of consciousness constituted through language with little regard for the ways that visual representation exceeds the linguistic structure of spoken language. Crary contends that nineteenth-century visual culture was founded on the collapse of classical subject-object duality and on the admittance of sensory activity that severs perception from any necessary relationship to an exterior world. Furthermore, Crary claims that at the historical moment in which visual perception is relocated as fully embodied—the period in the nineteenth century in which a series of photographic practices replaced the cultural importance of the camera obscura—the way was paved for the historical emergence of autonomous vision understood as a corporealization of sensation. Crary's latest effort demonstrates how the interplay between such a localized embodiment and modernism's shock and effect of alienation results in the physiological mapping of vision, making the modernist subject itself the consequence of narrowly materialized disciplinary effects of attention, fascination, and even distraction.

Crary's interest in writing the body back into the field of signification and his attentiveness to a historical rupture in the fixed model of classical spectatorship within a Foucauldian historiographic framework—against Hayles's belief in historical change as "patterns of overlapping innovation and replication"—sets up a dialectical relationship in which I wish to consider cinema's historical context.[6] Cinema depended on reconciling bodily experience (and cognitive understanding) to the ascendancy of vision as the privileged self-sufficient source of perceptual knowledge. In other words, if cinema is—as so many have claimed—the paradigmatic vision machine of modernism, it is so only by hyperbolizing vision in relationship to an embodied perceptual spectatorship. Rather than theorize cinema as a disembodied fantasy, I argue here that cinema attempts to effect and promise embodiment as a prophylactic against a world of continuing disembodiment. Indeed, this is the model against which *all* of cinema should be read (as promising embodiment in relationship to disembodiment): cinema represents a complex interplay between embodied forms of subjectivity and arguments for disembodiment.

I propose a model of cinema that shifts from a technologically determinist cinema as an ongoing effort for improved cinematic realism. In fact, cinema "at the cutting edge" always promises more than this: it promises to be *more than the movies*. As one critic has said about Imax, "Representation is boring because it has all been seen before. The actual subject of the film is superfluous. Imax is about the spectacle of seeing and the technological excess necessary to maintain that spectacle."[7] These films are not visions of cinema's future because of what they depict but because of the ways they represent an instantiation of the apparatus. They continue the oldest tradition of cinema: like the earliest film exhibitions where the name of the apparatus, not the names of the films, received billing on the programs, *Hale's Tours* or Imax supercede the name of any particular movie being shown. In fact, at a number of Imax theaters, employees introduce the equipment to the audience before each screening.[8] These techno-spectacles promise to perfect cinema's basic drive wherein the apparatus itself is organized, to quote Francesco Casetti, as a "snare ready to capture whoever enters its radius of activity."[9]

Movies at the technological edge are not about what is being depicted except insofar as they reveal the capacity of the apparatus for summoning novel points of view, for extending the panoptic gaze, and for eliciting wonder at the apparatus. It is no wonder then that beginning with *Hale's Tours* travel films have been particularly well suited for that purpose. *Hale's Tours* and its competitors offered virtual travel to remote areas that the railroad had recently opened up for tourism in the United States, Canada, and Europe (e.g., Niagara Falls, Rocky Mountain and Alpine passes, the Yukon). They also featured travel to colonial "frontiers" at the height of the age of industrial empire—China, Ceylon, Japan, Samoa, the Fiji Islands. Today's films are likewise dominated by voyages to new frontiers—pushing the envelope in speed and flight; outer space; lost civilizations; vanishing rain forests and other endangered "natural" worlds and species; remote areas of Africa, Asia, and the Arctic; inside the oceans; even inside the human body. Such travel is always presented as a cinema of attractions: it offers the transformation of the landscape into pure spectacle.

By conquering space not only with the gaze, such spectacles foreground the body itself as a site for sensory experience within a three-dimensionally contained space. They coordinate the cinematic images with a range of other cues: visual and auditory effects may emanate from different points in the auditorium; atmospheric or environmental stimuli affect skin responses and sensations; and there may even be efforts to produce kinesthesia (or actual movement). The degree to which these movies have been historically successful at these attempts may be exemplified by a continuous, unintended side effect: historian Raymond Fielding has suggested that *Hale's Tours* incited nausea in some of its participants.[10] His remark echoes modern observations that at Imax shows "even the slightest tilt or jiggle [of the projected camera shots] can be felt in the stomach"[11] or that an Imax movie about flying is "so realistic that viewers may feel a little airsick."[12] Furthermore, attendants often warn audiences at the beginning of today's motion simulation rides and Imax or Omnimax shows: "If you start to feel nauseous, simply close your eyes." Tourist cinema thus invokes the physical delirium of the senses, sometimes so much so that it overdoes it. But what is most important is the degree to which all of these examples bind vision to a wider range of sensory affect—cinema to a multimedia event.

Across the century, *Hale's Tours*, Imax, and modern ridefilms articulate a seemingly contradictory process for the spectator: they attempt to dematerialize the subject's body through its visual extension into the cinematic field while they emphasize the spectator's body itself as the center of an environment of action and excitement. They have to sensationalize and smooth over the gaps between the in-the-body experience (affect) and the out-of-the-body sense of panoptic projection. Their promise of an embodied spectatorship seemingly celebrates a heightened interactivity, although such resistance to a pure passive gaze may not generate a truly active spectator. Instead, these films simply require that we frame the history of moviegoing differently, as a spectatorship of sensory fascination, a *jouissance* instead of distraction.

Hale's Tours and Scenes of the World

American entrepreneur-promoter George C. Hale first introduced *Hale's Tours and Scenes of the World* at the 1904 Louisiana Purchase Exposition of St. Louis. His success led to a more permanent installation for the 1905 season at the Kansas City Electric Park. With his partner, Fred Gifford, Hale took out two patents for his "illusion railroad ride." [13] They licensed it to others for several years until it is likely that the increased systematization and consolidation of the movie industry forced them out of business sometime after 1910.

Hale's Tours was composed of one, two, or even three theater cars that each seated 72 "passengers." The company advertised that an installation could "handle as many as 1250 persons per hour with ease." [14] The movies shown out the front end of the otherwise closed car generally offered a filmed point of view from the front or rear of a moving train, producing the illusion of movement into or away from a scene while mechanical apparatuses and levers simultaneously vibrated, rocked, and tilted the car. Representative film titles include: *A Trip on the Catskill Mt. Railway*; *Grand Hotel to Big Indian*; and *The Hold-Up of the Rocky Mountain Express* (all produced in 1906 by American Mutoscope & Biograph). Steam whistles

The Hold-Up of the Rocky Mountain Express
(American Mutoscope & Biograph, 1906).

tooted, wheels clattered, and air blew into the travelers' faces. It was the first virtual voyage, a multisensory simulation of railway tourism.

By the end of the 1906 summer season, there were more than five hundred installations at amusement parks and storefront theaters in all major U.S. and Canadian cities. *Hale's Tours* also opened in Mexico City, Havana, Melbourne, Paris, London, Berlin, Bremen, Hamburg, Hong Kong, and Johannesburg.[15] They were highly successful and often were among a park's biggest moneymaker concessions.[16]

Imitators and variants that capitalized on Hale and Gifford's immediate success quickly followed. In New York and Chicago there were *Palace Touring Cars, Hurst's Touring New York,* and *Cessna's Sightseeing Auto Tours.* Another, *Citron's Overland Flyer,* differentiated itself merely by offering draw-curtains at the side windows that could be opened and closed in synchronization with the beginning and end of the motion and sound effects.[17] (Hale and Gifford eventually bought out Citron's patents.)[18] Other modes of transportation varied the formula only slightly. *Auto Tours of the World and Sightseeing in the Principal Cities* changed the railroad vehicle to an automobile and added painted moving panoramas to the sides of the open car. In addition, they "stopped the car" in order to take their passengers to an adjacent electric theater showing a variety of moving pictures.[19] *White & Langever's Steamboat Tours of the World* applied the *Hale's Tour* concept to water travel. They employed an actual ferry to transport patrons to a "marine-illusion boat," where moving pictures were projected in the front of a stationary boat that seated up to two hundred people. Mechanical apparatuses rocked and oscillated the mock boat, rotating paddle wheels beneath the deck "simulat[ed] the sound of paddle-wheels employed for propulsion," and fans blew breezes in the face of the audience to "give the impression that they are traveling."[20] The illusion boat included a steam calliope as well.

Hruby & Plummer's Tours and Scenes of the World appropriated all these concepts but made them more generic for traveling carnivals so that they could set up a train, boat, or automobile.[21] *Hruby's* rocked and oscillated both the seat bases and the upper portions of the chairs.[22] Other movie-illusion rides simulated hot air balloon travel, including one patented in 1906 by Pittsburgh film manufacturer Sigmund Lubin.[23]

A Trip to California over Land and Sea, however, may have been the most ingenious of the imitators. It combined railway and marine illusion travel. It offered first the fantasy of a cross-country rail journey to California, followed by the sensation of the car being dropped into the water to turn the vehicle into a boat for travel down the California coast. Its advertisement proclaimed that the effect was "the car being instantaneously transformed into a beautiful vessel which gives you a boat ride along the coast, the performance ending with a sensational climax (a Naval Battle and Storm at Sea)."[24]

Hale's Tours films typically featured the landscape as the train picked up speed so that the details accelerating into the foreground were the featured information. The films employed both editing and camera movements but usually only after presenting an extended shot (often one to two minutes or longer in a film seven to eight minutes in length) organized by the locomotion of the camera. The initial effect then was a continuous flow of objects rushing toward the camera. The camera, mounted at a slightly tipped angle, showed the tracks in the foreground as parallel lines that converge at the horizon, an important indicator of perspectival depth. Telephone poles, bridges, tunnels, and other environmental markers in the frame also marked continuous flow according to the lines of perspective. Passing through tunnels effected a particularly dramatic difference of darkness/light, no image/moving image, and interruption/flow. The repetition of all these elements contributed to an overall impression that the perceptual experience of camera motion is a re-creation of the flow of the environment.

Hale's Tours, however, did not have to maintain a strict cowcatcher point of view to get across its sensations. The emphasis on flow and perspective of travel was frequently broken in order to display dramatic incidents and bits of social mingling between men and women, different classes, farmers and urbanites, train employees and civilians, ordinary citizens and outlaws. Changes of locale occurred abruptly through editing, moving the camera position, or abandoning altogether the perspective from the front or rear of the train. When this happened, the film usually expanded its travel format to offer views of accompanying tourist attractions or to stretch the travelogue with comic or dramatic scenes. A 1906 advertisement in the *New York Clipper* for *Hale's Tours* listed five "humorous railway scenes" that could be included in *Hale's Tours* programs.[25] *Trip Through the Black Hills* (Selig Polyscope, 1907) covered "the difficulties of trying to dress in a Pullman berth."[26] In addition, the early film classic *The Great Train Robbery* (Edison Manufacturing Company, 1903) played in *Hale's Tours* cars.

It was not unusual for the films to cut regularly to the interior of a railroad car, producing a "mirror image" of the social space in which the ridefilm patron was seated. These films were thus not purely travelogues but also addressed the social relations and expectations connected with the experience of travel. They suggest that what was fundamental to the ridefilm was not merely the sight of the "destination" and the sensation of immersion in it, but the *experience*—both

Grand Hotel to Big Indian
(American Mutoscope & Biograph, 1906).

physical and social—of being in that place. Thus, *Hale's Tours* commodified the logic of a new experience—the inscription of being of
the world.

Early accounts of these ridefilms are reminiscent of the reception
of the earliest Lumiere films: "The illusion was so good that . . .
members of the audience frequently yelled at pedestrians to get out
of the way or be run down."[27] It is noteworthy that in the latter
report spectators do not jump out of the way (as they did in the
reports about Lumiere film showings) because they do not understand things coming at them inasmuch as they understand them-

selves moving forward; they instead yell at onscreen pedestrians to get out of the way. As film historian Noel Burch summarized: "These spectators . . . were already in another world than those who, ten years earlier, had jumped up in terror at the filmed arrival of a train in a station: [they] . . . are masters of the situation, they are ready to *go through the peephole*."[28] But Burch makes the mistake of thinking that *Hale's Tours* depended entirely on its capacity to effect this visual, out-of-body projection into the diegesis. He fails to see that these illusion rides were always *more than* movies; they were about a physiological and psychological experience associated with travel.

Hale's Tours riders themselves may have recognized this element. One reporter describes a rider: "One demented fellow even kept coming back to the same show, day after day. Sooner or later, he figured, the engineer would make a mistake and he would get to see a train wreck."[29] The "demented fellow," ostensibly a victim of hyperrealism, may have actually recognized the delicious terror of *Hale's Tours* better than Burch, because it is precisely the anticipation of disaster that provides the thrill at the heart of *Hale's Tours* and all other ridefilms. The new mode of railway travel that *Hale's Tours* worked so hard to simulate was not necessarily understood by its public as the simple, safe technology we assume it to be today. Wolfgang Schivelbusch has shown that railroad passengers generally felt ambivalent about train travel and that, despite their thrill at being part of a "projectile shot through space and time," passengers also had an "ever-present fear of a potential disaster."[30] The turn-of-the-century press certainly thrived on stories of streetcar and railway disasters and death.[31] Indeed, Lynne Kirby persuasively argues that *Hale's Tours* best unified "the perceptual overlap between the railroad and the cinema" and that the "imagination of disaster" represented the experience of both railway traveler and moviegoer.[32] The fantasy of seeing technology go out of control and the pleasure in the resulting terror is integral to the spectatorial process.

Illusion ride manufacturers understood this fact. Their advertisements privileged the motion effects and the physical sensation of travel. (Their patent applications, after all, asked to cover the motion effects and the installation rather than the projectors and screens, which were already patented to other companies.) They repeatedly emphasized the synchronization of visual, kinesthetic, and sound effects as the unique property of the apparatus. More than what was viewed out of the window, the cognitive convergence of sensory information provided the basis for the illusion that "you are really there."

The content of *Hale's Tours* was important for its contribution to the overall effect of the spectator made over into a traveler, and it did not require a visual point-of-view literalism for the realism of the experience. What was fundamental to the illusion ride was not merely the sight of the "destination" but the sensation of visual immersion, because vision was linked to the physical and social experience of being in that place—a place that extended the notion of the phantasmagoric space of cinema from the screen to the theater itself.

Imax

Imax is a Toronto-based international corporation that, since 1970, has made camera and projection systems that accommodate an exceptionally large screen format by turning standard 70mm film stock on its side.[33] Imax Corporation designs special viewing spaces and produces films using Imax cameras for exclusive distribution to Imax theaters (the name Imax is derived from "maximum image"). There are currently some 183 Imax and Omnimax theaters worldwide, whose combined attendance in 1995 was sixty million people.[34] While theater specifications may vary, they generally feature a wide screen that is five to eight stories tall, state-of-the-art digital sound systems that allow sound and music to emanate from and even travel across different points in the auditorium, laser light effects, and seats steeply banked in relationship to the screen. They may also include three-dimensional imaging systems (at least forty theaters have this capacity) or more futuristic systems such as that at Poitiers, where a transparent floor is a window to a second screen that runs synchronously with the regular forward or surround screen.[35]

Although they play to a much smaller market than does standard Hollywood fare, Imax films have been remarkably successful. *To Fly* (1976), one of the earliest Imax films, made over $150 million and is the highest-grossing documentary ever produced. Another film, *Everest*, on its initial release in 1998 was the fifteenth highest-grossing film in North America, despite the fact that it only played in thirty-two theaters.[36] Sony Imax theater in New York City, opened in 1994, has regularly been the highest-grossing screen in the United States, and Imax films overall have played to more than 510 million people since 1970.[37]

Imax films feature swooping, sailing, and soaring shots taken from a variety of vehicles in flight. One Imax film director explains, "[We applied] camera movement as much as we possibly could. This would help us move away from just another series of pretty postcards and also would allow for a more subjective experience . . . Slight perspective changes would bring the audience more of a feeling of being there . . . Camera movement is particularly necessary and effective."[38] Film scholar Charles Acland describes it similarly: "IMAX films soar. Especially through the simulation of motion, they encourage a momentary joy in being placed in a space shuttle, on a scuba dive, or on the wing of a fighter jet."[39] Imax has made movies about outer space, complete with views of the earth taken by astronauts on their expeditions (e.g., *Hail Columbia*, 1982; *The Dream Is Alive*, 1985; *Blue Planet*, 1990; *Cosmic Voyage*, 1996; *Mission to Mir*, 1997); about ecology and the balance of nature, complete with subjective views of swinging through the treetops or flying off a mountain (e.g., *North of Superior*, 1971; *Skyward*, 1985; *Mountain Gorilla*, 1991; *Survival Island*, 1996; *Africa's Elephant Kingdom*, 1998); about the oceans and their inhabitants (e.g., *Nomads of the Deep*, 1979; *The Deepest Garden*, 1988; *Titanica*, 1992; *Into the Deep*, 1995); and about flight and speed (e.g., *Silent Sky*, 1977; *On the Wing*, 1986; *Race the Wind*, 1989).[40]

Like Burch's description of "go[ing] through the peephole," advertisements for Cinerama, and Trumbull's claim of total immersion, Imax asserts its capacity to "put you in the picture." Charles Acland notes that "the filmic representation is less central than the effort to create the sensation that the screen has disappeared, that it is truly a window and that the spectator sits right in the image."[41] But the experience of total involvement is more accurately a set of coordinated sensations, a program for which the models of cinema and spectatorship by Acland, Burch, and Trumbull are inadequate.

Paul Virilio comes close to the experience when he describes his encounter with Imax as the "fusion/confusion of camera, projection system and auditorium."[42] He searches for an appropriate cinematic model but can only single out one lexiconic element of early cinema—the experience of the tracking shot. His models of cinema are equally inadequate for the task of understanding Imax's "logis-

tics of perception which subjugate auditorium/stage and spectacle
. . . to its passengers of the moment, travelers in a cinematographic
hemisphere" (173). His claim that the tracking shot is the progenitor
of Imax's status as a static audio-visual vehicle is true insofar as it is
also the semiotic foundation for *Hale's Tours*. Had he known about
Hale's Tours, he would have found a model that fully exemplifies the
cinema space reconfigured as an audio-visual vehicle, the simulation of motion, and the reconstruction of spectatorship as coordinated sensory involvement. Virilio does recognize, however, that
what is at stake is not merely visual projection into the screen space
but a reconfiguration of spectatorial presence to simulate physical
sensations of travel.

One might well argue that such films as *Alamo—Price of Freedom*
(1988), *Grand Canyon: The Hidden Secrets* (1984), *Behold Hawaii* (1983),
Yellowstone (1994), and *Niagara: Miracles, Myths and Magic* (1987)
are so good at replicating the sense of real travel while transcend-
ing it with a fantasy of spatial mastery that they have become the
ideal tourist simulation—a packaged replacement for the inconve-
niences and imperfections of travel while fulfilling tourist desires.
The Grand Canyon, Yellowstone National Park, and Niagara Falls
all have Imax theaters on site that feature the actual park in a compressed, idealized, physically intensified adventure that surpasses
direct experiences usually permeated by a range of physical discomforts, the psychological frustrations of competing tourists and
lengthy waits, and the restrictions of slow exposure, incomplete-
ness, or inaccessibility to all the reaches of the park or site.

The degree to which these tourist narratives have become necessary substitutes for our memories of lived experience is best illustrated not by any one example from these tourist centers but by the
experience of a group of travelers least likely to substitute a movie—
albeit one that preserves haptic knowledge in the body—for their
actual travel: the American astronauts. When several astronauts attended a special screening of the Imax movie *Destiny in Space*, they
reported that it changed their experience of their own space mission: "The Imax experience was so close to what it was like for them
in space. They said that in many respects it was actually better, because they didn't have the restricted view of being in their helmet.
They could sort of sit back and experience the gestalt of the entire
scene. They said that the Imax experience was replacing their own
real memories of what it had been like in space."[43]

Grand Canyon: The Hidden Secrets
(Douglas Memmott and Kieth Merrill, producers; 1984).

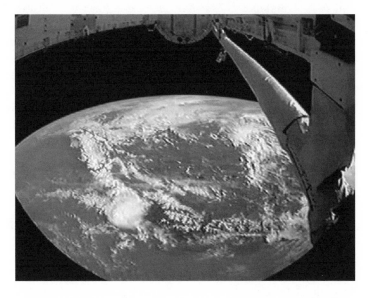

Blue Planet
(Graeme Ferguson, producer; 1990).

Modern motion simulation rides date from 1986, the year that Douglas Trumbull installed *Tour of the Universe* at Toronto's CN Tower. His tourist attraction was a simulated space adventure that featured Trumbull's high-speed Showscan process of 70mm film cinematography. It inspired *Star Tours,* the Disney and Lucasfilm collaboration the following year. *Star Tours* (eventually installed at all Disney theme parks) became the industry model. Like *Tour of the Universe, Star Tours* was designed to show only one film and used the theater's architecture as well as a lobby "preshow" to activate and advance the narrative. Since then, Disney has added a second motion simulation ride at its Epcot Center in Orlando (*Body Wars,* 1989), a *Fantastic Voyage*-like journey inside a human body where something goes wrong and the body becomes a cosmic force that wreaks havoc on the little ship. A handful of other companies supply motion simulation rides to Disney's park competitors, to shopping mall theaters, to hotels, and to other entertainment zones, and the largest companies use their own integrated systems: Imax Corporation, Iwerks Entertainment, and Showscan.[44]

In 1993, Trumbull's *In Search of the Obelisk* (part of a theatrical trilogy titled *Secrets of the Luxor Pyramid*) at the Hotel Luxor in Las Vegas marked the maturation of modern ridefilms. Designed and installed as part of the hotel's overall conception, it demonstrates the degree to which a motion simulation theater has become a standard feature for Las Vegas hotels and entertainment complexes. *In Search of the Obelisk* relies on the surrounding narrative associations of the hotel's pyramid structure and a video preshow to launch a fictional rescue mission through time into a lost civilization. The film itself is a combination of live action, computer-generated imagery, matte models, and other cinematic special effects: it results in a vertiginous diegesis that spins around and upside down so much that it eludes any references to north, east, west, or southerly directions. The only onscreen spatial anchor is the narrative's "pilot," who appears in the center onscreen and speaks over his shoulder to the audience/passengers "behind him."

While some ridefilms—like those at Disney parks, the Hotel Luxor, Universal Studios, or Busch Gardens—are fixed (one film only) so that they can coordinate the setting and the film, most motion simulation rides change films on a regular basis and are thus housed in more generic movie theaters, such as Iwerks's Turbo Ride Theaters. These ridefilms depend on computer technologies not simply for the movies' special effects but for software-driven movie products that can simultaneously control and synchronize the hydraulics of the seats. This, in turn, allows theater owners to change the bill of fare regularly and without the expense of continuously adapting the moviehouse for each new attraction.

Each of the major companies that builds such generic ridefilm theaters also produces films, but each also relies for a regular supply of films from independent production companies. These theaters offer a "preshow" only to the extent that video monitors displayed in the lobby and halls outside plain, boxlike auditoriums repetitively loop narrative prologues while the audience waits to enter the theater. Just a small sample of titles includes: *Alpine Race* (Showscan, 1991), *Space Race* (Showscan, 1991), *Sub-Oceanic Shuttle* (Iwerks Entertainment, 1991), *Devil's Mine Ride* (Showscan, 1993), *Asteroid Adventure* (Imax Corporation, 1993), *River Runners* (Omni Films International, 1993), *Robo Cop: The Ride* (Iwerks Entertainment, 1993), *Seafari* (Rhythm and Hues, Inc., 1994), *Dino Island* (Iwerks Entertainment, 1995), *Funhouse Express* (Imax Ridefilm, 1995), *Red Rock Run* (Iwerks Entertainment, 1996), *Smash Factory* (Midland Productions, 1996), *Days of Thunder* (Iwerks Entertainment, 1996), *Secrets of the Lost Temple* (Iwerks Entertainment, 1997), and *Aliens: Ride at the Speed of Fright* (Iwerks Entertainment, 1997).

Unlike *Hales Tours*, which emphasized picturesque travel, topographical landmarks, and tourist travel experiences, the independent ridefilms are dominated by fantasy travel that features the scenery of outer space, futuristic cities, and lost civilizations (especially inside mountains, pyramids, or mines), (although there are also representations of present-day automobile races, train panoramas, and amusement park views). Ridefilms rely on the same cinematic conventions as *Hale's Tours* and *Imax*, in effect persuading spectators to perceive their bodies as hurtling forward through time and space because they visually perceive a flow of environmental motion toward them. Most often, these visual cues consist of passing vehicles or features of the landscape represented in foreshortened animation and of colors rendered by computer-generated imagery that swirl and change. These cinematic light shows are not only indirect successors to Cinerama and other widescreen special effects but also are direct heirs to Douglas Trumbull's famous

"Stargate Corridor" sequence in *2001: A Space Odyssey* (1968) and owe their signification of moving forward in interplanetary space as much to the precedent of that film's representation of stroboscopic colored lights as to more conventional graphic indicators of perspectival foreshortening and depth.

Modern motion simulation rides not only offer physically jolting movements synchronized to the onscreen action, but they repeatedly inscribe technology run amuck. Vehicles that are out of control motivate the wild ride and dominate the field. The vehicles might be racecars, airplanes, spaceships, submarines, or mine carts and trains. Two producers of animated ridefilms say that practically all of the narratives of dangerous adventure depend on a small number of technological and mechanical crises—a bad landing, "something's wrong with our ship," "Oops! Wrong direction!" or an encounter with an evil creature—which may occur singly or in combination.[45] For example, *Star Tours* (1987) features an interplanetary shuttle trip with *Star Wars* androids who head the wrong way, then try to hide from and avoid enemy ships, and finally crash land the vehicle. The popular *Back to the Future—The Ride* (Douglas Trumbull, Berkshire Ridefilm, 1991), which plays at the Universal Studios theme parks in California and Florida, takes its inspiration from the Hollywood film after which it is named. It advances a simple plot using the movie's characters and narrative premise in order to combine outer space flight, time travel, the reckless pursuit of a villain, problems with the ship's mechanical systems, and the requisite bumpy ride that frequently and narrowly averts disaster.

Narrativization is an equally important marker of realism in the modern simulation rides, although it is employed differently than in *Hale's Tours*. This is interesting in light of the fact that the shift effected by the films in *Hale's Tours* was a novel one, a way of *introducing* narrative strategies to the cinema, whereas narrativization in today's ridefilms relies on a conservation of Hollywood's dominant strategy.

For example, *Secrets of the Lost Temple* (Iwerks Entertainment, 1997) offers a cinematically conventional exposition—all in third-person point of view—of a teenage boy finding a book on the floor of a mausoleumlike library. Opening the mysterious book, he is transported to another dimension in a blinding flash of light and dematerialization. Certainly, the prologue's purpose is not only to explain the narrative premise but also to offer up a figure for identification in the most traditional syntax of Hollywood cinema. At this point, the ridefilm begins and, as the audience is first lifted by the hydraulics and then dropped, the boy onscreen simultaneously experiences a fall to the floor in front of an "Indiana Jones" adventurer look-alike. The two converse and, as they are about to be whisked away on a raft down the waterways and chutes of the lost temple, the film switches to the boy's subjective point of view. Throughout the rest of their ensuing wild ride, the film steadfastly maintains the boy's point of view as the audience is asked to assume his place. At the conclusion of their journey the boy finds himself back in the library, and the film reveals this reentry with a return to the third-person point of view. The shift is synchronized with the grinding to a halt of motion shocks and effects. The movie effects narrative closure through the boy's discovery that he is clutching his hero's battered fedora (an exact duplicate of the one worn by Indiana Jones in the Steven Spielberg movies): he doffs the beloved hat and jauntily departs.

This return to a conventional movie "ending" in the context of the ridefilm is most jarring, however, in its shattering of a subjective position. The return to a third-person point of view occurs *with* the loss of motion and effects. Ride manufacturer and movie director Trumbull contrasts these two points of view: he calls the traditional cinematic one of "non-participating voyeurism" and the subjective point of view coordinated with kinesthetic effects "invasive."[46] Trumbull's binary opposition of spectator experience conflicts with his initial hype of total immersion to describe more accurately that what is important about this cinema is that it acts on the spectator's body rather than providing a peephole into which the spectator can dematerialize. In short, this cinema invades the body rather than inviting consciousness to leave behind the body and enter into the movie.

In this regard, today's ridefilms function differently than did *Hale's Tours*, which worked to inscribe its audiences into an idealized novel position of authoritative invisibility and surveillance. Toward this end, permanent installations improve on ridefilm experiences like *Secrets of the Lost Temple* by diffusing lines of demarcation between embodiment, character identification, and a dematerialized gaze and thus more gradually moving their audiences back and forth between them. *Star Tours, Back to the Future, Body Wars*, and other permanent installations extend the narrative to the social spaces of the building beyond the movie theater.

The lobbies outside the movie auditoriums especially carry an important atmospheric weight, providing a preparatory zone for the ride that prefigures the spectatorial processes inside the auditorium. *Star Tours*, for example, really begins with one's entrance into the waiting lanes in the lobby, an architectural space whimsically presented as a futuristic space airport. The lobby features a glassed-in control tower visible from the floor in which animatrons of the android characters in *Star Wars* go about their business. An animatron of the character C3PO greets visitors with a running commentary. The audience is already physically immersed in an interactive spectacle even though its role, similar to that of the movie spectator, is simply to move forward in the proper lane and to react without any possibility of altering the narrative that envelops the audience. At amusement parks, in particular, such an organization of space is both a pragmatic way of controlling noisy crowds and an effective means for maintaining efficient traffic circulation. But it also encourages rowdy crowds to behave like the distracted individuals of idealized mass movie audiences, who respond passively more to the stimuli of the spectacle than to each other.

More than wild narratives that reposition spectators, rides like *Star Tours* and *Secrets of the Lost Temple* also completely recover the gap between the index and the referent. It is not accidental that these movie-themed ridefilms appear more realistic to the rides' patrons than do the roller coasters, runaway trains, race cars, and bobsleds that are also the subjects of ridefilms. In movie-themed films, the referent is not a landscape to which the spectator might in reality have physical access but is a movie instead. In other words, the space landscape of *Star Tours* need not be measured against an ideal referent that it can never equal but only approximate because it *is* its own referent. The *image of* the landscape *is* that which it refers to—the cinematic space of *Star Wars*; it is, after all, a movie of a movie. As one computer artist put it: while it may be difficult for computer animation to look like the real world, it is easy for computer-generated imagery to look like computer-generated images.[47] These movie- or game-themed rides close the gap between index and referent, achieving a sublime realism that is the subject of postmodern fantasy, of being not so much in outer space as in, more properly, a well-loved movie or video game. Even the *New York Times* acknowledges this particular ridefilm effect: "It's like being inside, not just at, the movies."[48]

Conclusion

At both the beginning and now ostensibly at the "end" of cinema, a popular tourist cinema responds to dramatic technological shifts. *Hale's Tours* registered the newness of cinema's autonomization of vision and the process of its normalization by grafting the process itself onto a bodily sensation of motion and coordinating it with synchronized sound effects; it retained the experiential *across the site of the body*. Almost one hundred years later, Imax and motion simulation rides similarly compensate for the "threat" of digital imagery, a threat that stems less from the fact of digital simulation of the photographic than from the digital's tendency to undermine the subject's ability to *determine* whether or not an image has a real-world referent—whether it is a truthful or faithful image.

Even a sophisticated film critic responded to this point after his experience on a motion simulation ride. Amos Vogel, writing in the late 1950s, states: "The total impression [is] so vivid as to approach the actual experience. The jury is stumped: Has film left behind the 'illusion of art' and become reality itself?"[49] Vogel's words demonstrate the degree to which tourist cinema has always granted something similar to enthusiasts and skeptics alike. Alternative tourist cinema is always about the confusion of visual knowledge in the face of too many visual stimuli, and it is even about certainty over the image's truthfulness—its referentiality. Tourist cinema makes vision coherent by asserting its certitude in relationship to one's bodily experience of multiple sensations. Simulation rides rectify and compensate for the loss of a unified, embodied subjectivity by literally grounding a subject position in all its material and sensory capacities. The rides initially made possible a modernist subject position of visual omnipotence and the authority of panoptic surveillance because they registered them as bodily knowledge. Today, the spectacles of movie simulation nostalgically address their spectators as diegetic movie characters, who become for the moment unified subjects because they synthesize living inside of movies with the locatedness of living inside of their own bodies. They chronicle neither the realization of Hayle's nightmare of posthumanity nor her dream of a technologically powered feminist utopia, but rather the social reconstruction of memory so that retrospection and history—as an ongoing dialogue between embodiment and disembodiment—conforms to and transforms contemporary ideology.

Notes

1 See Emmanuelle Toulet, "Cinema at the Universal Exposition, Paris 1900," *Persistence of Vision* 9 (1991): 10–36.

2 For an introduction to the relationship between gunnery, military training, and cinema's development, see Paul Virilio, *War and Cinema* (London: Verso, 1986).

3 Although many people have commented on the "cinema of attractions," the seminal essay for defining this mode is Tom Gunning's "The Cinema of Attractions: Early Film, Its Spectator, and the Avant-Garde," in *Early Cinema: Space, Frame, Narrative*, ed. Thomas Elsaesser (London: British Film Institute, 1990), 57–58.

4 N. Katherine Hayles, *How We Became Posthuman: Virtual Bodies in Cybernetics, Literature, and Informatics* (Chicago: University of Chicago Press, 1999), 4.

5 Jonathan Crary, *Suspensions of Perception* (Cambridge: MIT Press, 1999), chapter 1.

6 Hayles, *How We Became Posthuman*, 15.

7 Charles R. Acland, "IMAX in Canadian Cinema: Geographic Transformation and Discourses of Nationhood," *Studies in Cultures, Organizations, and Societies* 3 (1997): 304.

8 Ibid. I have also experienced this introduction at both the Denver Museum of Natural History and the Langley Theater at the National Air and Space Museum in Washington, D.C. More recently, the Denver museum offers a preshow slide show that describes in hyperbolic language the equipment components.

9 Francesco Casetti, *Inside the Gaze: The Fiction Film and Its Spectator*, trans. Nell Andrew and Charles O'Brien (Bloomington: Indiana University Press, 1998), 8–9.

10 Raymond Fielding, "Hale's Tours: Ultrarealism in the Pre-1910 Motion Picture," in *Before Griffith*, ed. John L. Fell (Berkeley: University of California Press, 1983), 129.

11 Charles Acland, "IMAX Technology and the Tourist Gaze," *Cultural Studies* 12, no. 3 (1998): 42.

12 Richard Saul Wurman, *Washington D.C. Access* (New York: Harper-Perennial, 1998), 59.

13 For descriptions of Hale and Gifford's patents of an amusement de-

vice (patent no. 767,281) and a pleasure-railway (patent no. 800,100), see *The Official Gazette of the United States Patent Office*, vol. 111 (Washington, D.C.: U.S. Government Publications, August 1904), 1577, and vol. 118 (September 1905), 788–789. In 1906, Hale and Gifford sold the rights east of Pittsburgh to William A. Brady of New York and Edward B. Grossmann of Chicago for $50,000 (*Billboard*, 27 January 1906, 20). They sold the southern states rights to Wells, Dunne & Harlan of New York; additional licenses to C. W. Parker Co. of Abilene, Kansas, for traveling carnival companies; and the Pacific Northwest states rights to a group of men who incorporated as "The Northwest Hale's Tourist Amusement Company" in Portland, Oregon.

14 Hale & Gifford, advertisement, *Billboard*, 17 February 1906, 19.

15 *Billboard*, 3 February 1906, 20.

16 The *Billboard* reported that both *Hale's Tours* and the *Trolley Tours* "raised the standard of attractions" at amusement parks and were enjoying "great popularity" ("Parks," *Billboard*, 9 June 1906, 24). And as early as its initial 1906 season, *Hale's Tours* and its competitors became top-grossing popular concessions across the United States. See, for example, "Duluth's New Summer Park," *Billboard*, 28 July 1906, 28. At Riverview Park in Chicago, the nation's largest and best-attended amusement park, *Hale's Tours* was the fifth biggest moneymaker of the fifty concessions there, earning $18,000 for the season. It was topped only by the Igorotte Village ($40,000), the Kansas Cyclone roller coaster ($28,000), the Figure 8 roller coaster ($35,000), Rollin's animal show and ostrich farm ($26,000), and the dance pavilion ($22,000). It even surpassed the revenues from the park's other moving picture venue, the Electric Theatre, which took in $16,000 for the year ("Riverview," *Billboard*, 1 December 1906, 28).

17 *Official Gazette of the United States Patent Office*, vol. 126 (January–February 1907), 3292.

18 *Hale's Tours*, advertisement, *Billboard*, 18 May 1907, 29.

19 *Billboard*, 27 January 1906, 23. Their advertisement said: "The illusion of seeing the various countries and cities from an automobile is produced by a panorama of moving scenes attached to the wall beside the Sightseeing Auto upon which are seated the 'Sightseers,' and the throwing upon a screen in front of the Sightseeing Auto the moving pictures which were taken from a moving automobile, by this company, and which are the property of the Sightseeing Auto Co. By an original and clever idea the 'Sightseers' are given a side trip which enables them to view a variety of moving pictures, thus taking away from the patrons of the Sightseeing Autos that 'tired feeling' which is produced by a repetition of the same kind and character of moving pictures they would be forced to witness should they always remain on the auto" (*Billboard*, 27 January 1906, 23).

20 *White & Langever's Steamboat Tours of the World*, advertisement, *Bill-board*, 22 September 1906, 44. See also patent no. 828,791, *Official Gazette of the United States Patent Office*, vol. 126 (July–August 1906), 2246–47.

21 This concept was advertised as follows: "A moving picture show in a knock-down portable canvas car, boat, vehicle or ordinary tent that can be easily set up, quickly pulled down, readily transported, yet mechanically arranged that the bell, the whistle, and the swing of a moving train, boat or vehicle is produced. Trips or views can be constantly changed to suit your fancy, scenes of any railroad vehicle or boat ride, on land or water, produced with full sensation of the ride, together with 'Sightseers' sightseeing side trips covering Principal Cities of the world" (*Hruby & Plummer's Tours and Scenes of the World*, advertisement, *Billboard*, 3 March 1906, 25).

22 Patent no. 838,137, *Official Gazette of the United States Patent Office*, vol. 125 (December 1906), 1832–33.

23 Patent no. 874,169, *The Official Gazette of the United States Patent Office*, vol. 131 (December 1907), 1846.

24 *A Trip to California Over Land and Sea*, advertisement, *Billboard*, 31 March 1906, 31, and 26 May 1906, 31.

25 Edison Manufacturing Company, advertisement, *New York Clipper*, 28 April 1906.

26 Raymond Fielding, "Hale's Tours," 128.

27 E. C. Thomas, "Vancouver, B.C. Started with 'Hale's Tours,' " *Moving Picture World* (15 July 1916): 373.

28 Noel Burch, *Life to Those Shadows*, trans. Ben Brewster (Berkeley: University of California Press, 1990), 39. Emphasis added.

29 Thomas, "Vancouver, B.C. Started with 'Hale's Tours,' " 373.

30 Wolfgang Schivelbusch, *The Railway Journey: Trains and Travel in the Nineteenth Century*, trans. Anselm Hollo (New York: Urizen, 1977), 13–131.

31 Ibid.

32 Lynne Kirby, *Parallel Tracks: The Railroad and Silent Cinema* (Durham: Duke University Press, 1997), 57.

33 Using multiple large-scale screens in three separate viewing spaces; multiple sound systems; as many as 288 speakers; mirrors and flashing lights; and altered theater viewing spaces, the filmmakers extended the idea of cinematic innovation to the very listening and viewing conditions. Their idea was a large-scale version of what Gene Youngblood has labeled "expanded cinema," a type of experimental cinema then in vogue throughout North America that tried to push back the boundaries of cinema by celebrating the hallucinatory aspect of cinema in all its material and viewing conditions (see Acland, "IMAX in Canadian Cinema," 291).

34 There are eighteen theaters in Canada, nineteen in Japan, eighty-

five in the United States, eight in Mexico, seven in Australia, eight in France, eight in Germany, four in South Korea, four in Taiwan, four in Spain, two in Great Britain, two in the Netherlands, and one each in Austria, Belgium, Ireland, Portugal, Switzerland, Denmark, Sweden, Norway, South Africa, China, Indonesia, the Philippines, Singapore, and Thailand (Imax Web site, 10 March 1999, http://www.imax.com/theatres/.

35 Ibid.

36 "Imax Max," *Forbes* 168 (1 June 1998): 84.

37 William C. Symonds, "Now Showing in Imax: Money!" *Business Week* (31 March 1997): 80.

38 *American Cinematographer* (December 1985): 75, 78.

39 Acland, "IMAX in Canadian Cinema," 435.

40 For descriptions of all current Imax films, see the Imax Web site, http://www.imax.com/films/.

41 Acland, "IMAX in Canadian Cinema," 290.

42 Paul Virilio, "Cataract Surgery: Cinema in the Year 2000," in *Alien Zone: Cultural Theory and Contemporary Science Fiction Cinema*, ed. Annette Kuhn (New York: Verso, 1990), 173.

43 Bob Fisher and Marji Rhea, "Interview: Doug Trumbull and Richard Yuricich, ASC," *American Cinematographer* 75 (August 1994): 66.

44 Because the name "Iwerks" is well known—Ub Iwerks (1901-1971) was Walt Disney's original partner, an animator, and a technical genius—it is worth noting the use of the name for this company. Iwerks Entertainment, Inc. was started in 1986 by two former Disney employees, one of whom is Don Iwerks, son of Ib (see http://www.iwerks.com/.

45 Fitz-Edward Otis, Omni Film International vice president of sales, as quoted in Debra Kaufman, "One Wild Ride: Motion-Simulation Market Picks up Speed," *In Motion* (October 1993): 27.

46 Trumbull, quoted in Fisher and Marji, "Interview," 59.

47 Judith Rubin, "Something's Wrong with Our Ship: Animated Motion-Simulator Films in Theme Parks," *Animation World* 1, no. 8 (November 1996): http://www.awn.com/mag/issue1.8/articles/rubin1.8.htm/.

48 *New York Times*, quoted in Entertainment Design Workshop Web site, 1 March 1998, http://www.edesignw.com/.

49 Amos Vogel, "The Angry Young Film Makers," *Evergreen Review* 2 (1958): 175.

Judith Babbitts

STEREOGRAPHS AND

THE CONSTRUCTION OF A VISUAL

CULTURE IN THE UNITED STATES

More than a century ago the stereograph industry promised Americans that its three-dimensional photographs would transform their lives, much as the printing press had transformed Europe centuries before. Two major producers of stereographs, Underwood & Underwood and the Keystone View Company, claimed their images would "bring the world into one's parlor" and ensure viewers economic and social success in the fast-paced twentieth century.[1] Addressing middle-class anxieties about modernity and rapid social change, appealing to school systems grappling with large numbers of immigrants, and exploiting the nation's role as a Pacific power after the Spanish-American War, the industry declared its products a panacea for America's problems and the key to its future greatness.

A stereograph is actually two photographs that when viewed together produce a solid, three-dimensional effect. In the nineteenth century, the photographs were pasted side by side on a cardboard mount, and on casual inspection appeared alike. But on closer examination, the viewer could see that one extended slightly to the left, the other to the right, duplicating the left and right field of vision of the human eye. When placed in the holder of a viewing instrument called a stereoscope, the lenses of the instrument helped the viewer's eyes and brain fuse the two images into one. The two photographs that comprised the stereograph were taken either with a camera that had a slide that enabled the photographer to move the lens for the second shot, or with a camera that had two built-in lenses. If high-quality lenses, printing, and viewing apparatus were used, the result could be an extraordinary visual experience.

Stereographs illustrate the extraordinary prestige and ideological legitimacy of a *way* of acquiring knowledge in a given historical time. They demonstrate how new technologies acquire cultural meaning and are transformed from useful curiosities to necessities of life. Cultural meaning evolves not alone from the widespread *use* of a technology but equally from the widespread belief in a technology's value in society and its efficacy in fulfilling personal needs and desires. Commercial voices of cultural authority in the early twentieth century played a dominant role in creating the popular discourse that redefined *what* was important to know and *how* one should go about knowing it. As no knowledge industry had before it, the stereograph industry identified technology—the technology of the camera—as the essential factor in acquiring information. And from the late nineteenth century on, technology has become the standard for knowledge acquisition that is purportedly "modern" and better.

A study of stereographs provides insight not only into the emergence of a visual culture in the United States but also into our own digital culture. The stereograph industry had access to national and international audiences through widespread advertising, industry publications, and endorsements by prominent national leaders and cultural commentators. Educational administrators—if not teachers—embraced stereographs as valuable learning tools in the classroom. A visual education movement, fueled by stereograph companies and endorsed by educators, eventually applied the discourse of visual learning to filmstrips, film, and educational television.

The stereograph companies, however, did not single-handedly change paradigms of learning. They benefited from and exploited early-twentieth-century beliefs about the infallibility of science, the prestige of being "in the know," and the privileging of the modern over the "traditional." The stereograph industry created nothing less than a paradigm of visual knowledge and diffused that paradigm to homes and schools throughout the nation. They presaged contemporary cultural and technological studies of disembodied realities, such as virtual reality and simulated computer environments, and they deserve to be restored to that tradition.

Believing the world is "knowable" through visual images is a historically specific construction that emerged in the late nineteenth century. New commercial stereograph companies, such as Underwood & Underwood and the Keystone View Company, devised marketing strategies that ignored nineteenth-century debates among photographers, artists, and cultural critics about whether a photograph was a mere mechanical reproduction or a work of art that offered a grander purpose for visual images in American life. Heralding a new era in human history brought about by photography, stereograph companies proclaimed not only new ways of seeing but new ways of knowing. The question was no longer how do we see and what can we see, the companies said, but what can we know when we look. Stereographs, the industry explained, allowed viewers to understand the world as they never had before because the images enabled viewers to see beyond the appearance of things, beyond the old ways of knowing that had prevailed in the world up until then. By calling attention to what was implicit but previously unarticulated in photographic vision, the companies attempted to monopolize the definition of visual understanding.

Underwood's slogan, "To see is to know," may have resonated with Americans who increasingly found visual entertainments a part of their everyday experience during the first decades of the twentieth century. Both urban and rural Americans saw movies, browsed through illustrated catalogs, sent and received postcards, and saw pictorial advertisements and billboards. Millions of people attended the world's fairs or international expositions held in Chicago in 1893, in Buffalo in 1901, and in St. Louis in 1904. At each exposition, reconstructed native villages from Asia, Africa, and Latin America as well as artificial Indian reservations offered Americans face-to-face experiences with people and environments they had never before seen. The majority of visitors bought or Kodak-snapped photographs as souvenirs. In the museums opened during these decades, Americans saw objects from foreign countries displayed in glass cases and in panoramic exhibits. In popular amusement parks, they took simulated train rides with *Hale's Tours*, making believe they were traveling through unfamiliar landscapes while sitting in a seat that jostled them in imitation of real travel.

Accepted by most Americans as part entertainment, part education, and part science, these new leisure activities expanded the nation's collective visual imagination.[2]

Stereographs were part of what Neil Harris has called an "explosion" of visual sights characteristic of the modern world.[3] But as creators of new experiences for Americans, the stereograph industry was profoundly different from the producers of nickelodeons, world's fairs, and museums. While none of these visual or simulated environments were devoid of ideological content, only the stereograph industry constructed and disseminated a worldview that promised to transform all aspects of American life. Museums and world's fairs satisfied the nation's interests in ethnography, natural history, and technological innovation and promoted ideas of national progress and Western cultural and racial superiority. Early screen practices incorporated similar racial stereotypes and notions of patriotism and national hubris in many of their productions. None, however, set forth the theoretical assumptions that gave cultural meaning and efficacy to visual knowledge. Only the stereograph companies articulated the complex social, cultural, and scientific issues implicated in the conceptual shifts and technological changes of modernity, and placed disembodied realities and vision at the center of that change. Like the computer industry today, the stereograph industry, through both its products and its rhetoric, attempted to construct a new paradigm of knowing by identifying information, and how one acquired it, as crucial for success in the contemporary world.

Constructing a Model of Visual Knowing

Historians estimate that between the mid-nineteenth century and the 1930s, the stereograph industry published between three to six million *different* images. The number of images made from any one negative is impossible to determine, but by 1901 Underwood was publishing twenty-five thousand stereographs a day and three hundred thousand stereoscopes a year.[4] By the early twentieth century stereographs had become a ubiquitous feature of American life. Salespeople selling consumer goods carried stereographs of their products rather than the products themselves; cereal manufacturers put free stereographs in each box they sold; and Sears and Roebuck and other large businesses distributed stereographs of their manufacturing operations. Sunday schools used stereographs of the Holy Land to illustrate Bible lessons, and public library users borrowed both stereographs and stereoscopes. Before the widespread use of the halftone process in early-twentieth-century publishing, the most common way Americans viewed photographs was through a stereoscope.

To educate Americans about the importance of stereographs, both Underwood and Keystone disseminated monthly magazines for home consumers and scores of teachers' manuals and student guides to their school sets. They also provided lengthy descriptions on the back of each stereograph and, in the case of Underwood, guidebooks to its three hundred sets of travel images. Most important, however, were their armies of cultural missionaries who fanned out over the country and the world. Thousands of traveling sales agents carried the industry's message to rural farmers and small-town Americans. Their numbers swelled each summer as school teachers and college students working summer jobs joined their ranks.[5] In the face-to-face conversations that took place in parlors, front porches, and kitchens around the country, sales agents recited the industry's script that they had memorized from their sales manuals.[6] They lectured Americans about achieving modernity and efficiency through viewing stereographs. They quoted prominent American leaders and commentators who had endorsed the companies' claims, their statements printed in company publications and popular magazines. The presidents of Harvard University and Columbia Teachers College, the poets Carl Sandburg and Ernest Thompson Seton, world-renowned traveler Burton Holmes, and even Pope Pius X agreed that stereographs were the next best thing to real travel itself.[7]

The stereograph industry's task was to inflate the value of visual images beyond what consumers already believed about their usefulness. Ordinary Americans knew that photographs showed them sights they might never see with their own eyes. From its beginnings, photography had preserved the likenesses of loved ones, depicted the horrors of war, and revealed the strangeness of foreign landscapes and peoples.[8] The specific appeal of stereography lay in the illusion of reality created, because stereographs mimicked depth, solidity, and perspective, as if one were looking at a scene through a window. The stereograph companies capitalized on this illusion of three-dimensional space in order to argue for a new conception of photography, one that invited Americans to think about the nature of photographic vision itself.

In defining visual knowledge, the companies shifted the focus from the photograph—the thing seen—to the viewer and the act of seeing. Throughout history, they argued, viewers of art had been only passive observers. Stereographs were different, however, because they transformed viewers by vicariously transporting them to distant places, and just as real travelers moved through space—to look and be looked at—viewers' vantage points changed to those within the scene itself. By peering through a stereoscope, viewers would be introduced to a new field of vision and become a participant in a vast new world, a world no longer bound by actual face-to-face contact. Stereographs would reshape what it was to know and perceive reality.

In their publications, Underwood and Keystone offered pseudo-scientific theories about how people came to know the world. The introduction to Underwood's tour guide on China, for example, began with a simple statement: the world was not only out *there* but also in viewers' consciousness, in their mental or "soul life." Whether viewers went to the time, expense, and trouble of traveling to a country or visited it through a stereoscope, they were concerned with only *"two kinds of realities."* One was the earth, people, and trees of the physical world, and the other the thoughts, emotions, and desires of their mental world. The guidebook explained: "We can see that proving there is no real Canton, China before a man in the stereoscope does not prove there is no real soul state within him, no genuine experience of being in Canton. The object of travel is not the land. No traveller brings any material houses or fields back with him. He travels to get certain experiences of being in the country, and those *genuine experiences of travel* are possible in the stereoscope. In the stereoscope *we are dealing with realities*, but they are the realities of *soul states*, not the realities of outward physical things."[9]

Were these two realities equal? Underwood argued they were not. The superior reality was the mental one: "The physical realities which are so often thought of as the only realities, serve simply as the means of inducing the states of consciousness, the mental reality, the end sought" (iii). The end sought, the goal of travel, was to acquire experience in the form of feelings, and eventually, memories. Viewers would have the same feelings if they were on a stereoscopic tour or actually present in a country. Underwood assured viewers that their feelings would differ "in quantity and intensity, but not *in kind*" (iii). By quantity and intensity Underwood meant those aspects of travel that one might hope to avoid anyway—the rank odors, ear-splitting noises, stifling temperatures, and dirty hands and elbows of the "natives." Seeking sights that could be turned into memories was the goal of travel, Underwood declared, and the mind, like camera film, only recorded what the eyes imprinted on it. The stereoscope delivered "the same visual impressions in all essential respects that we gain if there in our bodies" (iii), Underwood concluded. By identifying vision, memory, and reality as the essential components of any experience, and by thinking about the mind's eye as itself a photographic process, Underwood legitimized "to see is to know" (iv) as the acquisition of knowledge.

Underwood and Keystone reassured viewers that knowing the world only through images was not naive or simplistic. It brought, they said, understanding of the deepest kind. By "translating oneself into the pictured situation," by living in the illusion created by the image, one's reality paradoxically was expanded and enhanced. In the *Stereoscopic Photograph*, a publication for home consumers, Underwood wrote: "But in the stereograph what we have to do with is not the bit of paper with its line-combinations and its spots and spaces of light and dark. It is out behind and beyond the card, a world into which we look *through* the card. What we hold in our hand is not, properly speaking, a work of art at all, but a key to everyday reality." [10] By seeing *through* the card, stereoscopic vision penetrated the facade of everyday life. True "insight" happened when the technology of the camera captured a scene on film. Only then, by looking at the photographic image, could viewers understand in another culture what often remained mysterious to them in their own. While immersed in the scene, they saw and understood the essence of things. The viewer's engaged, active looking was superior to his or her random, unaided sight because it offered "insights" more valuable and enduring than real travel could ever offer with its fleeting, chaotic perceptions.

Underwood redefined the body as necessary to travel, not in the body's sensory fullness but in its role as a marker of place. Knowing where one literally *stood* at a site was essential to getting the most out of an experience. The stereographic guide told viewers that "one must look intently and with some thought, not only at what is before one, but what is to the left and right and behind one, even though one could not see in all those directions."[11] To assist viewers in accomplishing this feat, the company designed an elaborate map system for its tours. Pasted into the back of each guidebook, the maps indicated with arrows and red lines the exact spot where the viewer was standing as he looked at the scene before him. It was, of course, the spot where the photographer had stood. Frequently throughout the tours the guide urged, directed, and cajoled viewers into consulting the maps, for without that sense of location, Underwood warned, viewers would be disoriented and lost, in the "helpless condition of a man who has been carried somewhere blindfolded or asleep, and who opens his eyes on a place whose identity is unknown" (iv).

But why was it necessary to know exactly where one stood on a street corner in Canton? Why this degree of precision? The maps helped to build a belief that vicarious experiences could be as credible as lived moments. The maps were one way that Underwood could deliver on its promise of transforming viewers into comfortable citizens of the world, "at home" among the narrow alleyways and wide boulevards of the world's major cities. But the maps also added a scientific and technological validity to the stereographs and placed them in the realm of "topographical studies." "In topographical studies," Underwood's guidebooks explained, "the points of the compass should always be determined," because not knowing one's exact location was "bewildering and a positive hindrance to a correct knowledge of locality" (v). The consequences could be disastrous, for "the disarranged compass will refuse to be adjusted and one's ideas of places and direction will thereafter remain forever erroneous"; without the maps, according to Underwood, viewers would find themselves in a "place whose identity is unknown" (vi). From the very beginning, then, it was vital that the maps precisely calibrate the compass for viewers. Diagrammatic and presumably accurate, the maps eliminated uncertainty and error and rooted stereographs in the prestigious world of science.

Underwood applied the rigorous procedures of laboratory work to its "modern," scientific approach to acquiring knowledge. Unlike the ever-changing reality that enveloped real travelers, Underwood said, stereographic scenes transformed nations into laboratory specimens, the home into a scientific laboratory, and the viewer into a scientist. Underwood described the importance of the laboratory method in the March 1901 issue of the *Stereoscopic Photograph*: "There is something tremendously real about a study that brings us in actual contact with things. Laboratory study has been the death of scholasticism and has revolutionized human thought. But . . . the humanities, as they were once called, have not held their old place in the college curriculum or in the esteem of mankind. Why not? Simply because we have not found a way to study them in the laboratory . . . Is there no such thing as a laboratory for history, for art and for civilization? . . . He who would study art must *see* art, he who would understand civilization must study it in the laboratory."[12] The laboratory method redefined culture itself so that it could be studied under a stereoscopic microscope, captured on film, or distilled into neat, comprehensible units fit for laboratory analysis. Underwood's stereographs reduced the chaos and mystery of the world to an orderly sequence of visual images.

Underwood's metaphor of the home as a laboratory reflected earlier changes in American society that had transformed bourgeois domestic life. As consumer products and services expanded and diminished the communal relations that had fulfilled families' household and emotional needs, the home had increasingly become a world unto itself. The stereoscope further privatized experience and erased the barriers between the private and public world. By declaring the home that possessed a stereoscope to be a laboratory, the industry infused the family parlor with notions of efficiency, exactitude, and the scientific method. Stereographs made the American home modern by putting the most up-to-date educational technology into the hands of every family member. Ironically, at a time when the discipline of science itself was becoming more bureaucratic, specialized, and professional, Underwood and Keystone conveyed the illusion that the average American could become a scientist merely by peering through a stereoscope.

While the stereograph industry shaped the language and ideas that fostered a visual culture, the photographers who created stereographic images gave that nascent culture its artifactual base. Images from afar, images of places Americans might never see and verify with their own eyes, underlay the industry's whole notion of a substitute reality. An examination of the industry's travel tours both illustrates how the stereograph companies' concept of visual knowledge was imbedded in its products and demonstrates the role that language played in its construction of a visual culture.

In 1897, fifteen years after the company was established, Underwood hired a staff of full-time photographers to travel the globe in search of pictures that had never before been seen. The Keystone View Company hired its full-time photographers in 1898.[13] Heavily promoted by their employers as cultural heroes, these stereographers portrayed themselves as image bounty hunters. Armed with cameras and guns, they purportedly devoted their lives to capturing and portraying the peoples of the world on film. In reality, they were working photographers aware of their responsibilities to their employers, and this awareness influenced what they photographed and how they understood their work. For the most part, their intention was not to challenge prevailing stereotypes but to find ever more exotic examples of national traits and characteristics that other travelers and cultural explorers had identified in their writings. The stereographers' images often provided visual proof that these written accounts were true.

Although the stereographers often followed the same routes as seasoned travelers and photographed the world through the prism of their own historical time, they believed that what they were doing was different. While they did not use the words "visual culture" they saw themselves as shaping a "modern" way of knowing. That new way was based on the camera as a technological gauge of modernity. The photographer's ease or difficulty in getting pictures and the eagerness or unwillingness of foreign people to be photographed marked in the photographer's mind a nation as primitive and backward or as progressive and modern. If visual knowledge underlay modernity, and the camera was a modern instrument of knowledge, then hostility to the camera revealed the absence of a modern sensibility. The willingness to sit for their portraits meant that indigenous peoples had rejected superstitious beliefs about photography and understood Western forms of visual representation. Photographers underscored this notion in their travel guides by depicting their cameras as laboratory instruments, precise enough to calibrate national character and distill the essence of a people's intellectual, moral, and ethical values.

While the images were indispensable as visual evidence of a culture, the companies' guidebooks explained and interpreted what viewers were seeing. Written in some cases by prestigious scholars, or by photographer-adventurers in others, the guides provided facts, anecdotes, history, and the personal commentary of their authors. For viewers, the one-line caption or brief explanation printed on the back of the stereograph could not compete with the knowledge and charm of a tour guide at one's elbow. Among the best guides was James Ricalton, perhaps the most famous of the industry's adventure photographers. Hired by Underwood in 1897 when he was forty-seven years old, Ricalton began a career with the company that took him around the world six times. In the twenty years he worked for Underwood, he traveled over half a million miles, crossing the Atlantic and Pacific Oceans forty-three times.[14] He wrote three guidebooks and numerous articles, and he took thousands of images of India, China, the Philippines, and many other countries, as well as of the Boxer Rebellion and the Russo-Japanese War. His stereographs of China, which Underwood boxed into a set of one hundred images and sold along with Ricalton's guidebook, were among the company's best-selling products.[15] As both image-maker and image-interpreter, Ricalton was in a unique position to teach Americans. The company could rely on him to tell viewers the significance of what they were seeing and not leave them to infer from looking at the image alone the importance of firsthand knowledge of the world. Ricalton gave viewers a ringside seat at the construction of each image and a personal introduction to learning from visual images.

Like other Underwood authors, Ricalton capitalized on the stereograph's experience of "being there." Before his China tour began, Ricalton told his viewers about "stereoscopic eyes" and how they differed from "natural eyes." He had seen China with both, he said, and "the genuine realism of the stereograph . . . has the power to produce vivid and permanent impressions on the mind that [are] scarcely less than that of one's natural vision. Furthermore [and here Ricalton repeats Underwood's motto], sight is our cleverest sense in the acquisition of knowledge; to see is to know."[16] The stereograph told no lies, Ricalton assured his viewers. What they would see was the real China. It should be noted, however, that Ricalton's viewers were "going" to China at a time when internal political and economic turmoil gripped the country. From early in the nineteenth century to its demise in 1911, the Manchu dynasty was beset by domestic and foreign threats to its sovereignty, and Ricalton's tour and images reflect this moment in Chinese history.

In his guidebooks Ricalton treated viewers as his fellow travelers. He used rhetorical devices to convince viewers that even though their bodies were in their parlors, their minds and emotions were traveling through the cities and countrysides of Asia. In Tien-tsin (Tianjin), for example, Ricalton dramatically conveyed a sense of imminent danger by anxiously shepherding viewers away from potential sniper firing, warning them not to turn and look at the bloody corpses lying nearby.[17] At a Chinese teahouse Ricalton told viewers, "Seated on one of these black stools we are permitted to look around; if you spy any drunken men about do not fail to call it to my attention, because I have been many times in these tea-houses, and I have never yet seen any in such condition" (45). At another time he gave viewers the feeling of being looked at by the Chinese in the image: "Two girls have spied us, and are gazing quizzically at our strange manner and appearance . . . Beyond the small house-boat two men in characteristic crouching pose are plainly watching the 'foreign devils' [meaning Ricalton and the viewers] and commenting thereon in a foul sarcasm only possible among Chinese" (61). In other stereographs and guidebook captions, Ricalton endured rural Chinese who jeered him and pelted him with stones; he searched for a woman with bound feet to photograph; and he bribed likely subjects. Ricalton constructed narratives and scenes to create an understanding of China that armchair travelers could get in no other way. The Chinese, however, remained hostile and suspicious of foreigners, and they defied and eluded Ricalton's camera.

Ricalton showed the strategic nature of his picture taking throughout his tour, and he documented the important part the Chinese people played in the process. Observation was always a two-way street, and Ricalton—and subsequently the stereograph viewer—was often the more uncomfortable of the pair. Through their resistance or compliance, the Chinese frequently determined which pictures he could take. Ricalton blatantly acknowledged that many of his stereographs were staged, but in his mind they were not untruthful. By describing the scene—the chaos and tumult he encountered taking the image—he believed it retained its authenticity. He distinguished between making the image and the image itself. A telling example of the difference between the two is illustrated in one of the tales in Ricalton's book, where he is describing for viewers his trek into rural China. A crowd of villagers and peasant farmers had followed him, scattering every time he pointed his camera in their direction, curious yet clearly hostile. They taunted and shouted at him. Before they reached the site where the image was actually taken, the crowd swelled, from the town, "a more belligerent element," Ricalton said. He continued:

> No sooner was my camera placed for this view than several small stones fell around us; it was not easy to ascertain the individuals throwing them. Many of them carried sticks and some poles. One bold fellow advanced, and with a pole uplifted threatened to smash my camera. Childs, [a friend accompanying Ricalton] stood near with a heavy stone in each hand and held them in check until this stereograph was hurriedly taken . . . We need not, however, let the rabble disturb our enjoyment of the landscape. Our faithful servant is before us and looks off into space, as though he were unconscious of the cowardly demonstration taking place behind him. (143–44)

The image here, a serene depiction of a lone figure sitting on a hill, the foreground surrounded by tea fields, is titled "Paddy Fields, Farm Houses and Patches of Tea at Matin, Kiangsi Province, among the Mountains of Interior China" (143).

For nineteenth-century viewers, knowing how an image was made appeared to underscore its credibility rather than to diminish its veracity. On the one hand, Ricalton grounded such images in a verbal description of their empirical construction and, on the other, he gave a cultural interpretation based on the stereographs of China that viewers saw through their stereoscopes. Seduced by his own images, Ricalton created a China that remained a land of mystery. Believing that only the camera caught China's true nature, he could neither see nor explain what could not be captured by his camera's lenses, and he thus failed to "see" China at all. At his side, viewers remained equally blind. Like an ancient traveler who brings back curious or unfamiliar objects from afar, Ricalton revealed hidden knowledge made visible by his camera. The more difficult his images were to obtain, the more revelatory they became. His organized, coherent images shaped viewers' knowledge of China and showed the power of technology to take inchoate reality and mold it into readily accessible nuggets of understanding.

Underwood encased Ricalton's images in the narrative of a travel tour, the vocabulary of "being there," and "scientific" explanations about the nature of vision. Grounded in specific localities in China, Ricalton's images bore some relationship to the historical and cultural contingencies of the country in the early twentieth century. But in 1907 Underwood extracted several images from the original set for home consumers and repackaged them for school children. In recombining the China stereographs with those of other countries, Underwood treated all images like random pieces of information that could move, unchanged, from set to set. Stripped of their context, the images represented what Underwood called "general truths," sparse abstractions that erased the differences or similarities among cultures. As seen through a stereoscope, the world became for American school children even more static and fragmented than for home consumers.

Stereographs as Visual Education in Schools

At the beginning of the twentieth century, the major stereograph companies struggled to hold their own in a fiercely competitive marketplace. Their tremendous production capacity forced several companies to seek new markets. Underwood established an educational department as early as 1895 and sold collections of stereographs made to order for school systems. In 1903 Keystone packaged its views for public schools in an attempt to sell the thousands of images a day it was turning out. From their millions of negatives, Keystone and Underwood selected, labeled, and arranged a relatively small number and put "the world in a box" for school children. Keystone issued what came to be known as the "600 sets," and Underwood sold sets of one thousand images. School systems bought stereographs in large numbers and, by doing so, conferred on them a legitimacy the industry alone could never have achieved for its products. In spite of its claims that stereographs were not entertainment but "educational appliances," the industry needed the endorsement of the educational establishment to validate its definition.

The industry's search for new markets coincided with the emergence of the education movement by the Progressive Party in the United States. Labor leaders, social reformers, and even farmers criticized schools for inadequately preparing children for the opportunities promised by complex industrial processes and scientific farming methods. These critics joined Progressive educators in calling for sweeping reforms and curricular innovations. John Dewey, one of the leading spokespersons for reform, argued that schools had the responsibility to connect a child's life inside the classroom to the world outside it.[18] National educators called on teachers "to equip each pupil for the thing he should do in order that he might make his maximum contribution to the welfare of all."[19] Society required teachers to train children to know their place in a complex world, a world that many educators believed robbed children of experiences rather than enriched them. In addition, politicians demanded that schools adapt to the pace set by modern business and industry. To them, educational methods seemed unscientific, crude, and wasteful.[20] They defined modern instructional methods as efficient, economical, and standardized. Industry and commerce provided the model; teachers had only to find ways to apply it to the classroom. These demands came at a time when large concentrations of immigrants and rural migrants strained city school systems to their limits. Newly enacted compulsory education and child labor laws, designed to insure a better life for all children, led to large classes filled with children of diverse backgrounds, interests, and abilities.[21]

The stereograph industry offered its products as the solution to the problems plaguing American schools. Keystone and Underwood promised that stereographs would "vitalize subject matter, provide vicarious experiences, and prompt the learner to engage in experimentation."[22] "Retardation and elimination," their terms for nonpromotion and dropping out of school, would disappear. They also exploited the commonly held belief that class distinctions could be ameliorated through educational and cultural "uplift." As Keystone's George Hamilton stated, "These things, however, when seen through the stereoscope, come to him [the disadvantaged school child] as very nearly real experiences. He is thus put on a par with the more fortunate child who has been able to travel and whose life has been enriched by first-hand contacts with the many facts of the world."[23] But the companies' ability to standardize school subjects and make instruction "teacher-proof" may have been a more persuasive selling point. In 1892, a national report on education had described a nation of "untrained teachers who blindly led their innocent charges in singing drill, rote repetition, and meaningless verbiage."[24] The companies' manuals for teachers were designed to instruct the nation's ill-equipped, poorly trained teachers as well as their pupils.

Keystone and Underwood published their first sets of educational images and accompanying teachers' manuals in 1903 and 1907, respectively. Keystone published its tenth and final revised teachers' manual in 1927. Competition between the two companies did not create alternative visions of the world for children but spurred each company to sell more vigorously the one worldview they both shared. In assembling their sets, the companies selected images that could be integrated into the school curriculum because the stereographs were not meant to be studied separately as a new subject area but were to serve as the essential material for every area of classroom learning. No matter what subject teachers wished to present, the companies assured them there was a stereographic view to illustrate it because the images could be assembled and reassembled in countless variations. Keystone's "600 set," for example, could be reshuffled into at least 6,293 different combinations.[25] Thus the system was not peripheral to learning but was meant to form the core of classroom pedagogy.

In 1907 Underwood divided its school set into roughly two parts, one devoted to what it designated "the twenty-three most important countries in the world" and the other to "Industries of the World." Subcategories under each country focused on home and family life, geographical surface features, transportation or waterways, and industries, commerce, or handicrafts. A student's workbook, called a "field guide," accompanied the stereographs. But independent "field" exploration was not the goal of using stereographs in the classroom. Underwood's teacher's manual explained the company's educational strategy: "The aim of instruction is not so much to acquaint pupils with individual facts as it is to secure their grasp of principles of broad application—general truths. This end is to be secured by the study and comparison of a number of cases that illustrate the one truth."[26] Those truths created a template based on cultural Darwinism that ranked nations on a progressive scale from primitive to civilized. "Our stereographs," Underwood said, "were carefully chosen not alone to show physical types, but also to illustrate and contrast the differences in temperament, mentality, etc., as shown by their various occupations, and the stage of progress indicated by processes of labor" (10). Agricultural methods, transportation, urban buildings, the presence or absence of telegraph poles, street lights, phonographs—all could be seen and measured in a stereograph. Children could determine which rung a particular country occupied on the cultural evolutionary ladder by counting the visible manifestations of its progress. Their judgment would be sound because the camera gave them empirical scientific evidence in the form of visual images.

But only by "putting themselves into the stereograph" could children learn those "general truths." Using similar language, but eschewing its theories about vision that had informed the company's explanations for adult consumers, Underwood instructed students to "imagine themselves playing or working" with the children in the image: "If a child actually reads himself into this situation and imagines himself aiding in the work that the members of the family are doing, he will gain a vivid idea of the conditions of life in this region and of the many ways in which these differ from the conditions under which he lives . . . By stepping into the image [children will] learn fundamental facts about the region that is being studied, its climate and surface features, its productions, occupations, industries, and the social customs of the people" (11). The manuals promised teachers that if children all focused on the same details in each image and interpreted what they saw in the same way, children would acquire uniform ideas about the foreign cultures they viewed. Stereographs of "subject matter entirely beyond his experience" would replace a child's individual images with standard stereographic ones.[27] American images of home, family, and patriotism would erase immigrant children's Old World memories and definitions. The result, Underwood promised educators, would be the creation of a collective national vision of the world.

In the introduction to its teachers' manuals, Underwood underscored that stereograph instruction was hard work. Stereographic learning was not "aimless pleasure" but as rigorous as "actual field work," according to Fred McMurry, a leading educator at Columbia Teachers' College.[28] Both Underwood and Keystone included exact instructions for organizing class activities around the most efficient use of the boxed sets. The movement of stereoscopes and views from child to child was precisely orchestrated. Like a factory assembly line, views and stereoscopes moved from hand to hand and images shifted from lesson to lesson like interchangeable parts. The end product was purportedly as standardized as any manufactured by industry. As in industrial processes, timing was critical: "The correct time to employ the stereograph is at the point when pupils are groping for concrete conceptions of the topic studied" (17). As the culminating distillation of a lesson, the stereograph jelled amorphous and ill-defined ideas into a visual mold.

In 1922 Keystone boasted that every American city with a population of fifty thousand or more had adopted the "Keystone System" of stereographs for its schools and that the United States government had placed its stereographs at West Point and in the "Indian Schools, because they are absolutely authentic and standard."[29] A 1924 study estimated that together the schools owned a total of 1,051,813 images.[30] By 1938, according to a U.S. Department of Education survey, two-thirds of all the public elementary and secondary schools in the country reported using stereographs.[31]

While the zeal for pictures that seized the American public was decried by some critics as a return to juvenile forms of communication, as encouraging illiteracy, and as distorting the ideas presented by the printed word, the idea of using visual images in the classroom appeared to have captured the enthusiasm and imagination of the education profession.[32] In 1914, the University of Wisconsin opened a Bureau of Visual Instruction. By 1922, seventeen of the thirty-seven colleges and universities responding to a U.S. Bureau of Education survey reported they maintained visual education distribution centers from which they loaned stereographs, stereopticon slides, and still pictures to schools in the area. In 1922, at the founding meeting of the Visual Education Association of America, the keynote speaker called the rapid spread of materials, methods, principles, and goals in visual education a "new movement that had swept through Europe and the United States."[33] A 1923 National Education Association study showed that over twenty institutions offered courses for teachers in visual education, and in that same year the association established its own official Department of Visual Education. Local organizations devoted exclusively to the promotion of visual education had already emerged by the second decade of the century.[34] Books, articles, pamphlets, conference reports, doctoral dissertations, and institute proceedings swelled the number of entries in the *Reader's Guide to Periodical Literature* from five entries in 1900 listed under "Pictures in Education" to several pages under the heading "Visual Education" by 1929.[35]

Stereographs achieved important acceptance in the educational community when researchers began to study the efficacy of visual education. A 1920 University of Chicago doctoral dissertation by Frank Freeman, published in 1924 as *Visual Education: A Comparative Study of Motion Pictures and Other Methods of Instruction*, compared stereographs to stereopticon slides, still pictures, teacher lectures with blackboard illustrations, and books. Measuring the efficiency, speed, and completeness with which children acquired facts in Illinois public schools, Freeman concluded that stereographs were better than other media for giving the children "new information that remained in pupils' memories and enabled them to achieve higher scores on fill-in-the-blank tests and composition writing."[36] Acknowledging that stereographs were no longer a novelty, or even a controversial "educational appliance," he found stereographs to be just as the stereograph companies claimed: efficient, modern ways to teach children about the world.

Other researchers later confirmed Freeman's findings.[37] Their conclusions could not have been otherwise because the researchers synthesized the industry's definitions of visual knowledge and converted the industry's marketing claims into test measurements. Freeman argued that stereographs were superior because: (1) the stereoscope removed distractions from the surrounding environment; (2) unlike moving pictures, stereographic images could be contemplated for a lengthy time and absorbed; and most important (3) stereographs presented the information to children as if they were "on the spot."[38] Such authoritative studies illustrated the degree to which the industry's concept of "knowing" had become embedded in the consciousness of professional educators.

Conclusion

In 1920, Keystone bought out Underwood's entire stock of negatives and became the sole remaining stereograph company. With a monopoly on visual images for the schools and with the support of the educational establishment, Keystone continued to play an important role in the visual education movement in the United States. In 1923, it attempted to regain its home market and published its most ambitious travel set, a collection of six hundred images called "A Tour of the World" with a guide by the famous travel-lecturer and filmmaker, Burton Holmes. At the beginning of the Depression in 1929, Keystone stopped issuing new stereographs but continued to fill individual orders for images until the company went out of business in 1960.

At the beginning of the century, however, Keystone and Underwood contributed to a redefinition of learning that emphasized visuality, efficiency, and the retention of facts. Their boxed sets categorized and standardized a large portion of the nation's nascent visual archives and promoted, if they did not actually create, a national collective vision of the world. Keystone and Underwood gave cultural meaning to their stereographic travel experiences by creating an ideology and vocabulary of visual knowing.

Advocates of school reform, educators, politicians, and opinion makers also equated technology in the classroom with curriculum innovation and with preparing students for the modern world. Keystone and Underwood's language of visual knowing and their theories of visual learning found their way into articles in national teachers' journals, and teacher training textbooks.[39] The central role stereographs assumed in the schools, however, was part of a larger shift in American culture toward a visual culture, a shift the stereograph helped to shape and define. By promoting its products in the nation's schools, the industry found its staunchest allies among American educators, and they became the most articulate proponents of that visual culture to the next generation of Americans, teaching them, in turn, that "To see is to know."

Notes

1   The idea of vicarious travel and acquiring experience of the world without leaving one's parlor is pervasive throughout the stereograph industry's advertisements and publications. For example, the *Keystone Review* stated: "Think what photography has done to bring the Holy Land over the seas and put it on our centre table" (December 1903): 3.

2   See Steven Conn, *Museums and American Intellectual Life, 1876–1926* (Chicago: University of Chicago Press, 1998); Charles Musser, *The Emergence of Cinema: The American Screen to 1907* (Berkeley: University of California Press, 1990); Robert Rydell, *All the World's a Fair: Visions of Empire at American International Expositions, 1876–1916* (Chicago: University of Chicago Press, 1984); Julie K. Brown, *Contesting Images: Photography and the World's Columbian Exposition* (Tucson: University of Arizona Press, 1994); and Lauren Rabinovitz, "More than the Movies," in this volume.

3   Neil Harris, "Iconography and Intellectual History: The Half-Tone Effect," in *New Directions in American Intellectual History*, ed. John Higham and Paul L. Conkin (Baltimore: Johns Hopkins University Press, 1979), 199.

4   William Darrah, *The World of Stereographs* (Gettysburg, Pa.: W. C. Darrah, 1977), 47.

5   George E. Hamilton, *Oliver Wendell Holmes, His Pioneer Stereoscope and Later Industry* (New York: Newcomen Society, 1949), 17.

6   Underwood & Underwood, *Manual of Instruction (To Be Followed by Our Agents)* (New York: Underwood & Underwood, 1899); and Keystone View Company, *The Keystone Review* 1899–1908, a monthly publication for the company's sales agents.

7   These endorsements appeared in Underwood's publications for its home consumers and in Keystone's monthly magazine for its sales agents.

8   Among the most useful interpretations of nineteenth-century photography are Martha Sandweiss, ed., *Photography in Nineteenth-Century America* (New York: N. A. Abrams, 1991); Alan Trachtenberg, *Reading American Photographs: Images as History, Mathew Brady to Walker Evans* (New York: Hill and Wang, 1989); and Weston J. Naef, *Era of Exploration: The Rise of Landscape Photography in the American West, 1860–1885* (Boston: New York Graphic Society, 1975).

9   James Ricalton, *China through the Stereoscope* (New York: Underwood & Underwood, 1903), iii.

10 *Stereoscopic Photograph* (September 1901): 58.

11 Ricalton, *China through the Stereoscope*, viii.

12 *Stereoscopic Photograph* (March 1901), 58.

13 William C. Darrah, *The World of Stereographs* (Gettysburg: W. C. Darrah, 1977), 49.

14 Christopher J. Lucas, ed. *James Ricalton's Photographs during the Boxer Rebellion* (Lewiston, N.Y.: Edward Mellen Press, 1990), 32–33.

15 Darrah, *The World of Stereographs*, 48.

16 Ricalton, *China through the Stereoscope*, 12.

17 Ibid., 34.

18 John McDermott, ed., *Philosophy of John Dewey* (Chicago: University of Chicago Press, 1981), 34.

19 Raymond E. Callahan, *Education and the Cult of Efficiency* (Chicago: University of Chicago Press, 1962), 60.

20 Ibid., 72.

21 Lawrence A. Cremin, *The Transformation of the School: Progressivism in American Education, 1876–1957* (New York: Knopf, 1964), 348. Cremin writes, "What Progressives did prescribe made inordinate demands on the teachers' time and ability . . . [and] required familiarity with a fantastic range of knowledge and teaching materials; while the commitment to build upon students' needs and interests demanded extraordinary feats of pedagogical ingenuity" (348).

22 Hamilton, *Oliver Wendell Holmes*, 4.

23 Ibid, 7.

24 Cremin, *Transformation of the School*, 3.

25 *Visual Education: Teacher's Guide to Keystone's "600 Set"* (Meadville, Pa.: Keystone View Co., 1911), 4.

26 Philip Emerson and William Charles Moore, eds. *Geography through the Stereoscope* (New York: Underwood & Underwood, 1907), 29.

27 Hamilton, *Oliver Wendell Holmes*, 12.

28 Fred McMurry, ed. *The World Visualized for the Classroom* (New York: Underwood & Underwood, 1915), 6.

29 Hamilton, *Oliver Wendell Holmes*, 12, 13.

30 C. E. Mahaffey, *Practical Visual Education—A Survey of the Use of Stereographs, Slides, and Motion Pictures in Education* (Bowling Green, Ohio: Department of Visual Education, NW Ohio Teachers' Association, 1925), 48.

31 Cline Koon, *School Use of Visual Aids: An Interpretive Study of the Data Collected in the National Survey of Visual Instruction in Elementary and Secondary Schools*. (Washington, D.C.: U.S. Department of the Interior, Office of Education, 1938), 6.

32 For a discussion of those who thought pictures were detrimental to American society, see Harris, "Iconography and Intellectual History."

33 "The Visual Education Association of America," *School and Society* 16, no. 414 (2 December 1922): 639–40.

34 Anna Verna Dorris, *Visual Instruction in the Public Schools* (Boston: Ginn and Co., 1928), 383–85.

35 In addition to the *Reader's Guide to Periodical Literature*, see the *Education Index* and *A Bibliography on Visual Education*, compiled by Theodor Schor (North Brunswick, N.J.: Middlesex County Supervising Principals' Association, 1936), Works Progress Administration Project no. 65-22.

36 Frank N. Freeman, *Visual Education: A Comparative Study of Motion Pictures and Other Methods of Instruction* (Chicago: University of Chicago Press, 1924), 123.

37 For a discussion of research in visual education before World War II,

see John Carroll, *Teacher Education and Visual Education in the Modern School: A Research Study* (San Diego: San Diego County Schools, Office of the Superintendent of Schools, Education Monograph 16, 1948). For individual research studies, see Helen Clark, "Visual Imagery and Attention" (Ph.D. diss., University of Illinois, 1916); *Visual Aids in Seventh Grade Instruction* (Chicago: Educational Screen, Inc., 1922); John V. Lacy, "The Relative Value of Motion Pictures as an Educational Agency," *Teachers College Record* (November 1919): 452–65; Walton Bliss, "Determination of Principles and Effective Procedures in the Use of Visual Aids in Secondary Education" (Master's thesis, Ohio State University, 1929); W. Crandall, "Report on Geography Tests Given to 6A Classes in Seven Schools Using Visual Instruction as an Aid in Teaching and in Seven Schools Following the Ordinary Methods of Instruction" (New York: Bureau of Reference, Research & Statistics, New York Public Schools, 1920). Additional information on research and teaching techniques may be found in Ella Callista Clark, *The Use of Visual Aids in Teaching* (Winona, Minn.: State Teachers College, 1925); Burton A. Barns, *A Course of Study in Visual Education* (Detroit: Department of Education, Detroit Public Schools, 1925); and William H. Johnson, *Fundamentals of Visual Education* (Chicago: Educational Screen, Inc., 1927).

38 Freeman, *Visual Education*, 238.

39 Among others, see Horace G. Brown, "Efficiency in Teaching by Pictures," *Education* 34, no. 3 (November 1913): 5; Sara Gallagher, "Pictures in the Classroom," *Classroom Teacher* (October 1912): 23; "Editorial," *Visual Education* 1, no. 5 (September–October 1920): 9–11; Jessie L. Burnall, "Sight-Seeing in School—Taking Twenty Million Children on a Picture Tour of the World," *National Geographic Magazine*, 35, no. 6 (June 1919): 50; Mark S. W. Jefferson, "Stereoscopes in School," *Journal of Geography* (December 1907): 151–60; "The Marvels of Photography," *The World's Work* (February 1906):7163–73; Willard Brinton, "Graphic Methods of Presenting Facts," *Engineering Magazine Company* (December 1914); Sherman Dickinson, "Visual Education for Teachers of Agriculture," *University of Missouri Bulletin* 26, no. 29 (1925): 23–25; Dudley Hays, *Suggestions on Visual Aids* (Chicago: Chicago Board of Education, 1924); Daniel Knowlton, *Making History Graphic* (New York: Charles Scribner's Sons, n.d.); Grace M. Findlay, "Visual Means in Elementary Science Teaching," *Visual Education* (May 1923); and F. W. Holmes, "Visual Aids as a Key to the Teaching of Sentences," *Visual Education* (November 1924). Additional articles on picture study in the classroom can be found in the *Grade Teacher, Instructor*, and *American Childhood*. The visual education movement waxed and waned throughout the twentieth century, its name changing to "visual instruction" and then "visual literacy" in the 1970s. The following texts provide information about

efforts after World War II to promote visual resources in schools: Mary Jo Read and Byron K. Barton, *A Selected Bibliography of Articles Dealing with the Use of Still Pictures in Classroom Teaching*, special publication no. 2, (Jacksonville, Ala.: National Council of Geography Teachers, January 1953); and *Proceedings of the First Conference on Visual Literacy*, ed. Clarence M. Williams and John L. Debes III (New York: Pitman Publishing Corporation, 1970).

Sharon Ghamari-Tabrizi

THE CONVERGENCE OF

THE PENTAGON AND HOLLYWOOD

The Next Generation of Military Training Simulations

Throughout the 1990s special effects technologies employed by the entertainment industry (including video game and film producers, theme parks, hotels, nightclubs, and casinos) contributed to the virtual reality (VR) capabilities of the professional military. But when in August 1999 the army awarded $45 million to the University of Southern California to establish the Institute of Creative Technologies (ICT), effects technologies by Hollywood and the Pentagon achieved a new, integrated purpose, one unlike any prior partnership between the two institutions.[1] While Hollywood has a lengthy tradition of producing training films for the American military, and universities have participated in defense contracts, the creation of an interdisciplinary team to pursue basic and applied research in VR technologies is unprecedented.

In 1999 ICT stated its plans to build two prototypes of military training simulations (a Mission Rehearsal Exercise and an Advanced Leadership Training Simulation); story lines for these two simulations, complete with character bibles for the artificially intelligent characters; "4-D" elements such as wind, temperature, humidity, and odor for the simulation environments; a high-performance game console for networked training; a VR theater as the primary gaming space at the ICT building; a general training system; and, finally, a Future Combat System projected for the year 2012.[2] In his public announcement of the venture, Secretary of the Army Louis Caldera said, "This will revolutionize the way the Army trains its soldiers and how it rehearses for missions."[3] While the main objective of ICT is to devise simulation technologies so true to life that the players in the simulation will behave as though their experiences are real, perhaps the most interesting aspect of this curious merger of the army, the academy, and the entertainment industry is that the roles of *story* and *character* have been foregrounded as the way to improve realism.

The convergence of defense modeling and entertainment simulation that focused on storytelling as the means to achieve realism began in the 1990s. In 1997, defense and entertainment simulation and game designers participated equally in a landmark conference in Monterey, California, that set the stage for future collaboration. A conference participant articulated the longstanding difference between defense and entertainment realism in their respective simulations: "Whereas DOD [the Department of Defense] has tended to emphasize the fidelity of interactions between objects in a simulated environment (using science-based models), the entertainment industry has tended to promote visual fidelity and uses principles of *good storytelling* to help participants suspend their disbelief about the reality of a synthetic experience (whether a VR attraction or a film)" (emphasis added).[4] The conference hosts hoped that in light of their expertise in "good storytelling" entertainment professionals could assist the Pentagon in remedying the still-alienating quality of their training simulations. Another conference participant remarked, "In this view, the goal of a simulation is not to approximate reality as nearly as possible, but to present individuals with *the appropriate set of cues* to produce the training effect desired. Creating the desired change in a person's mind requires a suspension of disbelief in the individual who is experiencing, interacting, and making decisions in the simulation. It requires a complex combination of attributes that engage and teach the user" (emphasis added).[5] In other words, expert storytelling could elicit an emotional engagement with the play of a simulation such that it emanated the quality of being real—or rather, comparatively more intensely felt than the training simulations currently in use.

If it is true that story form imposes constraints on action and feeling, then a clear-cut story could indeed render training simulations highly effective, but at the expense of reality testing. In the case of indoctrinating soldiers for combat, it is hoped that soldiers will, as much as possible, feel constrained by their environment to cleave to standard procedures (which are designed to be and drilled into the troops as the safest gestural repertoire of action and behavior). In other words, if a simulation is designed to limit the players' range of actions in order to enforce preestablished routines, then masterful storytelling could arguably have a role in prompting the desired behavior in the haze of battle, which requires single-point concentration, reflex action, and the suppression of distracting sense impressions and emotions. However, for these very reasons, the emotional and behavioral cueing suggested by a thrilling story form blocks a thoughtful reflection on the degree of probability entailed by the narrative thrust of the simulation's scenario and characters. Therefore, it is fitting to ask of contemporary simulations, how probable or reckless are stories that are designed to be emotionally compelling? Do they overstimulate the players? Do they exaggerate the threat in order to command a high order of concentration?

Further, given the brutality of the majority of action-and-adventure genre films and video games, should the collaboration between Hollywood and the Pentagon be regarded with alarm? Will it cultivate bloodthirstiness among simulation trainees? Will the incorporation of storytelling in defense training simulations produce pitiless cyborg soldiers that are overtrained, fused with their weapon system, vacant, and insensate? Surely, this describes the nightmare of cyberwar, obsessively depicted in science fiction stories of the last twenty years or more. Given the fact that the army seeks to build a 3-D virtual reality simulator for training and mission rehearsal (vowing "Not only will the Holodeck happen, but it's really mandatory")[6] how shall we appraise this? While it is unlikely that a radically dehumanized cyborg soldier will result from the comprehensive incorporation of simulation technologies into defense activities (dehumanization is more properly attributed to automated combat itself, especially the American casualty limiting strategy of relying on long-range precision munitions), nevertheless these developments prompt a searching review of the collaboration between the Pentagon and the entertainment industry in the 1990s.

In the first half of the 1990s the Department of Defense (DOD) embraced simulation for all dimensions of defense activities: part-task training; mission rehearsal; operational planning; strategic and tactical analyses; weapons systems modeling during research and development, testing and evaluation, and acquisitions; and long-range future studies. In 1997, the DOD budget for acquiring training systems was more than $1.5 billion. If one were to compound the budgets for modeling and simulation altogether (including research programs), the total allocation in 1998 exceeded $2.5 billion.[8]

The Pentagon's focus on simulation and modeling in the 1990s resulted from the consequences for the American military of the collapse of communism. By 1990, even before the dissolution of the Soviet Union, the defense budget had decreased 13 percent from its peak in 1985.[9] By 1991, Congress and the American people clamored for sharp cuts in the defense budget as the immediate windfall or "the peace dividend" of the unexpected transformation of geopolitical realities. In light of military base closings, cuts in personnel, and cancellations of long-term projects, the Congressional Office of Technology Assessment projected in 1992 that from 1991 to 2001, as many as 2.5 million defense-related jobs would be eliminated.[10]

One consequence of the squeeze on defense budgets was that the DOD altered its procurement practices.[11] Rather than underwriting research and development and acquisitions from defense contractors for specific military projects, the DOD was required to seek or modify already existing, commercial off-the-shelf (COTS) technologies and practices. Only in the absence of COTS items would defense contractors be authorized to create something new. Accordingly, during the 1990s there was a dramatic transformation of the defense sector: formerly stalwart companies merged or disappeared, accompanied by the diversification of products and services to non-defense areas. This was especially noticeable in the aerospace industry in Southern California, which contracted greatly in the 1990s. From 1988 to 1997, Los Angeles County lost 135,000 jobs in the aerospace and electronics industries. During that same period, the entertainment industry supplanted aerospace as the premier sectoral employer of the county, adding 144,000 jobs.[12] By 1999, for every job lost in aerospace the entertainment industry added two jobs. Since 1990, the entertainment sector has grown by 83 percent.

Defense budget constriction immediately gave rise to a boom in low-end simulation systems. Gone were the days when the Pentagon could pay for and justify massive field exercises such as the annual joint field exercise (called REFORGER) in Germany. Whereas the 1988 REFORGER exercise deployed 17,487 troops at a cost of $53.9 million, the 1992 REFORGER relied on the advent of new air force and army networking and interoperating capabilities to deploy 6,500 soldiers but to simulate 175,000 troops at a cost of $19.5 million.[13]

Another consequence of the defense drawdown was increasing reliance on reservist troops. Distributed simulation systems came into play as the answer to the problem of training weekend soldiers for sudden deployments. With a distributed simulation system, reservists could now join in elaborate exercises and maneuvers from their home bases, which has had a significant impact on force readiness in the era of a radically downsized standing army.[14]

The post–cold war strategic environment is substantively different from the earlier bipolar geopolitical template. In the new regime, how could the disciplined skills of the military services find their proper mission? In the 1990s, a new domain for army deployment, dubbed "Operations Other than War," rapidly filled out a menu of noncombat operations including: (1) peacekeeping by interposing troops between opposing forces following a cease-fire; (2) observation, positioning unarmed neutral troops to monitor provisions for human rights or cease-fire conditions; (3) collective security performed by a large international army to restore territory to its original borders and defeat an aggressor state; (4) election supervision; (5) humanitarian assistance during conflict, disaster relief, state/nation building including training police and security forces, aiding in the construction of infrastructure; (6) pacification of civil war, riots, disturbances; (7) preventive deployment by positioning troops in order to forestall violence or the spread of war across territorial boundaries; (8) arms control verification; (9) protective services such as guaranteeing rights of passage or creating safe havens for endangered populations; (10) drug interdiction and eradication; (11) antiterrorism; (12) intervention in support of newly elected leaders in fragile democracies; (13) sanctions enforcement such as enforcing blockades, restricting smuggling, punishing a transgressor state; and (14) aid to domestic civilian populations such as fire fighting, public health assistance, construction of infrastructure.

In terms of actual combat missions, potential foes shifted from the communist states to uncertain, emergent, and possible threats. Whereas the cold war emphasized strategic armaments, most new missions of the American military will likely supplant older notions of total warfare with restraint on force. Whereas during the cold war American forces had been dispersed to fixed forward bases abroad, future missions will require rapid deployment of small flexible forces to trouble spots around the world. Finally, the army may have to fight in joint operations with multinational forces, with or without United Nations or foreign senior command over its soldiers.[15] In an article published in the Army War College quarterly urging redoubled efforts in wargaming near-future military requirements, the authors present a condensed statement of all of the strategic changes wrought in the 1990s: "Traditional military missions, once separated in time, distance, platform, and function, are now being fused. This integration of surveillance, information, battle management, and precision strike has become known over the last few years as a 'system of systems.' "[16]

Perhaps the most significant means for cutting cost and redundant effort, as well as to recognize the organizational reform attendant on the post–cold war geopolitical situation, was the shift from individual service missions to joint operations. *Joint Vision 2010* (1996) and *Joint Vision 2020* (2000) codified the new stress on joint collaboration among the services and required new training and mission rehearsal simulations that would be globally integrated and interoperable.[17] Instead of the longstanding interservice rivalry of the cold war, the new joint doctrine highlighted a collaborative approach. Hence in 1992 the vice chairman of the Joint Chiefs of Staff and the deputy secretary of defense for research and engineering signed a memorandum of understanding that the Advanced Distributed Simulation systems scheduled to be implemented in the coming years should be aimed for joint (i.e., interservice) training, mission rehearsal, exercises, evaluation, and war fighting capabilities.

Many simulation platforms developed during the 1990s specifically addressed the need for collaboration. Whereas most training simulations were service or weapons-system specific and therefore not interoperable, the Joint Simulation System (JSIMS), for example, was designed to be the single, overarching mission rehearsal and command simulation environment within which all commands in all services could participate. Because it is a single, integrated system, commanders stationed at sea, abroad, and at bases across the United States will be able to participate in the same single joint exercise, which saves the DOD a great deal of money.[18]

Motivated not only by the loss of the defense allocations and manpower of the cold war era, the DOD turned to simulation for other reasons. The DOD fully recognized the fundamental differences that advances in computing, networking, graphics, and artificial intelligence had wrought in the arena of actual combat. What was once called the war-fighting *theater* had now taken on the electronic and communications dimensions embodied in the new jargon of the conceptual mission- or battle-space. In 1995, the Pentagon convened its Four-Star Summit on Modeling and Simulation to codify the terms of the changed technical environment. Distributed Mission Training (DMT) would henceforth be the object of all simulation activities and the pentagon announced that it was "a revolutionary training concept based on the need for multi-ship (multi-aircraft) full-mission training and mission rehearsal capabilities."[19] Consequently, the chief of staff of the air force proclaimed a campaign to "revolutionize training in the air force" in all commands by replacing as soon as possible stand-alone legacy (i.e., cold war era) fighter simulators with networked part-task trainers.

Not only will DMT systems be used for training and mission rehearsal, the same simulation systems and capabilities will be used for research and development, test and evaluation, acquisition, and operational planning. In a 1998 *Armed Forces Journal International* article, the authors explain that future DMT systems will collapse the synthetic environment of a hypothetical training space and the actual battle space: "As simulations and sensors result in a battlefield digitized layer by layer and entity by entity, a new hybrid environment will emerge from this augmentation and adjustment of the real world provided by advanced simulation tools, seamless networks, and high-fidelity visuals."[20]

The soldier's perceptions have for decades been technically mediated by computers and other aids embedded in various weapons systems but the augmented reality systems of DMT go beyond making the synthetic environment appear as close as possible to the actual sphere of combat and change soldiers' perceptions of the actual battlespace. An augmented reality system combines virtual and real environments in a single interface. For example, the authors of a National Research Council report on virtual reality explained, "In many such cases, information from the real environment is sensed directly by means of a see-through display, and the supplementary information from the virtual environment is overlaid on this display."[21] For many people enamored with the digitization of the military, the following exclamation from a brace of defense reporters expresses the hopes invested in the new technologies: "This capability to 'morph' the perception of the real world to our own designs will become the most dramatic contribution of simulation and D MT in the 21st century. It has already revolutionized the entertainment industry. Warfighting is not far behind."[22]

Cyberwar refers not only to augmented reality systems but also pertains to the ways in which information about the adversary can be exploited by military forces. Information warfare, the complement to cyberwar, refers to the panoply of technical and social communications and information systems that each antagonist possesses "in order to know itself: who it is, where it is, what it can do when, why it is fighting, which threats to counter first."[23] Virtually every information resource is potentially vulnerable to attack: satellite systems, telephone lines, power plants, television and radio stations, etc. Dorothy Denning, professor of computer security at Georgetown University, observed that the "information space of particular interest during wartime is the battlespace, which consists of everything in the physical environment, including communications signals traveling through the air."[24]

Information warfare is exceptionally difficult to achieve. The army of the future is expected to attain information dominance through instant access to pertinent battlespace data as well as through unobstructed access to space systems.[25] The army of 2025 will be characterized not only by its technical competence but by its speed. According to one defense reporter, "speed implies a great many things—faster data processing, faster decision cycles, faster logistics operations with just-in-time delivery methods—but most important, it refers to the speed of maneuvering fighting forces, strategically, operationally at the theater level, and across the tactical battlefield."[26] These requirements are extraordinarily steep. Former air force chief of staff General Larry Welch remarked that in the future battlespace, "decision makers at all levels are directing multifunctional forces; that is, forces who do several things simultaneously, forces that have to be quickly tailorable, quickly deployable, rapidly adaptable, and operating in situations for which there is no re-hearsal and in many cases for there is very little specific prepara-tions."[27] And yet, Pentagon planners must be mindful of the danger that the databases available to the commanders of the future do not lead to information overload; according to Collie Johnson, "DOD needs to limit the information pushed directly at the war-fighter and make a very rich set of relevant information available for the warfighter to pull when needed, that allows those warfighters at all levels across the spectrum to make decisions that are always better and faster than the adversary can make."[28] New simulations as well as scores of other long-range and medium-range future sys-tems currently underway elsewhere are touted as the royal road by which weapons designers, strategists, commanders, troops, and their civilian contractors will make the transition to the fully net-worked, information-based military of the twenty-first century.

The Intersection of Entertainment and Defense

In the early 1990s, Dr. Anita Jones, director of Defense Research and Engineering, dreamed up the idea of a symposium to bring together the defense and entertainment sectors in order to discuss common problems in simulation computing research and devel-opment. Their first meeting took place on 11 August 1995. Mem-bers from the Defense Modeling and Simulation Office (DMSO) met with commercial computer game designers and other entertain-ment professionals to see if they could find common ground for collaboration. The DMSO newsletter reported: "The workshop . . . was undertaken to begin a dialogue and to look for opportunities to leverage advances in commercial games and simulations—particu-larly in the areas of graphics, audio effects, and human interface and immersion."[29] The immediate objective of the symposium was to introduce the members of each group to one another and to lay the groundwork for a more intensive workshop to be sponsored by the National Research Council (NRC).

The NRC workshop in October 1996 invited participants from the film, video game, location-based entertainment, and theme park in-dustries, as well as representatives from the DOD, academia, and the defense industry.[30] The subsequent NRC report on the workshop centered on the technologies for world building that appeared to be the same for both groups (i.e., man-machine interfaces, networking technologies, computer-generated forces, and autonomous agents). Some comments, however, in the participants' position papers and in the report itself manifest the sense in mid-decade that entertainment professionals might indeed wield a specific set of skills in simulation realism that could aid the military in its pursuit of evermore efficacious training.

A prominent point of contact was the design intent—"a believable artificial world for participants." The NRC report describes the human operator's relationship to the synthetic environment as "experiential rather than cognitive."[31] Rather than situating virtual realism as the effect of design ingenuity, the criterion for believability is "the perception that a world exists into which participants can port themselves and undertake some actions" (28). More particularly, storytelling assists in the experience of verisimilitude: "Skilled storytelling techniques . . . help participants in a virtual environment sense that they are in a real environment and behave accordingly" (40). Storytelling complements the simulation's technical powers in order to enforce the emotional aspects. As workshop participant Danny Hillis of the Walt Disney Company explains, "if you want to make somebody frightened, it is not sufficient to show them a frightening picture. You have to spend a lot of time setting them up with the right music, with cues, with camera angles, things like that, so that you are emotionally preparing them, cueing them, getting them ready to be frightened so that when you put that frightening picture up, they are startled" (41). The report's author adds, "DOD may be able to learn additional lessons from the entertainment industry regarding the types of sensory cues that can help engender the desired emotional response" (41).

Thus, in contrast to didactic practices of lecture, drill, and testing, storytelling is a potent form of emotional cueing that appears to elicit desired behavioral responses during training. Moreover, and this is the surprise given the hoopla associated with new media, many conference participants argued that the preferred mode of experiential immersion in electronic media is not the unframed chaos of hypertext, but old-fashioned storytelling. Alex Seiden of the special effects and animation company Industrial Light and Magic, explained, "I've never seen a CD-ROM that moved me the way a powerful film has. I've never visited a Web page with great emotional impact. I contend that linear narrative is the fundamental art form of humankind: the novel, the play, the film . . . these are the forms that define our cultural experience."[32]

In 1999, defense and entertainment industry experts set out to test the hypothesis that a story-based defense training simulation yielded more intensive, more effective learning. Richard Lindheim, executive vice president of Paramount Digital Entertainment, and his colleagues developed multimedia materials to complement an annual political-military exercise at the Industrial College of the Armed Forces (ICAF) in the National Defense University (NDU). The ICAF's goal is to expose senior service officers (those with twenty or more years of experience) to broad geopolitical and strategic concepts and problems before promoting them to their final career posting. The materials set, titled *Final Flurry*, is projected ten years into the future and focuses on four hypothetical regional crises. The ICAF students role play political officers in agencies and branches of the national security complex coordinated into a crisis task force. They attempt to gather insight into the process of formulating joint, interagency (and occasionally multinational) security strategies under the pressured tempo of a crisis.

Paramount Digital's multimedia package, dubbed the "JMEANS computer interface," includes video and audio clips produced by an entertainment director and actors, a networked information system and database that gives players access to maps, (fictitious) intelligence assessments, teleconferencing, and e-mail. It was designed to mimic a national security (i.e., interagency) information network that senior political and military officers would employ in the course of their future duties. "These technologies reflect the increased use of information systems to support national security decision-making," explains the faculty guide to the 2000 NDU exercise. "Ready access to numerous informational data bases [will] facilitate effective decision-making."[33] A professional screenwriter developed the characters and worked with the NDU faculty on the crisis scenario. Lindheim's team stressed the critical importance of the role of story and character in the package: "Video and audio are the means to help you get to know the characters. But it is the characters and the story that draw the participant into the event and create a compelling feeling that it *is* 2010 and these are *real* crises."[34]

The databases and other game background material in the JMEANS system anticipate a host of possible scenario paths within the four games worlds, sorted into status quo, escalation, and deescalation branching points. Each morning of the five-day exercise, the faculty transmit a "scenario update," including a host of background international and political data as well as public and private comment and analyses. On the basis of these inputs, as well as occasional "scenario injects" selected by the faculty during the course of game play, the students attempt to shape the national security policy. The interactivity between the faculty and the exercise participants is reflected in the scenario updates and injects: "The updates and injects should teach by exposing erroneous assumptions, mirror-imagining, end-means disconnects, missed opportunities, incomplete considerations of likely opponents' actions. This flexibility offers many advantages: the faculty team can reward success by decreasing the level of tensions in a certain area, or it can make problems worse if student recommendations appear inappropriate, provocative or hostile."[35]

The *Final Flurry* test seemed to offer proof of the social and artistic dimensions of what VR enthusiasts have called "dramatic presence." In other words, the specific novelty of the interactive drama rests in the freedom offered to the exercise participant to determine the progress of the action. And yet, for a theater piece not to collapse into the wholly open form of improvisation (which seems hard to program, anyway), an autonomous agent or function called the "director" must orchestrate the participant's behavior. The essential problem for such interactive VR theater, then, is how to guide the participant without creating the suspicion that he or she is being manipulated; that is, how to maintain a "delicate balance between freedom and control . . . allowing the interactor maximum freedom of choice and response while still presenting a shaped experience."[36]

Indeed, Paramount's *StoryDrive* project for *Final Flurry* did allow for constraint on the participants' choices. Larry Tuch, Paramount's manager for the demonstration project, explains the design principles for *StoryDrive*'s interactivity: "In the *StoryDrive* experience the students are like a movie audience with the teachers as the director. He can orchestrate story events by sending the students e-mail, voice mail or electronic video mail, and specific information in the form of television newsclips, briefing documents, maps and intelligence reports. But, of course, this is more than movie. It's a simulation. And that means the students also have the power to react to and (affect) the direction of the story."[37]

In order to test the comparative efficacy of story and character, one third of the *Final Flurry* participants were exposed to Paramount's story elements as well as to audio clips of characters (performed by actors); another third received the video materials only; and the last third played a seminar game with paper and pencil. Postgame assessments determined that the participants who used the story plus character-enhanced materials felt a much greater degree of involvement in the exercise. Lindheim remarks: "When we put characters in, the students began interacting, such as deciding whether or not to believe a character, the experience was completely different, which was reflected in the way the students reacted and how the professors felt it went in terms of collaboration between students and the dynamic of the whole exercise."[38] Lindheim found an ally in Judith Dahmann, chief scientist of the Defense Modeling and Simulation Office. She states: "In the *StoryDrive Engine* applications, we tried to create that almost immediate sense of depth and reality you get in a movie. It's hard for decisionmakers to understand these complexities until they are actually in them, which is why we want to create synthetic worlds that help them understand that. It is a different kind of simulation that uses entertainment industry techniques and technologies to help us develop decisionmaking environments."[39]

The *StoryDrive* package produced for future exercises will eventually feature artificially intelligent characters whose responses will react to players' decisions. Rather than a live instructor, the director will be a computer agent who will orchestrate the behavior of the agents in the simulation and the synthetic environment. Chief scientist of the army's Simulation, Training, and Instrumentation Command (STRICOM), Mike Macedonia, explains, "By exercising control of these elements, the Director ensures that the exercise follows the intended story line so that the intended training goals can be achieved."[40] The director's program will include a menu of possibilities, so that even though the participant will be able to make choices as the simulation unfolds, the director will introduce the desired events so that the participants are "forced to confront the intended dilemma, thereby achieving the pedagogical goals for the simulation."[41]

The National Defense University's Crisis Decision Exercise 2000 used the same databases, some of the same scenarios, and the media package created for the previous year's game, with the difference that for the first time the exercise combined the faculty and students of ICAF and the National War College (NWC) in a single joint exercise. Postgame survey results found general enthusiasm for the multimedia JMEANS system.[42] For example, more than half of the ICAF faculty and students and 70 percent of the NWC students found that the new information technology "significantly enhanced the exercise learning experience."[43] Compared to other crisis exercises, more than half of the ICAF faculty and students and 83 percent of the NWC students regarded the information technology tools as more effective than previous games.[44] Interestingly, the video materials made the greatest impact on the faculty of ICAF, 85 percent of whom reported that they regarded the Paramount package as more effective than previous modes of delivering scenario updates.[45] The Paramount media package was immensely helpful in the exercise because its various modalities helped to sort out critical inputs. Rather than just providing a credible mise-en-scène of a crisis task force workroom, the media enhancements were wholly understood by NDU faculty as resources for information management. To the extent that story and character helped to sort, classify, and prioritize information, it had a cognitive dimension as well as a didactic one.

Beguiled by the talents of entertainment simulators, which do not share the blindspots and habits of a military culture attempting to reform itself after decades of cold war, the DOD sought to establish a stable simulation research and development resource at a university with strong ties to the entertainment industry. It found its academic host at the University of Southern California. At the press conference announcing the establishment of the ICT, Secretary of the Army Louis Caldera stated: "This will enhance the realism and thus the value of the individual, crew-served, and networked training simulators that we use to train our soldiers. It will permit our soldiers to do en-route mission rehearsals immersed in high-fidelity images of the actual terrain to which they are about to deploy, with very real story and character content to prepare them to accomplish the mission."[46] Other defense officials also rejoiced. "It's a marriage made in heaven," exclaimed Anita Jones, the former director of Defense Research and Engineering who had originally proposed defense industry and Hollywood technical collaboration.[47] Brigadier General William Bond, commander of STRICOM, wrote: "You've seen what they do. They tell the story. *Saving Private Ryan*, those first 30 minutes have been rated by veterans as the most realistic, most emotional they've ever seen of war. How do we take that same thing . . . to enhance training, to make it more realistic? So [the solider] remembers and the coaches remember. . . . We have to create realism with sound, smell, touch. These things are all now available with computer technology. Things that increase the heart rate, make you perspire, sweat, the real feelings of combat. The goal is to immerse a soldier so he'll forget he's in a training situation and react the way he would in combat."[48] The consensus was that Hollywood had a role to play in designing defense simulation.

Highly experienced film and television producers Richard Lindheim and Jim Korris were certainly the right choice to attempt the transfer of Hollywood storytelling to the DOD. Lindheim, ICT's executive director, had worked for NBC for years. His last appointment was executive vice president of the Paramount Television Group. He produced the *Star Trek* series, *Next Generation, Deep Space Nine*, and *Voyager* for close to ten years. Longstanding contact with the shows' technophile content, including collaboration with the various programs' chief scientists, prepared Lindheim to approach the DOD's simulation problems with visionary élan. For Lindheim, "the ICT is on a quest to envision and prepare for the future."[49] The series' look and feel had so much shaped his conception of future defense environments that Lindheim engaged the art director for *Star Trek*, Hermann Zimmerman, to design the offices and simulation studio of ICT's new building.

Korris, ICT's creative director, had been the executive director and CEO of the Entertainment Technology Center at USC's School of Cinema and Television. As a television and film producer Korris brought experience and taste to fuse together the two strands— narrative entertainment and technology—of the defense/entertainment collaboration. He commented: "Traditional Army simulations were boring and not quite engaging. The Army wants enlivening and energizing simulations to train their military. They want the Hollywood kind of storytelling capabilities."[50]

It is here, in the link between immersive technology and storytelling, that the DOD's recruitment of *Star Trek* series personnel is telling, and potentially troubling. Wholly immersive simulations necessarily capture the heart—the emotions—as well as the mind and body of the man or woman in the training environment. Representatives of STRICOM recognize that story and character produce *emotional immersion* and that ICT's concepts of story and character will increase the degree of immersion experienced by participants in synthetic experiences.[51] They understand that what the DOD is buying from their screenwriters is an unfailing prescription for capturing the attention and emotional investment of a mass audience. Or, as Lindheim put it, "the same engine can be used for education or entertainment, or for a networked game. What's the difference between fighting Saddam Hussein or fighting Klingons? It's just different applications of the same technology."[52]

Who Is the Enemy?

How is it that entertainment and defense experts alike profess the belief that the emotional coloration of life could be concentrated within the generic structures of story form? Is lived experience really like a story? Historiographer Hayden White explains that the enhanced realism offered by story and character in defense simulations are both aesthetic and ideological claims about the form in which life appears to human subjects. While he has not written directly on virtual reality, he has insisted that "we do not *live* stories, even if we give our lives meaning by retrospectively casting them in the form of stories."[53] Instead, the representation of the past in the form of a story could only be an expression of a wish for the shaping of experience that aesthetic intention can give to open-ended events. White argues that the desire to find a transparent meaning in the contemplation of past events expresses a wish to find "coherence, integrity, fullness and closure" in the world. "The notion that sequences of real events possess the formal attributes of the stories we tell about imaginary events could only have its origin in wishes, daydreams, reveries. Does the world really present itself to perception in the form of well-made stories, with central subjects, proper beginnings, middles, and ends, and a coherence that permits us to see 'the end' in every beginning?"[54] The formal coherence of a story is guaranteed by an ending that not only closes off the narrative but implicitly harkens back to and invokes the beginning in a meaningful way. This is one of the chief qualities of the story form. The child learns to make this reflection on beginnings from the position of endings, and sanctions the development in the narrative, thereby learning the cognitive act and aesthetic pleasure of understanding a story. Understanding, for White, involves grasping the meaning of the dynamic movement of the story from beginning to end.

Reflection on a historical event, regarded as a totality, resembles the kind of remembering forward and backward that understanding a story involves. White clearly intends to refer to the poetic capacity of the mind to conceive a gestalt: "To understand historical actions, then, is to 'grasp together,' as parts of wholes that are 'meaningful.' "[55] The formal coherence of narrative, in which the ending provides the shape and context for the beginning, is the shared ground of historical reflection, aesthetic pleasure, and the belle-lettristic satisfaction of perceiving within a cascade of successive happenings the dimension of purposeful continuity. Insofar as events appear to be *implicitly* meaningful, they always already assume a story form without the subject having consciously shaped it as such—which would be the reason that although human beings do not, in fact, live stories, *it appears to them as though they do* when they attempt to make sense of their experience. The totality of story form contributes to the possibility for meaning to be present to consciousness. As White states: "Form can be conceived as a 'shaping' or as a 'containing' principle. As 'shaping,' it can be thought of as a narrative; as 'containing,' it can be thought of as providing 'meaning.' "[56]

The historical past and stories display the sheen of a total world, fully comprehended and immanently meaningful insofar as historical or literary reality appears whole or "possesses fullness." People desire stories, or the past shaped into a story. As White puts it, "the historical narrative . . . reveals to us a world that is putatively 'finished', done with, over, and yet not dissolved, not falling apart. In this world, reality wears the mask of a meaning, the completeness and fullness of which we can only imagine, never experience."[57] The representation of past reality possesses the totality that present experience lacks. Insofar as the story form comprehends a whole movement, it articulates a closed-off world. It is "full" of meaning. It is here—in the meaning that stories deliver—that history, literature, and storytelling converge in mythic structures. Insofar as the historical event has been expressed in story form, this narrative will bring the mythic ideas associated with imaginary structures to bear on past realities. The plot structure provides a sequence of translations, *from* an indifferent sequence of phenomena *into* a story of a familiar kind (in the case of defense simulations, the action-adventure, or martial epic narrative).

White refers narrative closure and its moral investiture back to the mythic conception that originates generic plot structures. Story in this conception is always an "exemplification" of that generic plot. And the reader will understand the story to the degree that he or she correctly identifies its inherent mythic structure. The narrative prompts the reader as to what symbols and associations should be consulted in order to identify the proper feeling toward the event. As White states, "the historical narrative . . . tells us in what direction to think about the events and charges our thought about the event with different emotional valences."[58] Both reader and historian must share in this cultural literacy if the historian is to communicate the significance of the event and if the reader is to identify it. Insofar as defense training simulations—complete with character bibles, crisis scenarios, automated opposing forces, and a full complement of realistic visual, auditory, haptic, and kinesthetic effects—exhibit the same kind of fullness, the intentionality and causative thrust of historical narrative so that the simulation feels like a "living history" (in precisely the sense that history, in this view, is immanently meaningful), then the experience of the defense simulation will feel both real *and* mythic.

Contemporary defense simulations are purposive, deadly serious, and structured according to the intricate rules of engagement for waging combat or operations other than war. How does story form express itself within the context of defense training, mission rehearsal, operations planning, and long-range research? Let's ponder Lindheim's remark, "The same engine can be used for education or entertainment, or for a networked game. What's the difference between fighting Saddam Hussein or fighting Klingons? It's just different applications of the same technology." Was he referring to the *StoryDrive Engine* artificial intelligence technology for producing scenarios and animated characters, or the structural sense in which for the purposes of cueing the proper behavior, it mattered little whether the foe was a real tyrant or a mythic bad guy?

For several years after the end of the dissolution of the Soviet Union, defense planners cast about to identify America's remaining enemies. In spite of its "Most Favored Nation Trading Status," mainland China, as well as Libya, Syria, North Korea, Iran, and Iraq, became identified as viable strategic threats. Narco-terrorists, ethnic bullies, secessionists, environmental catastrophes, and biomedical threats to the free movement of goods and labor across national boundaries, outlaw computer hackers, and Islamic fundamentalists all took the place vacated by the former Soviet Union and the Warsaw Pact nations. Regional "rogue states" that possessed advanced weaponry; nuclear, biological, or chemical weapons; and access to high-tech communications systems—as well as terrorist cells willing to martyr themselves, murder scores of innocents, and wage low-tech unconventional (i.e., asymmetric) war—have also become the chief predators against the United States, the European Union, and allied states.

Given the fact that in the new post–cold war environment where it is not clear who future enemies might be, uncertainty dominates all trend analysis and forecasting. This is the terrain in which cultural inheritance comes into play. Where substantive evidence is lacking, incomplete, or nebulous, the vigilant imagination fills in the blanks with reference to conventional understandings of geopolitical and cultural realities. Who is the enemy? Uncertainty has tended to invoke the motif of an oriental, demonic character who is the favored villain in today's popular fiction. This kind of mythology is extraordinarily flexible: it was effectively cast against the Japanese in World War II; against non-European mystic Slavs immediately after World War II; against the Chinese communists, the North Koreans, and the Soviets in the Korean War; against the North Vietnamese and their allies in Vietnam; against the putatively irrationalist nations of Iran, Iraq, North Korea, China, Libya, and Syria. The construction of the post–cold war enemy is functional for acquisitions and modernization programs and for staving off the hemorrhage of the post–cold war defense budget drawdown.

In defense simulations, the mythic construction of enemy forces is the one point that appears to validate those critics who are troubled by the fusion of fact and fiction. And yet I don't believe that the makers of defense simulations cannot distinguish between the reality of experience, confirmed by common sense and good intelligence gathering, and the orientalist scenarios of the immersive worlds of tactical combat and video games. Just as some people are more susceptible to the realism displayed by the current state of VR technologies (especially within the genre of military techno-thriller novels, films, and games), so too will some fraction of the defense community, including its congressional and industry partisans, no doubt be more literal minded, more hypnotizable, more inclined to fear non-Europeans than others. Rather than deploring defense simulations as the means for indoctrinating troops into ever-more brutal American combat doctrine, I would suggest that the more prudent response to the convergence of the Pentagon and Hollywood would be to insist that both sides teach one another the merits of more complex story lines in place of folkish myth—something marginal, modest, and something that could be called "post-heroic warfare."[59]

At the time of this writing it is too soon to evaluate fully the quality of ICT's system simulations. Yet, from the perspective of sensitizing senior military members to the domestic political context, to interagency, intragovernmental negotiation, the package produced by Paramount- and ICT-anticipated products achieves a precise psychological function. The students of the crisis exercise *step into* the movie of the experiential environment not in order to evade the inchoate processes of unstoried life but in order to rouse their emotions and intellect to an intense pitch of concentration. War-gaming professor Alan Whittaker of ICAF remarked: "The issue is psychological acceptance. If they are skeptical about what they're playing, if the exercise is insufficient to their expectations of the actual characteristics of what you're trying to simulate, it affects their motivation to direct sufficient psychological and even physical energy to the activities that are required to respond to that simulated event. The issue is: is the person focusing all of their psychological and physical energy into solving this problem?"[60]

By turning to Hollywood in the 1990s, the military has not shifted its authority for shaping the subjectivity of its forces from seasoned professionals to the Scheherazades of sensation and sentiment. But it is important to remember that when the simulation tests more senior command levels and strategic policy making, what is needed most is depth and complexity in the crisis scenario. Leaders must be trained to deliberate over the relevant information, not to respond with a spasm of primal emotion.

Notes

1   "USC and U.S. Army to Sign $45 Million Contract to Develop Modeling & Simulation Technologies," USC News Service, release date 8/18/99, http://uscnews.usc.edu.

2   For more information, see "The Institute of Creative Technologies" at http://www.ict.usc.edu/projects.html.

3 "USC and U.S. Army to Sign $45 Million Contract."

4 National Research Council, *Modeling and Simulation: Linking Entertainment and Defense* (Washington, D.C.: National Academy Press, 1997), 5.

5 Ibid., 95.

6 James Heath, senior intelligence and technical adviser to the army's Land Information Warfare Activity, as cited in Dan Verton and Dan Caterinicchia, "Army Enlists Tinseltown," *Federal Computer Week* (1 May 2000): http://www.idg.net/go.cgi?id=256356.

7 For an excellent document collection on the revolution in military affairs, see the RMA debate page on the Commonwealth Institute's Web site: http://www.comw.org/rma/index.html.

8 Timothy Lenoir, "All but War Is Simulation: The Military-Entertainment Complex," *Configurations* 8 (fall 2000): 238–335.

9 U.S. Congress, Office of Technology Assessment, *After the Cold War: Living with Lower Defense Spending (Summary)*, OTA-ITE-525, (Washington, D.C.: Government Printing Office, February 1992), 8.

10 Ibid.

11 As codified in DOD Directives 5000.1 and 5000.2 in accordance with the Federal Acquisitions Streamlining Act of 1994.

12 Andrew Pollack, "From Science to Fiction: Military and Entertainment Industries Swap Expertise," *New York Times* (10 October 1997): 1.

13 U.S. Congress, Office of Technology Assessment, *Distributed Interactive Simulation of Combat*, OTA-BP-IS-151 (Washington, D.C.: Government Printing Office, September 1995), 24.

14 Rolando Rabines and John Mohler, "Battlefield Realism Flows via Distributed Simulation," *Signal* 45, no. 3 (November 1990): 48.

15 Daniel Druckman, Jerome E. Singer, and Harold Van Cott, eds., *Enhancing Organizational Performance* (Washington, D.C.: National Academy Press, 1997), 153–54.

16 Robert P. Haffa Jr. and James H. Patton Jr., "Gaming the 'Systems of Systems,'" *Parameters* 28, no. 1 (spring 1998): 110.

17 For *Joint Vision 2010* online, see http://www.dtic.mil/doctrine/jv2020/index.html; for *Joint Vision 2020*, see http://www.dtic.mil/doctrine/jv2020/index.html.

18 See "Models, Simulations Converge, Close on High-Level Architecture," *Signal* 51, no. 11, (July 1997): 43–48.

19 Col. Lynn Carroll, Dr. Dee Andrews, and Mary Wellik, "Distributed Mission Training," *Armed Forces Journal International* 136, no. 4 (December 1998): 46.

20 Ibid.

21 Nathaniel Durlach and Anne Mavor, eds., *Virtual Reality: Scientific and Technological Challenges* (Washington, D.C.: National Academy Press, 1995), 20.

22   Carroll, Andrews, and Wellik, "Distributed Mission Training," 49.

23   John Arquilla and David Ronfeldt, "Cyberwar is Coming!," *Comparative Strategy* 12 (1993); cited in Dorothy E. Denning, *Information Warfare and Security* (New York: Addison-Wesley, 1999), 67.

24   Ibid., 22.

25   William B. Scott, " 'Title-10' Games Shape Policies," *Aviation Week and Space Technology* (2 November 1998): 62. Wargames had determined that the military's dependence on commercially owned satellites and some imaging assets rendered American warfighting capabilities vulnerable to offensive assault.

26   Robert B. Killebrew, "Learning from Wargames: A Status Report," *Parameters* (spring 1998): 132.

27   Ibid.

28   Collie J. Johnson, "JAWS S3—Making Information Work for the Warfighter," *Program Manager* 28, no. 5 (September/October 1999): 51–52. See also Clarence A. Robinson Jr., "Warfighter Information Network Harnesses Simulation Validation," *Signal* 52, no. 5 (January 1998): 27–32.

29   "Entertainment Industry Symposium," *DMSO News* 1, no. 1 (fall 1995): 4.

30   National Research Council, *Modeling and Simulation: Linking Entertainment and Defense* (Washington, D.C.: National Academy Press, 1997). Workshop participants did not readily perceive a union of interests in the conjunction of defense and entertainment personnel. The report noted: "The entertainment industry and DOD have vastly different cultures that reflect different business models, capabilities, and objectives. It is unlikely that the cultures will converge, and bridging them may be difficult" (14). And, indeed, when the staff at Paramount Digital Entertainment attempted to work with their putative counterparts in the DOD, the culture conflict was intricate. Paramount vice president Richard Lindheim observed that "when Paramount began working with the Defense Department in 1996 . . . it took a full year for each side to understand the other" (Karen Kaplan, "Army, USC Join Forces for Virtual Research," *Los Angeles Times* [18 August 1999]: 1).

31   National Research Council, *Modeling and Simulation*, 33.

32   Appendix D: Position Papers, Alex Seiden (Industrial Light and Magic), "Electronic Storytelling and Human Immersion," in National Research Council, *Modeling and Simulation*, 170.

33   War Gaming and Simulation Center, National Defense University, *Crisis Decision Exercise 2000: Faculty Guide*, (Washington, D.C.: Government Printing Office, 2000), 1, 2.

34   Marnie Salisbury, "DMSO, Paramount Collaborate to Support ICAF's Final Flurry, Analyze Value of Multimedia," *DMSO News* 4, no. 2 (summer 1999): 9.

35 Ibid., 4.
36 Margaret Thomas Kelso, Peter Weyhrauch, and Joseph Bates, "Dramatic Presence," *Presence* 2, no. 1 (winter 1993): 1, 4.
37 Tuch quoted in Sherrel Mock, "DMSO, Paramount Collaborate to Support ICAF's 'Final Flurry,'" *DMSO News* 4, no. 3 (fall 1999): 8.
38 Lindheim quoted in J. R. Wilson, "Going Hollywood," *MT2* 4, no. 6 (1999): 24.
39 Dahmann quoted in ibid., 25.
40 Michael R. Macedonia and Paul S. Rosenbloom, "Entertainment Technology and Military Virtual Environments," unpublished manuscript, March 2000, 8.
41 Ibid.
42 "National Security Network system was operationally adequate: combination of strongly agree and agree: ICAF faculty 66%; ICAF students 84%; NWC Faculty 82%, NWC students 85%" (*Command Decision Exercise 2000: Final Survey*, 10). "Compared to previous, overall CDE learning environment was: Combination of strongly agree and agree: ICAF faculty 50%; ICAF students 63%; NWC Faculty 63%; NWC students 100%." (ibid., 56).
43 "Technology significantly enhanced exercise learning experience: Combination of strongly agree and agree: ICAF faculty 60%; ICAF students 61%; NWC Faculty 36%; NWC students 70%" (ibid., 17).
44 "Compared to previous, information technology tools were: combination of significantly more and moderately more effective: ICAF faculty 53%; ICAF students 60%; NWC Faculty 38%; NWC students 83%" (ibid., 63).
45 "Compared to previous, video materials were: combination of significantly more and moderately more effective: ICAF faculty 85%; ICAF students 56%; NWC Faculty 51%; NWC students 86%" (ibid., 64).
46 "USC to Put 'Virtual Reality' into Army Training," *Program Manager* 28, no. 5 (September/October 1999): 40.
47 Kaplan, "Army, USC Join Forces," 1. See also Bob Brewin, "DOD Scripts War Games," *Federal Computer Week* (30 August 1999): http://www.fcw.com/fcw/articles/1999/FCW.083099_1037.asp.
48 Brigadier General William Bond, "Bond Sees Unique Opportunity for Stricom to Support Training Enablers in New Digitized Army," *DMSO News* 4, no. 4 (winter 1999): 5. In an unpublished paper about the establishment of the ICT, Mike Macedonia made note of the following comparative data: "The Entertainment Industry has in many ways grown far beyond its military counterpart in influence, capabilities and investments. For example, Microsoft alone expects to increase R&D spending next year [2001] by 23% to $3.8 billion, compared to the US Army's $1.2 billion science and technology budget. The Interactive Digital Software Association estimates that in 1998, interactive entertainment businesses invested approximately $42

billion in new technology R&D, with an increase of more than 20%. This far outweighs current US Army Research and development for training and simulation technology" (Macedonia and Rosenbloom, "Entertainment Technology and Military Virtual Environments," 1).

49 James Der Derian, "War Games: The Pentagon Wants What Hollywood's Got," *Nation* 270, no. 13 (3 April 2000): 44.

50 Anne Wonsono, "Korris named ICT Creative Director," *Daily Trojan* 138, no. 34 (18 October 1999): 15.

51 Macedonia and Rosenbloom, "Entertainment Technology and Military Virtual Environments," 4, 6.

52 Wilson, "Going Hollywood," 25.

53 Hayden White, *Tropics of Discourse* (Baltimore: Johns Hopkins University Press, 1978), 90. And also, "Narrative becomes a problem only when we wish to give to real events the form of story. It is because real events do not offer themselves as stories that their narrativization is so difficult" (Hayden White, *Content of Form* [Baltimore: Johns Hopkins University Press, 1987], 4).

54 White, *Content of Form*, 24.

55 Ibid., 50.

56 White, *Tropics of Discourse*, 78 n.27.

57 Ibid., 21.

58 Ibid., 91.

59 I am using the term in a different sense than the man who appears to have originated the phrase. See Edward N. Luttwak, "Towards Post-Heroic Warfare," *Foreign Affairs* 74, no. 3 (May–June 1995): 109–22. Edward N. Luttwak, "A Post-Heroic Military Policy," *Foreign Affairs* 75, no. 4 (July–August 1996): 33–44.

60 Telephone interview with Dr. Alan Whittaker, 8 August 2000.

PART III

MATERIALITY, TIME, AND THE REPRODUCTION

OF SOUND AND MOTION

John Durham Peters

HELMHOLTZ, EDISON, AND

SOUND HISTORY

To know what eyes see today and ears hear today one would have
to explain what brought Helmholtz to Chicago to shake Edison's hand
before all his other colleagues.—FRIEDRICH A. KITTLER,
Grammophon, Film, Typewriter

The Messiah, said Walter Benjamin, comes in inconspicuous ways.
Thomas Alva Edison's tinfoil phonograph, a rather unprepossessing
instrument, divides history into two halves, a before and an after.
Prior to 1877, all sounds died. Indeed, dissipation is the very essence
of sound as we know it: if sounds did not die, no music or speech
would be possible. Hegel even made the fading of the voice a philosophical principle, a distinguishing mark of human temporality and
finitude.[1] The phonograph, however, redeemed sound waves from
the curse of transience. It achieved, in Edison's words, "the captivity
of all manner of soundwaves heretofore designated as 'fugitive.' "[2]
To be sure, the storage and playback of sound was an old dream,
comically expressed in Baron Münchausen's frozen trumpet that,
when it thawed, emitted the tones that winter had trapped inside. A
less cryogenic dream of acoustic storage is found, of course, in writing itself, which Plato's *Phaedrus* treats as a kind of phonography, a
recording of voices. The notion that writing captured human voices

and *kleos*—acoustic renown—was widespread in ancient Greece, an oral culture in which silent reading had little "raison d'être."[3] Plato's anxieties about writing's catching and throwing of voices recur in late-nineteenth-century commentary about phonographic inscription: both are held to simulate live presence, distort face-to-face dialogue, compulsively repeat themselves, and relate promiscuously with audiences.[4] Both sound recording and alphabetic writing lifted old limits that held voices in check—distance, dissipation, and discretion. A captured voice forfeits its body, mortality, and authorial control. With the ability to record, amplify, and transmit sound by machines, the voice apparently lost its finitude.

Of all technological and sensory transformations of electronic media, those pertaining to sound are perhaps the most radical. From time immemorial drawings and paintings have portrayed moments in time, but sound recording requires duration, a fourth dimension that the painted surface can only imply. To store sound events requires a sort of inscription that traces time in its serial flow.[5] Like the eye, their much more studied colleague, the voice and ear have fairly recently in our species history become subject to transmission, recording, and amplification. The disembodiment of ear and voice is as important a story about our times as the hypertrophy of the eye.

This disembodiment, however, did not begin abruptly with new phonographic instruments in the late nineteenth century. When Marshall McLuhan called media the extensions of the human nervous system, he thought he was simply offering a smart metaphor.[6] He did not seem aware of a long tradition of physiological investigation that understands the human nervous system as precisely an extension of media. The phonograph was only one of many mechanisms fabricated in the 1850s through 1880s as artificial portals to the human (or sometimes animal) nervous system, many of them derived from the telegraph. The electrical telegraph was the seedbed for the invention of graphic recording instruments in the nineteenth century. It not only enabled the compression of time and space and gave elites a means to manage distant properties and populations, as James Carey demonstrates,[7] but also inspired new arts of neurophysiological mimicry. Its automatic writing on spooled paper, dissociation of eye, ear, voice, and hand, and fine measurement of temporal intervals inspired around mid-century a variety of devices for registering minute physiological changes, such as Ludwig's kymograph (blood pressure), the myograph (muscle fatigue), and Marey's sphygmograph (pulse).[8] In addition, there are important efforts to record sound well before Edison in the 1850s through 1870s, such as Léon Scott de Martinville's phonautograph and Charles Cros's paléophone.[9] Recent research has traced the origins of twentieth-century media to diverse forms of nineteenth-century culture, but medical measurement devices designed to represent temporal processes are just as important a source for our entertainment machines today. Film, telephony, phonography, television, and human-computer interfaces are in diverse ways psychotechnical practices that derive from study—and simulation—of the human sense organs. Media are all fruits of the graphic method; they are "applied physiology," as Nietzsche defined aesthetics.

To understand the origins, subsequent trajectory, and larger cultural significance of the recorded voice and assisted hearing, we should look not only to Edison, who, as the inventor of duplex telegraphy, the phonograph, kinetoscope, and electric lightbulb (a technology crucial for the future of radio, with its vacuum tubes), not to mention his near misses in inventing the typewriter, microphone, and telephone, presides over the founding era of analog media, but also to the science of the sense organs that emerged a generation before Edison, and whose greatest representative was Hermann von Helmholtz (1821–1894). Perhaps the last great universal genius of science, Helmholtz—physicist, physiologist of the eye and ear, aesthetician, and epistemologist, among many other interests and accomplishments—played a key role in the externalization and instrumentalization of the senses, which forms a crucial but largely forgotten backdrop for modern media. Timothy Lenoir notes: "Helmholtz conceived of the nervous system as a telegraph—and not just for purposes of popular presentation. He viewed its appendages—sensory organs—as media apparatus" and adapted "a number of interrelated technical devices employed in telegraphy to the measurement of small intervals of time and the graphic recording of temporal events in sensory physiology."[10] McLuhan was right to link media and physiology, but he settled too quickly for poetic montage instead of historical research. To fathom the voice in the age of its technical reproducibility, one must appreciate the ways that it was already externalized before it was mechanized. Helmholtz is perhaps the best representative of externalization, as Edison is of mechanization.

The American inventor/entrepreneur and the German scientist share much, starting with a fascination for the telegraph, the seedbed of nineteenth-century media instruments. For Helmholtz the telegraph was a model of the nervous system and wellspring of instrumentation; for Edison, it was an early source of livelihood because he worked as an itinerant telegraphist in his youth. Edison proposed to his wife by signing Morse code into the palm of her hand, and his son and daughter were nicknamed Dash and Dot. Both Edison and Helmholtz occupied positions of institutional power: Helmholtz as director of the Institute of Physics at the University of Berlin from 1871 and of the Physikalisch-Technische Reichsanstalt in Charlottenburg from 1887 to his death in 1894; and Edison as director of his laboratories and factories. Both had learned the lesson of minute quantities, care for what Edison called "attention to many seemingly unimportant and minor details."[11] Both sorted through an immense variety of raw and cooked materials with near infinite patience, Edison supposedly having tested 6,200 different substances for the filament in his electric light. Both Helmholtz and Edison understood the isomorphism of the ear and eye. As Edison says of the origins of film: "In the year 1887, the idea occurred to me that it was possible to devise an instrument which should do for the eye what the phonograph does for the ear, and that by a combination of the two, all motion and sound could be recorded and reproduced simultaneously."[12] There are important differences as well: Edison was an empiric, Helmholtz an experimentalist; Edison cared about effects and applications, Helmholtz cared about theory. Edison recounts of the telegraph: "The best explanation I ever got was from an old Scotch line repairer who said that if you had a dog like a dachshund long enough to reach from Edinburgh to London, if you pulled his tail in Edinburgh he would bark in London. I could understand that. But it was hard to get at what it was that went through the dog or over the wire."[13] Helmholtz, in contrast, understood—and measured—exactly what went through the dog: one worked in an academic tradition of integrative science, the other in a vernacular tradition of mechanical invention. Still, Edison cared enough about theory to read and annotate the 1875 translation of Helmholtz's *On the Sensations of Tone*; he also built and tested Helmholtz resonators. Both are clearly two of the characteristic "geniuses," if this word can still be used, of the nineteenth century, and here I intend to use them as representatives of different moments in the history of sound recording rather than to tell a tight tale of influence.

Helmholtz

Later-nineteenth-century science and engineering constantly explored the large differences made by minute quantities: catalysts in chemical reactions, vitamins, trace elements (such as thallium), by-products of coal tar, phonograph grooves, radio signals, radioactivity, and electricity above all. Helmholtz was no exception. His pioneering work on reaction times, on blind spots and afterimages, and the effects of equal tempering on the development and destiny of Western music, for instance, all revealed the profound importance of small differences that had hardly been noticed before. Take, for example, his early research on the transmission speed of impulses in the sciatic nerves of frogs. Helmholtz had learned from his teacher, the physiologist Johannes Müller, that "the difference in the sensations due to various senses, does not depend upon the actions which excite them, but upon the various nervous arrangements which receive them."[14] Müller pushed the Kantian problematic of the all-coloring powers of apperception in a new physiological direction. Helmholtz went further: "Kant's question about the fundamental conditions of possibility of all knowledge is reformulated by Helmholtz into a question of experimental physiology about the conditions of spatial perception."[15] In an 1850 letter to his father, he wrote: "The reason why the time-span of [nervous] propagation seems so terribly small is that we just cannot perceive any faster than our nervous system works; for that reason, the time-spans that it uses for its operations are imperceptibly small to us."[16] The Kantian limits of pure reason are here measured and quantified. Just as the blind spot is filled in so that the eye cannot perceive its own junction with the optic nerve, so the structural inevitability of failure in introspection and self-knowledge lies in the fact that we cannot observe the slight delay it takes for our nerves to send their signals. There is no bootstrapping out of the nervous circuit. The soul's access to itself and to its body, in other words, always occurs across a gap. With Müller the a priori became physiological; with Helmholtz the qualitative structure of the sense organs became quantitative. William James states the consequences of Helmholtz's measurements of nervous propagation with characteristic eloquence: "The phrase 'quick as thought' had from time immemorial signified all that was wonderful and elusive of determination in the line of speed; and the way in which Science laid her doomful hand upon this mystery reminded people of the day when Franklin first *eripuit coelo fulmen*, foreshadowing the reign of a newer and colder race of gods."[17]

For this newer and colder race of gods led by Helmholtz, *aesthetics* assumed its ancient Greek tie to sensation (*aisthêsis*). Painting was subsumed by optics, music by acoustics. Beauty, and its emotional and cognitive overflows, became subject to physics, physiology, and psychology. To be sure, Helmholtz always retained a certain gracious modesty in the face of great artistic achievements, as he did of the more complex regions of mental life: although his method clearly was reductionistic, he did not claim to explain more than he could, even if the logic of his work reached more radically in the colder directions James indicated.

Hemholtz's two great contributions to the physiology of the eye and ear were his three-volume *Handbuch der physiologischen Optik* (1856–1867) and *Von den Tonempfindungen als physiologische Grundlage für die Theorie der Musik* (1863; fourth edition, 1877). The latter, on which I focus here, makes a number of fascinating contributions to musical theory; in spots Helmholtz sounds like Hegel in understanding dissonance as the condition of reconciliation; like Adorno on part-whole relationships in musical form; or even like Schönberg on the trend to dissolution of the tonal system. In the musical arguments of the book, Helmholtz states that the voice (and not the piano) is the preeminent musical instrument because it is all but infinitely fine in its tuning, having no fixed notes as do pianos, organs, and the open strings on a violin, all of which necessitate minor distortions in tempering. Modern ears, trained to hear the notes of the equally tempered piano, are largely corrupted because the piano and organ have taught us to accept notes as in tune that actually are as much as one fifth of a semitone off their true pitch. The voice is the tutor in natural tempering, the source of the minute quantities that make such gigantic qualitative differences. Helmholtz offers a kind of natural history of the voice, one that recognizes both its physical and its cultural basis.

The senses, most especially the ear and eye, were for Helmholtz apparatuses of measurement whose actions were not only qualitative but reducible to quantitative effects: "The organs of sense do indeed give us information about external effects produced on them, but convey those effects to our consciousness in a totally different form, so that the character of a sensuous perception depends not so much on the properties of the object perceived as on those of the organ by which we receive the information."[18] Seeing and hearing are structurally parallel: the hue, intensity, and saturation of colors are respectively like the pitch, volume, and tone quality (*Klangfarbe*) of sounds. An afterimage is to an image as harmony is to melody.[19] And yet the two organs are also different. The eye is synthetic; the ear, in contrast, has an astonishing analytic aptitude, a morphological gift. A single wave form can be heard by the ear as a stack of overlapping harmonics. "This analysis of compound into simple pendular vibrations is an astonishing property of the ear."[20] The eye, in contrast, never grasps elementary sensations, say, of color: all perception is admixture for the eye: "The eye has no sense of harmony in the same meaning as the ear. There is no music to the eye."[21] The eye and ear also have acutely different time sensitivities. The ear can distinguish, even if it cannot count, at least 132 beats per second, whereas the maximum for the eye, Helmholtz suggests, is 24 images per second, a number with an uncanny relevance for the eventual flicker rate of the movies.[22] The eye excels in grasping the all-at-onceness of space, but the ear perceives only a small portion of the sound ocean in which we swim because the ear canal, like a looking glass for the eye, narrows the field of sensation.[23]

Helmholtz's chief contribution in musical acoustics was to show that the infinitely diverse tone qualities of voices, musical instruments, and of all sounds derive from upper partials (*Obertone*). Pitch is a function of the frequency of sound waves, as volume is of amplitude, but tone quality owes to wave form, more specifically to the series of upper partials that a compound wave carries. The particular timbre of a musical instrument is not due to anything more mysterious than its upper partials. So, too, with much of human speech. Even vowels, the heart of speech and singing, are marked by a particular pitch for Helmholtz and a characteristic series of upper partials. (Helmholtz coined what is called "the fixed-pitch theory of vowels.") All sounds become, in principle, synthesizable. "It is quite indifferent whether they [sounds] are generated by the vibrating strings of a piano or violin, the vocal chords of the human larynx, the metal tongues of the harmonium, the reeds of the clarinet, oboe, and bassoon, the trembling lips of the trumpeter, or the air cut by a sharp edge in organ pipes and flutes."[24] Vowels can be aped by instruments and machines—by vowel bottles, pianos, and electrified tuning forks, and eventually, of course, by the phonograph and telephone.[25] Helmholtz levels all modalities and is indifferent to bodily origins: sound is sound is sound. What matters is the wave form and not the source (although, in practice, some sources are extremely hard to mimic, the voice above all). Ear and voice are in principle detached from a mortal body—immortal organs capable of diverse coupling with (and as) machines.

Central to Helmholtz's reductionistic method was the creative use of instruments both in experiment and as analogies. We have already seen the architectonic role of the telegraph: Lenoir states that "telegraphic devices were not only important as means for representation and experiment; telegraphy embodied a system of signification that was central to Helmholtz's views about mental representations and their relationship to the world."[26] But other devices encouraged his habit of conceiving the eye and ear as instruments, perhaps most notably his invention of the ophthalmoscope and resonators. The latter were specially shaped glass bottles tuned to pick precise pitches out of the air. They not only demonstrated the existence of upper partials but also trained the ear to recognize them. At first he covered one end of the bottle with a pigskin membrane that could register sonic vibrations visually by patterns in the sand placed upon it, quite in the manner of Chladni figures (self-inscribing sound pictures). Then, fitting the pointy end with wax and inserting it in the ear canal, "the observer's own tympanic membrane has been made to replace the former artificial membrane," the advantage of this design being that the resonator is brought into "direct connection with the auditory nerves themselves."[27] Once equipped with these resonators, the ear not only readily identifies upper partials in music, but the isle turns out to be full of noises: "The proper tone of the resonator may even be somehow heard cropping up in the whistling of the wind, the rattling of carriage wheels, the splashing of water."[28] Everything becomes, potentially, a voice! In Helmholtz's universe, all bodies are oscillating: the periodic oscillators produce sound, and the irregular ones produce noise. Even the eardrum, like all elastic bodies, is a resonator with its own pitch (around 2,640 to 3,168 vibrations per second), a range in which the human voice is particularly rich in upper partials. This sonic revelation is the fruit of instruments every bit as unprepossessing as the phonograph (a glass resonator stuck in the ear canal with wax) and of a clever substitution (a nervous membrane for an artificial one). According to Helmholtz, these resonators formed the very conditions of possibility of his acoustical studies.[29]

Von den Tonempfindungen is an illustrated catalog of mid-nineteenth century instruments. An index of Helmholtz's centrality in the social network of his time is his ready access to the very best scientific and musical instruments, including pianos by Steinway and Bausch and a Guadanini violin, as well as to musicians. He even measured the fingering of the foremost violinist of his era, Joseph Joachim, and found intuitive adjustments to produce natural as opposed to equal tempering.[30] But instruments are not only toys but also things with which to think with and command. As James, the founder of the first German-style psychological laboratory in the United States, noted of psychophysics, "every new problem requires some new electrical or mechanical disposition of apparatus."[31] For Helmholtz, the resonator educates the ear; but the resonator was already modeled on the ear—indeed, it is quite literally a hearing aid. His metaphorizing of the ear as instrument invites the instrumentalization of the ear.

Helmholtz's resonance theory of hearing is a fine example of the nervous system as an analogic extension of media. Helmholtz understood hearing as sympathetic vibration of elastic appendages attached to nerve endings. As his resonator substitutes a pigskin for an eardrum, so Helmholtz takes the ear as a gigantic piano, with strings tied not to tuning pegs on a sounding board but to nerves. Hearing turns out to be a particularly delicate operation that involves the magic of small quantities: the ear must "transform a motion of great amplitude and little force, such as impinges on the eardrum, into a motion of small amplitude and great force . . . to be communicated to the fluid in the labyrinth."[32] (The eardrum's movements, as we now know, are as small as the diameter of a hydrogen molecule.) The ear hears by sympathetic vibration, just as the strings of a piano with the damping pedal lifted will resonate, selectively, to the sounds that strike them. "Now suppose that we were able to connect every string of a piano with a nervous fibre in such a manner that this fibre would be excited and experience a sensation every time the string vibrated."[33] For Helmholtz, this is no mere flight of fancy. There are 4,500 or so outer arches in the cochlea, which gives us nearly 600 for each of the seven or so octaves that are musically usable (the young human ear can discern up to eleven octaves). Each sound in the universe sympathetically vibrates with one or more of these, which are placed "orderly beside each other, like the keys of a piano."[34] (He notes that combinations of sympathetically vibrating strings may be necessary to account for the full differentiation of a musically trained ear.) All sound, speech, and music, then, plays on our inner piano, a contraption of vibrating strings and nervous tissue in conjunction. Helmholtz belonged to his age in the project of mating mechanism and organism. For the romantics of an earlier generation, a Herder or Pestalozzi, everyone had a clavichord in the ear, an instrument of inwardness on which our thoughts were played. For Helmholtz, every person has a piano in the ear as a measuring instrument for the motions produced by periodically oscillating bodies.[35]

Although not without its critics (including James),[36] Helmholtz's theory of hearing remained dominant until the mid-twentieth century with Georg von Bekesy's Nobel Prize–winning work. The theory nicely catches Helmholtz's overall ambitions: "Physiologically it should be observed that the present assumption [of a sympathetically vibrating inner piano of sorts] reduces sensations which differ qualitatively according to pitch and quality of tone, to a difference in the nerve fibres which are excited."[37] Voilà! In one lucid stroke we find quality converted into quantity, sounds into sensations, art into physiology. He joins a piano key, a tuning fork, and the inner ear's most sensitive bone. Thus Helmholtz philosophizes with a hammer.

One gets dizzy trying to keep track of what is the model and what is the copy in the engineering and science of the sense organs, and, as we will see in Edison, sometimes the aim is precisely to mix them: "Psychotechnics connects [verschaltet] psychology and media technology under the condition that every psychical apparatus is also a technical one and vice versa."[38] Two years before his successful telephone call to Watson in 1876, Alexander Graham Bell tried to build a harmonic telephone based on Helmholtz's model of the ear, "a sort of piano-sized musical box-comb with between 3000 and 5000 tines to replicate the hair-like organs of Corti within the human ear." Bell kept these experiments under wraps for fear of ridicule, "especially by those unacquainted with Helmholtz's experiments"[39] (which he apparently read in French translation). Bell does not just envision the ear as a piano but builds a piano *as* an ear. Metaphors leap off of pages—and out of ears—into machines. Bell took to a monstrous extreme the logic in Helmholtz's analogies: the ear as an acoustic apparatus that could be reconstructed outside the body. Helmholtz, with the physiologists and psychophysicists of his day, rewrote the sound producing or receiving parts of human body as a collection of instruments: the voice is a musical instrument, a reed pipe or wood-wind; the throat is organ pipe, the vocal chords are membranous tongues; the eardrum is a resonator. Helmholtz's practice shows that metaphors, like media themselves, are time machines and matter replicators, able to reconfigure bodies and transport them across space and time.

Helmholtz may have stimulated the dream of building apparatuses that deviate from bodily bounds, but he also focused on a new kind of finitude in our sense organs. Never before had the lacks of the ear been so clearly revealed: its limited range of audibility, its microscopic (rather than panoramic) focus on the universe of sound, and the extremely fine quanta beyond which its sensitivities could not pass. Helmholtz repeatedly shows the routine fallibility of ordinary sensation, and a consequence of his work underscores the imperfections of the sense organs, the thresholds of perception (what Fechner called "just noticeable differences"), afterimages, optical illusions, the production of combinatorial tones, etc. Just as revealing the small intervals of nervous transmission helped make mind measurable, so analogies of the sense organs as artificial instruments and of artificial instruments as sense organs revealed, as we shall see in Edison, not only finitude lost but finitude regained. The new models of boundless hearing reacted backward on the ear, showing it to be a flawed instrument.

Edison

Edison's work continued along the lines Helmholtz had drawn for the ear and voice except for the stunning breakthrough of the capture of time in phonography. He was a rather astute commentator on the cultural significance of the phonograph except for one crucial blind spot: its eventual destiny as the centerpiece of a popular music industry. The first symphony recorded, for instance, was in 1914 (Beethoven's Fifth), almost forty years after the phonograph.[40]

Edison's original aim was the recording of voices, not the playing of music; conservation, not repetition; stenography, not entertainment. The need behind the phonograph lay in, again, the telegraph: to make a repeater that would store words without the labor of the human hand or errors of human attention. What started as an aid to transmission ended as a technique of recording. The aim to transcend distance led to the transcendence of time. As one 1896 phonograph enthusiast announced a trifle too prematurely: "Death has lost some of its sting since we are able to forever retain the voices of the dead."[41] Recording, after all, is transmission in reverse, and the phonograph reveals this reversibility—not the least of its achievements. To transmit, one must record the data in some form. Perhaps the key facts in the philosophy of the phonograph are, first, the reversibility of transmission and recording and, second, the reversibility of mouth and ear. These may be the same thing.

The cultural consequences of Edison's innovations in sound recording were diverse. First, as with Helmholtz, the phonograph's voices inaugurate a new era of blurred bodies, an interhuman blending of bees, dogs, angels, and humans. On first hearing the phonograph Edison is said to have said: "I was never so taken aback in my life." The phonograph took him back in time and history, to the mimetically rich conditions of childhood, animals, and primitivism.[42] Recording the children's song "Mary Had a Little Lamb," he foreshadowed the indefinite repeatability of advertising jingles. The phonograph made time itself a ventriloquist. An 1878 piece on "the papa of the phonograph" reported this gem: " 'A dog came along here the other day and barked in the mouthpiece,' said Edison, 'and the voice was admirably reproduced. We have hung up that sheet yonder, and now we can make him bark any time. That dog, perchance, may die and pass away to dog-heaven,' added he in a bloodcurdling voice and an impressive wave of the hand, 'but we've got them—all that is vocal survives.' "[43] Edison thus acts like a backward Cerberus, a man controlling the afterlife of a dog. The phonograph opens infra- and ultrahuman realms of sound: "Vibrations above the highest rate audible to the ear can be recorded on the phonograph and then reproduced by lowering the pitch [i.e., slowing the playback speed], until we actually hear the record of those inaudible pulsations."[44] Time axis manipulation allows eavesdropping on the speech and song of bees, dogs, and angels. No more do sonic dissipation and sensory thresholds delimit the range of possible experience. Like the microphone, which took its name from the microscope, the phonograph made "very faint sounds" accessible. As stated by Théodore DuMoncel, "Even a fly's scream, especially at the moment of death, is said by Mr. Hughes [inventor of the microphone] to be audible."[45]

Second, as with Helmholtz, the mimicry of the human vocal and hearing apparatus led to the confusion of originals and doubles. The rhetoric around early sound recording was often unclear about what kind of copy was made—an imitation, a Doppelgänger, or a copy. Edison thought the recording left no remainder once compared to the real: "The phonograph is the acid test of a voice, for it catches and reproduces the voice just as it is; in fact, it is nothing more nor less than a re-creation of the voice."[46] Intentional confusion of the voice and the machine reached a climax in the "tone tests" that were used to market Edison diamond disc phonographs and recordings in the United States from around 1915 to 1925. In over four thousand tests given to theatrical audiences that may have included two million, Edison's company teased listeners with the indiscernibility of the live and recorded voice.[47] As Edison explains, "the singer stands beside the phonograph and sings with a record he or she has previously made. Suddenly the singer stops, but the song goes on, and the audience cannot tell the difference except by noting that the singer's lips are closed."[48] The tests sought to permanently cross the two apparatuses. One 1915 ad from the beginning of the campaign humbly announced: "This New Edison was nature itself. It was the artist in all but form."[49] Despite the rhetoric, the "form" (mortal body) of the artist was not the only noticeable difference; some "live" singers admitted to coloring their voices to resemble the more metallic sounds of the phonograph (that is, as Helmholtz would remind us, to suppress certain upper partials). Obviously, human-machine mimesis is mutual. Like Helmholtz, Edison's tone tests sought to erase the difference between bodies and apparatus as sound sources. This doubling, of course, ultimately failed: mortality is too hard to match. "Speech, has become, as it were, immortal," said *Scientific American* in 1877 of Edison's contraption;[50] but ghosts dwell in the "as it were." Claims of interchangeability yield body doubles. Time travel is always matter replication, as all readers of science fiction or Stephen Hawking know, and the new bodies made are always slightly weird.

Third, sound media sought to argue that absence is as good as presence. "Live" human presence could be an impediment. A key episode is recounted in a letter Charles Batchelor wrote to the editor of the *English Mechanic* on 3 January 1878: "So accurately are the words repeated by the machine that a gentleman who was present at the exhibition would not believe that the sounds were made by it. He insisted that it was a ventriloqual performance, and would not be convinced that it was not until Mr. Edison retired into another room while the instrument was worked by someone else."[51] The proof of successful communication is obtained, curiously enough, by sending a human being into another room. As in the Turing test, the body is hidden so that the machine can fool you. Acoustic media are machines for transporting bodies from room to room—or banishing them.

In a late memoir, Edison's rival Alexander Graham Bell recalls his father's lectures in Edinburgh in the early 1860s on Universal Alphabetics, a system for representing vocal sounds by graphic marks. Before the phonograph and telephone, the aim was to reproduce sounds across gaps of time and distance. Young Alexander, acting as his father's assistant, would leave the lecture hall, and "volunteers were called to the platform, where they uttered the most weird and uncanny noises, while my father studied their mouths and attempted to express in symbols the actions of the vocal organs he had observed." On returning, Alexander would read his father's graphemes and produce the sound to the surprise and applause of the audience. A special triumph occurred when young Bell was able to produce a sound "correctly at the very first trial, without ever having heard the sound at all."[52] This is the primal scene of the supercession of presence by programming. The original is indifferent for a convincing performance. No interiority is needed for successful communication. We are in the realm of effects—of pragmatism, the philosophy fit for what Kittler calls the discourse network of 1900.[53] Bell thus found the Holy Grail of modern media: a code that can pass as an adequate substitute for the original. The ambition from Helmholtz to Edison, from Bell to Turing, has been to make communication channels immune to the troublesome fact of bodily presence.[54] It too has always failed—but only in the most inconspicuous ways.

The preferability of absence to presence pervades Edison's first essay on the phonograph. He brags that his assistants can transcribe "without the loss of a word, one or more columns of a newspaper article unfamiliar to them, and which were spoken into the apparatus when they were not present."[55] He further asserts that the phonograph generates sound waves in all their "original characteristics at will, without the presence or consent of the original source, and after the lapse of any period of time" (530). Here again, the old limits of distance, death, discretion avail not: "The phonograph letters may be dictated at home, or in the office of a friend, the *presence* of a stenographer *not being required*" (532). He even suggests that a telephone plus phonograph would remove the potentials for misunderstandings in face-to-face discussions: "Men would find it more advantageous to actually separate a half-mile or so in order to discuss important business matters, than to discuss them verbally" (535). Since the sound quality of the early phonograph was often terrible, the question was how to evoke the original without direct access to it. This is the classic problem in telecommunications of sending signals that carry information the receiver does not already possess, a problem that Claude Shannon was to formalize in 1948 with his mathematical theory of communication. His aim, again, was to produce a copy able to eliminate the need to be there.

Finally, the instrumentalization of the voice and ear retroactively imposed a disability onto the human being. The perfection of humanoid instruments invited the handicapping of our bodily organs. What had once been normal ears and voices are now revealed in all their deficiency. Edison, as is well known, had a hearing loss, and even boasted "I am a phonograph," because his high-frequency deafness helped him filter the same sounds in which the phonograph was also lacking. In his actively cultivated personal mythology,[56] Edison's deafness was not a mark of shame but a proof of authenticity. The text for a 1913 ad states: " 'I hear through my teeth,' said he [Edison], 'and through my skull. Ordinarily I merely place my head against the phonograph. But if there is some faint sound that I don't quite catch this way, I bite my teeth into the wood, and then I get it good and strong."[57] Here again is the oral primitivism of the phonograph: listening as mastication. If the ear doesn't work, use the mouth. Indeed, there is a perverse logic in Edison's chomping on the machine, because the phonograph (as opposed to the gramophone, which is ROM or read-only) also achieved the reversibility of mouth and ear, of recording and playback.

Human imperfection helped to sell the phonograph. Edward Johnson, an early Edison salesman, describes his adventures on the road wowing the natives with the uncanny little machine. Although he sings badly, he sings into the phonograph when he fails to get a volunteer from the audience: "The effect when they hear me singing is stupendous, but when they hear the Phonograph reproducing my song with all its *im*perfections they endanger the walls with clamor I then tell them they have negative proof that it will reproduce song—the whole thing proving the happiest possible exhibition of the work of the instrument."[58] New prosthetics make us gods, as Freud famously argued, but also into cripples by revealing what we previously missed.[59] What the phonograph offers, indeed, is negative proof.

William James, who knew Helmholtz's work backward and forward, gave perhaps the best insights on the disabilities that Helmholtz, Edison, and company impose on us. As a physiologically trained physician like Helmholtz, James saw in himself and his patients the dissolution of old forms of human sensation and embodiment amid late-nineteenth-century media instruments. But in these changes he saw an occasion not for despair but for reinvention. The great psychophysicist and mystic Fechner taught not the sad or stoic dissolution of our bodies into machines, thought James, but the possibility of "an altogether different plan of life": "Our animal organization comes from our inferiority. Our need of moving to and fro, of stretching our limbs and bending our bodies, shows only our defect. What are our legs but crutches, by means of which, with restless efforts, we go hunting after the things we have not inside of ourselves. But the earth is no such cripple; why should she who already possesses within herself the things we so painfully pursue, have limbs analogous to ours? Shall she mimic a small part of herself?"[60]

Disability (in this case, motoric disability) thus becomes part of the general human condition. James is far superior to the cultural pessimists who worry that machines that expand or mimic our senses will make us inhuman,[61] because he knows, like Saint Augustine, that humans have never been anything but creatures stuck amid artificial bodies and organs. James's descriptions of psychopathology in his massive *Principles of Psychology* (1890) constitute a catalog of the varieties of embodied experience in a media age: aphasia (the ability to hear but not speak, like radio listeners); agraphia (the ability to write but not read, like blind typists); cutaneous anaesthesias (the ability to see and hear but not feel, like the spectators in sound cinema or television). James states: "One of the most constant symptoms in persons suffering from hysteric disease in its extreme forms consists in alterations of the natural sensibility of various parts and organs of the body."[62] Then we are all, by James's definition, hysterics. Quite like what Deleuze and Guattari do with schizophrenia, the psychopathologies of his day provide James with descriptions of media-induced alterations of various organs and bodies.

Conclusion

McLuhan remarked that the content of a new medium was a previous one. The car, he said, was first known as a horseless carriage. Likewise, the telephone was a speaking telegraph, the radio a wireless telegraph. A new medium's most important effects work backward, not on the future. Thus Edison was taken aback. Media progressively reveal bodily imperfections. Humanity is what is left behind when all media have been stripped out of our bodies and souls. The uniquely human is established in a subtractive process: it is defined by what media machines cannot copy. The telephone made us all deaf to distant voices; the phonograph to past voices. Writing would make everyone forgetful, worried Socrates in the *Phaedrus*. The camera made our eyes forgetful to past sights. Artificial intelligence shifted the location of unique humanity to skin, handwriting, beauty, and birth: all the things that Turing took care to exclude from his game. Immortalizing media are mortalizing media. They not only make voices and other organs immortal, they also retroactively reveal the lacks of all our built-in instruments.

To understand the ways that media inscribe themselves on our bodies, we need a philosophy of history that recognizes the production of a "new already." New emergences reveal what was always there—but was never there *before*. Thus the fundamental principle of the phonograph for Edison was "the gathering up and retaining of sounds hitherto fugitive, and their reproduction at will."[63] The phonograph discovered a brand-new "hitherto." Before the phonograph, no sound had the option not to be fugitive. A historical rupture in the nature of sound arises that, in turn, rewrites its entire history. Charles Sanders Peirce, the single man of science in the nineteenth century who might rival Helmholtz as a polymath, contemplated an archaeology of vanished voices: "Give science only a hundred more centuries of increase in geometrical progression, and she may be expected to find that the sound waves of Aristotle's voice have somehow recorded themselves."[64] Like Charles Babbage, who claimed that "the air we breathe is the never-failing historian of the sentiments we have uttered,"[65] Peirce dreams the analog dream of ever-smaller tracings reverberating forever in an airborne archive. But not only does Peirce contemplate the retrieval of departed voices from the air, he imagines the past being transformed by the future in such a way that the passage of time makes infinitesimal tracings more—and not less—accessible. He understands that new media give us sense organs to perceive old things that were never, and always, there before. "Apparemment, c'est le phonographe qui fait prendre conscience à l'homme de sa voix" [Apparently, it was the phonograph that made people conscious of their voices].[66] Perriault is almost right: before sound recording, Helmholtz and his resonators and tuning forks made us aware of the voice, as echoes and laryngitis did from time immemorial.

The lesson of media history as philosophy of history is the retroactive redescription of the previous standard as limited. Finitude consists of media's leftovers, what they have not yet copied, or more precisely, what they reveal in their attempts at mimicry. In sum, the phonograph and its fellow devices of sound recording liberated the voice from its finitude, because voices can now live forever, travel far, and fall under the command of many besides their "owners." But acoustic media of recording, transmission, and amplification also revealed the grain of the voice, its lacks, breath and whispers—its mortality, in short—to a degree unprecedented in history. The phonograph, like many other media, is a memento mori, a source of the dour wisdom that the closer we approximate to the gods, the more our disabilities are made manifest.

As new media proliferate, all of which must adapt to hands, eyes, ears, mouths, mind, and bodily fatigue, we can expect an ongoing rediscovery of past amenities. Current cosmological theory speaks of a "chronology protection conjecture": the notion that the inventors of a time machine could never travel to an era historically prior to the invention of the machine, because time travel did not exist before the invention of the machine (and lest the travelers accidentally invalidate the very basis of their invention).[67] As far as I can tell, media history has no such protected chronology: new media, as vehicles that carry our senses and bodies across the space-time continuum, introduce us to old modes of experience that we never recognized we had before and therefore seem new. Media thus bear the messianic power, in Benjamin's special sense of that word, to forever alter the past.

Notes

I would like to thank Clark Farmer, Lisa Gitelman, Jim Lastra, Allison McCracken, Lauren Rabinovitz, Cornelius Reiber, Mark Sandberg, Ingo Titze, Katie Trumpener, and Steve Wurtzler for suggestions and sources. The Lilian Voudouris Music Library of Greece was a crucial resource. Much of my research was enabled by a Special Projects in the Arts and Humanities grant from the University of Iowa. An earlier version of this essay was published as "Helmholtz und Edison: Zur Endlichkeit der Stimme," trans. Antje Pfannkuchen, in *Swischen Rauschen und Offenbarung: Zur kulturellen und Medien-geschichte der Stimme*, ed. Friedrich A. Kittler, Thomas Macho, and Sigrid Weigel (Berlin: Akademie Verlag, 2002), 291–312.

1 Josef Simon, *Das Problem der Sprache bei Hegel* (Stuttgart: Kohlhammer, 1966).

2 Thomas A. Edison, "The Phonograph and Its Future," *North American Review* 126 (1878): 530.

3 Jesper Svenbro, *Phrasikleia: Anthropologie de la lecture en Grèce ancienne* (Paris: Éditions la Découverte, 1988), 183.

4 John Durham Peters, *Speaking into the Air: A History of the Idea of Communication* (Chicago: University of Chicago Press, 1999), 36–51, 160–64.

5 Friedrich A. Kittler, *Grammophon, Film, Typewriter* (Berlin: Brinkmann und Bose, 1986).

6 Marshall McLuhan, *Understanding Media: The Extensions of Man* (New York: McGraw-Hill, 1964).

7 James W. Carey, *Communication as Culture: Essays on Media and Society* (Boston: Unwin Hyman, 1989), chapter 8.

8 Thomas L. Hankins and Robert J. Silverman, *Instruments and the Imagination* (Princeton: Princeton University Press, 1995), 113–47.

9 Jacques Perriault, "Une autre genèse du phonographe," in *Mémoires de l'ombre et du son: Une archéologie de l'audio-visuel* (Paris: Flammerion, 1981), 121, 160.

10 Timothy Lenoir, "Helmholtz and the Materialities of Communication," *Osiris* 9 (1994): 185–86.

11 Edison, "The Phonograph and Its Future," 528.

12 *The Diary and Sundry Observations of Thomas Alva Edison*, ed. Dogobert D. Runes (New York: Greenwood Press, 1968), 84.

13 Ibid., 216.

14 Hermann von Helmholtz, *On the Sensations of Tone as a Physiological Basis for the Theory of Music*, translated from the fourth German edition by Alexander J. Ellis (1877; New York: Dover, 1954), 148.

15 Quoted in Timothy Lenoir, "Helmholtz, Müller, und die Erziehung der Sinne," in *Johannes Müller und die Philosophie*, ed. Michael Hagner and Bettina Wahrig-Schmidt (Berlin: Akademie-Verlag, 1998), 208.

16 Ibid., 217.

17 William James, *The Principles of Psychology* (1890; New York: Dover, 1950), 1: 85–86.

18 Hermann von Helmholtz, "Goethe's Scientific Researches," in *Science and Culture: Popular and Philosophical Essays by Hermann von Helmholtz*, ed. David Cahan (1853; Chicago: University of Chicago Press, 1995), 13.

19 Helmholtz, *On the Sensations of Tone*, 364.

20 Ibid., 128.

21 Ibid., 64–65; Hermann von Helmholtz, "On the Physiological Causes of Harmony in Music," in *Science and Culture*, 74.

22 Helmholtz, *On the Sensations of Tone*, 173.

23 Ibid., 26–29.

24 Helmholtz, "On the Physiological Causes of Harmony in Music," 40.

25 Helmholtz, *On the Sensations of Tone*, 123ff. Alexander Ellis, Helmholtz's English translator, includes an extended appendix in the 1885 edition on the relevance of the Edison phonograph for the study of vowel sounds (538–43).

26 Lenoir, "Helmholtz and the Materialities of Communication," 206–7. For a key passage using the telegraph as an analogy for Hemholtz's theory of the sense organs, see *On the Sensations of Tone*, 149.

27 Helmholtz, *On the Sensations of Tone*, 43–44.

28 Ibid., 44.

29 Ibid.

30 Ibid., 325.

31 James, *Principles of Psychology*, 1: 88.

32 Helmholtz, *On the Sensations of Tone*, 133.

33 Ibid., 129.

34 Helmholtz, "On the Physiological Causes of Harmony in Music," 60.

35 Wolfgang Scherer, "Die Stimme und das Clavichord: Medientechnische Bedingungen der musikalischen Empfindsamkeit im 18. Jahrhundert," in *Zwischen Rauschen und Offenbarung: Zur Kultur- und Mediengeschichte der Stimme*, ed. Friedrich Kittler, Thomas Macho, and Sigrid Weigel (Berlin: Akademie Verlag, 2002), 288.

36 James, *Principles of Psychology*, 2: 170.

37 Helmholtz, *On the Sensations of Tone*, 148.
38 Kittler, *Grammophon, Film, Typewriter*, 238.
39 Brian Winston, *Media Technology and Society: A History from the Telegraph to the Internet* (London: Routledge, 1998), 38.
40 Jacques Attali, *Bruits: Essai sur l'économie politique de la musique* (Paris: Presses universitaires de France, 1977), 201.
41 "Voices of the Dead," *Phonoscope* 1 (1896): 1.
42 Michael Taussig, *Mimesis and Alterity: A Particular History of the Senses* (New York: Routledge, 1992), 211–14.
43 William Croffut, "The Papa of the Phonograph: An Afternoon with Edison, the Inventor of the Talking Machines," in *The Papers of Thomas A. Edison*, ed. Robert A. Rosenberg (1878; Baltimore: Johns Hopkins University Press, 1998), 4: 218.
44 Edison, "The Perfected Phonograph," 642.
45 Théodore DuMoncel, *The Telephone, the Microphone, and the Phonograph* (New York: Harper and Brothers, 1879), 145–46.
46 *The Diary and Sundry Observations of Thomas Alva Edison*, 83.
47 Thompson, "Machines, Music, and the Quest for Fidelity," 153.
48 *The Diary and Sundry Observations of Thomas Alva Edison*, 83.
49 Steve Wurtzler, "The Social Construction of Technological Change: American Mass Media and the Advent of Electricity" (Ph.D. diss., University of Iowa, 2001), 35.
50 "A Wonderful Invention—Speech Capable of Indefinite Repetition from Automatic Records," *Scientific American* (17 November 1877): 304.
51 *The Papers of Thomas A. Edison*, 7.
52 Alexander Graham Bell, "Prehistoric Telephone Days," *National Geographic* 41, no. 3 (1922): 228–29.
53 Friedrich A. Kittler, *Aufschreibesysteme, 1800/1900*, rev. ed. (Munich: Wilhelm Fink, 1995).
54 Alan M. Turing, "Computing Machinery and Intelligence," *Mind* 59 (1950): 433–60. See also Peters, *Speaking into the Air*, 233–41.
55 Edison, "The Phonograph and its Future," 528–29.
56 Portia Dadley, "The Garden of Edison: Invention and the American Imagination," in *Cultural Babbage: Technology, Time and Invention*, ed. Francis Spufford and Jenny Uglow (London: Faber, 1996), 81–98.
57 Wurtzler, "The Social Construction of Technological Change," 37.
58 *The Papers of Thomas A. Edison*, 4: 44.
59 Sigmund Freud, *Civilization and Its Discontents*, trans. Joan Riviere (1930; New York: Norton, 1961).
60 William James, *A Pluralistic Universe* (New York: Longman, Green, and Co., 1909), 158–59.
61 For example, see Günter Stern (later known as Günter Anders), "Spuk und Radio," *Anbruch* 2 (1930): 65–66.
62 James, *Principles of Psychology*, 1: 202.

63 Edison, "The Phonograph and Its Future," 527.
64 Charles Sanders Peirce, *Collected Papers*, ed. Charles Hartshorne and Paul Weiss (Cambridge: Harvard University Press, 1931–1958), 5: 543.
65 Charles Babbage, *The Ninth Bridgewater Treatise*, 2nd ed. (1838), in *The Works of Charles Babbage*, ed. Martin Campbell-Kelly (London: William Pickering, 1989), 9: 36.
66 Perriault, *Mémoires de l'ombre et du son*, 192.
67 Michael White and John Gribben, *Stephen Hawking: A Life in Science*, 2nd ed. (London: Penguin, 1998), 296–98.

Lisa Gitelman

MEDIA, MATERIALITY, AND

THE MEASURE OF THE DIGITAL; OR,

THE CASE OF SHEET MUSIC AND THE

PROBLEM OF PIANO ROLLS

> The notion of property starts, I suppose, from confirmed
> possession of a tangible object and consists in the right to exclude others
> from interference with the more or less free doing with it as one wills.
> But in copyright property has reached a more abstract expression.
> The right to exclude is not directed to an object in possession
> or owned, but is *in vacuo*, so to speak.
> —JUSTICE HOLMES, *White-Smith v. Apollo*

Media tend to be very slippery historical subjects, at least because media—so often portentously "the" media—of any generation tend to become naturalized; they start to seem inevitable and then transparent, or transparent and then inevitable. Much has been written, for example, regarding the identity of communication and transportation before the advent of the telegraph. The electric telegraph, we are told, decisively severed the age-old connection between point-to-point communication and point-to-point travel. Much has also been written of the ways in which digital technologies make the means of communication "virtual," freeing information from the limits of physicality, from tangible things like pages, books, and files. These narratives stand at the center of the way media are understood today. The former conceptualizes an electronic age while the latter conceptualizes the information age. Both stories are technically false, at least because they forget the precedence of optical telegraphy on the one hand, and on the other because they occlude the presence of physical keys, screens, and silicon. Yet both seem to possess resilient explanatory power; both are tenacious, valorizing narratives of *dematerialization*. Together they suggest that it is partly in relationship to their *materiality* that media become mystified—that is, slippery—as historical subjects.

The purpose of this essay is to catch a glimpse of slipperiness in itself by looking at a specific moment of media transition, when things seemed particularly contingent and far from inevitable or natural. Moments of media transition are periods in which the perceptual and semiotic patterns, the technological forms, social practices, economic structures, and legal constructions later defining a particular medium within a dominant media system remain unsettled and under negotiation. Indeed, negotiation makes a better point of historical comparison than media forms themselves: "new media" resemble each other to varying degrees in their *newness*, whether they happen to have been new a long time ago or new today. So the phonograph records and piano rolls of 1900 or 1910 compare to downloaded MP3 files only in the most banal regard because they are all musical forms for private consumption. More telling comparisons, and equally important contrasts, attend the respective newness of such forms, the negotiation and emergence of listening habits, technical standards, new corporate structures, copyright strictures, and the like.

In this essay I focus on one material. Stated in the extreme, before "the digital" and even before "information" were culturally constructed as such, *paper* was one way (and I think a major way) in which ordinary people experienced the materially diverse economy of meaning that modern communications entail—part of what gets called "synergy" today. Paper remains vital to the "social life of information" in our digital era, although that fact has slipped from awareness in many ways.[1] This essay addresses an earlier moment when assumptions or habits associated with paper broke down, caused open conflict, and had to be reestablished in a new configuration.

In May 1906, an American appeals court handed down a ruling having to do with perforated music rolls, the long punched-paper scrolls that work in player pianos. On one side of the lawsuit was a successful manufacturer of piano rolls. On the other side was a music publishing company that argued that certain music rolls violated the copyright it possessed for sheet music. When consumers bought music rolls instead of buying sheet music, music publishers and the authors they represented lost royalties. Although phonograph records caused the same problem and were even more popular, the issue came up in the courtroom according to its hardest test case, printed sheets and punched rolls, which were intuitively the same—they were both paper—and yet just as intuitively different. This quarrel about media was also a quarrel about materials and about issues of materiality, issues central to copyright laws, where, as Justice Holmes observed, authors possessing copyrights have a vital and yet paradoxically vacant interest in materiality, in what intellectual property law understands as the tangible *expressions* of an author's mental *conceptions*.

This case, *White-Smith v. Apollo*, had come up from a federal court in New York and was soon on its way to the U.S. Supreme Court, and thus the decision of 1906 and the debates it provoked in Congress and in the press provide a look at the terms of the quarrel at midstream. (The same terms were later integral to the U.S. Copyright Act of 1909 and were replicated to an extent in wrangling over revisions to the Berne Convention in Europe.) The appellate judge rejected the idea that the perforations of the music roll might be a form of "notation or record" of the music (and therefore a violation of copyright). To admit that rolls contained notation, he reasoned, would be to admit that phonograph records also contained notation, when anyone could plainly see that they did not. Holes in a music roll, in other words, were not "a varied form of symbols substituted for the symbols" used in music. It was not the perforated paper that published the composer's conception but rather the mechanical action of the player piano, of which the paper roll was adjunct, that made the music publicly available. Phonograph records were not notational records, and air holes could not be symbols.[2]

John Philip Sousa, the popular American composer and bandleader, published his response to the ruling in an essay titled "The

Menace of Mechanical Music."[3] Sousa's marches had been and continued to be wantonly and profitably appropriated by the makers of records and music rolls, and Sousa reasonably wanted to recover payment for all of the sheet music royalties he was losing. He argued from personal interest, but he dressed up that interest as best he could for the occasion. Most of his essay treats the damage to American music caused by phonographs and player pianos. He even coins the pejorative "canned music" in thinking of the can-shaped, cylindrical phonograph records of the day, and he points out that "[mechanical reproductions] are as like real art as the marble statue of Eve is like her beautiful, living, breathing daughters" (279). When he did get down to his own grievance and the matter of "fair play," he responded to the court by asking, "is a copyright simply represented by a sheet of music? Is there no more to it than the silent notation? The little black spots on the five lines and spaces, the measured bars, are merely the record of [the] birth and existence of musical thought. These marks are something beyond the mere shape, the color, the length of the pages" (283). Sousa wanted the abstract "musical thought" not the "silent notation," "black spots," or "marks" to be his property, because that musical thought was "conceived" by him. Printed notes, spots, and marks were no more equal to his musical thought or "living theme," he was sure, "than the description of a beautiful woman is the woman herself" (284). Music is a lady in many of Sousa's conceits, and here notational representation proves just as pale an imitation of her as mechanical reproduction.

Neither Sousa nor the judge explored the implications of what Sousa was saying with regard to symbols and material forms. The court's analogy between music rolls and phonograph records was functional—both embodied music for mechanical reproduction—but that functional comparison made stark the contrast between symbols and what can now be called "machine-readable text." For the judge, machine-readable text was nonsymbolic, although its embodiment on or as paper helped assure him that it *was* text. On Sousa's part, the "little black spots" of notation might be symbolic but they were not real *music* at all, because resident on the silent stuff of paper. Real music was intuitively "something beyond" dead matter, and Sousa wanted musical authorship reconstructed accordingly under the law. Each man possessed a different, necessary, and forensic (one might also say "bibliographic") interest in the materials of music and its public circulation. The material properties of the piano rolls can be seen freshening the logic of their dispute in subtle ways, just as the physical shapes of phonograph records less subtly influenced the meanings of recorded sound. The term "canned" proved to be a very powerful descriptor, even after records were all disk shaped, while the earliest phonograph audiences had apparently been quick to believe the machines were "reading" records, in part because the very first records were incised on sheets of tinfoil, just like sheets of paper.[4]

The material meanings of music rolls became an issue of controversy when the popularity of "self-playing" pianos at the beginning of the twentieth century challenged the material meanings of printed music. "Material meanings" in this sense are that nexus of cultural practices, economic structures, and perceptual and semiotic habits that make tangible things meaningful. Music rolls and sheet music each helped to call the varied properties of the other into question as changes in American musical practices associated with mechanical music inspired litigation and eventual legislation about musical copyright. The properties at stake were economic and semiotic at their heart, while the social experience of these properties involved varying uses for paper, new modes and patterns of leisure, varying and diverse tastes for music, as well as the ongoing reconnaissance of the machine in modern life. Paper became recomplicated within contemporary musical culture as that culture itself continued to change. As Sousa recognized, amateur home music making waned in the face of mechanical music. More and more Americans played music mechanically rather than making it themselves.

For most of the first decade of the twentieth century, composers, record and roll producers, congressmen, jurists, and musicians quarreled over the material meanings of music rolls. Further, the flux continued when the quarrel over music rolls was settled and attentions turned elsewhere. If the popularity of self-playing pianos helped to challenge the material meanings of printed music at the beginning of the twentieth century, one need hardly be surprised that the popularity of Internet downloads is helping to challenge the material meanings of compact discs at the beginning of the twenty-first century.

How robust is the analogy? Like Jacquard looms and barrel organs, player pianos form part of the prehistory of computing because self-playing depended on a calculated series of binary terms, of zeros and units, or, in this case, of holes and paper. Scholars and player piano enthusiasts today are quick to call them digital.[5] But digitized data could hardly have mattered to the material meanings of the perforated rolls over which Sousa and the federal judiciary wrangled, before anyone had formulated "the digital" or, indeed, data, in quite the way we do now. Instead, one must look to the material meanings of published sheet music as well as to the rolls themselves and the musical practices that self-playing pianos engaged and helped to transform during the first decade of the twentieth century.

Sheet music and piano rolls can retrospectively be considered the "software" of the early twentieth century, if "software" is defined narrowly as a form of market relation. Each kind of paper formed the component supplies of "a primarily hardware-driven industry." The terms "hardware" and "software" might not have been applied at the time, but something of the relation that later emerged between them was already recognizable, working in the construction of "self-playing," as it would in the construction of machine-readability and of digital " 'wares." The sale of piano rolls, of course, depended on the consumer's possession of a player piano while "printed sheet music suitable for home entertainment" had succeeded and continued to prosper reciprocally with home keyboard instruments.[6] Practically speaking, sheet music publishers had their market relations pretty well worked out. They took advantage of long-established, flexible networks connecting themselves to music stores, department store music counters, music teachers, live performers, and the individual subscribers to musical periodicals like *Dwight's* or *Etude*. By contrast, the newer makers of music rolls suffered the hardware obsession of the music trades. One symptom of that obsession was what insiders called the "music roll problem" or the lack of any agreed-on system for selling rolls. Some dealers in player pianos simply gave them away as premiums, dampening the rest of the trade, while others established music roll subscription libraries that resembled today's video rental businesses.[7] "The man who buys a piano does not expect a library of sheet music," one observer complained; "The man who buys a talking machine does not get nor expect an exchange library of records; the man who buys an automobile does not expect free tires or gasoline."[8] Soft wares depended on hard, but the commercial specifics of that dependency remained undefined in the case of piano rolls. The sheer size and competitiveness of the piano trade appears to have eclipsed the stature of music roll manufacturers as participants in the definition of relevant market relations. Additionally debilitating to that definition was the seeming reluctance of roll manufacturers to adopt a standardized format.[9]

The market for pianos, with or without player mechanisms, was nothing short of staggering—riding, as it did, on a widely shared ideology of womanly accomplishment. According to one observer, the market for pianos was completely saturated by 1900, a year in which American manufacturers alone produced another 171,000 pianos.[10] Piano makers got busy selling upgrades, among them pianos with self-playing action. The number of instruments manufactured peaked in 1909 at 364,000 a year, then slowly tapered back toward 200,000 a year before plummeting with the stock market in 1929.[11] (For a variety of reasons, self-playing pianos never recovered from the crash.) Market saturation in this case seems to have meant that in towns and cities across the United States something like half of all households possessed a piano of some sort by the mid-1920s. In 1929 Robert and Helen Lynd reported that 43 percent of the homes in Middletown (Muncie, Indiana) contained a piano, although "music, like poetry and the other arts, is almost nonexistent among the men."[12] A good or "high-class," upright piano, one that might grace "the drawing rooms of the wealthy or the aspiring middle class," cost about $600 in 1916 (the same year that Henry Ford reduced the Model T price to $345). A "low-grade," cheap piano cost $200. Buying "on time" was a common feature of the trade.[13]

Such distinctions between "high-class" and 'low-grade" were the bread and butter of the piano trade, which helped to project homologous distinctions onto society. Hierarchies of price mirrored hierarchies of wealth, which were quickened by presumed hierarchies of class and of taste. Pianos formed both the subject and the instrument of middle-class aspirations as they became markers for and makers of middle-class domesticity. Piano playing was freighted with the sanctity of home and family in a conflation of aesthetic and moral values.[14] It was according to this logic that the explorer Robert Scott took along a piano when he first set off for the Antarctic in 1901. Far from home, family, and the company of women, the piano would signify them all. Lacking women to play the instrument, Scott brought along a pianola, probably one of the early *vorseitzer* player mechanisms that sat in front of a conventional piano and played with felt-covered "fingers" as someone pumped the pneumatic pedals in front. Chopin on ice proved "a perfect godsend," as it somehow introduced an appropriately masculine vehicle for homesickness—particularly among the officer class—performing and reperforming, producing and reproducing the experienced distance between home and away.[15] What got lost in the distance, of course, was musical literacy, which remained detached enough from hierarchies of taste and class to allow player mechanisms an entry into the "cultural" status of music without all of the accumulating baggage of "canned" music. Pianolas and player mechanisms played live music on real pianos, not bottled, pickled, or canned. What they sidestepped was the skill of reading music and, for many, the obscurantism of musical notation, the tedium of practice, and the widely remarked discomforts of listening to imperfect, amateur playing.[16]

Player pianos promised the democratization of "good" music well played. Classical music dominated the commercial conception of the instruments and the music rolls, even if, practically speaking, more "popular" music probably comprised the lion's share of the market. Player manufacturers hyped the advantage of the player over the "straight" piano, as it was termed in contrast, and managed to persuade many people, as well as themselves, that the player was "destined" to become "the musical instrument for the home of the future."[17] All player pianos could be used as conventional, "straight" pianos, but they also offered the opportunity to hear the music played without reading and without fingers, without hands. Advertising copy indicates that music *appreciation* was sold as the stand-in for home musical performance, while performance was thus disembodied, or reembodied, in the person who played "by foot" rather than by hand or "manually."[18] Users sat before the keyboard, pumped the pedals, and watched as the keys moved. They moved as if pressed by invisible hands, although those hands could not have suggested an entire invisible body very convincingly because the pedaling user sat squarely where such an invisible player would have been. Thus the playing of the piano remained (somewhat mystically) an extension of the self on the piano stool, while that self, normatively a woman's self, became at once dismembered, handless, and subject to the fragmentation of attention and agency across body and machine. Salesmen hinted, meanwhile, that using a player piano to produce good music would inspire users to learn to read music and play it themselves. Invisible limbs might create embodied desire, which might lead (with plenty of practice) to a "straight"—that is, holistic—playing body and intentioned, reading self: fingers for the keys, eyes for the music, feet for the piano pedals. Player pianos and music rolls rendered broad or democratic access to music because they appeared to de-skill it. Hinting at some of the social renegotiations taking place, one advertiser assured, "The American player piano in the home is the delight of the American girl," while another later maker of player pianos prospered in the dissemination of its trademark picture of a diapered infant crawling onto the pedals and thus playing the player piano.[19] At pedal height, a baby could not even pretend to read music as the instrument played. For their part, sheet music publishers had no comparable recourse—reading and playing or singing music *is* a skill—except in trying to ensure that customers could really use the sheet music that they bought. A few printed difficulty ratings in their catalogs beside the titles listed for sale; Woodward & Company of New York used a scale from one to six; John Church Company of Cincinnati used a scale from one to seven.[20] Once purchased, sheet music still required the addition of musical literacy, technique, practice, and—apparently—an American Girl, before much elevating musical appreciation could take place.

Democratization came with certain risks, and the trade literature makes clear that anxieties surfaced with the notion that "even a child" could play the player piano. Of paramount importance was the question of taste; democratization suggested universal access but taste required discrimination. Good taste was an accomplishment, a form of accumulated cultural capital, not—as much as it might be assumed in some quarters—an instinct available to the babies of the wealthier classes. In short, the dis- or reembodiment of musical performance was one thing, but outright mechanization was entirely another. The short-lived trade magazine *Player Piano* urged dealers and salesmen to avoid words that might connote the contamination of the musical ideal by what Sousa had already painted as "a mathematical system of megaphones, wheels, cogs, disks, cylinders, and all manner of revolving things."[21] The magazine advised salesmen to emphasize the artistic: "As far as possible, the mind of the purchaser should be diverted from the idea that he is buying a piece of mechanism . . . The player-piano should never be referred to as a 'machine.' The very terms 'machine' and 'music' are antagonistic . . . By the same token the player instrument should never be referred to as a 'self-player' or 'automatic' . . . Never use the word 'operator' when referring to one who uses or demonstrates a player-piano. A person operates a sewing machine or a lathe . . . [but] it requires intelligence and musical taste to play a player-piano, and such a person is a 'performer' as much as one who uses the fingers."[22] The semantic province of the player piano was meant by its producers to be the semantic province of the piano. The equation worked in part because the same producers made both instruments. (*Player Piano* likely failed because the player business was not a wholly separate trade within the musical trades; the dominant *Music Trade Review* continued to run its player piano columns and advertisements.) The makers of quality pianos eventually offered quality players. Consumers were urged to be careful in discriminating between "Steinway & Sons" and the cheaper, so-called stencil pianos, with names painted on the front by dealers using names like "Steinwebb," "Steinweg," "Stein & Sons," "Steinbay," and "Steinberg & Co."[23]

Emphasizing the artistic or musical over the mechanical took a number of more subtle forms as well. Although player pianos did not require musical literacy, they did quickly become involved within the construction of different paraliteracies. With the notable exception of the "reproducing" player piano (discussed below), every make of player piano required its own technique, and technique was familiarly associated with music, not—however mistakenly—with machines. Users needed to master an "artistic use of the pedals," as well as the available "phrasing levers," "expression" knobs, "speed pointers," and "loud buttons" that their players possessed.[24] These techniques in turn required that instructions be added to the music rolls. As one writer noted in his booklet *How to Play the World's Most Wonderful Musical Instrument, The Player Piano*, "The best Music Rolls have signs or helps printed upon them," which form "a guide to the intention of the interpreter or composer."[25] Another explained the technique in the publication *Musical Expression through the Player Piano* by giving pedaling instructions as well as by explaining "the various marks of expression," the "dotted or continuous line," "together with special accent and stop marks" that appeared on the roll.[26] And a third assured readers that "women and children can play without tiring when they use the pedals properly," and followed by dilating on the subject of "lines" and "accent marks" necessary to his "system" of playing the player piano.[27] Although they were never required to read music, users of the player piano were encouraged to sit and read music *rolls* as they—the user, the player piano, and the roll—all "played." The rolls remained emphatically empty of musical notation but just as emphatically marked with legible signs.

Makers of music rolls cropped up everywhere to supply the trade. Most were not subsidiaries of individual player piano makers and none appear to have been music publishers. Each trumpeted the advantages of its own rolls, usually glossing over the intricate differentiation that the lack of a standardized format entailed in favor of noting differing aspects of readability. For example, the Billings Player Roll Company boasted of its "Staffnote Rolls" that "all that pertains to music is printed on the roll." The American Piano Company claimed that its "Flexotone Music Rolls" contained "a simple and musically effective guide to the intelligent use of the expression devices of any type" of player piano. "Mellographic Rolls," made by the Mellographic Roll Company, included "expression marks acknowledged most correct by professional musicians." Finally, "Vocalstyle" rolls had "special interpretation marks," and were "word rolls," just like Columbia's "Truly Synchronized" rolls and Imperial's "Songrecord" rolls.[28]

"Word rolls" became a generic term for rolls that contained the lyrics of a song stenciled beside the perforations. Users read the lyrics as the player mechanism "read" the air holes. Consuming "word rolls" differed from other reading, one writer explained, because sheet music is "printed to read from left to right; [while] the music roll unwinds downward on the Player-Piano and the words and interpretation marks are printed on the roll to be read upward. Each word or syllable of the song is directly opposite the note to be sung, and should be pronounced as it passes over the tracker bar or mouth piece of the Player-Piano."[29] The "note to be sung" in this case is a sound, not a mark, which emerged from the piano in synchrony with an air hole passing over its "mouth piece." (The player piano "reads" with its mouth and plays with hammers and strings like any "straight" piano.) Music rolls wind down into the player mechanism (turning in the direction opposite to a typewriter platen, for instance), so that lyrics and other readable facts appear and disappear from bottom to top, something like this:

```
       Wa.
       O-
↓      I-
       In
       Down
↓      Way
       Way,
       A-
       Hide
↓      I'll
```

The eyes must move up the scroll as the paper moves down. The direction of tracking upends the direction of reading. Word rolls thus thoroughly inverted the logic of reading sheet music, separating musical and nonmusical literacy. They turned reading on its axis, as left-to-right became top-to-bottom, and then flipped it upside down. Even more, by offering lyrics without musical notation, word rolls presumed a performance for which singers know the tune but do not know the words. Knowing the tune relied on the repeated operation of the player piano, which "read" and "reread" the accompaniment as people read and sang the words. The rolls both assumed and facilitated repetition as a musical practice but departed radically from the age-old repetitive logic of "practice, practice, practice."

Long were the debates in American courtrooms and in Congress over whether musically literate people might not be able to read the air holes, to decode what the machine decodes in playing music rolls. If readable, the perforations were more likely to be copies of legible, copyrighted scores. Senator Reed Smoot (a Republican from Utah) pressed witnesses before the Joint Committees on Patents in 1906, "Are there people that can read that roll?" It seemed self-evident to him that people could, because "every slit or cut or dash in that paper represents a note, does it not, just the same as the notes are differently represented upon the paper that Mr. Sousa exhibited" during his testimony before the committee.[30] Smoot was persuaded by the one-to-one correspondence between notes or keys pressed on the keyboard and holes in the paper. But a representative of the National Piano Manufacturers' Association quickly assured him that no one "can take that music roll and tell you what particular note any particular slit or dash represents." The individual holes each formed "a notation" only *by relation to* the mechanical parts of the player piano.[31] This was in denial of a certain tacit knowledge that did accrue to the makers of music rolls, but even the U.S. Supreme Court would be persuaded by "the weight of testimony" that—as much as some patient and skilled operator might read them—the rolls were neither regularly read nor "intended to be read as an ordinary piece of sheet music."[32] As the appellate judge had ruled in 1906, the holes were instrumental, not symbolic.

In effect, the quarrel was about whether the piano rolls were analog or digital. Did the perforations have an indexical (one-to-one mapping) relation to musical notes, or were they just an arbitrary machine code? It is this quarrel that gets lost in the rush by so many authors today to call music rolls and player pianos "digital." It is true that the rolls do form part of the prehistory of computing, but their dubious legibility proved an experience of the incipient *question* rather than the accomplishment of digitized sound. As it happens, the perforations in a conventional music roll have an indexical relationship to the keys of the piano: there are eighty-eight potential holes across the roll at every moment. More sophisticated music rolls used in so-called reproducing pianos added a series of arbitrary, nonindexical perforations in both margins of the roll as a means of reproducing the dynamics of performance.

Rolls for reproducing pianos, like the Welte-Mingon and the Duo-Art, reproduce an individual performance by an individual pianist because they are based on scrolls marked with key strokes and dynamics that add sustaining and soft pedal movements during a single performance. "What may be called the 'film of the music camera,'" one advertiser explained, "receives impressions of every detail" of fingering and pedaling.[33] Some of the greatest pianists and composers of the era made reproducing rolls, and the owners of reproducing pianos could buy rolls "played" by Jan Paderewski, Sergei Rachmaninov, and Maurice Ravel. George Gershwin and Igor Stravinsky made them too, although possibly with differing motivations. Sold with slogans like "The master's fingers on your piano," the rolls were usually printed with ornate, engraved "leaders" attesting to the authenticity of the performance, complete with the autograph of its celebrated performer. Users fed the leader into their reproducing piano and then stood back to watch an invisible master depress the piano keys, particularly in later models when electric motors replaced the pneumatic pedals. The musical quality of these reproducing rolls is still controversial in some quarters, but pianists reportedly liked them because they allowed corrections to be made before the "master" roll was used to produce saleable versions of the master. Mistaken keystrokes could be fixed, the timing of notes comprising a chord might be evened out, repeats pasted in exactly, and—as careful, musically astute listeners can attest—extra "fingers" and "hands" could be added to the roll as desired for particularly intricate compositions or to gain a richer sound.[34] Although never a large proportion of the self-playing market, the expensive reproducing pianos proved important conceptually in the construction of "self-playing" and still offer unprecedented access to the interpretations of dead pianists. The reproducing piano fully displaced the user's body: after loading the roll and setting the tempo, the user had no knobs or levers to fiddle with during the performance and therefore no incentive to sit and watch or read the roll. Displaced users heard and watched invisible pianists depress the keys with *virtual* fingers and hands.

Predictably attended by a rhetoric of authenticity—the *real* Steinway & Sons, the *real* Rachmaninov—music rolls helped to open the question of a virtual reality. Virtual fingers and hands provide a reminder that the "self" in "self-playing" proved as malleable as the "playing." Pianolas, player pianos, and reproducing pianos involved new subjectivities, in other words, as the activities of both playing and reading became with greater force something that machines as well as people could do. In vernacular parlance, users, master pianists, rolls, pianos, and player mechanisms all "played" at once. Further, the mechanisms "read"—and read paper, it turned out—without reading anything by an actual author, at least as far as the federal judiciary could discern. Composers and music publishers were seemingly out of luck in their suit for "fair play."

John Philip Sousa was no jurist. American copyright is a statutory construction, not a natural law, and it is based on the varied material forms that express an author's conception. Authors' rights are *in vacuo* in the sense that their exercise depends not on any *thing* an author can point to but rather on future, potential, material expressions that may eventually be found to be infringements. Ironically in the case of musical copyright and sheet music, the material expressions that the future rendered so problematic were themselves vacuous—holes that suggested musical notes (and their absence) to members of the bench. But John Philip Sousa tried to go even further to evacuate materiality. By arguing that he had a natural right to the *sounds* he had composed, however they might be expressed or embodied in black spots or air holes, Sousa headed where neither the courts nor Congress could constitutionally follow. Fortunately for the bandleader, the U.S. Copyright Act of 1909 soon contrived a statutory fix, a two-cent royalty payable to musical authors on every record and roll. The records and rolls remained readable but not authored under the law, until their meanings were called into question by the material meanings of cassette tapes in the 1970s, which then inspired Congress to extend copyright to recordings.

For litigants and jurists today, *White-Smith v. Apollo* is less important to the *legal* construction of the digital or the potential authorship of data than *Baker v. Selden*, another Supreme Court case alluded to at the time, which involved the "utilitarian instrumentalities" of blank paper forms used for bookkeeping.[35] Culturally, however, the matter of music rolls is vital to an understanding of where the idea of the digital (its utilitarian instrumentality) comes from and just how intricate the material meanings of any new medium can be. Music rolls meant what they meant to Sousa, Smoot, and their contemporaries in part because of the ways they challenged and adapted the familiar economics and semiotics of published sheet music. It seems particularly telling that music rolls offered a new form of *access* (to music well played on one's own home piano) that was immediately enrolled within a rhetoric of democratization by some and painted as trespass by others. It is equally notable that the makers of rolled software struggled to prosper in a market variously shaped by hardware commitments and that Congress acted to protect one business sector while under the fear of monopoly in another.[36] Meanwhile, the experience of music itself as specifically "cultural" helped to inspire anxieties about mechanization: mechanization remained thoroughly if dynamically invested by the gendered constructions of users, *appreciation* was valorized as a form of mass consumption, and the suggested (oft-lamented) decline in traditional music literacy was accompanied by the construction of numerous paraliteracies required in part by interface conventions.

Taken with and against the popular dissemination of music rolls in the protracted moment of discomfiture that self-playing pianos helped to provoke, musical publishers countenanced some of the

arbitrariness of both statutory authorship and "little black spots."
Paper and meaning and the meaning of paper had been briefly
and narrowly interrogated. Reading entered new relations with machines and with people. As music rolls addressed, adapted, and sub-
verted the material meanings of sheet music, they helped to open
an unsettled semantic field, one that would be organized later in
the century by terms like "machine-readable text," "program," and
"the digital," which function today in descriptions of an imminently
immaterial future, the supposed *apparition* of the eBook, e-Paper,
and "shared" MP3 files. The resemblance between the quarrels over
music rolls and those over Internet downloads certainly relies far
less on words like these than on long-standing patterns of capital-
ization and trade, jeopardized and thus so much more evidently
contrived and contingent. Resemblance further relies contextually
on varying investments in materiality as such. The specifics of materiality continue to *matter* much more to authors, to publishers, to
"labels"—that is, to potential owners—than they ever can, could, or
will to listeners.

Notes

I would like to thank Donald Manildi, curator of the International
Piano Archives, University of Maryland, for discussing the germ of
this paper with me, and the Obermann Center for Advanced Studies,
University of Iowa, for supporting its completion.

1   See John Seely Brown and Paul Duguid, *The Social Life of Information*
(Cambridge: Harvard Business School Press, 2000): "To make better
progress against paper, to make better document technologies, designers of alternatives need to understand paper better" (175).
2   *White-Smith v. Apollo*, 139 Fed. 427 (1906).
3   John Philip Sousa, "The Menace of Mechanical Music," *Appleton's
Magazine* 8 (September 1906): 278–83.
4   I've tried to make this argument regarding tinfoil sheets in "The
First Phonographs: Reading and Writing with Sound," *Biblion* 8 (fall
1999): 3–16.
5   See, for one example, Michael Chanan, "The Player Piano," in *Piano
Roles: Three Hundred Years of Life with the Piano*, ed. James Parakilas
et al. (New Haven: Yale University Press, 1999), 72–75. The analogy
to the Jacquard loom appears early in Alfred Dolge, *Pianos and Their
Makers* (Los Angeles: Covina Publishing, 1911), 1: 131. For a detailed history of mechanical music, see Alexander Buchner, *Mechani-*

cal Musical Instruments, trans. Iris Urwin, (Westport, Conn.: Greenwood Press, 1978). For a technical history and description of players, see Arthur W. J. G. Ord-Hume, *Pianola: The History of the Self-Playing Piano* (London: George Allen & Unwin, 1981).

6   This is Paul Théberge's point, which I am making more explicit; see his *Any Sound You Can Imagine: Making Music/Consuming Technology* (Hanover, N.H.: Wesleyan University Press, University Press of New England, 1997), 28–29. See also Thomas Christensen, "Public Music in Private Spaces: Piano-Vocal Scores and the Domestication of Opera," in *Music and the Cultures of Print*, ed. Kate van Orden (New York: Garland, 2000), 67–94.

7   Chanan, "The Player Piano,"74.

8   "One View of the Music Roll Problem," *Player Piano* 1 (July 1911): 6; see also *Player Piano* (October 1911): 3, and (November 1911): 12, for different sides of the issue.

9   A number of authors claim that roll manufacturers met and agreed on a standard-format roll. See, for example, for 1905, Théberge, "Any Sound You Can Imagine," 29; for 1908, Harvey N. Roehl, *Player Piano Treasury: The Scrapbook History of the Mechanical Piano in America*, 2nd ed. (Vestal, N.Y.: Vestal Press, 1973), 12; or for 1910, Ord-Hume, *Pianola*, 116. But I have seen neither convincing, independent evidence of this meeting nor anything except the gradual emergence of 88-note rolls (able to play the whole piano) as a standard around 1910; see "The Standardization of Music Roll Catalogues: The Player Monthly Makes a Carefully Considered Plea for an Understanding on this Subject—Suggests Standardized Numberings and Classification—Why not English Instead of German or French Titles?—Interesting Subject Interestingly Treated," *Music Trade Review* 50 (18 June 1910): 35. The unidentified author of this article notes the recent success of 88-note rolls, urges accessible standards for music terminology, and wants more rolls: "The literature of music rolls must be made coextensive with that of the printed scores" (35).

10 Dieter Hildebrandt, *Pianoforte: A Social History of the Piano*, trans. Harriet Goodman (New York: George Braziller, 1988), 79.

11 The value (as opposed to the number) of pianos produced annually in the United States peaked in 1919 at $94.5 million, suggesting that Americans were progressively buying "better" (i.e., more expensive) instruments, whether as upgrades or as first pianos (Department of Commerce, Bureau of the Census, "Musical Instruments and Phonographs," in *Census of Manufactures, 1921* [Washington, D.C.: Government Printing Office, 1924], table 7, 15).

12 Robert S. Lynd and Helen Merrell Lynd, *Middletown: A Study in Modern American Culture* (New York: Harcourt, Brace & World, 1929), 244. For the 50 percent figure, see *Zanesville and 36 Other American*

Communities: A Study of Markets and of the Telephone as a Market Index (New York: The Literary Digest, 1927).

13 Quoted here is Craig H. Roell's *The Piano in America, 1890-1940* (Chapel Hill: University of North Carolina Press, 1989), 74. For full details, see William Geppert, *The Official Guide to Piano Quality*, 4th ed. (New York: n.p., 1916), 12.

14 See Roell, *The Piano in America*, chapter 1.

15 Edward Wilson, *Diary of the Discovery Expedition to the Antarctic Regions, 1901-4*, ed. Ann Savours (New York: Humanities Press, 1967), 48. Wilson's comment that he made "old Shakle[ton] very homesick" with the machine indicates something of the class-bound banter of the officers' mess where Chopin and other "old friends" helped pass the time.

16 Implicit in such remarks was a swipe at dilettante women *readers* of music, just as male pundits two generations earlier had sniped at supposedly dilettante women *writers* "scribbling" fiction.

17 Dolge, *Pianos and Their Makers*, 1: 131, 160.

18 Geppert, *The Official Guide to Piano Quality*, 19.

19 For these and other advertising copy see Roehl, *Player Piano Treasury*, 17.

20 Catalogs of 1884 and 1899, respectively, Library of Congress, Division of Performing Arts, Washington, D.C.

21 Sousa, "The Menace of Mechanical Music," 279.

22 "Player-Piano Nomenclature: Words to Use and Avoid," *Player Piano* 1, no. 5 (September 1911): 5-6.

23 See Geppert, *The Official Guide to Piano Quality*, 131-32; and Roell, *The Piano in America*, 74-75.

24 Roehl, *Player Piano Treasury*, 54.

25 Jessie B. Broekhoven, *How to Play the World's Most Wonderful Musical Instrument, The Player Piano* (Cincinnati: Church-Beinkamp Co., 1916), 5.

26 Fred James Hill, *Musical Expression through the Player Piano* (Chicago: n.p., 1913), 5, Library of Congress, Division of Performing Arts, Washington, D.C.

27 Lester C. Singer, *Singer's System of Player Piano Instructions* (Chicago: n.p., 1919), 7-14, Library of Congress, Division of Performing Arts, Washington, D.C.

28 These details are from advertisements quoted in Roehl's *Player Piano Treasury*, 54.

29 Broekhoven, *How to Play the World's Most Wonderful Musical Instrument*, 7.

30 *Arguments before the Committees on Patents of the Senate and House of Representatives, Cojointly, on the Bills S. 6330 and H.R. 19853; To Amend and Consolidate the Acts Respecting Copyright, June 6, 7, 8, and 9* (Washington, D. C.: Government Printing Office, 1906), 119, empha-

sis added; reprinted in E. Fulton Brylawski and Abe Goldman, eds., *Legislative History of the 1909 Copyright Act*, vol. 4 (South Hackensack, N.J.: Fred B. Rothman and Co., 1976).

31 Ibid. Emphasis added.

32 209 U.S. 1 (1908). The tacit knowledge or sense that the holes *are* a form of notation is readily available to users of the rolls, because there is a potential hole across the roll for each key of the keyboard. The roll in effect offers tiny, consecutive pictures of the keyboard, with keys depressed (holes) or not (paper).

33 Auto Pneumatic Action Co., quoted in Roehl, *Player Piano Treasury*.

34 See Robert Craft, "The Composer and the Phonograph," *High Fidelity* 7 (June 1957): 34–5, 99–100 which mentions Stravinsky's piano rolls. See also Denis Hall, "The Great Piano Roll Controversy," *ICRC* (May 1995): 57–67; and Gregor Benko and William Santaella, "The Piano Roll Legacy," *High Fidelity* (July 1967): 51–53; and clipping file, International Piano Archives, University of Maryland, College Park. What is called "overdubbing" today was also available to the makers of standard (nonreproducing) rolls. Remember that the success of ragtime coincided with the success of the player piano.

35 *Baker v. Selden* involved a system of bookkeeping, and the Court had ruled that Selden was not due any protection for the blank forms or "utilitarian instrumentalities" of his system just because he had published a book describing them. The decision drew a distinction between Selden's book and "the art" it illustrates. It continues to be cited in cases regarding the nonauthorship of data and helps explain why computer programming languages are in the public domain and why source code can be such a vigilantly kept trade secret. The term "utilitarian instrumentality" was used by Albert H. Walker, a patent expert who testified in *Hearings before the Committees on Patents, March 26, 27, and 28* (Washington, D.C.: Government Printing Office, 1908), 279; reprinted in Brylawski and Goldman, *Legislative History of the 1909 Copyright Act*, vol. 5. The ruling (101 U.S. 100 [1880]) continues to be cited, for example, in *Feist Publications, Inc. v. Rural Telephone Services Co., Inc.* (499 U.S. 340 [1991]), on instrumentality and authorship with regard to telephone books. Programming languages are difficult to protect as intellectual properties because while *descriptions* of them (i.e., manuals, help files) are easily protected with copyright, their instrumentality is not. Patents might work, but to be patented an invention must be thoroughly described, and thereby revealed to competitors. Secrecy thus remains an attractive alternative to intellectual property.

36 During the copyright hearing it became clear that the Aeolian music-roll company had maneuvered to protect itself in the event of the passing of the bill by signing exclusive contracts with virtually all of the American music publishers.

Scott Curtis

STILL/MOVING

Digital Imaging and Medical Hermeneutics

Digital technology has changed the image of medicine, just as it has touched and transformed nearly every other aspect of our lives. From the mundane tasks of billing and recordkeeping to the weightier duties of diagnosis and prognosis, computers have revolutionized all aspects of medical care. Nowhere is this "digital revolution" more visible than in the radiologist's laboratory. Imaging technologies such as computed tomography (CT), magnetic resonance imaging (MRI), and positron emission tomography (PET) have captured the imagination of doctors, patients, and the media, while fundamentally changing the way analog technologies, such as X rays, are used. Yet for all the novelty of these ways of seeing, they are, in many respects, not new at all; in a way, digital technology has revolutionized nothing in medical research and diagnosis. The rapid dissemination of these techniques and the voracious appetite for new processes and technologies (recalling the fervor for X rays at the turn of the century) indicate, in fact, the extent to which these imaging methods are part of a well-established tradition in medicine. This tradition certainly includes Western medicine's long-standing dependence on technology,[1] but more important, it includes the ways in which these technologies are created and used in daily medical routine. In other words, the digital revolution in medical imaging, like all revolutions, did not completely overthrow what preceded it; indeed, this particular revolution owes much to the analog approaches that came before.

There are any number of points of entry for a comparative history of analog and digital medical imaging. One could focus on the history of the technology by examining the similarities and differences in "hardware" and "software" design.[2] We could emphasize the history of production by comparing the adjustments to the apparatus (as well as those required of the patient and the doctor) necessary to create a "legible" image. Or we could stress a history of reception by concentrating on the function of analog and digital images in day-to-day operations. I am interested in a specific problem within this last approach: how physicians "read" medical images—specifically, moving medical images—and how their interpretative procedures have changed with the advent of digital technologies. I will argue that, in fact, not much has changed. Physicians use digital images in much the same way that they have used analog images. This is, in itself, perhaps not surprising. After all, how else would we expect doctors to use them? I do not want to discount the novelty of these digital imaging technologies, but the *use* of images has implications for their production. If digital images are used just as analog images were employed, then it also follows that the very design of these "new" technologies has appropriated "old" procedures and practices. Once appropriated, these established protocols risk being subsumed into the category of "the new"—their history forgotten—and the "revolution" becomes complete. In the name of historical accuracy, if nothing else, it is important to demonstrate just how much these new technologies owe to their historical antecedents.

On a grander note, I also believe there is an essential continuity between the way physicians *understand* analog and digital medical images, which points to hermeneutic dilemmas at the basis of modern medicine. Grander still, a study of medical hermeneutics reveals the deeper connection between medicine and the humanities. Not only do they share a common object—our mortality or finitude—they share an interpretive approach. If medicine concerns itself with the confrontation between life and death, and if the humanities similarly focus on the human condition, ultimately both attempt to understand their objects (the human body, cultural texts) in the same way. That is, both approach their objects with a common hermeneutic strategy. This strategy, as we shall see, involves conceptual movements between part and whole, depth and surface, past and present, and stillness and movement.

I believe that medicine and film studies have an especially strong connection in this regard; a shared interpretive approach that is evoked by *moving* medical images, which challenge physicians with the same problems of understanding as the living human body. Moving medical images recapitulate especially clearly some of the fundamental, confounding issues of medical representation, such as the creation and interpretation of "legible" images. How does one create an image of the human body that captures only the pertinent details but still can be understood by one's audience? This is also an issue in film studies, where histories of production are tempered by histories of reception due to the constant negotiation between filmmaking and moviegoing, and where the interpretation of moving images must take into account issues of textuality and temporality. "Legibility," therefore, is one of the most important issues shared by medicine and film studies.

"Legibility" is not a given in medical imaging. Since the sixteenth century, at least, medical illustrators have had to contend with the overwhelming, often mysterious detail of the human body. Given the pedagogical function of medical illustration, the doctor and/or illustrator found it necessary to "interpret" the detail and to manage it by means of visual emphasis or omission. That is, illustrators could not conceivably replicate every detail of the section of the body under scrutiny—they had to make choices about what to emphasize and what to omit in the illustration.[3] With the emergence of photography in the nineteenth century, this problem of managing detail became even more acute, because it seemed that the camera recorded without emphasis, or at least that this new medium required different methods of "visual pointing." With both medical illustration and photography, physicians tried to strike a balance between construction and recording, between subjectivity and objectivity. The same is true for digital technologies; the magnetic resonance imager generates an overwhelming amount of information in an acceptably "objective" way, but that information must be modulated, selected, and processed by the radiologist and his or her staff in order to create a legible—that is, readable, interpretable, productive—image.

The techniques for managing detail in medical imaging have a history of their own. In 1543, for example, Andreas Vesalius pro-

vided a familiar, hence immediately legible, context for his anatomical illustrations by giving the bodies shapes that recalled classical sculpture.[4] Nineteenth-century medical photography organized
its images using conventions borrowed from studio portraiture,
demonstrating that, despite claims to total objectivity, aesthetic
standards have always played a significant role in medical illustration.[5] With the introduction of *moving* images to medical research and diagnosis, the question of detail was complicated by an
additional factor—time—which required another set of "management techniques." These techniques balance the aesthetic and scientific, the subjective and the objective. Digital medical imaging—
although dominated by the *still* image—incorporates management
techniques learned from the *moving* medical image.

In this essay, then, I try to accomplish two things. First, in an effort
to historicize digital imaging technologies and their use, I briefly
survey the history of three techniques for managing and interpreting the moving medical image: the spot film, the looped film strip,
and the act of tracing images from motion pictures onto paper. Each
of these techniques finds its echo in digital medical imaging, such as
the captured "screen shot" from an echocardiogram, the repeated
cycle in a cine-MRI of the human heart, or the edge-enhancement
techniques common to most image-processing software. I argue
that the function and even the design of digital medical imaging
technologies incorporate methods of analysis common to analog
medical images.

Second, and perhaps more important, in an effort to draw connections between medicine and film studies—and to understand the
hermeneutics they share—I argue that even though medical imaging is overwhelmingly "still," it cannot be understood apart from
the "moving." The dialectic of stillness and movement plays an important role in understanding the creation and interpretation of
medical images in general. But in a broader sense, moving images in
medical diagnosis and research enact important dilemmas of representation and interpretation at the very heart of medicine. Just as
medicine must contend with an ephemeral, moving, vital object—
the human body—so must physicians who integrate moving images
in their research (for precisely its ersatz vitality) come to grips with
an elusive, temporal object. The human body is oppugnantly *alive*,
frustratingly resistant to contemplation, study, and interpretation;
the history of medicine could be written as a history of attempts

to tame—to hold *still*—the unruly body through such techniques as autopsy and illustration. In this sense, medicine's foundational hermeneutic dilemma rests on a dialectic of movement and stillness that is mimicked by the use of motion pictures in medicine and is reenacted in digital medical imaging techniques.

This dialectic is significant for its close relation to the line between life and death, which I explore throughout this paper. The essay is divided into six sections. I begin with a discussion of hermeneutics and its relation to the human body and its representations, before arguing for the privileged status in medicine of moving images of the human body. Foucault's *Birth of the Clinic* will offer an opportunity to discuss the relation between life and death, while a discussion of film and photographic theory will connect that relation to stillness and movement. Finally, I present a survey of a variety of management techniques in digital medical imaging and end with their implications for changing conceptions of life and death.

Medical Hermeneutics

The pillars of Nature's temple are alive and sometimes yield perplexing messages.—BAUDELAIRE, *Les Fleurs du Mal*

Before we can discuss the relation between movement and stillness in medicine—and in the use of moving images in medicine—we need to clarify the concept of "medical hermeneutics." First, what is hermeneutics? Hermeneutics has been defined traditionally as the theory and method of interpretation, especially of the Bible. If, theoretically speaking, the presence of the speaker behind his or her spoken word ensures clarity and comprehension, the absence of the author of a written text generates a gap in understanding that must be bridged by interpretation.[6] Difficult passages of the Bible required some interpretation in order to square them with other passages, as well as with the goals and standards of the community. In the early nineteenth century, Friedrich Schleiermacher extended hermeneutics to include all texts, not just the Bible, and theorized the method by which we interpret them. According to Schleiermacher, this method, the means to bridge the gap between the text and understanding, entailed a conceptual movement between the text and its parts. "Complete knowledge always involves an apparent circle," Schleiermacher says, "that each part can be understood only out of the whole to which it belongs, and vice versa. All knowledge which is scientific must be constructed in this way."[7] This is known as the "hermeneutic circle": understanding's incessant movement between levels of the text.[8]

Other theorists expanded the notion of hermeneutics to include other types of "texts," each type requiring a different kind or number of "hermeneutic circles."[9] Johann Gustav Droysen applied hermeneutics to history and argued that historians circle between past and present.[10] Sigmund Freud, as Paul Ricoeur argues, saw the human mind as a text and based his hermeneutic method on a surface/depth model.[11] With these models and with hermeneutics in general, there are (at least) two types of circularity. There is a movement between levels of the object (part/whole, past/present, conscious/unconscious), and there is a circularity in the process itself: the object of study is tailored by the interpretation, which simultaneously calls for a retooling of the mechanics of interpretation brought to bear on the object. In other words, the gap between text and understanding is bridged by the circle, but it leaves neither untouched. There is always a mutual dependence and intermingling between "text" and "reader." Hermeneutics implies, then, a "dialectic" that—for the purposes of this essay—connotes analysis, transformation, and recursion (repeated action).[12]

So what is the role of "reading" and "interpretation" in medicine? What is unique about medical hermeneutics? And, perhaps more fundamentally, what, exactly, does the medical profession "read"? Is there a text in this examination room? In one sense, modern medicine has always tried to make the body legible; if Biblical hermeneutics recalls the incarnation of God's word in text, or the Word made flesh, then medical hermeneutics reverses this equation to give us the flesh made word. Yet even the body itself is not the sole "text" of the clinical encounter. Beyond the physical examination of the patient, there is the patient's medical "history" and the images, charts, and graphs from the laboratory, not to mention the patient's own experience of the illness that prompted the call to the doctor.[13] But it is not as if these are static texts just waiting to be explicated.[14] Like the historian, the physician must actively bring these texts into being before/while bringing to bear the interpretative procedures. In any case, the text of medicine is constantly shifting and multiple. This is even more true if the ostensible object of study in medicine is not the body but disease and death. The healthy human body is important as a model or ideal of normalcy, but even that is defined against and dependent on a conception of pathology.[15] Judging from healthcare's current focus, disease seems to be the real object of medicine; the human body is only its localization, its *visualization*. The body makes disease manifest, but disease itself is imperceptible; is cancer the collection of cancerous cells, the process that created the cancerous cells, or a category that encompasses all the symptoms brought on by the cancerous cells? These questions are disputed even today. Medicine, therefore, attempts to describe and diagnose things that it cannot see, imperceptible processes or inaccessible entities. The relatively modern attempts to visualize lesions requires an apparatus—both technological and interpretive—that signals a fundamental blindness in the medical gaze.

It is not that physicians are groping in the dark, but they deal with inherently ephemeral, transient, and imperceptible phenomena: fleeting fevers, real and phantom pain, invisible internal functions. Doctors read signs and symptoms as clues to processes that are inaccessible to direct observation, making medical hermeneutics a *semiotic* enterprise. Interpretation in medicine means reading signs (which are usually illegible to the lay public) against a larger context in order to arrive at a diagnosis or prognosis. (Of course, this larger context involves institutions and power relations, not only between doctor and patient, but between doctor and administrator, between doctor and staff, and between doctors.) Indeed, the hermeneutic circle in medicine encompasses not only part/whole, but also present/past (life/death), surface/depth, and—as we shall see—stillness/movement.

This hermeneutic activity is fundamentally speculative. Herein lies an interpretive model that, as Carlo Ginzburg notes, has informed the human sciences generally. Art history and history, literary criticism and psychoanalysis also see visible signs (e.g., brushstrokes, aphasia) as clues to deeper, imperceptible patterns (e.g., authorship, childhood trauma). For Ginzburg, the humanities owe their hermeneutics to an age-old semiosis at the core of medical practice. Furthermore, Ginzburg argues, both medicine and the human sciences are "highly qualitative disciplines, in which the object is the study of individual cases, situations, and documents, *precisely because they are individual*."[16] This focus on the individual case —even if it is meant to represent a larger group—limits the ability to quantify the data. In other words, because no two cases are exactly alike and no two manifestations of disease identical, medicine will remain an inexact science. Medicine can never attain the certainty of, say, classical physics because medical knowledge, like historical knowledge, is "indirect, presumptive, conjectural."[17] Each human body, like each historical event, is slightly different from the next, which makes it difficult to arrive at universal laws. The living human body and the past are both fundamentally resistant to quantification and direct perception.

What makes the body so imperceptible, so resistant to quantification? Not only are its internal functions hidden, but the body itself is dynamic. It *moves*. It is difficult to measure something when all the variables are constantly changing, or when the object itself won't stand still. Indeed, it is hard to *comprehend* (from the Latin: to grasp or to seize) something that is alive. This conundrum recalls the troubled philosophical relationship between the real and the ideal: what is the relationship between the individual, disorderly, *temporal* object and the *intemporal* form it takes in our concept of that thing? How do we comprehend that which exists in time?[18] Baudelaire's lines above remind us of this cognitive dilemma as it relates to medicine: the body ("Nature's temple") is "alive" and, for that very reason, unreadable, or at least "perplexing."

All this is not to say that doctors cannot make good (hence lifesaving) guesses. They do, and they work around these hermeneutic dilemmas quite well. Medical images and imaging techniques are an important part of the solution. Medical images (photographs, CT scans, etc.) make the imperceptible perceptible, hold the body still, and can provide the basis for quantification. An anatomical illustration, for example, reveals the hidden structures of the human body, allows the physician time to contemplate and to study these structures, and, if exact enough, can provide a sense of scale or even the grounds for measurement. Despite the fundamentally unquantifiable character of the human body and disease, modern medicine has gone to great lengths to ground its uncertainty in the certainty of science and its quantitative methods. These strides began in the late eighteenth century, accelerated in the late nineteenth century, and today have turned into a full gallop.[19] Imaging techniques have been integral to this scientific, quantitative approach. Even more important, however, medical images have allowed physicians to *comprehend*, however briefly, the elusive human body. From Vesalius's engraved sections to the Visible Human Project's digitized sections of human anatomy,[20] representations of the human body have been medicine's conceptual prosthesis, its central, illuminating trope.

Medicine and the Moving Image

The fixation onto a corpse of a segment of immobile space
may resolve the problems presented by the temporal developments
of a disease. — Foucault, *The Birth of the Clinic*

Moving images of the body are a privileged example of medical imaging. Projected, these images come "alive" and mimic the detail and continuity of the living body. As such, they present physicians or researchers with the same hermeneutic problems as the living body: they are temporal and ephemeral, hard to read and difficult to grasp. But whether on celluloid, on videotape, or on digital media, moving images are also much more readily manipulated than the living body, much more malleable and controllable. In this regard, they are analogous to the cadaver — the domesticated and revealing, but also meager, version of the vibrant body. Foucault's comment above indicates that dissection and autopsy were at one time important solutions to the physician's hermeneutic dilemma. The temporal conundrums presented by disease and by the body were to some extent solved by medicine's ability to examine the intemporal cadaver. In other words, the corpse played a vital role in the formation of modern medicine. Both incarnations of the moving image (the projected image and the celluloid) compare more favorably to the living and the dead than medical drawings or photography, and this physical and functional analogy is the basis of a more profound and complicated relation between life, death, and moving medical images.

In other words, there is a deeply *philosophical* connection between film and modern medicine, a structural homology, affinity, and shared hermeneutic that commentators have neglected. Walter Benjamin's comparison between the surgeon and the cameraman comes the closest. In a discussion of the changing perception of art and reality in the age of their mechanical reproducibility, Benjamin explores the difference between painting and cinema by way of a medical analogy:

Here the question is: How does the cameraman compare with the painter? To answer this we take recourse to an analogy with a surgical operation. . . . The magician heals a sick person by the laying on of hands; the surgeon cuts into the patient's body. The magician maintains the natural distance between the patient and himself. . . . The surgeon does exactly the reverse; he greatly diminishes the distance between himself and the patient by penetrating into the patient's body. . . . Magician and surgeon compare to painter and cameraman. The painter maintains in his work a natural distance from reality, the cameraman penetrates deeply into its web.[21]

From this analogy, Benjamin finds two opposed ways of representing reality. On one hand, painting presents a view of "immediate reality" from a distance; there is a "natural" distance between the object viewed (such as a landscape) and the painter, a distance that is respected in the painter's appropriation of a scene. On the other hand, a movie set's view is so cluttered with technology that the "immediate reality" must be *extracted* by a special, almost "surgical" procedure involving correct camera placement and editing before it is presented on screen. Cinema's illusion of an immediate reality free of all artifice is possible only *because of* its highly mediated, technological nature. The difference between these two art forms, then, is the difference between the physical and psychic distance associated with painting's "aura" (comparable to the aura of the magician) and the physical and psychic penetration associated with motion pictures (and the surgeon).

Benjamin therefore theorizes the common connection between cinema and medicine to be one of technique, attitude, or approach. It tells us much about technological mediation and the relation between subjectivity and objectivity. The apparently "objective" (i.e., unmediated) medical image of the human body is also highly mediated by technology. The medical image, as a "pure aspect of reality,"[22] is extracted by a variety of techniques and technologies. Indeed, in the twentieth century, the very possibility of anything even approaching "objectivity" in science and medicine depends on technological mediation.[23] The moving image is only one weapon in this arsenal. Benjamin's is an important point of comparison, but it does not touch on the connections between medicine's preoccupation with life and death and cinema's essential relation to this duality.

Likewise, the comparatively few book-length studies of medicine and cinema tend to focus on either questions of technique (how these films are made) or on the political and ethical implications of the close historical connection between medicine and moving images. For example, Anthony Michaelis's valuable survey of scientific cinema, *Research Films in Biology, Anthropology, Psychology, and Medicine*, outlines in detail the technical issues involved in filming the human body and other natural phenomena. For Michaelis, however, film's legitimacy as a scientific instrument is obvious and uncontestable. Commenting on the astonishing variety of techniques employed in scientific cinema, he states, "In all of these we have discovered that only the quantitative use of cinematography, combined with frame-analysis, has produced the maximum amount of research data of which the motion picture film is inherently capable."[24] In scientific cinema, there is a double "extraction": the camera penetrates and captures a reality otherwise invisible, and then, through quantitative analysis, useful, objective data is "extracted" from the image itself.

On the other hand, Lisa Cartwright's important study, *Screening the Body*, is concerned primarily with the status of the human body under the medical gaze, and with cinema's contribution to and complicity in this disciplinary surveillance. Cartwright argues that "the cinematic apparatus can be considered as a cultural technology for the discipline and management of the human body, and that the long history of bodily analysis and surveillance in medicine and science is critically tied to the history of the development of the cinema as a popular cultural institution and a technological apparatus."[25] While Michaelis is interested in what Benjamin might call the process of penetration and extraction, Cartwright is interested in the trials of the human body as a consequence of this process. Concepts such as "discipline" and "medical gaze" immediately signal Cartwright's debt to Michel Foucault. But because of her interest in the political consequences of the relation between cinema and the body, her theoretical framework depends primarily on the investigation of power and the body in *Discipline and Punish*, rather than on Foucault's earlier work on medicine proper, *The Birth of the Clinic*.[26] There are, however, important insights in *Birth* that have been overshadowed by his later work. In the following section, I chart a course between Michaelis's interest in the purely technical and Cartwright's interest in the ethical, and explore, with the help of Foucault, the philosophical affinity between medicine and cinema.

Life / Death

We say, for instance, that man is mortal, and seem to think that the ground of his death is in external circumstances only; so that if this way of looking were correct, man would have two special properties, vitality and—also—mortality. But the true view of the matter is that life, as life, involves the germ of death, and that the finite, being radically self-contradictory, involves its own self-suppression.
—HEGEL, *Hegel's Logic*

Foucault's *The Birth of the Clinic* is an "archaeology of medical perception," an account of the reconception of disease around the turn of the nineteenth century. During the seventeenth and eighteenth centuries, a "botanical" model of disease flourished, with accompanying ontological and taxonomic implications. Disease was conceived as a foreign essence; it had its own "life cycle" independent of its human host. Indeed, its connection to the human body was only coincidental. Like a plant, disease flourished in its "natural environment," which was thought to be the home (as opposed to a hospital), and to diagnose the illness correctly it was necessary for the physician to let the disease develop and reveal its true essence. Once the disease displayed itself fully through its signs and symptoms, it could be placed in a classificatory scheme—that is, placed in relation to other diseases—and thereby accurately named and understood. Foucault calls this the "medicine of species"; disease existed conceptually, as an essence that was part of a larger taxonomy.

In the early nineteenth century, a new conception of disease grew out of and alongside changes in medical practice, especially the rise of case-oriented, hospital-based medicine and pathological anatomy. The existing knowledge of diseases and their symptoms was superimposed on the relatively new study of pathological tissues. Recordkeeping and autopsy, for example, changed the structure of medical knowledge, eventually localizing disease in the human body, specifically in lesions. Contrary to the medicine of species, this approach advocated intervention and eventually recognized the hospital as the "natural" environment for disease. New forms of observation—what Foucault names "the medical gaze"—grew out of this intersection of hospitals, medical education, case histories, autopsies, and dissection. Foucault chooses to focus on the clinic (a hospital department or stand-alone institution devoted to a particular group of diseases) as an exemplary case study because its attention to individual case *histories* and its intense description of individual facts and their variations brought to light the *temporal* character of disease in a new way. As a result of these configurations, disease was no longer conceived as an ahistorical essence but, as Karl Figlio succinctly describes, as a "historical mode of life which the new pathological anatomy of tissues could visualize, from the moment of insertion until its death with that of the organism, as the rooting, growth, and spreading of lesions. The 'space' of the disease, including its essentially historical character, had become identical with that of the body," a concept that we now find ridiculously obvious, but which Foucault uncovers as being historically constructed.[27]

The most profound effect of this change in the conception of disease is the concomitant reconsideration of the relation between life, disease, and death. Autopsies especially, relatively uncommon before the nineteenth century, became more routine, brought death under closer inspection, and played an important role in the transformation of ideas about life and death. Before the nineteenth century, the dichotomy was clear: life was considered an abundance, death an absence. Death was a boundary designating the absence of vitality, having no positive content of its own: a negativity, a purely quantitative subtraction. According to Foucault, "In eighteenth-century medical thought, death was the absolute fact,"[28] but as pathological anatomists inspected corpses immediately after death, it became clear that death occurred in stages, "multiple and dispersed in time" (142). Death was recognized to be not an "absolute, privileged point at which time stops and moves back," but like disease itself, death "has a teeming presence" (142). And this "teeming presence" spread back into life in the form of lesions, what Figlio aptly characterizes as "lesser and localized deaths."[29]

Autopsy, then, cast doubt on the clear dichotomy between life and death. Death was no longer an ultimate threshold but perhaps the very origin of disease, even an integral part of life itself. Life is not merely riddled with death; the two are absolutely *correlative*, mutually interdependent. And this reciprocity even implies that life is inherently pathological and degenerative. On one hand, death determines a priori the conditions of life, in that the forms of internal organization of the organism could be understood only as different ways of meeting the threat of death.[30] On the other hand, under this scenario life becomes the principal source of its own destruction. When Claude Bernard, one of the most influential physiologists of the nineteenth century, said that "life is death," he meant that "when a part functions, such as muscles, glands, nerves, brain, the substance of these organs is consumed; the organ destroys itself."[31] Even before Bernard, physicians prominent in Foucault's study had concluded that the normal functioning of the organism itself was intrinsically pathogenic, that the action of the organism gave rise to organic lesions; the parts of the body, by the very fact of their action, are pathologically altered (153).[32]

In other words, nineteenth-century physicians conceived a dialectic between life and death. But this discovery was possible only *because of* death—that is, as a result of autopsy and dissection. At this point in the early 1800s, as Foucault notes, "life, disease, and death now form a technical and conceptual trinity. . . . It is from the height of death that one can see and analyse organic dependencies and pathological sequences. . . . The privilege of its intemporality, which is no doubt as old as the consciousness of its imminence, is turned for the first time into a technical instrument that provides a grasp on the truth of life and the nature of its illness" (144). Death not only becomes an object of study, in the form of pathological anatomy—it becomes the basis of study itself: "The analysis of the disease can be carried out only from the point of view of death" (144). It is therefore precisely because of death's intemporality that medicine can obtain a measure of certainty: "Medicine discovered that uncertainty may be treated, analytically, as the sum of a certain number of isolatable degrees of certainty that were capable of rigorous calculation" (97). That is, physicians found the rigor required by professionalization (and compensated for medicine's essentially speculative nature) not in "generality, but in the small number of endlessly repeated elements" (99) accumulated in the hospital and on the autopsy table. "Death," says Foucault, "is the great analyst" (144).

This figurative relation between death and analysis points not only to a relation between stillness and hermeneutics but to the nature of scientific method. "Analysis" and its counterpart "synthesis" are fundamental concepts for scientific investigation. They have been around at least since Plato, but they were most often considered separate procedures for investigating and demonstrating philosophical concepts, different ways to conduct one's thoughts in an orderly fashion.[33] But Sir Isaac Newton, in his *Opticks*, saw "analysis" and "synthesis" as two methods constituting a single procedure. The investigation of empirical phenomena (not concepts) required two mutually interdependent steps: "This Analysis consists in making Experiments and Observations, and in drawing Conclusions from them by Induction." Synthesis, on the other hand, "consists in assuming the Causes discover'd, and establish'd as Principles, and by them explaining the Phaenomena proceeding from them, and proving the Explanations."[34] Analysis consists of breaking the empirical phenomena into manageable units (isolation by experiment), while synthesis means recombining these units into a larger picture. Synthesis is therefore a control mechanism, a method of verification absolutely vital to the entire procedure. In scientific method, then, analysis and synthesis are two sides of the same coin: decomposition and recomposition, breaking down and building back up.

Condillac, the patron philosopher in Foucault's history, offers this similar definition of analysis (and also refers to the philosophical function of this procedure): "Be that as it may, to analyze, in my opinion, is nothing more than an operation arising from the concurrence of those operations which went before. It consists only in compounding and decompounding our ideas, in order to compare them differently, and to discover the relations among themselves, together with the new ideas which they are capable of producing. This analysis is the true secret of discoveries, because it makes us attend to the origin of things."[35] Foucault's contribution to the history of medicine is his description of the way in which clinical practice, through "the medical gaze," incorporated the correlative relation between analysis and synthesis. Even though it is called a "gaze," Foucault stresses that "the medical gaze embraces more than said by the word 'gaze' alone" (164).[36] Newton's discussion of method in the context of a project on light and optics does not make an explicit connection between analysis and vision. But Foucault's discussion of medical perception recognizes both that, while perhaps dominated by the visual register, the gaze encompasses other forms of observation and that analysis is necessarily bound up with the scientific employment of these tools. It is a "gaze that touches, hears, and, moreover, not by essence or necessity, sees" (164). Not just close observation, not just the trained touch of the physician, not just descriptive language, but all three and more, the gaze is "an act . . . that joins, in a single movement, the element and the connection of the elements among themselves" and is therefore "really no more than Condillac's analysis put into practice in medical perception" (94). The gaze is not merely a way of seeing; it incorporates the scientific method by mapping the correlative relation between analysis and synthesis onto the mutual interdependency of death and life.

"This explains the enthusiasm that Bichat and his disciples immediately felt for the discovery of pathological anatomy," writes Foucault, "they rediscovered analysis in the body itself; they revealed, in depth, the order of the surface of things; they defined for disease a system of *analytical classes* in which the element of pathological decomposition was the principle of generalization of morbid species" (131). In other words, these physicians were excited by the discovery of a homology between object and method on a variety of different levels: Condillac's method of "compounding and decompounding" is discovered to be also a principle in how tissues function. The "isolatable degrees of certainty" found in "the small number of endlessly repeated elements"—that is, the trend toward isolation and quantification in method—finds its match in lesions, those "lesser and localized deaths."

This last analogy between "death" and "certainty" is not flippant. It is no mere coincidence that pathological anatomy developed as a discipline during the same period that clinicians were defining their method, for this method depended on "the stable, visible, legible basis of death" (196). Nor is it simply that modern medicine is based on, as some have argued, an "epistemology of the corpse."[37] It signifies a breakthrough in medical hermeneutics, a work-around to the fundamental dilemma of medical diagnosis: the living body. Death offers the time to contemplate, to study; it holds still the body. At the same time, the knowledge that comes from the corpse is meaningful only in relation to the living body and the historical, temporal nature of disease. As one medical historian put it: "As soon as one used the ear or the finger to recognize on the living body what was revealed on the corpse by dissection, the description of diseases, and therefore therapeutics took quite a new direction."[38] The gaze and the language of description rests on the stability of the corpse, but moves as well, newly informed, to the living body. This back-and-forth movement—between life and death, present and past, part and whole—exemplifies the medical task.

Still/Moving

Words move, music moves
Only in time; but that which is only living
Can only die. Words, after speech, reach
Into the silence. Only by the form, the pattern,
Can words or music reach
The stillness, as a Chinese jar still
Moves perpetually in its stillness.
—T. S. ELIOT, "Burnt Norton"

So what does Foucault's archaeology of medical perception mean for the subject at hand? How does the relation between life and death concern the way physicians read the medical moving image? If, before the nineteenth century, "one knows death only by its opposition to life, in the same way that rest is manifested by its direct contrast with motion,"[39] the history outlined by Foucault troubles this strict polarity on both levels: between life and death, and between stillness and movement. Certainly, the connection between the pairs is not coincidental: "still" connotes "inanimate" or even "dead"—as in "still life" (*nature morte* is the French equivalent)—as well as "timeless," "motionless," and "unchanging." Yet its relation to movement should not be considered one of strict opposition, as Eliot's lines above indicate. The complex relationship between stillness and movement, discontinuity and continuity, divisibility and indivisibility go back as far as Zeno of Elea's paradoxes, which were intended to deny the reality of motion for the sake of a monistic philosophy, or a philosophy of "the one" (i.e., indivisible reality).[40] Zeno did this by contradicting the commonsense belief in the existence of "the many" (i.e., distinguishable qualities and things capable of motion). For Zeno, therefore, movement and indivisibility are opposed; his paradoxes were designed to reduce to absurdity our assumptions about the divisibility of phenomena. Modern science, intent on this division, overcame Zeno's paradoxes when it created logically consistent mathematical concepts of continuity and infinity that could promote quantitative approaches.[41]

Henri Bergson returned to this issue in *Creative Evolution*, where he found, contra Zeno, that movement and indivisibility are not opposed but inextricably linked. Bergson maintains that the universe is in a perpetual state of flux; change and movement are the only constants, the only true reality. Our common perception cannot hope to grasp this flux, it can only extract determinate moments and hold them up as reality. Therefore, Bergson says, "our perception manages to solidify into discontinuous images the fluid continuity of the real." Furthermore, he argues, the mechanism of cinema follows this pattern and reflects, therefore, our perceptual process, which science codifies into experimental method. In its insistence on finding the moments of "stillness" in the constantly moving flux, modern science is essentially "cinematographical."[42] Science, then, works like cinema in that the uncertainty of flux is traded for, or finds its basis in, lots of "little certainties" (which gives new meaning to Jean-Luc Godard's dictum that "cinema is the truth 24 times a second").[43]

In modern science, we can find stillness in movement: the "determinate moments" of discontinuity extracted from our perceptual impression of constant movement. In modern art, by contrast, we find movement in stillness: Eliot's Chinese jar; futurism's "visible motion"; or cubism's "vision in motion."[44] Photography seems to capture this tension best, especially since the development of instantaneous photography in the 1880s. As Tom Gunning notes, instantaneous photography cast the human body in a different light, or more precisely, in a different time: the time of the instant, caught in awkward and ungraceful (even "disgraceful") poses.[45] The snapshot ripped the instant out of its temporal flow. That flow is nevertheless deeply imbedded within it; its moments are "explosive," just waiting (forever) to detonate. Surrealist André Breton described this dialectic of stillness and movement within the photograph as "convulsive beauty": "There can be no beauty at all, as far as I am concerned—convulsive beauty—except at the cost of affirming the reciprocal relations linking the object seen in its motion and its repose. I regret not having been able to furnish, along with this text, the photograph of a speeding locomotive abandoned for years to the delirium of a virgin forest."[46] Breton's imagined photograph captures several registers of time at once: the blinding speed of modern technology, the geological slowness of nature, and the stillness of repose.

Life and death are echoed in cinema and photography not merely through the representation of movement and stasis. The dialectic between life and death is also captured by the very nature and social functions of film and photography. As André Bazin argues, photography, like all the representational arts, has a "mummy complex" in its attempt at immortality: "By providing a defense against the passage of time," the mummy "satisfied a basic psychological need in man, for death is but the victory of time. To preserve, artificially, his bodily appearance is to snatch it from the flow of time, to stow it neatly, so to speak, in the hold of life."[47] The paradox of photography (and the mummy) is that in this attempt to stow appearance in the hold of life, in this effort to hold life and time, the specter of stasis and death still reigns. Photography, like the mummy, is a double, an effort to preserve the past against what Bazin calls a "second spiritual death."[48] Freud's formulation of the psychological function of the double—and its relation to death—recalls photography's paradox:

> For the "double" was originally an insurance against the destruction of the ego, an "energetic denial of the power of death," as [Otto] Rank says; and probably the "immortal" soul was the first "double" of the body. . . . The same desire led the Ancient Egyptians to develop the art of making images of the dead in lasting materials. Such ideas, however, have sprung from the soil of unbounded self-love, from the primary narcissism which dominates the mind of the child and of primitive man. But when this stage has been surmounted, the "double" reverses its aspect. From having been an assurance of immortality, it becomes the uncanny harbinger of death.[49]

Furthermore, the photograph is like a mummy or a death mask in that there is an *indexical* relationship between the object and its representation, and this necessary relation distinguishes photography and film from the other arts. That is, like a fingerprint or a footprint, the photograph results from a physical connection between the object and the film as the result of a chemical process. Therefore, the object *and* the duration of the photograph is inscribed onto the film. Because it refers not only to the represented object, but also to the (already passed) time of its impression, the photograph is imbued with the tinge of death. For Roland Barthes, this connection to death is tied to photography's immobility: "However 'lifelike' we strive to make it (and this frenzy to be lifelike can only be our mythic denial of an apprehension of death), Photography is a kind of primitive theater, a kind of *Tableau Vivant*, a figuration of the motionless and made-up face beneath which we see the dead."[50]

Barthes finds death also in the photograph's indexicality: "In Photography I can never deny that *the thing has been there*. There is a superimposition here: of reality and of the past. And since this constraint exists only for Photography, we must consider it, by reduction, as the very essence, the *noeme* of Photography. . . . The name of Photography's *noeme* will therefore be: 'That-has-been,' or again: the Intractable" (76–77). And finally: "For Death must be somewhere in a society; if it is no longer (or less intensely) in religion, it must be elsewhere; perhaps in this image which produces Death while trying to preserve life. . . . *Life/Death*: the paradigm is reduced to a simple click" (92). Bazin argues that cinema "embalms time";[51] Barthes, on the other hand, defines photography in opposition to cinema. For Barthes, cinema's temporal rush animates and thus obscures the subtle links to time and death delicately layered in the photograph. Garrett Stewart, however, argues against this strict dichotomy found in most theories of photography.[52] If each frame of a motion picture were counted as a single photogram—a "lesser, localized death"—then cinema, as Bazin implies, is more like a walking mummy, the undead, or the reanimated corpse of Frankenstein's monster. If the photograph implies, in Barthes's terms, "*that-has-been*" and thus death, then cinema only gives the dead a semblance of life. Furthermore, if narrative fiction film must ignore this deathly basis in order to keep going, as Stewart argues, then I would suggest that scientific film, in order to keep its project going, must revel in these fatal moments and ignore their narrative (dramatic) potential.

Barthes mimics the scientist when he admits "what Marey and Muybridge have done as *operators* I myself want to do as *spectator*: I decompose, I enlarge, and, so to speak, I *retard*, in order to have time to *know* at last" (99). And "I have the leisure to observe the photograph with intensity; but also, however long I extend this observation, it teaches me nothing. It is precisely in this *arrest* of interpretation that the Photograph's certainty resides: I exhaust myself realizing that *this-has-been*" (107). The photograph teaches him nothing, refuses real understanding, because its certainty simply *is* (or "*has-been*"). The immobility of the photograph allows us to examine it at leisure, to *know*, but its stasis is ultimately frustrating, I would argue, because stillness alone reveals nothing. Death, by itself, has no meaning. It is only as part of an interpretive dialectic between stillness and movement that the object of the photograph comes to light. The binarisms themselves are heuristic; it is the movement *between* them that brings them to life.

This movement is implied even in the opposite conceptions of death held by Foucault and Barthes. Foucault stresses the stasis of death, its function as stable ground, yet he recognizes its temporal dimension, not only in the unfolding of death in the living body but also in the *necessary* movement from dead to living in the process of analysis. On the other hand, Barthes's emphasis on the "*that-has-been*" gives his conception of death a particularly poignant, temporal character, even while he focuses on the still photograph. For both theorists, the nature of death can be understood only through its opposite: if static, through temporality; if temporal, through stillness. The corpse or the photograph are comprehensible only through the movement of analysis or the passing of time, each of which, likewise, contain within them the tinge of stasis and death.

Medical film and photography have a relationship to the medical profession's foundational dialectic between life and death that is not merely analogous or metaphorical but ontological as well. Medical films offer a convenient record of phenomena that meets the profession's requirements for objectivity and transmissibility, but their function in medicine is not reducible to this criteria. They are not used simply because they are available; indeed, their function and use in medicine can reveal so much precisely because they are so overdetermined. Specifically, the dialectic of medical hermeneutics—the back-and-forth outlined above—is rehearsed in miniature in the design and interpretation of medical imaging techniques. With medical imaging, of course, the stakes (life and death) are not so high, but the rehearsal is nonetheless inevitably, ontologically tinged with real-life drama. Just as there is a movement from death to life in medicine, so there is a movement from still to moving in medical imaging. This dialectic is embedded in the techniques of reading and managing the detail of the image. In the next section, I focus on a variety of techniques in radiology to illustrate this point.

The individual is understood in the total, and the total from
the individual. . . . The process of understanding is as truly synthetic
as analytic, as truly inductive as deductive.
—DROYSEN, *Outline of the Principles of History*

Probably the best example of the tension between movement and
stillness in radiology is fluoroscopy's "spot film" technique. Invented by Thomas Edison about a month after X rays were publi-
cized in December 1895, the fluoroscope produces a simultaneous,
real-time image of the patient on its translucent screen, which is
coated with a material that fluoresces when exposed to X rays.[53] The
fluoroscope is still in use today; fluoroscopy now refers to the whole
process of presenting a moving X-ray image on a television screen
or on motion picture film. But its advantage (a moving image) is
also its key disadvantage: for decades the image could not be controlled or captured with ease. Because it was not reproducible, the
fluoroscopic image could not be displayed to a group, and therefore
the information obtained by the technique remained "subjective":
the correlation of the images remained completely within the mind
of the physician.[54] On the other hand, the still image of the X-ray
film (or even the moving image of X-ray cinematography) could
be shared and thus was "objective." Submitting a record to group
scrutiny ratifies its objectivity; judgment is not limited to the single
point of view of the physician, but is validated by the group. Objectivity resides in the exchange.

With the development of the "image intensifier" in the 1950s,
the fluoroscope could participate in this exchange. The intensifier
amplified the fluoroscope's dim light (which before could only be
viewed in a darkened room) many times, allowing physicians to
view the image in daylight and record the image on motion picture film or, later, videotape. It also allowed the attachment of a still
camera that could take "spot films" during the examination. As the
examination takes place, the radiologist views the moving image on
the monitor and punctuates the event by taking a still image of certain "determinate moments."[55] Not all moments need to be stilled;
spot films are not, in other words, a Marey-like decomposition of
the event. Instead, these still images function primarily as evidence
of diagnostically significant phenomena, but they also help the radi-

ologist remember his or her "place" within the examination. That is, they function as "bookmarks," they remind the radiologist of the duration of the examination. Bookmarks in novels mark passages, not stoppages; when one returns to a bookmark, the flow of the narrative resumes. The marked point makes sense only in relation to the passage, to the larger contextual movement. In the same way, the spot film indicates a correlative relation between stillness and movement. The spot film makes some sense on its own, but its status as evidence is dependent on the duration of the examination. Likewise, the moving image is more legible when accompanied by the determinate moments marked by the spot films.

This explicit relation between movement and stillness recalls the first moving pictures themselves. As Tom Gunning notes, "the initial reception of motion pictures foregrounded their relation to—and transcendence of—the still image."[56] Inventors and audiences alike associated motion picture cameras and projectors with developments in instantaneous photography. Gunning argues that the first projections by the Lumière brothers in 1895 emphasized this relation between photography and cinema by "starting each projection with the first image as a still, then cranking the machine into motion and endowing that image with life and movement."[57] From the Lumière brothers' projection technique to Hollywood's fondness for Frankenstein's monster and his legacy, the back-and-forth between life and death, between stillness and reanimation, has been a favorite theme in cinema.

Today radiologists reenact that relation between stillness and "life and movement" with the pause button on a videotape player and with digital screen shots of MPEGs. Fetal sonograms, echocardiograms, X-ray angiograms, and others are routinely recorded on videotape or on digital media by the technician and reviewed by the physician, who stops and starts, cues and reviews back and forth. If early cinema audiences were "astonished" by the sudden animation of the lifeless image, and if this animation is the essence and pleasure of cinematic art, then the essence and function of the scientific moving image lies somehow in the opposite approach: the urge is not to start but to stop, not to animate but to suspend. Yet it is never quite so simple. Physicians analyze and synthesize simultaneously, even intuitively, after years of internalizing case studies and methods. Analysis and synthesis become part of the same operation. The relation is akin to that between anatomy and physiology in medicine. Anatomy as a discipline focuses on structure, stillness, the corpse, death; physiology on function, process, the living body, life. The historical relation between them has sometimes been competitive,[58] but they are just as correlative as the other pairs examined here. Each contains part of the other. Analysis and synthesis, like anatomy and physiology, are never in strict opposition nor are they merely complementary, but in practice they are pressed so closely together that they form a single procedure.

The spot film is one way of managing the detail of the image, of controlling its temporal flow for analytical purposes, even if the exact timing of the spot film requires an intuitive relation to movement. Another technique for managing the moving image is the "cine loop." In digital medical imaging, this technique is fairly uncommon, although it is becoming more popular as computer memory and processor speed catch up with the information-intensive requirements of digital moving images. Basically, the term cine loop refers to any sequence of digitized movement that has been set to repeat; the technique is not technology-specific—it can be used in CT, MRI, PET, or even echocardiography. Rhythmic cycles, such as the movement of the lungs during breathing, the bending of joints, or the beating of the heart, are ideal subjects for this technique, but cine loops are used most often in cardiology, which prizes the ability to see the heart function in real time. (The paradox here is that a loop of a heartbeat cycle is not "real time," but only a "virtual" representation of the heart's own repeated, looplike action. In effect, the loop *acts* "real.") To create a digital cine loop, a CT or MRI scanner captures the information and creates still images. Selected, sequential images (for example, at five-degree intervals) are then stored in computer memory and strung together to form a loop. This loop is recorded on videotape or as an MPEG, where it can be examined at leisure and compared to the original sequence of isolated images. The advantages of the loop are obvious: it allows physicians to examine the movement at their leisure while also providing, because of its correlation of space and time, a means of quantification.[59]

Again, this technique recalls forms of early cinema. Precinematic devices such as the zoetrope and the zoopraxinoscope are basically repeating loops. The work of Muybridge and Marey—which focused on finite, rhythmic events, such as a woman descending stairs or a pole vaulter's attempt—also implies repetition. Edison's Kinetoscope contained a looped filmed sequence that would repeat with every new nickel. The content of the scenes filmed for these machines matched the form: a group of blacksmiths hammering rhythmically, a somersaulting dog, circular dances, etc. Even after celluloid was freed from the confines of the peepshow, early cinema continued to feature "latent loops," so to speak: 360-degree panoramas, parades of passing policemen, chases that merely show the same thing over and again.[60]

But the cine loop also has a long history in medicine. As early as 1912, doctors were recording physical conditions and projecting them in loop form.[61] Rudolf Janker, one of the leading radiologists in pre– and post–World War II Germany, developed techniques for representing complete heartbeats on film with looped strips.[62] Ever since, the loop has been a common method of viewing rhythmic action in radiology.[63] Medicine's loop has much in common with both Marey's experiments and Edison's. Marey was less interested in movement for its own sake than as a check against his analytical methods. Marta Braun elaborates: "Marey had cut apart the pictures that made up these earliest film bands and recomposed their movements in slow motion in an electric zoetrope to confirm his analysis in real time. . . . He was working on a projector whose sole function would be to mechanically synthesize the results of his analyzer, slowing down some movements and speeding up others. He was not after a machine that would replicate the continuity of perceived movement: such an apparatus would have been no use to him in his work."[64]

Marey, as one would expect, follows scientific methods scrupulously: movement exists only in relation to stillness, synthesis only in relation to analysis. The cine loop in medicine also embodies this tension between fluidity and fragmentation. However, movement is not merely an experimental control, it also demonstrates what cannot be otherwise seen. While movement in science is reduced and dependent on analysis, movement in medicine still has value unto itself, precisely to the extent that the body itself has value. More important, the repeated action of the loop allows analysis and synthesis to occur at the same time. That is, the loop moves, but its short length and recursion allows one to grasp the movement by holding it in one's mind for a moment. Like a treadmill, on which we move while remaining in the same place, the loop clearly "moves" but is conceptually "still."

Finally, if the loop is in many ways the very basis of cinema, it is also, according to Lev Manovich, the basis of the digital: "Programming involves altering the linear flow of data through control structures, such as 'if/then' and 'repeat/while'; the loop is the most elementary of these control structures."[65] If these control structures allow the data to be modified as it passes from input to output and back again, we have the famous "feedback loop" so central to theories of cybernetics.[66] From the repeated application of algorithms (known as "recursive functions") in programming code to animated GIFs, the loop appears to be the most basic element of the digital world. In medical technology, the design of CT and MRI scanners also implies a loop. Computed tomography and magnetic resonance imaging differ from conventional X rays in that they are not fixed to a single point of view. The machines are shaped like a big doughnut; in CT, X rays are emitted from all around the inside of the ring, in the middle of which lies the patient. (In MRI, strong magnets align the molecules within the patient's body, which then emits electrical energy that is captured by the doughnut.) These scanners therefore capture axial, or cross-sectional, views of the patient's interior. The information is therefore based upon a 360-degree slice of multiple, shifting views that evokes a circle or loop in both design and content.[67]

When physicians today discuss "image analysis," they are usually not referring to the decomposition of movement but to a panoply of digital techniques designed to create more legible images. "Image analysis" refers to the process by which digital information is manipulated to create an image and elements are added so that the image is easier to read. For example, a CT scan of the brain might undergo some colorization in order to illustrate circulation patterns. Or these CT or MRI "slices" may be submitted to "voxel processing" and rendered as a three-dimensional, animated image. In echocardiography, "color flow Doppler" technique generates color-coded images of blood flow velocity. Similarly, echocardiograms are usually processed by the accompanying ultrasound software to generate a cross-sectional view of the heart in order to measure chamber dimensions and wall thickness.[68] Digital images are more manipulable than their analog counterparts; image analysis is a common technique that uses this advantage in order to manage detail digitally and thereby produce more legible images.

Yet even this technique is not new to the digital revolution. Edge-enhancement technology, while standard in the digital realm, is also common in the history of medical cinematography. The filmic image also contained too much information: often researchers would stop the film, project it onto a desk or wall covered with white paper, and trace by hand the outlines of the image, thereby focusing on the significant elements of the frame. Tracing was a standard technique in scientific and medical cinema. R. F. James demonstrated in 1935 how to trace the outlines of organs recorded through X-ray cinematography, and tracing has been repeated often as an analytical procedure throughout the history of radiology.[69] In the sciences, Hans Fortner projected his films of single-cell life-forms onto huge sheets of paper in order to trace cellular movement as a function of time, as did German biologist Willi Kuhl in the 1940s.[70] Arnold Gesell, one of the preeminent experts on child development, made tracings a standard procedure for his work, arguing that "the cinema registers the behavior events in such coherent, authentic and measurable detail that for purposes of psychological study and clinical research the reaction patterns of infant and child become almost as tangible as tissue."[71] And so on. Scientists investigating everything from the pecking speed of pigeons to the horse's gait have hoped to "hold" the cinematic image even closer by tracing it.[72] Even today, some radiology texts recommend tracing an image by hand in order to obtain quantifiable information.[73] Tracing the image onto paper is a way of "dissecting" the image: tearing away, finding the important detail, extracting, quantifying. Image analysis and tracing rehearse the dialectic between the mental and the manual also found in the dissection of cadavers.[74]

Each of these techniques for managing the detail of the filmic image—the spot film, the loop, and the traced image, common to both medicine and science—have been around for as along as there have been scientific and medical films. What is striking is not so much their longevity but the way in which they have been appropriated. That is, these techniques are now built into the apparatus itself, rather than being ad hoc reconfigurations of or additions to the machine. If the spot film was possible only with the addition of a camera to the image intensifier, the pause button and image-capture software now function to "hold" the image still for a moment. If the looped film strip required some manipulation of the celluloid and a special device for projection, now it is built into the very structure of the digital image. If tracing required extra steps and patience, now image distillation and enhancement is an option for any physician with money and a mouse. Every version of these techniques, however, has embedded within it this "back-and-forth" between stillness and movement, and with it a shadow of the drama of life and death. So is there any difference at all between the analog techniques and their digital counterparts? Does digital imaging express this drama differently?

Death and Digitality

Is not the animal organism revealed uniquely as a machine—extremely complicated, undoubtedly, but all the same manageable and obedient as any other machine?—PAVLOV, "Experimental Therapeutics as a New and Exceedingly Fruitful Method of Physiological Investigation"

In Western culture today, death is almost immoral. We treat death as something foreign, to be staved off at all costs, to be denied. Not that humanity hasn't always feared death, but since the late nineteenth century, our medical conception of the relation between life and death has changed. The relationship is no longer correlative; now death and life are once again opposed. Death is not the organically inevitable element it once was; we have come to believe that a cell could live forever if properly maintained.[75] That the organism is incapable of maintaining that balance by itself does not mean that death is a part of life, only that we have failed to keep the organism alive, due to technological ignorance or accident. Death is no longer internal to the organism—now it is external, contingent, accidental. Think of how doctors phrase the bad news: "there was nothing more we could do," which signals, on one hand, a certain powerlessness in the face of inevitability but also implies, on the other hand, that the power over death is *theoretically* in their hands, if only all the elements (environment, technological know-how, etc.) were aligned just right. Preventative medicine, organ replacement, life support—all have made the criterion of death technological rather than biological, robbing death of its privilege and authority and giving it to those in control of the technology.[76] Death still reigns, but modern medicine does not believe in it any more.

This modern opposition between life and death recalls the preclinic conception of death as an absolute boundary, the opposite of life. But there is an important difference between that opposition and today's. Consider brain-death criteria: "A comatose patient today whose loss of spontaneous brain functions is irreversible by existing resuscitation techniques is 'dead.' Another comatose patient tomorrow, *in exactly the same physiological state* as the first one today, is 'not dead' if in the meantime a new resuscitation technique has been introduced that can be used to reverse the coma."[77] So in the twentieth century, life is not the opposite of death in the same way that the active is the opposite of the inert, because the same level of organic activity or inactivity can count as life or death, depending on the level of technology of the time. The criterion for death lies with us, not with God or Nature.

It would be tempting to argue that digital imaging expresses that change, that if death backed the photograph's indexical image, guaranteed the photograph's authenticity by its peculiar absent presence, then the lack of an indexical image in digital media means that death is no longer the absolute, no longer the guarantor of certainty. But this would be to misunderstand the nature of the digital medical image.[78] While it is true that the images created by the CT or MRI scanner are not "pictures" of the body in the same way that X-ray films are, this does not mean they are not indexical. Even though the information gathered by the machines travels to the computer in the form of binary oppositions, ones and zeros, that information is nonetheless "indexical" in the sense that there is a necessary physical connection—even if only at the molecular level—between the object and its representation. It must be so; otherwise, the images would have no informational value.

If the digital medical image expresses our modern idea of death at all, it is in the "practically infinite manipulability" that the digital image promises.[79] The ability to cut, paste, and replace at will; to be able to generate copy after copy without any "degeneration"; to be able to make changes with greater and greater rapidity—these are the hopes of modern Western medicine as well. Organ transplants, gene therapy, cloning: what are these except "energetic denials of the power of death," attempts to extend the ultimate deadline? Of course, that deadline prevails, despite the digital. So what does the digital revolution really offer, especially if the techniques outlined in the previous section are merely newer versions of older practices? Convenience, or more bluntly, time. Time is the real currency of the digital realm, both in terms of time extended and time saved.

And this is, perhaps, the reason for their rapid infiltration of modern medicine. In the end—*at* the end—however, the fact that these technologies are "digital" means less than that they are "medical": all these imaging technologies carry within them the drama of life and death.

Cinema, too. Like the human body, motion pictures are pathogenic. That is, films die just a little bit whenever they are projected; their very functioning brings about their own deterioration. After months of lifelike activity, a print must be "retired" because it has become worn and frail. Even when a new print has been struck from the original negative, that negative gives up part of its usable life to create that print. And so the cycle continues, until one day, through use or neglect, the line eventually dies out.[80]

Many people hope that digital media will stall this pathetic cycle. Film archives experiment with digital techniques to "clean up" worn prints, while archivists debate the viability of DVD technology as a storage medium. We hope that the digital will extend the deadline, but film preservation, like medicine, eventually comes to the point where "nothing more can be done." Again, the extent to which digital technologies owe their content, form, and function to older, analog models makes their digitality almost irrelevant. Instead, faced with that inevitability, in the struggle to hold on to a vanishing past or life, we try to find ways to understand and appreciate. Hence, the importance of hermeneutics.

Historicizing digital medical imaging technologies allows us to pause, replay the past, and cue forward to the present. In doing so, we not only find striking similarities but we mimic the hermeneutic strategy so important to medical understanding, and thereby partake of the appreciation of the human condition that medicine first provoked. Thinking about medical films brings out the relation of this condition to the dialectic of stillness and movement. Whether digital or analog, medical imaging techniques present doctors with the possibility of stopping time, of holding on to the unruly body and thereby—just maybe—holding disease and death at bay. Yet in the rush to seize, to hold, to read, and to analyze, physicians must still come back to movement and synthesis. In this hermeneutic movement, this back-and-forth, doctors productively, if perhaps unconsciously, remind themselves of the line they cross every day between life and death.

I would like to thank Jennifer Barker, Lester D. Friedman, Court-
ney Podraza, and two anonymous readers for their insightful comments on an earlier draft, as well as Tom Gunning, Jim Lastra, and
the members of University of Chicago's Mass Culture Workshop.
Thanks also to Lauren Rabinovitz, Abe Geil, and the members of
the 2000 Obermann Seminar for their patience and encouragement.
This essay is dedicated to the memory of Dr. W. J. "Grandpa Doc"
Mack (1922-2001).

1 See Stanley Joel Reiser, *Medicine and the Reign of Technology* (Cambridge: Cambridge University Press, 1978).

2 For a technological history of medical imaging, see Bettyann Kevles,
Naked to the Bone: Medical Imaging in the Twentieth Century (New
Brunswick: Rutgers University Press, 1997), and Tibor Doby and
G. Alker, *Origins and Development of Medical Imaging* (Carbondale:
Southern Illinois University Press, 1997).

3 Martin Kemp, " 'A Perfect and Faithful Record': Mind and Body in
Medical Photography before 1900," in *Beauty of Another Order: Photography in Science*, ed. Ann Thomas (New Haven: Yale University
Press, in association with the National Gallery of Canada, Ottawa,
1997), 120-49.

4 See Andreas Vesalius, *The Illustrations from the Works of Andreas Vesalius of Brussels*, ed. and trans. J. B. de C. M. Saunders and Charles D.
O'Malley (Cleveland: World Publishing Co., 1950), and Glenn Harcourt, "Andreas Vesalius and the Anatomy of Antique Sculpture,"
Representations 17 (winter 1987): 28-61.

5 Chris Amirault, "Posing the Subject of Early Medical Photography,"
Discourse 16, no. 2 (winter 1993-1994): 51-76.

6 Paul Ricoeur, "Human Sciences and Hermeneutical Method: Meaningful Action Considered as Text," in *Explorations in Phenomenology*,
ed. David Carr and Edward S. Casey (The Hague: Martinus Nijhoff,
1973), 13-46.

7 Friedrich Schleiermacher, *Hermeneutics: The Handwritten Manu-
scripts*, trans. James Duke and Jack Forstman, ed. Heinz Kimmerle
(Missoula, Mont.: Scholars Press for the American Academy of Religion, 1977), 113.

8 Martin Heidegger went one step further, arguing that even what
we conceive to be simple perception is an act of interpretation. All
understanding implies a "fore-conception" of "something as something," even before we begin to interpret it thematically. For Heidegger, then, the "hermeneutic circle" refers to the fact that "interpretation always already has to operate within what is understood
and nuture itself from this" (Heidegger, *Being and Time: A Translation*

of Sein und Zeit, trans. Joan Stambaugh [Albany: State University of New York, 1996], 143).

9 Wolfgang Iser, *The Range of Interpretation* (New York: Columbia University Press, 2000).

10 Johann Gustav Droysen, *Outline of the Principles of History,* trans. E. Benjamin Andrews (Boston: Ginn and Company, 1893).

11 Paul Ricoeur, *Freud and Philosophy: An Essay in Interpretation* (New Haven: Yale University Press, 1970).

12 This formulation of "dialectic" borrows from Plato's conception of dialectic as "division and collection" (*Phaedrus* 265–66, *Sophist* 253–54, *Statesman* 261–68, and *Republic* 531–34) and Hegel's conception, which includes both necessary movement and transformation. On Hegel, see Karl Popper, "What Is Dialectic?" *Mind* 49 (1940): 403–26.

13 Drew Leder, "Clinical Interpretation: The Hermeneutics of Medicine," *Theoretical Medicine* 11 (1990): 9–24.

14 Richard J. Baron, "Medical Hermeneutics: Where Is the 'Text' We Are Interpreting?" *Theoretical Medicine* 11 (1990): 25–28.

15 Georges Canguilhem, *The Normal and the Pathological,* trans. Carolyn R. Fawcett (New York: Zone Books, 1991).

16 Carlo Ginzburg, "Clues: Roots of an Evidential Paradigm," in *Clues, Myths, and the Historical Method,* trans. John and Ann C. Tedeschi (Baltimore: Johns Hopkins University Press, 1989), 106.

17 Ibid.

18 Hans Ulrich Gumbrecht, "Perception versus Experience: Moving Pictures and Their Resistance to Interpretation," in *Inscribing Science: Scientific Texts and the Materiality of Communication,* ed. Timothy Lenoir (Stanford: Stanford University Press, 1998), 351–64.

19 See, for example, W. F. Bynum, *Science and the Practice of Medicine in the Nineteenth Century* (Cambridge: Cambridge University Press, 1994), and Theodore Porter, *Trust in Numbers: The Pursuit of Objectivity in Science and Public Life* (Princeton: Princeton University Press, 1995).

20 See The National Library of Medicine's Visible Human Project Web site: http://www.nlm.nih.gov/research/visible/visible%5Fhuman. html. See also Lisa Cartwright, "A Cultural Anatomy of the Visible Human Project," in *The Visible Woman: Imaging Technologies, Gender, and Science,* ed. Paula A. Treichler, Lisa Cartwright, and Constance Penley (New York: New York University Press, 1998), 21–43, and Gordon Grice, "Slice of Life: How a Convicted Killer's Corpse Brought Anatomy into the Digital Age," *New Yorker* (30 July 2001): 36.

21 Walter Benjamin, "The Work of Art in the Age of Mechanical Reproduction," in *Illuminations,* ed. Hannah Arendt, trans. Harry Zohn (New York: Schocken Books, 1969), 233.

22 Ibid.

23 For important discussions of objectivity in science, see Lorraine Daston and Peter Galison, "The Image of Objectivity," *Representations* 40 (fall 1992): 81–128, and Allan Megill, ed., *Rethinking Objectivity* (Durham: Duke University Press, 1994).

24 Anthony R. Michaelis, *Research Films in Biology, Anthropology, Psychology, and Medicine* (New York: Academic Press, 1955), 371.

25 Lisa Cartwright, *Screening the Body: Tracing Medicine's Visual Culture* (Minneapolis: University of Minnesota Press, 1995), 3.

26 Michel Foucault, *The Birth of the Clinic: An Archaeology of Medical Perception*, trans. A. M. Sheridan Smith (New York: Pantheon Books, 1973), 140; Foucault, *Discipline and Punish: The Birth of the Prison*, trans. Alan Sheridan (New York: Vintage Books, 1979).

27 Karl Figlio, "Review of *The Birth of the Clinic*," *British Journal for the History of Science* 10 (July 1977): 167.

28 Foucault, *Birth of the Clinic*. Subsequent citations appear as parenthetical page references in the text.

29 Figlio, "Review," 167.

30 W. R. Albury, "Ideas of Life and Death," in *Companion Encyclopedia of the History of Medicine*, ed. W. F. Bynum and Roy Porter (New York: Routledge, 1993), 255.

31 Claude Bernard, *Lectures on the Phenomena of Life Common to Animals and Plants*, trans. Hebbel E. Hoff, Roger Guillemin, and Lucienne Guillemin (Springfield, Ill.: Charles C. Thomas, 1974), 30, 252.

32 Hence, degeneration—the idea that all systems degrade into entropy—became the guiding principle in biology as well as thermodynamics. See the essays collected in *Degeneration: The Dark Side of Progress*, ed. J. Edward Chamberlin and Sander Gilman (New York: Columbia University Press, 1985).

33 The most famous statement on this use of analysis and synthesis, even though he does not call it such, is René Descartes, *Discourse on the Method*, in *Selected Philosophical Writings*, trans. John Cottingham, Robert Stoothoff, and Dugald Murdoch (Cambridge: Cambridge University Press, 1988), 111–51, especially 116–22. For an overview of scientific method, see A. C. Crombie, *Styles of Scientific Thinking in the European Tradition* (London: Duckworth, 1994), and Neal W. Gilbert, *Renaissance Concepts of Method* (New York: Columbia University Press, 1960).

34 Sir Isaac Newton, *Opticks* (1730; New York: Dover, 1952), 404–5.

35 Etienne Bonnot de Condillac, *An Essay on the Origin of Human Knowledge*, trans. Thomas Nugent, (1746; Gainesville, Fla.: Scholar's Facsimiles and Reprints, 1971), 74.

36 To drive this point home: "le régard médicale" deliberately evokes Sartre's "le régard," which is primarily but certainly not exclusively

visual. Jean-Paul Sartre, *Being and Nothingness: An Essay on Phenomenological Ontology*, trans. Hazel E. Barnes (New York: Philosophical Library, 1956); see especially "The Look," 252–302.

37 Drew Leder, "A Tale of Two Bodies: The Cartesian Corpse and the Lived Body," in *The Body in Medical Thought and Practice*, ed. Drew Leder (Dordrecht, Neth.: Kluwer Academic Publishers, 1992), 17–35.

38 Charles Daremberg, *Histoire des sciences médicales* (Paris, 1870), 2: 1066; quoted in Foucault, *Birth of the Clinic*, 164.

39 Jean Joseph Ménuret de Chambaud, "Mort (*Médicine*)," in *Encyclopédie, ou dictionnaire raisonée*, ed. Denis Diderot and Jean Le Rond D'Alembert (Paris, 1751–1765), 10: 718; quoted in Albury, "Ideas of Life and Death," 252.

40 Zeno's paradoxes are to be found in Plato's *Parmenides*, trans. Mary Louise Gill and Paul Ryan, in *Complete Works*, ed. John M. Cooper (Indianapolis: Hackett Publishing Company, 1997), 359–97.

41 See, for example, Adolf Grünbaum, *Modern Science and Zeno's Paradoxes* (Middletown, Conn.: Wesleyan University Press, 1967).

42 Henri Bergson, *Creative Evolution*, trans. Arthur Mitchell (New York: Modern Library, 1944), 328, 332.

43 *Le Petit Soldat* (Jean-Luc Godard, France, 1963); or *Le Petit Soldat*, a film by Jean-Luc Godard, trans. Nicholas Garham (New York: Simon and Schuster, 1967), 39.

44 Dynamism in art is not exclusive to the modern period, of course; *Laocoön*, the Hellenistic sculpture now in the Vatican Museum, prompted Lessing to think about precisely this issue. See Gotthold Ephraim Lessing, *Laocoon: An Essay upon the Limits of Painting and Poetry*, trans. Ellen Frothingham (1766; New York: Noonday Press, 1957).

45 Tom Gunning, "New Thresholds of Vision: Instantaneous Photography and the Early Cinema of Lumière," in *Impossible Presence: Surface and Screen in the Photogenic Era*, ed. Terry Smith (Chicago: University of Chicago Press, 2001), 71–99.

46 André Breton, *Mad Love*, trans. Mary Ann Caws (Lincoln: University of Nebraska Press, 1987), 10.

47 Andé Bazin, "The Ontology of the Photographic Image," in *What Is Cinema?* vol. 1, trans. Hugh Gray (Berkeley: University of California Press, 1967), 1: 9.

48 Ibid., 10.

49 Sigmund Freud, "The 'Uncanny,'" in *The Standard Edition of the Complete Psychological Works of Sigmund Freud*, trans. and ed. James Strachey (London: Hogarth Press, 1953–1974), 17: 235.

50 Roland Barthes, *Camera Lucida: Reflections on Photography*, trans. Richard Howard (New York: Hill and Wang, 1981), 31–32. Subsequent citations appear as parenthetical page references in the text.

51 Bazin, "Ontology of the Photographic Image," 1: 14.

52 Garrett Stewart, *From Film to Screen: Modernism's Photo Synthesis* (Chicago: University of Chicago Press, 1999), especially chapter 1.

53 Reiser, *Medicine and the Reign of Technology*, 62–63.

54 Ibid.

55 My discussion of spot film technique is indebted to an interview with Dr. Joel Leland, Attending Radiologist at Michael Reese Hospital, Chicago, and Assistant Professor of Radiology at the University of Illinois at Chicago, 17 November 2000.

56 Tom Gunning, "The Ghost in the Machine: Animated Pictures at the Haunted Hotel of Early Cinema," *Living Pictures* 1, no. 1 (2001): 4.

57 Ibid. See also Tom Gunning, "An Aesthetic of Astonishment: Early Film and the (In)credulous Spectator," in *Viewing Positions*, ed. Linda Williams (New Brunswick: Rutgers University Press, 1995), 114–33.

58 See the essays collected in *Physiology in the American Context, 1850–1940*, ed. Gerald L. Geison (Bethesda, Md.: American Physiological Society, 1987).

59 J. C. Waterton et al., "Magnetic Resonance (MR) Cine Imaging of the Human Heart," *British Journal of Radiology* 58 (August 1985): 711–16. See also J. S. Garrett, C. B. Higgins, and M. J. Lipton, "Computed Axial Tomography of the Heart," *International Journal of Cardiac Imaging* 1, no. 2 (1985): 113–26, and T. R. Miller and J. W. Wallis, "Cardiac Nuclear Medicine," *Current Problems in Diagnostic Radiology* 17, no. 5 (September–October 1988): 157–93.

60 For an interesting treatment of chase films in this light, see Jonathan Auerbach, "Chasing Film Narrative: Repetition, Recursion, and the Body in Early Cinema," *Critical Inquiry* 26 (summer 2000): 798–820.

61 A. E. Stein, "Ueber medizinisch-photographische und -kinematographische Aufnahmen," *Deutsche medizinische Wochenschrift* (Berlin) 38 (1912): 1184.

62 Rudolf Janker, "Das endlose röntgenkinematographische Band bei der Röntgenuntersuchung des Herzens," *Fortschritte auf dem Gebiete der Röntgenstrahlen* 71 (1949): 345.

63 For representative articles, see R. J. Reynolds, "Cineradiography: Its Technique and Applications," *British Journal of Radiology* 23 (1927): 33; T. Motloch, "Vorführung eines Laufbildes darstellend den weichen Gaumen und die Tubenmündung beim Schluckakt," *Zentralblatt für Hals-, Nasen- und Ohrenheilkunde* 44 (1938): 359; B. S. Holmgren, "Roentgen Cinematography as a Routine Method," *Acta Radiologica* 26 (1945): 286; I. K. R. McMillan, R. Daley, and M. B. Mathews, "A Method of Studying the Action of Fresh Post-Mortem Aortic and Pulmonary Valves by Colour Cinematography," *British Heart Journal* 14 (1952): 42; A. Benchimol and K. B. Desser, "Advances in Clinical Vectorcardiography," *American Journal of Cardiology* 36, no. 1 (July 1975): 76–86; and K. R. Burnett, C. L. Davis, and

J. Read, "Dynamic Display of the Temporomandibular Joint Meniscus by Using 'Fast-Scan' MR Imaging," *American Journal of Roentgenology* 149, no. 5 (November 1987): 959–62.

64 Marta Braun, *Picturing Time: The Work of Etienne-Jules Marey (1830– 1904)* (Chicago: University of Chicago Press, 1992), 170, 173–74.

65 Lev Manovich, "What Is Digital Cinema?" in *The Digital Dialectic: New Essays on New Media*, ed. Peter Lunenfeld (Cambridge: MIT Press, 1999), 189.

66 See Norbert Wiener, *Cybernetics: Control and Communication in the Animal and the Machine* (Cambridge, Mass.: Technology Press, 1948), and Wiener, *The Human Use of Human Beings: Cybernetics and Society* (Boston: Houghton Mifflin, 1950).

67 For a discussion of the implications of this technology for vision and point of view, see Lisa Cartwright and Brian Goldfarb, "Radiography, Cinematography, and the Decline of the Lens," in *Incorporations*, ed. Jonathan Crary and Sanford Kwinter (New York: Zone, 1992), 190–201.

68 My discussion of echocardiography is indebted to an interview with Dr. Catherine L. Webb, associate professor at Northwestern University Medical School, 5 November 2001. See also A. Rebecca Snider, Gerald A. Serwer, and Samuel B. Ritter, *Echocardiography in Pediatric Heart Disease*, 2nd ed. (St. Louis: Mosby, 1997).

69 R. F. James, "Roentgen Cinematography," *Journal of the Society of Motion Picture Engineers* 24, no. 3 (March 1935): 233–40.

70 Hans Fortner, "Die Punktweg-Methode: Ein Verfahren zur quantitativen Auswertung von Mikrokinematogrammen," *Zeitschrift für wissenschaftliche Mikroskopie und für mikroskopische Technik* 50, no. 1 (1933): 1–63; Willi Kuhl, *Die technischen Grundlagen der Kinematischen Zellforschung* (Berlin: Springer, 1949).

71 Arnold Gesell, *Arnold Gesell: My Contribution to a History of Psychology in Autobiography* (Worcester, Mass.: Clark University Press, 1952), 4: 123–42; quoted in Louise Bates Ames, *Arnold Gesell: Themes of His Work* (New York: Human Sciences Press, 1989), 171.

72 Otto Koehler, O. Müller, and R. Wachholtz, "Kann die Taube Anzahlen erfassen?" *Verhandlungen der Deutschen Zoologischen Gesellschaft* 37 (9–11 July 1935): 39–54; Etienne-Jules Marey, *Movement*, trans. Eric Pritchard (New York: D. Appleton and Company, 1895).

73 See Snider, Serwer, and Ritter, *Echocardiography in Pediatric Heart Disease*, 134, and N. B. Schiller et al., "Recommendations for Quantitation of the Left Ventricle by Two-Dimensional Echocardiography," *Journal of the American Society of Echocardiography* 2 (1989): 358.

74 Wax or plaster models of organs (such as the heart or eye) also evoke this dialectic between the mental and manual. These life-size models help the student and physician correlate two-dimensional information to three dimensions. For more on the relation between

the mental and manual in dissection, see Barbara Maria Stafford, *Body Criticism* (Cambridge: MIT Press, 1991), 48–54.

75 For an important statement of this idea, see Ivan Petrovich Pavlov, "Experimental Therapeutics as a New and Exceedingly Fruitful Method of Physiological Investigation," *Bulletin of the New York Academy of Medicine* 50 (1974): 1018–30 (originally published in 1900), and Alexis Carrel, "On the Permanent Life of Tissues Outside of the Organism," *Journal of Experimental Medicine* 15 (1912): 516–28.

76 Albury, "Ideas of Life and Death," 272.

77 Ibid.

78 My thanks to the members of University of Chicago's Mass Culture Workshop for pointing out *my* misunderstanding in an earlier version of this essay.

79 I borrow this phrase from Philip Rosen, "Old and New: Image, Indexicality, and Historicity in the Digital Utopia," in *Change Mummified: Cinema, Historicity, Theory* (Minneapolis: University of Minnesota Press, 2001), which provides an extensive exploration of the relation between the digital and the indexical.

80 For more on this idea, see Paolo Cherchi Usai, *The Death of Cinema: History, Cultural Memory, and the Digital Dark Age* (London: BFI Publishing, 2001).

PART **IV**

DIGITAL AESTHETICS, SOCIAL TEXTS,

AND ART OBJECTS

N. Katherine Hayles

BODIES OF TEXTS, BODIES OF SUBJECTS

Metaphoric Networks in New Media

For a long time now, writers and readers have acted as if books have bodies. They draft headnotes and footnotes, tack on appendices, inadvertently crack spines. The metaphoric mappings not only flowed from flesh to word but also from word to flesh.[1] Human bodies became texts to be read, whether the writing was visible on the face or buried in the heart, encrypted into physiognomic features or coded into DNA. Given the long and rich tradition of mapping books onto bodies and bodies onto books, we may suppose that if literary works were to undergo dramatic and profound changes in embodiment, the disturbances would shake up these metaphoric networks, resulting in new configurations. As texts decreasingly take the material form of durable marks inscribed on paper and increasingly manifest themselves as electronic polarities, the bodies represented within (and without) electronic documents undergo correlated transformations in embodiment.[2] Flesh is conceived as data, the body as cyborg circuitry, blood as information carrier, genomes as codes. In these wide-ranging and pervasive changes, electronic literary texts have a special role to play, for they employ the resources of literary language to interrogate the plexed relation of body to text in digital media. At the same time they self-consciously interrogate their own status as flickering signifiers rather than durable marks. To indicate this interplay between the body of the text considered as a material-semiotic artifact and the bodies represented within the imaginary worlds that texts create, I use the phrase textual body/bodies in the text. My claim is that changes in the physical forms of texts take place in correlation with how bodies are imagined within the text. When the physical form of the text mutates, shockwaves reconfigure its internal landscapes as well.

To explore how the connections between flesh and word are both troubled and reinscribed in New Media, I take as my tutor texts Deena Larsen's *Disappearing Rain* and Stuart Moulthrop's *Reagan Library*.[3] When bodies are in question, gender remains a relevant category of analysis, however complex and transfigured in digital media.[4] To interrogate the subtle differences in perspective that gender orientations create in the reconfigured relation of flesh to electronic word, my analysis juxtaposes a text by a man and a woman. Identifying textual strategies with an author's gender—always a tricky strategy—is especially risky when the statistical sample is limited to two. Nevertheless, these texts clearly are gender-inflected, particularly in their conceptualizations of bodies and their visions of how bodies are constituted through cultural and semiotic practices. Larsen shows a family where the women do most of the work of knitting together lives and maintaining the everyday fabric of communal life; yet this pattern is also disrupted by the daughter's choice to escape into a masculinized space of a cyberspace lover. In contrast, Moulthrop depicts landscapes devoid of "normal" embodiment. One narrator has been badly burned in a plane crash and must use virtual reality prostheses to interface with the world; another is dead; and a third seems to have lost his body altogether. The care-work so pervasive in Larsen's text appears nowhere in Moulthrop's piece, where the narratives (such as they are) appear in settings largely stripped of family connections and kinship ties.

Even more striking is how words are embodied in Larsen's text compared to Moulthrop's work. For her interface, Larsen inscribes English words into Japanese kanji ideograms, thus creating a hybrid writing that visually conveys the differences and convergences between ancient calligraphy and contemporary electronic media. The kanji symbols for water and river mark the two main sections entitled "Water Leavings" and "River Journeys." When clicked, the

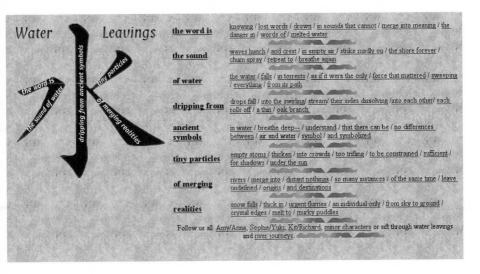

Deena Larsen,
Disappearing Rain (2000).

alphabetic text inscribed into these symbols opens onto the main narrative sections. The narratives can also be accessed by clicking the mouse over phrases in the lines of the poems that run horizontally below the symbols. The interface is further complicated by having the initial words of the horizontal lines form another poem if read vertically down the screen. Thus the screen invites the user to see the space as multiply encoded, simultaneously functioning as visual image and alphabetic text, wavy lines of text running horizontally across the screen and poems dripping down in a vertical stream of words. The complex interplay between horizontal currents and vertical flows is enhanced by the metaphoric association of the text as an electronic body with the bodies represented electronically within the text. The electronic text, manifesting itself as transitory images created by a scanning electron beam, serves as a metaphor for flows of subjectivity, as the textual body/bodies in the text mutate and change state, as the borders of the family are torn between maintaining old customs and adapting to a new homeland, and as characters experience the fractal complexities of passionately merging with a loved one as opposed to maintaining one's identity intact.

Reagan Library, by contrast, launches its imaginary world not from words but from spaces. When the user opens the work, she is presented with the image of an island landscape on which various objects are scattered. She can navigate by holding the mouse down, clicking on the landscape, and pulling the cursor right or left. Clicking the mouse while the cursor is on an object plunges the user into one of four world levels, signified by the image of an object with text below. Unlike books, which create imaginary spaces for the reader to inhabit as she decodes the words, *Reagan Library* presents spatial images that open onto words. It thus marks an important transition phase between first-generation hypertexts, which were primarily conceived as screens of text with little or no images, and second-generation works, which make full use of the multimedia capabilities of electronic environments, including graphics, sound, images, animation, and object behaviors.[5]

Whereas the aspect of electronic textuality foregrounded by *Disappearing Rain* is the fact that screen text constantly refreshes in a quicksilver flow, *Reagan Library* focuses on the fragmentation electronic text undergoes as data strings are scattered throughout the hard drive and/or distributed on remote servers. Instead of watery text, its dominant metaphor is text as assemblage.[6] This work constantly reminds the user that to represent a body at all—textual or human—requires that fragments scattered throughout an information space be collected and reassembled. Fragmentation affects the text at every level, from words and sentences to larger narrative blocks. In reassembling the (textual) bodies, the user can never be sure if the emerging coherence is an artifact of her imagination or a pattern intrinsic to the work. No wonder, then, that the bodies represented in the text are highly mediated by everything from technology to death, for the text constantly reminds us that the textual body/bodies in the text are contingent assemblages whose forms are as much a result of chance as necessity.

Fluid Subjectivity and Watery Flow in *Disappearing Rain*

In *Of Two Minds: Hypertext Pedagogy and Poetics*, Michael Joyce observes that "print stays itself; electronic text replaces itself."[7] What Joyce has in mind here, among other things, is the constant refreshing of the CRT screen. But he is also glancing at the hypertextual link and the movement from lexia to lexia in electronic writing, an aspect of electronic textuality that he evokes in the lovely phrase "writing on water."[8]

The observation is relevant to Deena Larsen's *Disappearing Rain*, where watery text is a pervasive trope. *Disappearing Rain* revolves around the disappearance of Anna Mizunami, a college student at Berkeley. *Disappearing Rain* flirts with being a murder mystery, although it finally draws back from this form that so many literary hypertexts have adopted. Larsen tells us that Anna's conversation, even with her twin sister Amy, stayed close to the surface, focusing on clothes and friends. We also learn that Anna was so isolated at Berkeley that it took weeks for anyone there to notice she was missing. Amy recalls Anna wearing an elaborate makeup of Lancôme cosmetics, a detail that suggests she needed a mask to face the world. Given these details, we can understand Amy's surprise when she learns that Anna had created an erotic Web site. She is even more shocked to discover on Anna's computer passionate letters from a cyberspace lover. The lover writes as if he lives *behind* the screen, lingering at her Web site and knowing that "somehow we will touch between these panes of glass that separate us" (Water Leavings/The word is/drown). His desire bespeaks excess, for he yearns not merely to possess Anna but to merge with her, past the molecular and down to the subatomic-particle level: "I want you to come into me./Join my world/Let our bodies touch, merge/show the electrons of our atoms/how to share orbits" (Water Leavings/the word is/the danger in).

In the context of Anna's disappearance, this excess can be read as deeply threatening, for it is as much annihilation as fusion. As mentioned earlier, the words that serve as a clickable index to the narrative sections also form poems. The poem in which the narrative about the hidden letters appears, "knowing/lost words/drown/in sounds that cannot/merge into meaning/the danger in/words of/melted water," evokes the twin dangers of dissipating sense and dissipating senses. The fluidity of bodily transformation is gruesomely represented in an image Amy glimpses in *Discovery* magazine, where a decomposing body is of scientific interest because the time of death can be estimated by how far advanced the life cycles are of the insect decomposers: "This is the picture that Amy cannot shake from her mind. The atoms of her sister Anna have sunk so far into the atoms of the ground that the orbits are indistinguishable"

(Water Leavings/tiny particles/empty atoms). While Anna's lover imagines atoms merging in passionate consummation, Amy "sees only horror filling the empty spaces between the atoms. She cannot recognize features in the close-up of the face. There is nothing there but the far off orbits of hair intersecting ground, air intersecting flesh. Water seeps through, merging the edges." The photograph turns out not to be of Anna at all, although we are allowed to think so long enough to register the full horror of this decay, which is also a return to fluidity as water seeps through the body, "merging the edges."

Larsen extends this fluid dynamic to words and language, as the poem "Water Leavings" hints when it speaks of the word "dripping from/ancient symbols/tiny particles/of merging/realities." Yuki, Anna and Amy's great-grandmother, begins losing her memory and is diagnosed with Alzheimer's. To help her hold onto language, her daughter Sophie makes flash cards with English words and kanji symbols on them, but the day comes when Yuki cannot read the words. Frustrated, she creeps out of her room late at night and throws the cards into a fountain in the family garden. The paper turns to mush and the purple ink dissolves into the water. Seeing language literally wash away from her, Yuki scrambles into the fountain, scraping her skin as she tries to retrieve the words. Two interfaces become permeable in this scene—the material boundary between words and water, and the biological boundary of skin and world. Language and body together feel the undertow of "merging realities."

The connection with the fluidity of electronic "writing in water" emerges through Sophie's belief that credit card companies are trying to steal her identity, as well as the identities of her granddaughter Anna and their ancestors, and imprison them somewhere in cyberspace. It begins with a routine call from a credit company in which they say her account is overdue. Confronted with the demand to produce the usual identifying information, Sophie suspects the company of "identity theft," not to defraud her of money but actually to steal her identity. Because they have evidently confused her with Anna, she deduces that they are responsible for Anna's disappearance. Why should they stop there? If they can steal one identity they can steal many, so she believes they have also stolen the identities of her ancestors, who are now trapped in cyberspace and so cannot visit the ancestral shrines. Just as Anna's dissolution into atoms can be seen as both erotic fusion and fatal dissolution, so the fluidity of cyberspace lends itself both to the freedom of untrammeled imagination and incarceration of ancestral spirits.

Sophie, in despair over the imagined conspiracy, plunges into the cold, fast-flowing creek behind their house and lies down in the shallow water, scraping her skin on the rocks. Although Amy eventually comes and pulls her out, she lies there long enough to feel the watery coldness inside her bones, hovering at the interface between coherent identity and watery dissolution. As with Yuki's memory loss, the fluidity of writing is associated with a punctured body surface. It is as if the lacerated skin serves as preparation for subjectivity to leak out of the body in a watery flow that is at once painful and somehow promising.

Larsen's blend of traditional rituals and electronic data from which Sophie fashions her conspiracy narrative makes an integrated (if not entirely coherent) story. Sophie's family has struggled with the tension between tradition and melting-pot assimilation throughout the generations. When she is losing her memory, Yuki dreams she flies back to her homeland. Seeing her birthplace again, she senses that if she were to land, her legs would become rooted in the soil, growing thick as trees. She rejects this solidity in favor of continuing to fly, finally preferring the fluidity of the new country to the static rootedness of the old. Sophie's daughter Kit—Anna and Amy's mother—insists that her daughters be given American names, although the family compromises by finally choosing names close to Japanese equivalents. In her own way, Sophie insists on mingling old traditions and new culture more fiercely than anyone. She attends a night class and learns to create a Web site to which the ancestors can return. Then she realizes that a street Web cam is passively broadcasting pictures of her neighbor's house. She seizes the opportunity to stream her messages into cyberspace by posting large placards in her neighbor's window, scolding the credit card company and encouraging Anna and the ancestors to return.

Although there are men in the household—Anna and Amy's father Richard, along with memories of their grandfather and great-grandfather—the care-work of knitting together the fabric of family life falls primarily on the women. Although Kit has a demanding job at a law firm that keeps her at her office most of the time, she is keenly aware she can do this only because her mother is at home to care for Yuki as she grows old and the twins as they grow up. When

Anna disappears, Kit starts seeing virtual waterfalls spilling out of the computer screens at work. When she thinks she discerns Anna's face in the flowing pools and hears her voice in the falling waters, it is as though a dam has broken and the accumulated guilt rushes to merge with her worry about her daughter, creating a turbulence that refuses to be neatly parceled into work and home.

One way to read Larsen's plot is through the generations of women and the choices they make. Yuki is torn between Japan and America, Sophie between her mother's traditionalism and her daughter's determination to be American, Kit between work and home as she tries to have it all—the burden of her generation of successful women. As the narrative progresses, it becomes increasingly clear that Anna may have *chosen* to disappear, and Amy comes to suspect she has gone to live in cyberspace. In the climactic sequence, Anna dives through the screen to join her: "Her hand reached out to touch the water and passed through the monitor as if it were merely the reflection of a window . . . She felt the warm smooth plastic of the monitor . . . Bent her head in the proper dive position . . . And soared into the computer" (River Journeys/in rivers/with our realities). Why does she make this choice? If it is to rejoin her twin, the question is only displaced onto Anna: Why did she make this choice? Anna's Web site and the electronic love letters suggest that cyberspace is here configured as a space of unconstrained imagination that can actualize whatever it can conceive. In view of this (highly problematic) freedom, one way to read the twins' decisions is as a refusal of family burdens. Whereas Kit tries to have it all by working eighty-hour weeks, Anna and Amy decide to have it all in a different way, leaving behind the space of physical reality and going to frolic with electronic lovers in computer-visualized meadows.

Complicating this problematic cyberspace fantasy is the tension between the narratives and poems. Whereas the narratives slide with alarming ease into mysticism, the poems are not so easily resolved. The vertical poem to "River Journeys" draws into question fusion as means of knowing the other: "If there are/other waters/we can not/know them/all we see/in rivers/is their presence." If the first horizontal lines of "River Journeys" proclaim that "joining the/river's flow/is the only/way to/welcome in/anything beyond/our skin," the penultimate lines draw a watery demarcation between individual subjectivity and flowing water, warning that "a river's secrets/depend on/how much/we need to/configure/its destinations/with our realities." From where does this need come? From dealing with the gritty and not always pleasant realities of connected lives and mutual responsibilities. Set in tension with Anna and Amy's choices is Sophie's decision to connect with cyberspace by building an ancestral shrine there, Kit's determination to keep working so she can provide for her extended family, and Yuki's attraction to her homeland and her desperate attempts to recover the dissolved words back out of the fountain. Although "the sound/of water" may drip from "ancient symbols," the wavy lines of the horizontal poems do not dissolve into the narrative sequences but maintain a distinct identity that remains in dynamic tension with the prose resolution.

Amid these complexities, what is clearly established is not the superiority of cyberspace to the real world but metaphoric networks that map electronic writing onto fluid bodies. As the body of the text is transformed from flat, durable marks to flickering signifiers, bodies within the text undergo similar disturbances: skin is scraped off, ancient traditions are reconfigured in electronic spaces, and writing is dissolved into water. The shift in the materiality of writing technologies that electronic textuality instantiates is registered on skin as well as screen. To create a new kind of textual body is inevitably to write new human bodies, which in turn serve as metaphors for the textual body that has imagined them. Textual bodies/bodies in texts co-evolve together.

Fragmented Bodies and Disappearing Memory in *Reagan Library*

The dark irony of the title *Reagan Library*—naming a memorial for an ex-president and Alzheimer's victim who cannot remember—invites meditation on the library's function in the late age of print. In addition to memorializing presidents, libraries function as external memory storage. At the dawn of the new millennium they appear on our cultural maps as systems of distributed cognition, augmenting the human neural system by reminding us what we have forgotten or never learned. Libraries instantiate a cultural memory too vast for an individual to grasp, a kind of meta-brain with which our individual brains can hook up to transfer a minute portion of its vast information store. An entire science has grown up figuring out how to create interfaces that will let users chart navigable routes through the knowledge cartographies of the modern library; the limiting factor ceased long ago to be what we can amass and became what we can remember. Of course, the library also remains the great repository of the codex book, its architectural monumentality testifying to the massive solidity of the material within it, even as the nano-technologies of electronic media are also becoming part of its central nervous system. In *Reagan Library*, Stuart Moulthrop marshals these connotations to create a text that embodies a dynamic struggle between remembering and forgetting, making connections and suffering disconnections, processing noise and struggling with information.

In addition to his creative writing, Stuart Moulthrop is a gifted critic, and his theoretical writing gives valuable insight into the workings of *Reagan Library*.[9] Although he has devoted much of his career to promoting and explaining fictional hypertexts, he recognizes that hypertext cannot be a panacea to authors. Taking his cue from Robert Coover's observation that the expansiveness of hypertext can be "paralyzing," Moulthrop writes that: "One will feel the need, even while using these vast networks and principles of randomness and expansive story lines, to struggle against them, just as one now struggles against the linear constraints of the printed book."[10] His reasoning implies that resistance to hypertext is bound to erupt because artists inevitably push the envelope of whatever form in which they work. Here the project turns tricky, for how does one push the boundaries of a form that celebrates its ability to break the boundaries of narrative form? Clearly it will not do simply to reinscribe traditional structures, which, rather than pushing the envelope, would amount to stamping and mailing it.

In meditating on how one might resist hypertext while writing within it, Moulthrop distinguishes between hypertext created to annotate a print book and hypertext with an entirely electronic orientation, which he calls "native hypertext."[11] Native hypertext, although frequently presented as an assault on what he calls the Line (the linear sequentiality of the codex book), must not be mistaken as pure anarchic resistance to dominant culture. As detractors of literary hypertexts delight in pointing out, in many ways native hypertext epitomizes the dominant culture because it depends on the hardware and software created by the cutthroat capitalism of such industry giants as Microsoft and IBM. Moreover, on a more abstract level, the logos that rhizomatic hypertexts seek to undermine is deeply embedded in the design of the computer, which is nothing if not a logic machine.

Given these complexities, Moulthrop envisions a double mission of resisting both the Line (which includes, along with print books, the logocentrism of capitalistic culture) and the Web (the rhizomatic anarchies of hypertext). The agent that will carry out this double mission is the "mutant machine." The mutant machine resists dominant culture through mutations that disrupt the exact replications on which the Line depends. Crossing to the other side of the Line, the mutant machine struggles against the anarchy of hypertext by making visible within the text the underlying logocentric structure of native hypertext, thus exposing conceptual limits to the narrative expansiveness and principles of randomness that native hypertext likes to flaunt. Moreover, Moulthrop insists that these double strategies should interpenetrate, taking place in dynamic tension with one another. It is not enough to send the Line off to hulk in one corner and the Web to bounce off the ropes in opposite corner, as if they were wrestlers torn apart by a referee. Less referee than *provocateur*, the mutant machine must find ways to resist both at once.

Moulthrop's theoretical agenda finds concrete expression in *Reagan Library*, the mutant machine of his dreaming. Moulthrop tells the reader in his introduction that much of the text the reader sees on first visiting a screen is "generated by a set of simple random-assembly programs." The computer tosses together a word salad using phrases and sentences the author has scripted into a database. Not all of the text, however, is random. Some of it is anchored to a specific screen and remains on that screen through repeated readings. At first the word salad predominates, but on each successive visit to a screen more pre-scripted text appears, until finally, on the fourth visit, the text stabilizes into coherence and does not change any further. The program maintains this state during a given reading. If the reader closes the program and re-opens it, the program goes back to the beginning of its routine, with the text again reaching stability at the fourth visit to a given screen. Small colored squares at the bottom record how many times the screen has been visited, so it is easy for the reader to ascertain when stasis has been reached.

Mixing word salad with coherent narrative, *Reagan Library* makes the reader acutely aware that the text evolves as a dance between information and noise. Moreover, it is not easy to tell which conveys more meaning, information or noise. Although the phrases from the data base are randomly placed on the screens, the phrases themselves are far from random, echoing key ideas from the critical discourse on hypertext. "This is not a game," one declares, while another announces, "This is serious hypertext," and yet another proclaims, "Not that this is not a game." One of the characters in the nonrandom text chides the reader for expecting "locks to lift, puzzles to pick, ciphers to crack." This protest notwithstanding, there clearly are game aspects to the work, including deciphering the clues that allow the reader to predict when the dance between noise and information will end.

In realizing that noise as well as information may have something to tell us, the reader ponders how far to follow the suggestive allusions that present themselves. Consider the word salad phrase "Please say more about that." Readers familiar with the ELIZA program, created by Joseph Weisenbaum to simulate a session with a psychotherapist, will recognize this as a phrase the program uses to prompt its human interlocutor to further revelations. The phrase is evoked when the program cannot find an obvious noun in the human's previous response that the machine can pick up for its next question. In a subtle way, then, the phrase reminds us of the limits of machine intelligence, carrying out the mutant machine's assignment of disrupting the Net as well as the Line. Moreover, the phrase eerily connects with another bit of word salad, "There is no simple way to say 'this.'" Readers of Michael Joyce's *Afternoon, a story* will recognize this phrase from his work.[12] They will also realize that Moulthrop has altered the source phrase by placing quotation marks around "this," a mutation that transforms the word from an unremarkable relative pronoun to a marker pointing toward the complexity of reference.

Other phrases are even more elusive. "More grass than a tree" will recall for some readers Deleuze and Guattari's *A Thousand Plateaus* in which they argue for the superiority of rhizomatic networks over arboresque hierarchies, but fewer readers will be likely to remember that with the quoted phrase the authors are referring specifically to the operation of the human brain. Fewer still will recall that Moulthrop picks up this phrase in "No War Machine" and mutates it by associating it with "this great Brain of culture," which "has what it imagines to be a new idea," namely hypertext.[13] The reader who follows this increasingly tenuous network of associations will find herself performing those side glances that made Vannevar Bush argue associational thinking is more natural for the human mind than linear sequences, an argument that has become canonical among proponents of hypertext.[14] At the same time, the associations have by now become so diffuse that the reader, if she has come this far, has likely lost all track of narrative continuity, which in any event has already been disrupted by the insertion of word salad. Thus the associations evoked by the phrase "more grass than a tree" serve both to enact rhizomatic connections and illustrate how the anarchical tendencies of hypertext can run wild.

"Change for the machines," another word-salad phrase, operates in the opposite direction of deconstructing the Line. The phrase is a citation from Pat Cadigan's *Synners*.[15] It appears when Visual Mark hears someone asking for change for vending machines and (mis)interprets it as a directive to change his life so he can interface more profoundly with intelligent machines. Cadigan's readers will remember that Visual Mark agrees to have electrodes planted directly in his brain so his visualizations will have more power (and more commercial appeal for Diversifications, the company exploiting him), a move that culminates in him having a stroke, which also brings down the Net. In this context, the phrase reminds us that changing oneself for the machines may lead to more cortical activity than we bargained for. In the context of *Reagan Library*, the phrase alludes to how the reader's decoding strategies are forced to change when an intelligent machine interjects noise into the narrative.

As the word salad phrases are tossed around, appearing now in one context and now another, the reader is teased with juxtapositions that often appear nonsensical but occasionally seem to make sense. Is it sense, however, when the processes that construct the connections are random? Does meaning occur only when a human writer crafts the sequences in which phrase follows phrase, sentence runs after sentence? Or is it sufficient that we can find meaning in chance operations, as Visual Mark did in (mis)interpretation of "Change for the machines"? One of the sites where these questions historically have been debated is information theory. Although a full discussion of information theory is outside my scope here, I have written elsewhere about the crucial intervention that Claude Shannon made when he argued that information has nothing to do with meaning.[16] According to the equations Shannon set forth, the maximum quantity of information is conveyed by a message that cannot be predicted. This result comes about because information is expressed mathematically as a probability function inversely related to how likely it is a given element will appear in a message. By definition, noise is random and cannot be predicted; therefore we arrive at the counterintuitive conclusion that noise is maximum information.

Reagan Library evokes this history through a word-salad phrase that mutates an old adage: "Like cutting off your noise to spite your face." From an information-theoretic viewpoint, noise *is* information; it is just not information intended by the receiver. If one finds merit in John Cage's philosophy that human intentionality prevents us from encountering the infinitely varying surprises the world has to offer, then letting noise come through our perceptual filters is one way to circumvent human intention and open ourselves to the ongoing creativity that bubbles all around us.[17] From this perspective, one who regards the word salad as an obnoxious nuisance that must be endured to get to the stable text is indeed cutting off one's noise to spite one's face because the most interesting connections may be the aleatory ones. Maybe. Yet who among us returns to reread *Mureau*, the work John Cage created by performing chance operations on Thoreau's *Walden*, compared to the multitudes who return over and over to *Walden* itself?[18] I suspect that most readers—let me confess at once this is true of me—still want something like a coherent narrative as a reward for investing a few acres of cortical real estate in a text. Does a narrative finally emerge from the froth of noise that swirls through *Reagan Library*, or will readers find only the meanings that our diffuse associations attribute to this enigmatic text?

Working on the principle that navigation in hypertext cannot be separated from its meanings, let me approach this question by giving a brief description of the work's navigational apparatus. Each screen presents the reader with an image and a block of text. By clicking on the image and dragging the cursor, the reader activates a QuickTime movie that rotates the perspective along the horizon until it comes back to its starting point, as if one were turning around in a circle. Thus the world has, as one of the characters remarks, a "basic circularity." Words with links are underlined in the text; in the panorama, objects with links are indicated by a change in cursor shape. The world has four levels or states, signified by the color of the sky (and a color band at the left margin), with a different narrator for each level. All four states have similar topographies—an island landscape dotted with clickable objects—and some of the objects (although not all) appear in more than one state.

In the Black state, so dark that land and water can scarcely be distinguished from one another, the narrator is a prisoner who cannot remember anything, including the offense for which he has been sentenced. Paraphrasing Mephistopheles in Christopher Marlowe's *Dr. Faustus*, he tells us, "This is the library, nor am I out of it." On the Blue level, where a deep blue ocean meets an equally blue sky, the narrator is Emily St. Cloud, a filmmaker whose most famous work is a cinematic adaptation of T. S. Eliot's *The Waste Land*. The notes tell us "Emily is dead." In contrast to the prisoner, she is very good at remembering, although she wonders (echoing her idol Stephen Hawking) why we can remember the past but not the future. In the Teal state, fluffy clouds in a light blue sky drift above the island landscape, which continues to be dotted with clickable objects. The narrator here is a stand-up comic who has been burned in a plane crash. His comments indicate that he has been badly injured, a reality his jokes do not altogether mask. His therapist, Dr. Ramchandra, has hooked him up to a virtual reality apparatus, presumably as therapy for his damaged sensorium. From his comments we can infer that Dr. Ramchandra is asking him to interpret the objects that appear in the QuickTime movie, suggesting that his therapy is a weird science combination of visualization technology and a Rorschach test.

The fourth state is Red. Here the narrative voice is not so much a character as a guide giving information on how to interpret the other states and the world as a whole. Some of this information appears in notes (recalling Eliot's famous notes to *The Waste Land*) and some in comments that have a sibylline tone (also reminiscent of *The Waste Land*). Clicking the mouse over a word or image in any state except the Red often results in being plunged into a different state. In the Red state, however, clicking the mouse over an image moves the reader to another location in that state. Hence the Red state has a kind of self-referential stability that the other states lack. But this stability is offset by a reading dynamic that operates in the opposite direction from the rest of the world. Whereas in the other states the text becomes more coherent as the reader makes repeated visits to a site, in the Red state the Notes are most copious at the beginning, decreasing in number and importance as sites are revisited. As the world as a whole becomes less noisy for us, the Red state responds by becoming less informative, thereby reminding us that there is a cognitive cost to stability as well as to instability.

Confronted with the Black, Blue, and Teal states, the reader naturally looks for connections between them. One way to correlate them is to concentrate on objects that appear in multiple states; among these is an image titled variously "The White Cone" and "The Black Cone." For Emily, the cone is associated with a cosmological vision. She recounts that at the age of ten she wanted to be Stephen Hawking and insisted on sitting in a wheelchair, talking through a computer prosthesis, and mimicking symptoms of his disorder. But when she saw the cone she snapped out of her obsession because she experienced firsthand what Hawking symbolized for her, a privileged vision of the cosmos: "The cone was the form of light streaming out into spacetime. Part of this form was taken away to show the interior, which was the world as we know it and see it, the world of light. But the vision included ground as well as figure—not just the cone, inside and out, but also the blackness all around, the space outside of space, the time that carries time." Before she had her vision, she had been "halfheartedly playing" with herself; afterward, she sees that her hand is covered with blood. Coinciding with her menarche, the vision also inaugurates her professional calling: "that was the first time I thought of becoming a film director." The cone's light thus is associated with her art (in a literal sense, film is light congealed through chemical processes), while the surrounding blackness makes it possible for her to situate the vision and realize its full implications.

For the prisoner in the Black state, the cone is black. Its signification is opposite to the white cone of Emily's vision; it operates as a taboo excluding him from power, knowledge, and memory. He understand the black cone as "not a happy site" because it is the "seat where the archon sits," a place where "No one can take that seat and live." He sometimes sleeps on the sands facing its backside, only to find when he wakes that it has silently turned toward him, as if it wants him to look inside its red maw. When he does so, however, nothing happens. For him, "There's no one home"—no vision, no calling, no cosmological knowledge.

For the stand-up comic, the cone again mutates in ways consistent with his perspective on life. He associates it with his brief career as a television actor, when he played a heavy in a remake of "the old *Prisoner* series for South African TV." This allusion promises to forge a connection with the Black state where the prisoner does not remember the offense for which he has been sentenced. The protagonist of *The Prisoner* TV series kept trying to escape from a mysterious place where he was being held for reasons he did not understand. The connection is strengthened by a rumor that "there was a tag on the back [of the cone] that read PROPERTY OF RONALD REAGAN LIBRARY." There are associations with Emily's state as well. The cone the comic describes appears physically similar to the one in Emily's vision, complete with "a light show in the belly." However, in his world it is reduced to a movie prop shaped like a "white metallic witch hat" to which "nobody in cast or crew would come within arm's length." It hums in an ominous way that makes him sure he wants nothing to do with it.

What are we to make of these glancing connections? Although the narratives in different states seem occasionally to reflect, invert, or mutate each other, it is difficult to know if the juxtapositions are chance combinations or meaningful connections. For example, Emily tells us that she has prepared a garden of remembering, and she echoes a line from Borges's "Garden of the Forking Paths": "I . . . bequeath to certain of the ways . . . my garden of first-class objects." Moreover, we know that she is obsessed with connecting the past to the future because she takes the trouble to bury a time capsule (in the form of her car) filled with a heterogeneous collection ranging from a pistol to a box of Kleenex to stolen plastic food. As she covers over the car she yells, "God help posterity," a statement, she confesses, that "I said a lot in those days." Emily can thus be seen as a devotee of the Line, at least in temporal terms, for she wants to connect past to present to future. In her art she preferred to see the world "through a lens of fire," a desire that took literal form when she tried to burn the cameras in the final scene of *The Waste Land*. As a filmmaker, she is exquisitely sensitive to light. She wanted to make a film about her dreams of God, but "it came out wrong in any light," appearing more like a "short film on the kingdom of death."

These narrative fragments may or may not shed light on the prisoner's dark state. Could he be trapped in the "short film on the kingdom of death" that was Emily's failed attempt to record her dreams? Or is his world running the lost minutes that the comic tells us are missing from Emily's film *The Waste Land*? The prisoner remarks that he burns continuously in a fire of purgation and that he sees the world through this fire, although he cannot remember the sin for which he should be purged. Whatever one wishes to make of these conjectures, it is clear that the prisoner is condemned to the Net in the same way that Emily is condemned to the Line, for his inability to remember goads him to create more and more stories about his situation. In the text that appears with the image of a high-tech sphere sitting on metallic legs, the prisoner insists he has been abducted by aliens, spinning a lurid yarn about the throbbing pink interior of their spaceship. But in the next line he admits the story is fabricated. He points out that if *real* aliens had abducted him, they would make sure he did not remember them. By this reasoning, the fact that he can remember a story is *prima facie* evidence it is untrue; the only true stories are those he cannot remember. Thus the sphere functions for him as a signifier for which there can be no referent. For Emily, by contrast, the sphere marks the X where she had her vision and found her vocation, an assertion of presence opposite to the prisoner's experience of the sphere as a self-consuming artifact.

Emily wanted to see the world through a lens of fire; the prisoner, who has no body, burns in a fire he cannot feel. For the comic, fire takes on searing physical reality when he falls burning from a plane wreck. Unlike the prisoner, he has a body, and unlike Emily, he is not dead. But neither is he wholly present. He tells us that he lost body parts in the crash, and he alludes to bandages swathing his head. He makes tasteless jokes about his condition—referring to himself as once the toast of the town and now toast in another sense—but it is clear that he is suffering: he tells the therapist, "If you have to throw the switch, Doc, please put out all the lights." His version of the landscape is a virtual reality simulation, and it connects glancingly with the other states. His allusion to the missing minutes of Emily's film of *The Waste Land* comes when the doctor asks him what he thinks is at the top of the steps to the Marble Building. The point for the comic is that he will never know what is at the top, because the powers that be will make sure he won't reach it. The Marble Building also appears in Emily's world, where it is associated with a speaking voice that seems to be a dream or memory of Emily's rather than Emily herself, since the voice speaks of her in the third person. It is this voice that recounts her dream in which God manifests himself as a landscape. Although no words are exchanged, the dream (or dreamer) has a sense of dialogue, a feeling of shared presence. Given that space is the generating medium from which words appear, we may suppose that God is figured here as the space from which logos emerge—a configuration that Shelley Jackson echoes in her work *Patchwork Girl*, where one of the narrators, living inside a landscape that is also a body, looks up at the "intelligent sky."[19]

This vision contrasts sharply with the prisoner's condition. He sees "nobody home" in the black cone and never senses any other presence in his world, as devoid of companions as it is of memory. The comic sees objects in the virtual landscape he tours, but he frequently does not know what they are or what they signify: "This is the altar of I-can't-say, this is your brain off drugs," he jokes about the colonnade that in Emily's state is associated with her dream of God-as-landscape. If God is space, his presence is felt only in Emily's level. In other states, the characters sense his absence, or a presence so unreadable that at most it counts as the tenuous possibility of meaning rather than meaning itself.

In light of these glancing connections, what are we to make of *Reagan Library* as a hypertext fiction? Does it desire to be a narrative as well as a mutant machine? We are given a clue in a phrase from the word salad: Error 404. In much the same way that the text is partly anchored and partly random, the links are partly pre-assigned and partly generated randomly by the computer, so the reader can never be certain where she will end up when she activates a given link. The importance of "Error 404" is reinforced when Emily calls herself "Inspector Four O Four." Web users will recognize Error 404 as the message that appears on the screen when a link has failed to connect, accompanied by the dismal announcement, "The object you requested could not be found on this server." In "Error 404: Doubting the Web," Moulthrop expounds on what he sees as the deeper philosophical implications of this error message.[20] He points out that the *visible* part of a hypertext is only part of its signifying structure. As important as the explicit text, he argues, are the gaps. These gaps can be understood in multiple ways (not all of which he explicitly enumerates). They include the spaces that the links leap over; the inferences the reader must make to render these leaps significant; the invisible machinery that performs the "go to" statement underlying the link; and the link understood as a poststructuralist articulation in which, like the purloined letter, it fails to reach its addressee even when it is performing properly.

The uncertain operation of the links in *Reagan Library* makes kinesthetically real to the reader that the computer is an active player in constructing this hypertext. It also confronts the user with surprises that are not always pleasant, as for example when the reader finds herself falling through to another state just when she has gotten interested in the previous one. The phrase "Between flying and falling" occurs both in the word salad and the stable text. This phrase accurately describes the reader's condition when she clicks on an object in the comic's fluffy sky and finds herself in the prisoner's dark world. In exploring the significance of links that fail, Moulthrop draws both on the poststructuralist arguments of Terry Harpold and on Terry Winograd and Fernando Flores's application of Heideggerean philosophy to computer design.[21] Moulthrop endorses the Heideggerean view that it is when breakdown throws us into unexpected situations that we are jolted out of our normal routines and opened to revelations about the true nature of our practices. If the uncertainty of the links in *Reagan Library* is one of the ways Moulthrop makes us experience breakdown, then what is revealed to us at these moments? To ask the question another way: to what insight are we brought by the operation of the mutant machine as it resists both the Line and the Net?

We may find a clue in the traumatized body of the comic. In "Error 404," Moulthrop makes the fascinating point that the physical trauma so often suffered by characters in electronic fiction may in some deep way reflect the injury that the electronic work conceives itself to be inflicting on the (print) body of literature.[22] We have seen that the comedian's burns link metaphorically with the lens of fire through which Emily wants to sees the world, as well as with the purgatorial fire the prisoner endures. To what assault on the (print) body of the novel do these fiery traumas correspond? Let us return to Moulthrop's train of thought in "No War Machine," where he picks up on Peter Brooks's suggestion that the plot of the novel represents a prolonged negotiation with death, in which the narrative struggles against reaching the quiescence of the ending.[23] Eventually, every plot loses this battle because it necessarily comes to an end. But hypertext, Moulthrop suggests, may have other strategies for prolonging the negotiation. With multiple narrative trajectories and no linear sequence of pages to which it is bound, the plot of a hypertext fiction may not have to end, or at least not end in any definitive way. This lack of closure may have something to do with the physical states in which the three characters find themselves. The prisoner experiences a death of memory. He has no body, and this physical trauma implies that if the book lost its body, it too would have no memory. In print culture it is not merely a metaphor to say that the printed page is memory and memory is the printed page. If acid paper crumbles, if the book is defaced or destroyed, if the ink fades into illegibility, then the archive is lost. Although electronic texts can scarcely boast of greater durability than print, they have the advantage of being able to replicate themselves at virtually no cost. Moreover, these copies can be transported over great distances essentially instantaneously, again at virtually no cost. It is significant that the prisoner makes no mention of artifacts, other than the objects he sees on the landscape. His state represents a zero condition of internal *and* external memory. The loss here is not merely the eradication of his personal recall, but also the much more traumatic loss of the Library as a repository for cultural memory. It carries Borges's Library of Babel one step further, moving from a library devoid of sense to a library devoid of books.

Emily's work emphasizes the movement of books into other media. In this way the book maintains a presence in the world, but increasingly it does so as it is adapted for other media rather than an object in its own right. Emily is good at remembering, but she is also dead — a state some have predicted for print culture. Even when alive, she mourned the fact that she could remember only the past, not the future. Her attempt to make a connection with the future by burying a time capsule fails; instead of carrying a message forward in time from the past, her time capsule is uprooted and destroyed by "one of those big convenience stores run by cargo cults." The future supplants the past, junk food crowds out food for thought, mass media replaces the book.

Finally, let us return to the comedian's body. Traumatized by his injuries, he no longer experiences the world directly but through the mediation of virtual reality simulations. As if bearing witness to the truth of Marshall McLuhan's argument that humans create media as prostheses to compensate for the auto-amputation they experience through the trauma of the modern world, the comic has literally lost body parts and tries to compensate for his damaged sensorium by using virtual reality as a prosthesis. In "Error 404," Moulthrop reminds his readers of this argument as well as McLuhan's insight that forms of subjectivity are linked to the nature of the dominant medium.[24] McLuhan argued, that the idea of the "public," with its Enlightenment connotations of intelligent general readers, was associated with print books, whereas the "mass" of the twentieth century was associated with the rise of broadcast media. What kind of subjectivity, Moulthrop asks, will emerge from computer technology?[25] The comedian's experience suggests that the paradigmatic citizen of the computer age is the cyborg, a traumatized human body that needs to be spliced into an integrated circuit with intelligent machines to function efficiently. Reading the comedian's experience as an assault on the book suggests that for environments that become ever faster, more complex, and consequently more traumatic, the book will inevitably lose out to the interactive media of computer texts and virtual reality simulations. Lest we leap too easily to this conclusion, however, we should remember that Moulthrop dreamed of a mutant machine that would resist the Net as well as the Line. The text finally does stabilize, narrative trajectories do emerge, and connections suggest themselves that could grow into something like a plot. If this were not so, how many readers would stay engaged with the text? Death by quiescence is perhaps to be preferred to death by indifference.

In his criticism, Moulthrop repeatedly engages in rhetorical moves that represent, if not a habit of mind, at least a habit of writing. He customarily builds an argument by evoking an idea, engaging with it, then swerving from that to another idea, engaging with it, and so forth. His essays proceed not as a Line but a series of feints and swerves, as if his mind were a football player ricocheting toward the goal through a field studded with muscular opponents. In the face of such strategies, the critic attempts to fix the writer's position at her own peril. I am not confident that Moulthrop intended *Reagan Library* to be read as a commentary on the fate of print; in any event, the subversion of authorial intention would seem to be part of the point. Nevertheless, if we read the text this way, *Reagan Library* becomes as dark as its ironic title. Read as an assault on the body of print, it takes no prisoners — or rather it takes one but punishes him by robbing him of memory. It carries the dispersion of narrative about as far as one could go and still preserve some hint of plot; it forces the reader to find her way between flying and falling; and it makes the reader endure many repetitions before the text stabilizes into narrative coherence. Conceptually fascinating, *Reagan Library* hovers on the border of hypertext fiction, pushing the limits of narrative pleasure as well as the limits of narrative form.

The tropes that *Disappearing Rain* and *Reagan Library* use to construct their metaphoric networks are positioned antithetically to one another. Whereas Larsen emphasizes connectivity, fluidity and mutating subjectivities, Moulthrop focuses on fragmentation, erasure, and gaps. This alone would be enough to indicate that electronic environments are radically under-determined with respect to how the materiality of the technology affects literary production. Where one writer sees connection, another sees rupture; where one perceives embeddedness, another emphasizes separation. Considered as a collection of abstract categories, the physical characteristics of electronic media are essentially infinite, from the CRT screen to logic gates to the power cord. What matters is how writers mobilize these characteristics as resources in creative work.[26] Although the technology's constraints and enablings shape the range of possibilities, the technology does not by itself dictate what can be signified with it. Rather, the changing configurations of textual bodies/bodies in the text are the result of complex dynamics between technological possibilities, cultural formations, generic traditions, and individual creativity.

Nevertheless, it is also undeniable that electronic textuality offers different resources than print. The flickering nature of electronic signifiers, the underlying code required to generate screen text, the networked and programmable capabilities of the medium, the inherently processual qualities of screenic text and images, and the multimedia convergences made possible by digital technologies are attributes that distinguish electronic textuality from durably inscribed ink marks on the pages of bound books. Deeply influenced by print, electronic environments also reflect reading and writing practices associated with traditions other than print, including Web browsing, video and computer game playing, and previous works of electronic literature. While these differences do not dictate any particular construction of textual bodies/bodies within texts, they comprise resources that in the aggregate are clearly distinct from those offered by print. Not better or worse: different.

That said, I also note that print and electronic textuality are in dynamic and robust conversation with each other. While electronic textuality offers new possibilities for thinking about texts and bodies, print has not remained static in the face of information technologies. A stroll through a bookstore is enough to demonstrate that contemporary books have become highly visual. Cookbooks, how-to books, popular histories, and travel books are among the many genres that have taken advantage of digital technologies to produce works with strong visual impact and graphic design. In a process that Jay David Bolter and Richard Grusin have called remediation, print recycles the visual tropes and design practices of electronic texts even as electronic texts recycle the tropes of print.[27] Moreover, almost all print books now produced in this country are digital texts throughout most of their production: from composition on a word processor to electronic copyediting to layout using a computer program. It would be more accurate to call print an output modality of digital text than to speak of it as if it were an entirely separate technology. Print is interpenetrated by electronic text at every point, a merging complexly reflected in the bodies of contemporary books.

These considerations suggest that as we struggle to understand how textual bodies and bodies in texts are transforming in the face of these developments, it is necessary to perform two gestures simultaneously. On the one hand, attending to the specificity of media enables us to understand how new media offer different resources for corporeal transformations of textual bodies/bodies in texts. On the other, analyzing the effects of convergence allows a deeper grasp of a dynamic media ecology in which different media compete and cooperate as they co-evolve together. Rather than standing apart from these processes, textual bodies/bodies in texts are co-constituted with them in a complex dance that Donna Haraway, following Marilyn Strathern in another context, calls ontological choreography.[28] As the Irish poet, dreaming of the strange bodies of swan and scarecrow put it, "How can we know the dancer from the dance?"[29]

Notes

1 Elizabeth Grosz has an informative discussion of the textualization of bodies in *Volatile Bodies: Toward a Corporeal Feminism* (Baltimore: Johns Hopkins University Press, 1994).
2 This point has been forcefully made by others. See George Landow, *Hypertext 2.0.* (Baltimore: Johns Hopkins University Press, 1997);

Michael Joyce, *Of Two Minds: Hypertext Pedagogy and Poetics* (Ann Arbor: University of Michigan Press, 1995) and *Othermindedness: The Emergence of Network Culture* (Ann Arbor: University of Michigan Press, 2000); and Espen Aarseth, *Cybertext: Perspectives on Ergodic Literature* (Baltimore: Johns Hopkins University Press, 1997). Among scholars working primarily with print texts, Jerome McGann argues that linguistic codes should be supplemented with equally rigorous attention to bibliographic codes. Jerome McGann, *The Textual Condition* (Princeton: Princeton University Press, 1991). D. G. McKenzie makes a similar point in *Bibliography and the Sociology of Texts* (Cambridge: Cambridge University Press, 1999, 1986).

3   Deena Larsen, *Disappearing Rain*: http://www.chisp.net/~textra/rain. Stuart Moulthrop, *Reagan Library*: http://iat.ubalt.edu/moulthrop/hypertexts/rl/ (available as a CD-ROM, *Gravitational Intrigue* [New York: Little Magazine, 1991]). All quotations in the text are taken from the Web sites given here.

4   The work on gender in cyberspace is too extensive to be referenced in this essay. Of particular relevance to my arguments here, however, are Allucquère Roseanne Stone, *The War of Technology and Desire at the Close of the Mechanical Age* (Cambridge: MIT Press, 1996); Anne Marie Balsamo, *Technologies of the Gendered Body: Reading Cyborg Women* (Durham: Duke University Press, 1996); Thomas Foster, Carol Siegel, and Elle E. Berry, *Bodies of Writing, Bodies in Performance* (New York: New York University Press, 1996); and Sue-Ellen Case, *The Domain-Matrix: Performing Lesbian at the End of Print Culture* (Bloomington: Indiana University Press, 1997).

5   For a discussion of first- and second-generation hypertexts, see N. Katherine Hayles, "Deeper into the Machine: The Future of Electronic Literature," *Culture Machine* 5 (2003): http://culturemachine.tees.ac.uk/frm_f1.htm.

6   The idea of assemblage is, of course, indebted to Gilles Deleuze and Felix Guattari, *A Thousand Plateaus: Capitalism and Schizophrenia*, trans. Brian Massumi (Minneapolis: University of Minnesota Press, 1987).

7   Joyce, *Of Two Minds*, 186.

8   Ibid.

9   See, for example, Stuart Moulthrop, "Error 404: Doubting the Web," in *Metaphor, Magic, and Power*, ed. A. Herman and T. Swiss (New York, Routledge, 2000). Stuart Moulthrop, "No War Machine," in *Reading Matters: Narrative in the New Ecology of Media*, ed. Joseph Tabbi and Michael Wutz (Ithaca: Cornell University Press, 1997). Stuart Moulthrop, "Traveling in the Breakdown Lane," *Mosaic* 28, no. 4 (1995): 55–77.

10   Robert Coover, as quoted in Moulthrop, "Traveling."

11   Moulthrop, "Traveling."

12 Michael Joyce, *Afternoon, a story* (CD-ROM. Watertown, Mass.: Eastgate Systems, 1987).

13 Moulthrop, "No War Machine."

14 Vannevar Bush, "As We May Think," *The Atlantic Monthly* 176, no. 1 (July 1945): 101–8.

15 Pat Cadigan, *Synners* (New York: Four Walls Eight Windows, 2001).

16 N. Katherine Hayles, *How We Became Posthuman: Virtual Bodies in Cybernetics, Literature, and Informatics* (Chicago: University of Chicago Press, 1999).

17 For a sampling of John Cage's chance operations as a way to do an end-run around intentionality, see Marjorie Perloff and Charles Junkerman, eds., *John Cage: Composed in America* (Chicago: University of Chicago Press, 1994).

18 John Cage, *M: Writings '67–72* (Middletown: Wesleyan University Press, 1974).

19 Shelley Jackson, *Patchwork Girl* (CD-ROM. Watertown, Mass.: Eastgate Systems, 1995).

20 Moulthrop, "Error 404."

21 Terence Harpold, "The Contingencies of the Hypertext Link," *Writing on the Edge* 2 (1991): 126–38; Terry Winograd and Fernando Flores, *Understanding Computers and Cognition: A New Foundation for Design* (Boston: Addison-Wesley, 1987).

22 Moulthrop, "Error 404."

23 Moulthrop, "No War Machine."

24 Moulthrop, "Error 404."

25 Ibid.

26 For a more extensive discussion of media specificity, see N. Katherine Hayles, *Writing Machines* (Cambridge: MIT Press, 2002).

27 Jay David Bolter and Richard Grusin, *Remediation: Understanding New Media* (Cambridge: MIT Press, 1999).

28 Donna Haraway, "The Companion Species Manifesto: Dogs, People, and Significant Otherness," Lecture at University of California, Los Angeles, 28 April 2003.

29 The poem is, of course, "Among School Children" by William Butler Yeats, *The Collected Poems of W. B. Yeats*, edited by Richard R. Finneran (New York: Scribner, 1996), 215–17.

Thomas Swiss

ELECTRONIC LITERATURE

Discourses, Communities, Traditions

Technology has put art to the rout.
—DAVID LEHMAN, *The Last Avant-Garde*

For a long time everybody refuses and then almost without pause
almost everybody accepts.—GERTRUDE STEIN, "Composition
as Explanation"

To hear the critics tell it, one problem with emergent digital literary and art forms is that they don't yet have established stars.
Where's our Shakespeare of the Screen? Our Pixel Picasso? How
long before we have a Digital DeMille? The assumption is that we'll
have them eventually—undisputed geniuses working in what is now
generally called "New Media." But behind this assumption is another assumption, one with a long, sometimes thorny history—
that the "best" or "most important" art is created by an individual,
a single pair of hands in the study or studio. As a poet, I began
collaborative, Web-based work with visual and sound artists several years ago—with a sense that the opportunities and demands
of Web-based poetry, like many other New Media practices, have
their roots in the shared notion of community that was integral
to the development of the Internet. I was also increasingly interested in what Hal Foster calls "the twin obsessions of the neo-avant

Thomas Swiss and Skye Giordano, *Genius* (2000).

garde": temporality and textuality.[1] Web-based poems—especially those involving links, animation, and attention to the pictorial elements of writing—suggest novel approaches to thinking about time and the text. Collaborative work redefines artistic labor in what is for me new and complicated ways: What is the relationship, for example, between my language and the images and sounds that others create, even if under my "direction"? How do the images and sound "change" the meaning of the language (and vice versa) and in what ways can the piece be said to still be a "poem"? Collaboration allows writers and artists—like myself and those with whom I compose—to reconsider both our work and our identities, to literally see them anew, as we move from individual to composite subjectivity. Yet while the art world has sometimes been open to collaborative work—in the long shadow of Marcel Duchamp's experiments with Man Ray, the shared labor of producing art in Warhol's Factory, the many hands needed to make a film—the literature world has always had a hard time accepting collaborative work, even in our digital age.

With the advent of digital technologies, new forms of electronic writing challenge already-contested terms such as "literature" and "text" and further complicate boundaries between literary genres. What is electronic literature? As Marjorie Luesebrink notes, it is a concept still slouching toward definition.[2] Among those who regard literature as a form of essential and authentic experience, there is a persistent historical tendency to vilify "technology"—including computer-based digital technologies—as a corrupting force. Alternatively, among those who champion the use of technology in the creation of literature, the tendency has been to glorify it as a form of liberation for both writers and audiences alike.[3] Among writers and critics in both camps, their narratives embody profound desires, hopes, anxieties, and fears about digitally based literature.

These narratives have less to do with "technology" and more to do with "culture"—in this case, literary culture. They are a response to the growing electronic literature community that in complex ways—in addition to the ever-quickening development of digital technologies, more powerful authoring software, and increasingly sophisticated work—brings together artists, graphic designers, sound technicians, musicians, and computer programmers. This new community constitutes an artistic underground, an avant-garde literary movement that alternately challenges and ignores the institutional apparatus for "traditional" or "mainstream" literature.[4]

In the broadest sense, electronic literature includes all writing that is produced in digital form. This would include everything from the reproduction of, say, Shakespeare's plays on the Web, to Sylvia Plath's poems reproduced for reading on newly developed electronic devices such as the Rocket e-Book. It would also include Stephen King's novel *The Plant*, which was downloaded from the Internet and paid for by readers in installments, starting in the summer of 2000. King's experiment brought a lot of public attention to developments in digital technology, to their impact on the materiality of texts, and to the economics of publishing. His high-profile (and seemingly successful) venture suggested a powerful new publishing model that dispenses with both traditional publishing "houses" and even with "the book" itself. It is not surprising, then, that in the second half of 2000, publishing companies like Random House and Time-Warner rushed to set up electronic publishing divisions—planning to compete not only with each other but also, in some cases, with "their own" authors.

More narrowly and currently less visible, another category of electronic literature is "hypertextual"—literature meant to be read on a computer screen (not printed out, as the King novel typically was), and characterized by multiple links from pages or sections, multilinear structures, and recursive loops. Hypertextual literature, which is primarily or exclusively language-based, generally employs temporal or spatial organizational styles that fall outside the conventions of most print texts. The best-known, most widely circulated literary hypertexts continue to be published by a small company in Maine called Eastgate Systems. Eastgate has been producing, for more than fifteen years, disk-based and CD-based hypertexts such as the widely reviewed *Patchwork Girl* (1995) by Shelley Jackson; *afternoon: a story* (1990) by Michael Joyce; and *Victory Garden* (1991) by Stuart Moulthrop. But hypertextual literature—or what Katherine Hayles, following Umberto Eco, calls "open work" —has been available on the Web, too, for the last half-dozen years.[5]

More recently, the example of hypertextual electronic literature has encouraged another subcategory—that of "hypermedia" or "New Media." Hypermedia literature may or may not have a multilinear form, but it nearly always uses graphics, sound, animation, or video as part of the content. It is typically Web based, employing specific technologies developed for the Web and accessible at a site *on* the Web. Works such as Carolyn Guertin's *Incarnation*, a hyperlinked "walk" through a maze of language with accompanying music and graphics, is a good example. So is Jennifer Ley's *Daddy Liked His with Heart*, which uses animated images and midi tracks to explore stereotypes and clichés associated with the word "heart."[6] Like hypertextual literature, hypermedia literature is a genre in flux; both are sometimes called "Web-specific writing," "cyberliterature," or even, in the case of hypermedia work, "netart." This last term clearly acknowledges its hybridity, its relation to images and sound. But the term that seems most likely to stick, at least for a while, is "New Media literature."[7]

The specific technologies that enable hypertextual and New Media literature are so new that the rhetoric of and about this literature is still emerging and therefore particularly unstable and contested.

This rhetoric nevertheless carries plenty of historical baggage because there are always already material and historical relationships between text-producing machines and the texts produced through them—whether the machine is a nineteenth-century phonograph and typewriter or today's networked computer. Lisa Gitelman reminds us in her study of inscription devices around the turn of the twentieth century that "accounts of digital textuality rely upon historically comparative explanations."[8]

Of course, historically comparative explanations also govern, more broadly, our changing notions of the Web itself. Consider, for example, the automobile-age language of the Internet "information superhighway," which functioned as the dominant metaphor in the early years (1994–1997) of the Web. While it enabled, shaped, and governed the widespread development and use of the Web, it has now largely faded from public view. Do our understandings and experiences of the Web, and the material construction of the Web itself, change—if only in subtle ways—as this key phrase becomes less productive in the social imagination and finally runs out of gas? And what terms, what ways of describing electronic literature are already beginning to shift within and against a modernist genealogy on which they draw for their imagery as well as their approach?

Hyping, Sniping, Almost Reconciling: Popular and Academic Discourses

Digital literature in a hypertextual mode, developed during the mid-1980s, was immediately trumpeted—by those who wrote it and by those who wrote *about* it—as a new arena where writing practices, aesthetics, and identities could be staged, negotiated, and transformed. From the outset, then, "electronic literature" was an ideology and discourse in addition to being a technology and a genre. Like other avant-garde literatures, it was often understood in the first phase of its development to be in opposition to or at least in competition with "conventional" writing.

By many early accounts, hypertextual writing aspired to the condition of noise, not music. It meant to jam the normal literary frequencies, create a disruption, introduce some useful static. To quote George Landow, an early supporter of and writer about hypertextual literature, "[Hypertext will] overthrow . . . all kinds of hier-

archies of status and power. . . . [It is] radical, revolutionary."[9]
Published in 1992, Landow's influential book, *Hypertext*, articulated
many of the things that early hypertext writers had been saying
about their work.[10] As Matthew G. Kirshenbaum notes in his brief
history of hypertext, Landow fused specific strands of postmodern
theory to specific works, most of them published by Eastgate Systems.[11] Starting with the straightforward fact that readers "follow"
links (by clicking on them) to create their own "paths" or "trails"
through connected bits of language or documents, Landow explains
that this means not only that no two readers read a hypertext in
exactly the same way but that the reading process is "active" and
"exploratory" rather than passive and predetermined. From this
modest if contestable definition, Landow then celebrated hypertext
as the "embodiment" of postmodernism, the technological realization of large-scale changes in human thought and perception.[12]

Landow wrote his book for an academic audience. But a "popular" version of this argument, more widely read and discussed, soon
appeared in the *New York Times Book Review* under the sensational
headline "The End of Books." Robert Coover, a well-published
writer and colleague of Landow's at Brown University, suggested
that the print novel had reached the end of its useful life and that
hypertextual literature would free writers and readers from "the
tyranny of the line." The new, computer-assisted fiction "with beginnings, middles and ends no longer part of the immediate display . . . accrete meaning, just as the passage of time and events does
in one's lifetime."[13] In addition to these extremely broad claims,
Coover, like Landow, also attempted to locate the new writing more
narrowly in literary history. He noted a number of "innovative"
nineteenth- and twentieth-century writers—Laurence Stern, James
Joyce, Italo Calvino, Jorge Luis Borges—whom he claimed inhabited
the same landscape as the new crop of hypertextual authors.

Academic writing and scholarly conference papers over the next
five years debated many of the issues initially raised by Landow
and Coover.[14] They increasingly theorized hypertextual writing as
"postmodern" collage or as "participatory" and "interactive" writing that opened up the closed, "immersive" narrative of the traditional print fiction.[15] Meanwhile, in 1994, Sven Birkerts published
The Gutenberg Elegies: The Fate of Reading in an Electronic Age, a book
that attacked electronic literature. Birkerts argued for the fixed stability of the printed page and against "putting ourselves at risk"

with computer-mediated writing.[16] As Landow's book had done for Coover, Birkerts's work provided a rich source for Laura Miller's 1998 publication in the *New York Times Book Review*—the provocative "www.claptrap.com." Few essays crystallize as nicely as does this one a set of opposing ideological and discursive relations as they resonate through an emerging literary practice.

Reading literary hypertexts, writes Miller, "is a listless task, a matter of incessantly having to choose among alternatives, each of which . . . is no more important than any other . . . The experience feels profoundly meaningless and dull."[17] While unusually harsh in tone, Miller's piece indeed represents a common enough view of early hypertextual writing in a literary mode: it's pointless. Not that literary hypertexts have always gotten such bad press, as I have noted. In fact, Miller references "The End of Books," writing that "six years after Coover's essay was published . . . I've yet to encounter anyone who reads hypertext fiction. No one, that is, who isn't also a hypertext author or a journalist reporting on the trend" (43). By the end of her piece, Miller has declared not only the popular triumph of traditional fiction but—touché!—the death of hypertextual literature.

Miller's "www.claptrap.com" is a one-sided view that is wildly unfair to the literary hypertexts she mentions. Nevertheless, her noisy partisanship brings into focus something of what was at stake—and for whom—in what I am calling the first phase of critical writing about electronic literature. Two different ways of generalizing about hypertextual writing surfaced in the 1990s with very different implications. On one side are those who find the terms "hypertext" and "literature" to be oxymoronic. Like Miller, they argue that literary hypertexts distort the true processes of both creating and reading literature. On the other side are those interested in the ongoing constitution of literature in and through technological media. They see "hypertext literature" and "New Media literature" as literature first, the way "kinetic sculpture," for example, is adamantly sculpture.

These are, for the most part, old arguments played out in a new age. Transformations in the materiality of literary texts, the relationship between literature and technology, between literature and other arts—such issues have been worried over by critics and writers at least since the invention of the printing press. By the early twentieth century, the multiplication of print technologies along with new technologies of reproduction and transmission, inspired the French avant-garde to call for poetry that would recuperate reproductive technologies. Writers such as Guillaume Apollinaire and Arthur Rimbaud, for example, argued that "mechanically produced" writing might successfully compete in a more broadly defined cultural market.[18] Later, in the 1960s, American writers like William S. Burroughs and Richard Kostelanetz made a similar case. Both writers explored mechanical and computer technologies in relation to composing literature (Kostelanetz called one of his projects *Kinetic Writings*), arguing that the barriers between symbolic and commercial fields should not be rigid.[19]

All of these writers believed that changing the structures and strategies of literature—as indeed the use of typewriters, photographs, video, and other technologies have changed writing and reading throughout this century—is inevitable, useful.[20] But Guillaume Apollinaire and Arthur Rimbaud, like William S. Burroughs and Richard Kostelanetz, remain to this day "outsiders."[21] In the popular imagination and—to a somewhat lesser extent—in the academy, the still-dominant tradition situates literature in opposition to "technological" mediation. "Technology" is seen negatively —as intrusive, disruptive, "mechanical." Indeed, electronic writing often does disrupt narrative conventions and, especially, the closural tendencies of more traditional ways of reading, but not all readers or critics see that as a bad thing.[22] In fact, some critics don't see disruption as even being something new. Joseph Tabbi points out: "Given the material constraints on print narratives, we tend to forget that, at any point within the covers of the book, the inevitability of ending may be resisted or put off."[23]

Like Birkerts in his musings on hypertext, Miller invokes a populist "we" in "www.claptrap.com" to speak for the imagined masses —as if literary tastes and consumption habits were one simple thing and were not always fragmented, distributed across an array of niches. At one point, Miller writes about literary hypertext: "No one really wants to read it, not even out of idle curiosity."[24] Later, she notes what "the common reader craves [is] . . . the intimacy to be had in allowing a beloved author's voice into the sanctums of our minds" (43). While the writing in this passage may strike some readers as approaching the purple prose found in fan magazines or the dreamy talk about literature heard on *Oprah*, Miller's point is nevertheless clear. And so is her anger a manifestation, as I have noted, of the anxieties many share about digitally based literature and its effects on literary culture, both "high" and "low." But who is Miller angry with?

Although she doesn't quite come out and say it, Miller's real beef may be less with hypertextual literature (which, finally, she does not waste many words on or read closely) than with "hypertext's champions" and the critical, academic discourse that has thus far defined the genre. "How alienated academic literary criticism is from actual readers and their desires," Miller writes, here echoing a long-standing complaint that scholars have created a critical language so specialized that it excludes "actual readers" (43). To a large extent, then, the first discourses surrounding electronic literature—writing by defenders such as Landow and Coover as well as writing by detractors such as Birkerts and Miller—may have had more to do with the diffusion of "theory" and the popular reaction against it over the last twenty years than it did with literary writing practices per se. In this way, the arguments are not only about canons but also about institutions and communities, resembling many other insider/outsider debates generated by experimental and avant-garde literary works in the twentieth century.[25]

Is this "first phase" of discourse about hypertextual writing really over? Probably not, although the increasing prevalence of the Web with its plentiful New Media and hypertextual stories, poems, and art projects seems to have made a difference in lessening critical resistance. Still, certain viewpoints persist. In a recent essay titled "Link to Nowhere" found on the well-known britannica.com site, Neal Pollack argues about hypertextual writing: "However beautifully written, however cleverly constructed, it's simply too busy dissecting itself to be of any real interest to the general reader."[26] He notes that most hypertextual literature lacks "deep content." While he never says what "deep content" is, and how readers might recognize it, the thrust of Pollack's argument seems to suggest that he, like Laura Miller, understands the purpose of literature to be "making sense of the chaos of this world, and our passage through it, because making sense of it is humanity's great collective project."[27] The broad ideological assumptions made by both Pollack and Miller are merely asserted, never examined. Grudgingly, however, Pollack does indeed differ from Miller when he announces, late in his piece, that "it seems possible, even likely, that hypertext literature will soon slip the bounds of its medium and seize the popular imagination."[28]

Even Pollack's qualified expression of the "possible" popular acceptance of hypertextual literature is problematic, however, as it suggests a wish for transcendence over the materiality of language. How, exactly, might hypertext literature—or *any* literature —"slip the bounds of its medium?" Visible here again is the rift between particular ideological and historical representations of reading practices—a rift often articulated today in the competing discourses of cultural journalism versus academic writing. The notion that the materiality of writing—its distinctive shape, its typographical or digital character—should or even *can* be transcended or "slipped" is one that has been mostly disregarded in the context-oriented materialist scholarship of contemporary literary and cultural studies. Said another way, most academic critics would argue that literary language is not a window to be seen through —not, as Marjorie Perloff writes, "a transparent glass pointing to something outside it, but a system of signs"; indeed, systems and signs mostly ignored in press accounts of hypertextual literature as critics continue to look through language for "deeper meaning."[29] As Nancy Kaplan writes: "Rather than lying outside the word and therefore providing a container for the work's content, the decisions that determine the page boundaries [in hypertextual literature] not only affect how a story or an essay looks; they also form constituent parts of the work's design."[30] Kaplan's description brings us back to Apollinaire. That is, while newly applied to electronic literature, Kaplan's argument is rooted in the early-twentieth-century explanations of the typographic revolution brought about by futurism, cubism, and dadaism, and, in the 1950s and 1960s, by concrete or visual poetry.

Among the proponents of electronic literature, I think we can see clearly the signs of what we might think of as a *second phase* of critical writing. This turn mirrors what Robert Coover, speaking about the production of literary hypertexts, has recently called "the passing of the golden age": "A decade or so ago, in the pre-Web era of the digital revolution, a new literary art began to emerge . . . This was, in retrospect, what might be thought of as the golden age of literary hypertext. For those who've only recently lost their footing and fallen into the flood of hypertext, literary or otherwise, it may be dismaying to learn that they are arriving after *the golden age is already over*, but that's in the nature of golden ages: not even there until so seen by succeeding generations" (emphasis added).[31] At any rate, if the early rhetoric in support of hypertextual writing was, to quote Miller, "warlike, full of attacks launched against texts that can offer no defense, prove vulnerable, and ultimately yield,"[32] that rhetoric seems to be passing into history as this literature attempts—as experimental and avant-garde writing often has—to move from the margins to the mainstream, from noise to music. By enlisting different arguments, borrowing from often-neglected work on writing as a material form, such established writers as Jackson, Joyce, Moulthrop, and Hayles are increasingly, and wisely, calling for medium-specific analysis. According to Hayles: "As we work toward crafting a critical theory capable of dealing with the complexities of electronic texts, we may also be able to understand for the first time the full extent to which print technologies have affected our understanding of literature. . . . The juxtaposition of print and electronic texts has the potential to reveal the assumptions specific to each."[33]

Other critics, such as Carolyn Guertin, have argued that hypertextual and New Media literature are not out to displace conventional print-based writing but should simply be seen as a new subcategory—the way, for example, under the broad term "fiction," "mysteries," "science fiction," "romances," and so on are already included. Still other proponents make different or even contrary arguments, noting, for example, that hypertextual literature is not a single genre, but multiple genres with different forms, structures, and grammars.[34] As Nancy Kaplan writes about hypertextual literature's critics in "Literacy beyond Books: Reading When All the World's a Web": "Ignoring the manifold differences among particular hypertexts as well as among the authoring systems by which they were produced, they have gathered the similarities into an essence or set of essential features to postulate and then attack."[35] In this essay, she makes a spirited argument for the work of learning to read this new literature, the work of puzzling out its particular literary codes and conventions.

New Literary Communities

Electronic literature, as I have suggested, is still thought of by some mostly in terms of "computers"—a great "daisy chain" of scanners and software programs, digital cameras and recording devices—rather than in terms of practice. Of course "practice" includes not

only the various uses of computers in the composition of hypertextual and New Media writing but also, more generally, the organization of production and consumption of this work.[36] In considering
this organization, what can be said about some of the still-emerging
institutional practices of the electronic literature community as
they reflect (and diverge from) the standard practices of production
and consumption in the historical literary avant-garde?[37]

Eastgate Systems, the pioneering company that was instrumental
in first publishing (on disks and, later, on CD-ROM) and distribut-
ing literary hypertexts, managed by the early 1990s to create a kind
of "local" scene for hypertext writers. Because of the use of e-mail,
news groups, and Web pages, however, I mean "locality" here to
denote less a place than a space: a network that brings people and
their ideas together. In this way, the electronic literary community,
which typically works and meets in cyberspace, diverges from the
historical avant-garde in that *geographical* place has not been a defining feature as it had been, say, for earlier outsiders, including mid-
twentieth-century collectives such as the San Francisco Beat writers
and the New York school of poets. Specializing in "serious" hypertexts, Eastgate's stable of writers included such influential authors
and critics as Landow, Moulthrop, and Joyce. In its early years especially, from the late 1980s to the mid 1990s, this pre-Web literary
community created what might be thought of as a countercultural
literary strand—reminiscent of many avant-garde literary movements in the twentieth century, each with their own brand of revolutionary "outsider" attitudes and insights. In its early years, this
community developed aesthetic approaches and language largely
outside of and in opposition to the dominant institutions of American literary culture.

Eastgate supported the fledgling hypertext community and, like
any small business needing to make a profit, hoped eventually to
alter hypertextual literature's outsider status by helping to move
this work into the mainstream. Resembling other "niche" publishers of avant-garde work—e.g., City Lights bookstore in the
1950s, which provided the Beat writers an early home; or Roof Press,
which still provides a publishing outlet for "language" poetry—
Eastgate offered hypertext writers a site for the community as it
grew. It also offered writers a business model for selling their work,
a model that included aggressive marketing. Using the tag line "serious hypertext" in all of its promotional materials, Eastgate wisely

marked out a "high" literary space early on for its products, making in effect a preemptive strike on those critics who refused to take seriously anything seriously composed in hypertext.[38]

Eastgate single-mindedly committed to promoting an aesthetic revolution not only by marketing hypertextual literature, however, but also by selling its own software for composing in hypertext (the well-known Storyspace software) and serving as a clearinghouse for books and other materials about hypertextual literature.[39] Around the same time, starting in 1990, the journal *Postmodern Culture* began as an experiment in scholarly publishing on the Internet and eventually became a leading electronic journal of interdisciplinary thought on contemporary culture. While not directly connected to Eastgate, the first editors of *Postmodern Culture*, including Eastgate author Stuart Moulthrop, shared an interest in encouraging thinking and theorizing about electronic literature.

By the mid to late 1990s, the influence of Eastgate had diminished for a number of reasons, including the fact that Eastgate was still wedded to selling its Storyspace software, which was now only one of a number of proprietary authoring programs available—some of them more powerful and less expensive than Storyspace. Its status was also diminished by the fact that the Web had made the development and promotion of New Media literature easier, as well as more various and free. Thus, a greater number of authors began to experiment with hypertextual and New Media Web-based literature, placing their work on private Web sites and finding each other —and forming communities—through search engines and portals like Michael Shumate's "hyperizons" and Alan Liu's "Voice of the Shuttle."[40] These sites gathered and linked related sites from all over the world.

Further, in the last five years a number of important Web-based journals have emerged, providing outlets and encouragement for literary experiments. Like the American "little magazines" that helped create the modernist canon in the years between 1912 and 1920, these resolutely noncommercial electronic journals with their minuscule staffs seem poised to create version 1.0 of the New Media literary canon. Their editorial stances and missions echo those of earlier magazines like the *Little Review*, the partisan avant-garde journal that since its start in 1914 published early work by American writers such as Wallace Stevens, T. S. Eliot, and Amy Lowell. The relationship between old and new can be seen, for example, in the journal of electronic writing and art *lume*, which takes an argumentative stance similar to that of the historical literary avant-garde. As it declares its "mission" on its Web site: "*lume* is devoted to the exploration of possibilities for electronic writing—the possibility of form, the possibility of meaning, the possibility of a writing that is more (or less) than it was in print. Our hope is that by creating a site focused entirely on electronic writing and art we can avoid the failures of imagination that have thus far attended the debates over the value of a medium that is still very much in the process of coming into being, and to suggest new possibilities for writing that are not dependent upon the authority of the printed word for their validation."[41] Like the *Little Review*, the *Dial*, or *Close-Up*, little magazines that questioned the literary canon of their time, contemporary electronic journals such as *lume*, as well as *Beehive*, *Riding the Meridian*, *Drunken Boat*, and the *Iowa Review Web* (an offshoot of the well-known literary journal), solicit the work of promising new hypermedia writers along with "more established" experimental writers like Joyce and Jackson.

In an interesting twist on the tradition of gathering writers of a particular stripe into an anthology—a tradition that has often, by its collective nature, been able to bring visibility to certain kinds and "schools" of new literature—online journals also have begun publishing "surveys" of New Media literature. Of special note is *Riding the Meridian*, an online journal that has published two large and influential surveys, the first of which brought together Web-specific work by women in 1999. The survey's title, "The Progressive Dinner Party," is a nod to the tradition Judy Chicago pioneered in her well-know installation piece, "The Dinner Party," a recognition and celebration of women's contributions to art and culture.[42] As Katherine Hayles notes in an introduction to the survey of thirty-nine works, many of the pieces—while not all classifiable, perhaps, as New Media "literature"—encourage interactive explorations of visual language in a Web-based environment that is visually and conceptually intriguing.[43] The second anthology, "Jumpin' at the Diner," surveys Web-specific work by forty men, including pieces that mix language, image, and sound by such electronic literature innovators as John Cayley and Jim Rosenberg.[44] Rosenberg's work is striking in that he often uses the visual trope of the "diagram." His poems employ word clusters, by analogy to the musical concept of tone clusters, as a way of disrupting syntax.

Like the early little magazines, too, the new Web-based literary journals are shaping a new literary canon by providing a forum in which New Media writers can act as critics, writing about and supporting each other's work. They reproduce the role assumed earlier in this century by poets acting as critics who began to give what has become the received high-modernist canon its first, tentative shape.[45] At least for now, it seems to be the New Media artists themselves who are following in the tradition of the *Little Review*, which once proudly (and amusingly) announced itself as the journal "read by those who write the others."[46]

Other emerging institutional support for the production and reception of electronic literature includes several dozen university courses, including those at Brown University, Georgia Institute of Technology, the University of California at Los Angeles, and other colleges. There are also online working groups for writers such as the monthly Online Workshop for Electronic Literature, begun in 1998 by writer Deena Larsen. Borrowing the traditional "workshop" approach to critiquing creative writing, authors meet in an Internet MOO space (an object-oriented multi-user dimension) to discuss works in progress, give and get suggestions for improvement, and learn more about electronic writing.[47] Trace, started in 1996, is another well-known online community for writers, including hypertext and New Media writers.[48] Based at Nottingham Trent University in England, the community conducts its business by e-mail, sponsors live meetings and events via the Internet, and has a large site on the Web.

The Electronic Poetry Center, started in 1996 and housed at the University of Buffalo, shifts the focus from writers to readers, serving as a popular gateway to resources in electronic poetry and poetics. "Our aim is simple," the home-page statement reads, "to make a wide range of resources centered on contemporary experimental and formally innovative poetries an immediate actuality."[49] Finally, The Electronic Literature Organization, formed in 1999, is also a community that plans to grow; its "ultimate goal is an expanded readership of literature written for electronic media." Of all current groups serving as proponents for electronic literature, its mission may be the best-funded and the most ambitious: "While Austria, Australia, and the United Kingdom are making cultural investments in electronic literature, by sponsoring governmental and nonprofit organizations with programs that help to enable the development of new electronic art forms, we have not yet seen that level of commitment in the United States, the center of the Internet economy. The Electronic Literature Organization is committed to filling that gap in our cultural landscape."[50]

Of course where there are Web sites, there are also advertising banners and Web site awards—in this case, both are mostly geared to encourage networking and community among those interested in electronic literature. *Beehive*, for example, carries advertising banners for Eastgate Systems, Trace, the Electronic Literature Organization, and other similar sites and groups. The Electronic Literature Organization carries logos for its various Web site awards, which, as Greg Elmer notes in "The Economy of Cyberpromotion: Awards on the World Wide Web," "speak to a hypertextual politics of finding and being found . . . promoting a hypertextually linked community of like-minded resources and interests outside of the . . . subject-based default portal, search engine or net guide."[51] While many writing communities begin as collective and egalitarian enterprises, however, they often change as they flow or attempt to flow from "noise" to "music." Institutional awards and prizes often signal this change.

Thus while Web site awards may be more about building community than building a literary canon, other awards and prizes—and there have been a number of them—can't help but contribute to the canonization of individual writers and texts. By 2001, New Media literature prizes had risen to: $10,000 for an entry in poetry; an equal amount awarded in fiction.[52] Entries in both categories are being juried with the following criteria: "Innovative use of electronic techniques and enhancements; literary quality, understood as being related to print and electronic traditions of fiction and poetry, respectively; and quality and accessibility of interface design."[53] What is most interesting about these criteria, perhaps, is not only that they preserve the traditional genres of "poetry" and "fiction" (therefore presumably excluding the genre-blurring "net-art," etc.) while simultaneously emphasizing innovativeness, but that they also situate "literary quality" in print and electronic "traditions," thus downplaying the more fiery language of the avantgarde and playing up historically comparative relationships and judgments.

Like other avant-garde literatures before it, hypertextual and hypermedia fiction and poetry are self-consciously experimental. Now
moving into a second phase, the practices of and discourses about
electronic literature in the age of the Web are increasingly mature
and expanding. In the fashion of most experimental writing, however, writers and critics of electronic literature began by defining
the work through its differences from "traditional" literature. Early
commentaries often highlighted the aesthetics of "rupture" and
"disruption," the ways in which electronic literature challenged
common assumptions about reading and writing. As Jay Bolter, an
early theorist of and software developer for hypertextual literature,
reflects in his introduction to a recent anthology of Web-based writing: "Enthusiasts for new media tend to be unitarians. They ask us
to believe that one media form will come to be dominant and to
define our digital culture . . . But in fact nothing in our current media
culture suggests that a single form will dominate all the others."[54]

Indeed, recently there has been an attempt on the part of both
authors and critics to understand electronic literature in a historical context that locates the work alongside other kinds of creative
work, including extraliterary or nonliterary art practices such as
sound art, illustration, photography, graphic design, and even film.
Francesca da Rimini's "Los Dias y Los Noches de las Muertas," for
example, employs streaming graphics, photographs, and audio in
combination with a haunting political text that takes its cues from
both the language of the military and the "statement-art" of Barbara
Kruger.[55] Young-hae Chang and Marc Voge, creators of "Dakota"
and "Lotus Blossom," reinforce this approach:

> In our work there is: no interactivity; no graphics or graphic design;
> no photos; no illustrations; no banners; no millions-of-colors; no play-
> ful fonts; no fireworks. We have a special dislike for interactivity. To
> us it's a paltry, laughable thing, like getting a kick out of pulling the
> trigger of a gun: click: bang. We don't get it. When we click on inter-
> active art, we get the feeling we're the rat in the Skinner box, except
> there's only the miserable reward, not the shock. Art isn't reward, it's
> shock, or something approaching it, something we would call beauty.
> Our Web art tries to express the essence of the Internet: information
> and disinformation. Strip away the interactivity, the graphics, the de-

sign, the photos, the illustrations, the banners, the colors, the fonts and the rest, and what's left? The text.[56]

One of the distinguishing features of electronic literature, one of the things that make it "new," is that it generally contests the presumed clear distinction between poetry, prose, exposition, and other literary genres. Yet, as hypertextual and New Media literature attempt to move from the margins to the mainstream, from "noise" to "music," its growing community of artists and critics represent and institutionalize this new work in time-honored ways: through its explanatory and theoretical writings; through venues such as meetings and conferences; through prizes, contests, and other public awards; and through the development of publishing outlets. Indeed, looking at the rhetoric of and about electronic literature as it plays out among texts, audiences, and institutions is a powerful reminder that the meaning of the term "literature" itself is always up for grabs—and that "electronic" literature, whatever the future might hold for it, is currently the site of many important conversations, struggles, and debates.

Notes

1 Hal Foster, *The Return of the Real*, (Cambridge: MIT Press, 1996), 32.
2 Marjorie Luesebrink (interview by author) "Literature in a Hypermedia Mode" *Popmatters* 11 (September 2000) (http://www.popmatters.com/a-and-i/000909.html).
3 Paul Theberge, "Technology," in *Key Terms in Popular Music and Culture*, ed. Bruce Horner and Thomas Swiss (Oxford: Blackwell, 1999), 245. Theberge makes this argument related to technology and popular music.
4 Any use of the term "avant-garde" may be problematic, of course, but coded as it is in this chapter in terms of specific resistant/alternative articulations of literary practices, I hope it might be useful. Like surrealism, constructivism, and other historical avant-garde forms that aimed to expand the writer's authority as aesthetic innovator, New Media writers have developed a critique of the print-based conventions of traditional literature. Further, New Media literature has increasingly forced an investigation of the *institution* of literature, its perceptual and cognitive, structural and discursive parameters. Hal Foster's genealogy of visual art and theory from minimalism and pop to the mid-1990s is instructive in its reading of

what he calls the "neo-avant-gardes," and it has shaped my own in regard to New Media literature (see Foster, *The Return of the Real*).

5 N. Katherine Hayles, "Flickering Connectivities in Shelley Jackson's *Patchwork Girl*: The Importance of Media-Specific Analysis," *Postmodern Culture* 10.2 (2000) (http://iath.virginia.edu/pmc/current. issue/10.2hayles.html).

6 Guertin's work is at http://trace.ntu.ac.uk/traced/guertin/incarnation/maze.htm/; Ley's piece is at http://www.heelstone. com/heart/felt.html.

7 "New Media" seems to be the term writers and critics have settled on for now, using it to describe the Web generally as well as certain kinds of work being done on the Web: New Media journalism, New Media art, New Media fiction, and so on. Richard Grusin and Jay Bolter helped popularize the term among academics with their book *Remediation: Understanding New Media* (Boston: MIT Press, 1999). Museums, especially, have begun to use the term New Media, perhaps following the lead of Lev Manovich's art-friendly book, *The Language of New Media* (Boston: MIT Press, 2000). Two widely covered art shows in New York in 2001 have helped popularize the term among journalists and the public: "010101: Art in Technological Times" at the Museum of Modern Art and "BitStreams" at the Whitney Museum. Throughout this chapter, I use the term New Media literature as a synonym for hypermedia literature: Web-based or CD-based literature that mixes language, images, and sometimes sound. But I also note that electronic literature is a broader category and that hypertextual literature, which predates hypermedia or New Media literature, typically does not contain images or sound.

8 Lisa Gitelman, *Scripts, Grooves, and Writing Machines* (Stanford: Stanford University Press, 1999), 5.

9 George P. Landow, *Hypertext: The Convergence of Contemporary Critical Theory and Technology* (Baltimore: Johns Hopkins University Press, 1992).

10 Jay Bolter and Stuart Moulthrop were among the early hypertext writers and critics who worried over and wrote about issues such as narrative closure; hypertext's precursors; the relationship between computers and literature, and so on. See Jay David Bolter, *Writing Space: The Computer, Hypertext, and the History of Writing* (Hillsdale, N.J.: Lawrence Erlbaum Associates, 1991), and Stuart Moulthrop, "Containing Multitudes: The Problem of Closure in Interactive Fiction," *Association for Computers in the Humanities Newsletter* 10 (1988): 29–46.

11 Matthew G. Kirschenbaum, "Hypertext," in *Unspun: Key Concepts for Understanding the World Wide Web*, ed. Thomas Swiss (New York: New York University Press, 2001), 135.

12 Landow, *Hypertext*, 27.

13 Robert Coover, "The End of Books," *New York Times Book Review* (21 June 1992): 25.

14 Hypertext issues mapped out by Landow, Moulthrop, Coover, and others were debated on panels and in individual papers most notably, perhaps, at the many high-profile worldwide conferences sponsored each year by the Association for Computing Machinery. See http://info.acm.org/ for an archive of some of the conference programs from these years.

15 Indeed, the notion of "immersion," of an *embodied* versus a disembodied readership/spectatorship, is one that continues to haunt arguments about not only electronic writing but also cinema. See, for example, Lauren Rabinovitz's essay in this volume. Moreover, comparing "interactive" stories with traditional print-based stories, critic J. Yellowlees Douglas writes: "highly conventionalized plots, stereotypic characters and settings make for an ease and more even pace of reading that absorbs readers' cognitive capacity more completely, leading to the absorption and trancelike pleasures of ludic reading" (Douglas, *The End of Books—or Books without End?* [Ann Arbor: University of Michigan Press, 2000], 146).

16 Sven Birkerts, *The Gutenberg Elegies: The Fate of Reading in an Electronic Age* (Boston: Faber and Faber, 1994).

17 Laura Miller, "www.claptrap.com," *New York Times Book Review* (15 March 1998): 43. Also at http://www.nytimes.com/books/home/.

18 See Carrie Noland, *Poetry at Stake: Lyric Aesthetics and the Challenge of Technology* (Princeton: Princeton University Press, 1999).

19 Thomas A. Vogler, "When a Book Is Not a Book," in *A Book of the Book*, ed. Jerome Rothenberg and Steven Clay (New York: Granary Books, 2000), 460.

20 The arguments described here, grounded in the literary world, are similar to ongoing discussions and debates about "the digital" also taking place in the fields of art, photography, and film, among others. Historically, media shifts create anxiety among artists and critics—the creation of photographic engraving early in the twentieth century, for instance, revolutionized commercial advertising, but more controversially it also encouraged literary editors to include additional illustrations in their publications. It resulted, too, in the development of modern visual poetry.

21 Even more "outside"—in that their books are less available and they are infrequently taught in the United States—are those writers and groups of writers who took more radical positions involving both aesthetics and literary politics. I am thinking here of the dadaist Tristan Tzara, for example, and Raymond Queneau and the Oulipo writers who invented or reinvented restrictions of a formal na-

ture and composed accordingly. Walter Abish's *99: The New Meaning* (Providence: Burning Deck, 1990), for instance, consists of five sections composed wholly of collaged material taken from other writers.

22 For a discussion of Apollinaire's role in this debate, see Noland, *Poetry at Stake*, 4–15. Other versions of this debate have pitted literature and literacy against television (the well-known and nationally discussed "Why Johnny Can't Write" article in *Newsweek* in the 1970s) and against video games and computers more recently. See Nancy Kaplan, "Literacy beyond Books: Reading When All the World's a Web," in *The World Wide Web and Contemporary Cultural Theory*, ed. Andrew Herman and Thomas Swiss (New York: Routledge, 2000), 211.

23 Joseph Tabbi, "Narrative," in *Unspun: Key Concepts for Understanding the World Wide Web*, ed. Thomas Swiss (New York: New York University Press, 2000), 139.

24 Miller, "www.claptrap.com," 43.

25 Examples include the French symbolist poets, as well as futurist and cubist poets in the early 1900s, the concrete poets and lettrists in the 1950s and 1960s, and the language poets of the 1980s and 1990s, among others. See Johanna Drucker, *Figuring the Word* (New York: Granary Books, 1998).

26 Neal Pollack, "Link to Nowhere," 30 March 2000 (http://www.britannica.com).

27 Miller, "www.claptrap.com," 43.

28 Pollack, "Link to Nowhere."

29 Marjorie Perloff, *Poetry On and Off the Page* (Evanston, Ill.: Northwestern University Press, 1998), 171.

30 Kaplan, "Literacy beyond Books," 211.

31 Quoted in N. Katherine Hayles, "Literary Hypertext: The Passing of the Golden Age," *Feed* (http://www.feedmag.com/document/do291_master.html).

32 Miller, "www.claptrap.com," 43.

33 Hayles, "Flickering Connectivities in Shelley Jackson's *Patchwork Girl*."

34 Carolyn Guertin, 1 November 2000 (http://www.ualberta.ca/%7Ecguertin/Guertin.htm).

35 Kaplan, "Literacy beyond Books," 211.

36 Theberge, "Technology."

37 A few words about the term community may be helpful here. I define "community" as a group of writers and supporters with shared interests, goals, or orientations. As Christopher Beach points out in *Poetic Culture* (Evanston, Ill.: Northwestern University Press, 1999), writers' communities are "the link between individuals and institutions" (80). As I have noted, experimental literary communities have been

fundamentally important to American writing throughout history, creating powerful subcultures that can address issues outside the artistic mainstream—issues that challenge the literary canon, itself an institutional structure.

38 Eastgate still uses this tag line (see http://www.eastgate.com).

39 Storyspace, hypertext software for writers, enabled writers to create fairly sophisticated links. Michael Joyce and Jay Bolter developed the software in the mid-1980s (see Bolter, *Writing Space*).

40 The URL for hyperizons is http://www.duke.edu/~mshumate/ hyperfic.html; Voice of the Shuttle is http://vos.ucsb.edu/.

41 See http://epc.buffalo.edu/ezines/lume/moment1/contents1.html.

42 *Riding the Meridian*'s "The Progressive Dinner Party" site is at http:// califia.hispeed.com/RM/dinner2.htm.

43 Hayle's comments on the survey are at http://califia.hispeed.com/ RM/haylesfr.htm.

44 "Jumpin' at the Diner" is at http://califia.hispeed.com/Jumpin/ jukeframe2.htm.

45 Alan Golding, "The Dial, The Little Review, and the Making of the Modern Poetry Canon," unpublished paper, 6.

46 Ibid.

47 The Online Workshop for Electronic Literature workshops, organized by Deena Larson, meet in Lingua MOO at http://lingua. utdallas.edu:700.

48 The URL for Trace is http://trace.ntu.ac.uk/.

49 The Electronic Poetry Center site is located at http://wings.buffalo. edu/epc/.

50 The Electronic Literature Organization site is located at http:// www.eliterature.org/.

51 Greg Elmer, "The Economy of Cyberpromotion: Awards on the World Wide Web," in *The World Wide Web and Contemporary Cultural Theory*, ed. Andrew Herman and Thomas Swiss (New York: Routledge, 2000), 189.

52 While the $10,000 prize for electronic literature is a source of legitimization and economic support, the amount pales by comparison with cash prizes awarded on a regular basis to print poets. These prizes include the Tanning ($100,000), the Ruth Lilly ($75,000), and the Lannon ($75,000).

53 Electronic Literature Organization. "Judging Criteria," http://www. eliterature.org/Awards2001/criteria.php.

54 Jay David Bolter, "Sampling the Jukebox," 1 January 2001, http:// califia.hispeed.com/Jumpin/bolter.htm.

55 The piece is located at http://califia.hispeed.com/RM/fdarimini. htm.

56 The site is located at http://www.yhchang.com/.

Vivian Sobchack

NOSTALGIA FOR A DIGITAL OBJECT

Regrets on the Quickening of QuickTime

It is as though all this material represented an underground network
in which the only visible landmarks were the boxes and collages,
and the difficulty of communicating their meaning was a
source of both regret and satisfaction. —DAWN ADES,
"The Transcendental Surrealism of Joseph Cornell"

Whenever I watch QuickTime "movies" (a nomination I want to interrogate here and thus keep under quotation), I find myself drawn
into someone else's—and my computer's—memory. Even when the
content speaks of the contemporary moment, the form itself seems
a remembrance of times—and things—past. Faced with its strange
collections, its moving collages and juxtapositions of image-objects
whose half-life I can barely remember, I tend to drift into the space
and time of a reverie not quite my own. Indeed, as QuickTime
"movies" play out and often repeat their brief, ambiguous animations and elusive, associative narratives in those "little boxes" that
I "open" on my computer "desktop" (or Web "browser"), the form
most frequently evokes from me the kind of temporal nostalgia and
spatial mystery I feel not when I go to the movies, but when I try
to "inhabit" the worlds of Joseph Cornell's boxed relics, or wan-

der among the enigmatic exhibits in the Museum of Jurassic Technology in Culver City, California, or leaf through pictures of the personalized collection of "curiosities" found in the *Wunderkammer* of the sixteenth and seventeenth centuries.[1]

Most of all, however, QuickTime "movies" remind me of Cornell boxes.[2] Both preserve "under glass" the selected and static fragments of a "read-only" memory that, paradoxically, evokes memory as "random access"—that is, as dynamic, contingent, and associational. Both QuickTime "movies" and Cornell boxes also do not open out onto worldly horizons of space and time. Unlike big-screen, live-action movies, they draw us down and into their own discrete, enclosed and nested poetic worlds: worlds recollected and remembered; worlds more miniature, intensive, layered, and vertically deep than those constructed through the extensive, horizontal scope and horizonal vision of cinema.[3] Both QuickTime "movies" and Cornell boxes also salvage "the flotsam and jetsam" of daily life and redeem it as "used" material whose recollected and remembered presence echoes with bits and traces of an individual yet collective past: personal memories, narratives, histories that were, from the first, commodified and mass-mediated. And, through reverential framing, both QuickTime "movies" and Cornell boxes construct what might be called "reliquaries": they preserve and cherish "the fragment, the souvenir, the talisman, the exotic" as precious matter, and treat "the ephemeral object as if it were the rarest heirloom."[4] In sum, both QuickTime "movies" and Cornell boxes contain "intense, distilled images that create a remarkable confrontation between past and present."[5]

Indeed, this "remarkable confrontation between past and present" is furthered by QuickTime's stuttering attempts to achieve "real-time" movement—or to capitulate to and embrace the temporal and spatial lacunae that visibly mark its expressions. While cut-out statues and matted silhouettes may float gracefully like collaged dreams across photorealist backgrounds that effortlessly warp and melt, "live-action" and "real-time" balk and stiffen in contrast. Strangely static and consequently moving, the temporal field of QuickTime "movies" is oneiric and uncanny—and its animations more effluvial than continuous. Full of gaps, gasps, starts, and repetitions, made "precious" by their small size and "scarce" memory, QuickTime "movies" seem to intensify our corporeal sense of the intensive molecular labor and matter of human and worldly "becoming." Thus, they evoke for me not the seamlessly lived and wholly present animation of "real-time" and "live-action" movies, but, rather, the "half-life" of certain time-worn and ambiguous kinetic objects: wooden puppets with chipped paint, forsaken dolls with gaping head wounds or missing limbs, Muybridge-like figures in old flip books hovering with bravado and uncertainty between photograph and cinema, images of nineteenth-century strong men or belly dancers hand-cranked into imperfect action through old Kinetoscopes found deep in the dark corners of amusement arcades. What comes to mind as I watch QuickTime "movies" is not "live-action" and "real-time" cinema at all; instead, I associate them with those forms of animated film that foreground the cinema's usually hidden struggle to achieve the "illusion of life"[6]—with the works of Jan Svankmajer or the Brothers Quay in which kinetic objects inhabit miniaturized worlds and achieve a laboriously animated life that somehow (and at some deep and molecular level) reminds us of the labor of our own. Hence, I take pleasure in the rumor that the thin-faced master puppet who gets caught up in and subjected to the intense, time-encrusted, miniature world of the Quays's *Street of Crocodiles* was modeled after Joseph Cornell.[7]

At the risk, then, of sounding retrograde and nostalgic, I don't want QuickTime "movies" to get any quicker. I also don't want to watch them get any bigger. Furthermore, given the value and pleasure I find in their fragmented temporality and intensely condensed space, I don't want them to achieve the "streaming" momentum of "real-time" and "live-action"—measured, although it need not be, against the standard and semblance of cinema. Indeed, precisely because QuickTime's miniature spatial forms and temporal lacunae struggle against (as they struggle to become) cinema, they poetically dramatize and philosophically interrogate the nature of memory and temporality, the values of scale, and what we mean by animation. In sum, I don't want them to become "real movies" at all.

Nonetheless, they will. At least that's what every computerphile enthusiastically tells me. It's just a matter of time—and compression and memory and bandwidth—before the "limitations" of the medium in relation to moving images no longer display themselves in their peculiar specificity as "different" and "other" and (for many) "less" than the space-times of cinema or television. Before that happens, however, before QuickTime "movies" as we see them today disappear (becoming both an extinct aesthetic form and a computergraphic expansion of cinema and television), I want to consider—and celebrate—them for what they presently are.

Refusing the "Myth of Total Cinema"

In QuickTime, a set of time-based data is referred to as a *movie*.
—"Introduction to QuickTime"

All this is to say that it is a shame that QuickTime "movies" were ever called movies: in being so named, their extinction as a specifically discrete and computergraphic form of aesthetic expression was virtually preordained. And this need not have been—yet could it be otherwise? Digital theorist Lev Manovich has made the astute observation that the basic metaphors reified by computer interfaces —metaphors such as the "desktop" with its "files" and "trashcan" or the "cinema" with its practices of "cutting," "compositing," and virtual "camera movement"—are also, and more significantly, *cultural interfaces*: preexisting and widespread cultural forms of conceptually organizing and visualizing data borrowed on by a new medium that, after all, had other options.[8] Consider, for example, the developers' documentation for QuickTime, "a set of functions and data structures" that permits applications to cooperatively "control time-based data." QuickTime itself, we are told, is not an application, but a "true multimedia architecture": a specific "enabling technology . . . comprised of pieces of software [that allow an] operating system to handle dynamic media [so as to] integrate text, still graphics, video, animation . . . and sound into a cohesive platform." However, this rather open initial description turns proscriptive at its end: hence the emphatic epigraph that introduces this present section of my essay and reduces QuickTime to a "*movie*."[9]

Long ago now, André Bazin wrote "The Myth of Total Cinema," an essay that argued that the novel technical discoveries "basic" to cinematic invention were "fortunate accidents but essentially second in importance to the *preconceived ideas* of the inventors." That is, "in their imaginations they saw the cinema as a total and complete representation of reality; they saw in a trice the reconstruction of a perfect illusion of the outside world in sound, color, and relief." Thus, "the cinema was born . . . out of a myth, the myth of total cinema."[10] And the myth of "total cinema" still remains—

this despite technical discoveries that have allowed the invention of a "new medium" (one that digitizes, integrates and, in so doing, transforms all others). In this regard, as a primary cultural interface with the computer, the cinema and its mythic teleology have, on the one hand, merely carried on and extended the representational imagination and realization of cinema from sound and color to "relief" (QuickTime 3 now incorporates 3-D graphics and virtual reality navigation and interaction), and, on the other hand, blindly or willfully asserted *the primacy of cinema in the face of its transformation into "something else" by another medium*.[11]

Again, the developers' documentation is telling. Its very first sentence introducing the "set of time-based data" on which Quick-Time operates as a *"movie,"* the documentation nonetheless continues: "A traditional movie, whether stored on film, laser disk, or tape, is a continuous stream of data. A QuickTime movie can be similarly constructed, but it need not be . . . . *The movie is not the medium; it is the organizing principle.*"[12] Here we have the significance of cinema as a primary cultural interface: while its very principles of organization enable a certain comprehensible use of the new medium, they also constrain its capacities and influence the trajectory of its "development" and practice. Thus, for all that the cultural interface of cinema allows, it also causes a certain "blindness" to both the phenomenological and material differences between QuickTime "movies" and cinematic movies. The aesthetic values of the former are measured against those of the latter—and the true computergraphic "novelty" of QuickTime works becomes historically inverted and transformed into a false cinematic "primitivism." Hence the desire to make QuickTime "movies" quicker and bigger rather than stopping to wonder at and privilege the strangely stalled momentum of their animation and the heightened intensity condensed by their miniaturization and framing.

Indeed, I would have much preferred naming QuickTime works "memory boxes" rather than "movies." Such a nomination not only evokes Joseph Cornell's work but also the essential nature of the new medium that is the fundament of QuickTime's existence: the *computer* in both its physical form and essential function. Also, insofar as it refers to a range of diverse containers (from reliquaries to children's "treasure" boxes to shoe boxes filled with photographs or souvenirs), "memory box" is a nomination that—particularly in the present technological moment—insists on memory's immaterial and dynamic status as well as the historical transformation of the material conditions of its preservation. The computer (and all its extensions) is nothing else but a fathomless "memory box"— one that collects, preserves, and allows for the conscious retrieval and remembering, the visible recollection, of selected fragments of all the possible memories "cached" in the "enormous, underground network" of past images, sounds, and texts that constitute the utopian totality of a potentially infinite and hyperlinked database.

"Memory Boxes" and the Database

A well-calculated geometric description is not the only way to write a "box."—GASTON BACHELARD, *The Poetics of Space*

In *The Poetics of Space*, Gaston Bachelard writes of a character in a novel who basks in the solidity and order of his oak filing cabinet: "Everything had been designed and calculated by a meticulous mind for purposes of utility. And what a marvelous tool! It replaced everything, memory as well as intelligence. In this well-fitted cube there was not an iota of haziness or shiftiness."[13] Despite its lack of solidity, I get the same feeling from my computer "desktop." It reassures me with hierarchy, with clarity and order, with principled and logical menus, commands, and systems through which I can access vast amounts of information (if not intelligence). This database of information, while unseen, does not seem "hidden" to me; rather, it is "filed" away in "folders" and, more deeply, in "records" and "fields." It is rationally organized and always hypothetically available for retrieval and display. Indeed, the "well-fitted cube" that is my computer gives me access to what seems an infinite store of information (if not knowledge)—and I take comfort in the hierarchical logic of its "unhazy" and "unshifty" memory (of an order quite different from my own). Here is the logical—and "official"—organization of the "office," of the catalog, the library, the museum, and the stockroom. Here, everything has been "designed and calculated by a meticulous mind for purposes of utility." Here, I've no sense of the "secretive" or "unconscious": at worst, information gets bureaucratically "classified," misplaced, or erased (not repressed). In sum, the phenomenology of comfort afforded by the "file cabinet" and the "database" refuses ambiguity, ambivalence, poetry.[14]

Human memory and its recollections don't compute so neatly. The orderly and hierarchical logic of the file cabinet and the database is not that of *Kunstkammern* or *Wunderkammern*, of Cornell or Quick-Time "memory boxes." Some other rationale—and phenomeno-logic—operates here: one more associative than hierarchical, more dynamic than static, more contingent than determined (even when "given" to us as spectators or users in "read only" form). Its search engines driven to the past by a present moment of desire (not utility), this is the eccentric, ever-extensible, yet localized logic of the *hyperlink*. The contingent nature and function of personal desire as well as the nonhierarchical and associative logic of the hyperlink transform the organization—and phenomenology—of the file cabi-net and the database into something quite other than it was. The file cabinet becomes charged with experience, temporality, and desire, and its hierarchical order becomes jumbled by logically incom-patible—if psychologically comprehensible—functions. Following Cornell's description of just one of the file folders relating to his work, we could say that the entire file cabinet is now transformed into "a diary journal repository, laboratory, picture gallery, mu-seum, sanctuary, observatory, key . . . the core of a labyrinth, a clear-ing house for dreams and visions."[15] And the database? No longer hierarchical, its order becomes that of a comprehensive but incom-prehensible labyrinth: a vast and boundless maze of images and sounds, dreams, and visions in which one follows, backtracks, veers off, loses oneself in multiple trajectories, all the time weaving tenu-ous threads of association in the logically endless teleology and tex-ture of desire. Here, the materials of the world are never fixed data or information merely requiring *recollection*; here, from the first, they are unstable bits of experience and can only be *remembered*.

The poetic and phenomenological power of both Cornell and QuickTime "memory boxes" emerge explicitly from their relation to a larger totality of material and memorial possibilities: they and their found objects exist not only as fragments of personal experi-ence but also as "emblem[s] of a presence too elusive or too vast to be enclosed in a box. These missing presences crowd the imagina-tion."[16] Thus, in differentiating QuickTime "memory boxes" from "movies," it bears pointing out that while watching a film I usually don't have a profound sense of all the images that weren't shot or all the stuff left on the cutting-room floor; yet while watching a Quick-Time "memory box" I always feel the presence of an "elusive" and "vast" absence, a sea of memories shifting below the surface and in the interstices of what I watch. In other words, I am always aware of an effluvial database.

Thus, by virtue of their framing, their miniaturization, their valuation of the fragment, and the slightness and ambiguity of their associational links, both Cornell and QuickTime "memory boxes" point to their own presence as the poignant and precious "visible landmarks" of an unseen, lost, and incomprehensible field of experience. And what Carter Ratcliff says of Cornell's "memory boxes" is equally true of QuickTime's: "Ultimately, the mode is enchanted by fragmentariness itself, which serves as an emblem of a wholeness to be found in other times and places," and it produces "an aura of loss which is as perfect in its own way as reunion would be." [17] And thus, as James Fenton notes: "Here was a place for private contemplation of the beautiful and curious. The important thing was to stay alone with these boxes for a while . . . allowing them to exert their slow influence." [18] And under this slow influence, states Ratcliff, "the panic of loss gives way to nostalgia." [19]

Frames within Frames

Two kinds of space, intimate space and exterior space, keep encouraging each other, as it were, in their growth. —GASTON BACHELARD, *The Poetics of Space*

Yet Ratcliff's notion of "a mode enchanted by fragmentariness" that serves as "an emblem of a wholeness to be found in other times and places" cannot stand as a complete description—for we cannot ignore the presence of Cornell and QuickTime "memory boxes" and their fragments as themselves *containers*. Furthermore, their miniature size, their collector's sensibility, and the discretion of their enclosures gain particular power from and exist always against their own *containment* by a larger—and marked—visual field. Both externally and internally, works by Cornell and by QuickTime provoke a structural and poetic tension between two different logics: one represented by the hierarchical and rational organization of the "file cabinet" and computer "desktop" where everything has its place in some comprehensive master plan; the other by the associational organization that is the psycho-logic of the "memory box" and the "hyperlink" in which everything has a relative and mutable order that, as a totality, cannot be mastered. This tension is simultaneously *framing* and *framed*.

As a framing device, this tension exists in—and as—a space *exterior* to, and containing and juxtaposing, the associational logic of the Cornell box and the museo-logic of the vitrine in which it sits, or the hyperlink logic of a QuickTime "memory box" and the hierarchical logic of the computer "desktop" on which it is opened. That is, the larger frame of the museum vitrine or computer desktop allows the smaller frame of the "memory box" an intensified condensation and concentration of its visible contents into an *aesthetic totality*: a personally meaningful and contained microcosm structurally homologous to—and nested within—all the potential order and meaning (not meaninglessness) of the macrocosm that surrounds them. In this aspect, both Cornell and QuickTime "memory boxes" take on the magnitude and function (if not the geometric size) of the *Wunderkammer* and *Kunstkammer,* chambers of curiosities and art curated less on logic and rational principle than on the personal sensibility and desire of their wealthy collectors.

Writing of these condensed collections, Anthony Grafton wonders what sixteenth- and seventeenth-century visitors sought in them; he concludes it was the experience of totality and plenitude: "They hoped, that is, to encounter the universe in all its richness and variety, artfully compressed into the microscopic form of a single room that showed all the elements, all the humors, all the musical intervals, all the planets, and all the varieties of plant and animal creation."[20] Neither hierarchically arranged nor meant to serve utilitarian or scholarly purpose, the compressed totality of the *Wunderkammer* was also not fraught by the implications of its own contingent desire and arrangement nor overwhelmed by its (to our eyes) chaotic clutter. Indeed, historicized, its totalizing impulse can be read as a celebration of mastery, order, harmony, and structural homology; that is, man's comprehension of the "universe in all its richness and variety" was represented mimetically in a single chamber complacently "nested" within the larger frameworks of both the master's residence and God's "master plan." Certainly, there are similar compressions and homologies articulated in the smaller *Wunderkammern* of Cornell and QuickTime "boxes" as they emerge structurally and figurally as both "framing" and "framed" within a larger field. But this "compression" of a homologous "universe" is apparent also in the *content* of these more contemporary "memory boxes." Their multilayered and rich imagery is marked repeatedly by the recurrence of maps; planetary and astrological charts; hourglasses, clocks, and other measuring devices; diagrams and schematics of optical devices from the microscope to telescope; evolutionary and devolutionary biological images of microbes and spores and skulls and skeletons. In sum, by consistently asserting homologies of shape and structure across a scale from the microscopic to the macrocosmic, much like the *Wunderkammer* these "memory boxes" position themselves as both framing and framed by larger cosmologies and cosmogonies.

Nonetheless, times and cosmologies change. While contemporary manifestations of the *Wunderkammer* may situate themselves in homologous relation to smaller and larger worlds, their relation to "totality" and its "mastery" is historically transformed. The assertion of homologies between the microscopic and macrocosmic is not emblematic of man's security and mastery in Cornell's boxes—and, in QuickTime boxes, this assertion foregrounds a relativism quite other than the comforting and "nested" unity of God's master plan. Cornell's references to, as well as containment of, macroscopic and microcosmic images seem nostalgic—indeed, elegiac—in relation to a totalized harmony and order, homologies between quotidian and cosmic objects thus provoking a sense of the great loss—and mystery—of perfect "comprehension." (Here we might remember Ratcliff's description of the boxes as generating "an aura of loss . . . as perfect in its own way as reunion would be".) In QuickTime "memory boxes," homologies between the microscopic and macrocosmic are also not about mastery or a sense of security and "nestedness": here the revelation of self-similarity across scale and structure constitutes a disconcerting and chaotic relativism, often evoking the vertiginous and nonhierarchical totality of "infinite regress" and "cosmic zooms"—and thus undoing an entire hierarchical history that positions and privileges the mastery and rationality of both "man" and "God." Indeed, in QuickTime it is not God's rational master plan mimetically framing or framed by the "memory box" opened on my computer desktop or browser: rather, these images of maps, measures, microbes, and constellations mimetically contain and figure and point to the total containment and mastering structure of a more contemporary—and secular—"main" frame: the computer.

As indicated earlier, the tension between the two different logics that organize the objects and structure of these contemporary "memory boxes" emerges not only in the juxtaposed relation between the interior space of the boxes and the external space that frames them. It also emerges *framed within* the intimate space of the boxes themselves—revealed in imagery that manifests both an appreciation and fear of the associational contingencies, oneiric secrecy, and mysterious material poesy that pervade lived experience and yet threaten to overwhelm it. Bachelard writes: "For many people, the fact that there should exist a homology between the geometry of the small box and the psychology of secrecy does not call for protracted comment."[21] Nonetheless, it is worth noting that within both Cornell and QuickTime "memory boxes," we see such a homology *literalized* again and again: the associational vagaries and "hyperlinked" debris of contingency, dream, and secret desire *overlaid* and in palimpsestic relation with the hierarchical and "orderly" order of the rational "file cabinet." Cornell's work evidences this internal tension even in name: his boxes exist in a taxonomic series titled "Jewel Cases," "Museums," "Pharmacies," "Aviaries," and "Habitats." Furthermore, as Ratcliff notes, "when Cornell feels the clutter becoming too oppressive, he sweeps it into those compartmented formats which draw on the orderliness of Victorian cabinetry and the museological devices of natural historians." His "Museums" and "Pharmacies," in particular, are "works which tuck images into drawers and vials and grids."[22] Compartments, grids, drawers, slots, and boxes within boxes: these manifestations of hierarchy and order do not only point to potentially larger (and smaller) frameworks of organization so that "scale is more than flexible, it is multiple, in Cornell's art";[23] such nesting also frames and contains potentially uncontrollable fragments of temporality and experience that are infinitely extensible in their generation of memory and meaning and secrecy.

The same is true of QuickTime "memory boxes." Frequently "overlaying" the image fragments and detritus of their remembered experience are orderly grids and schematic diagrams, geometry in the form of mattes that segment and compartmentalize. And more specific to the particular medium, this compartmentalization and gridwork point not only to the larger order and framework of the surrounding "desktop" but also to the smaller geometries and hidden, "secretive," orders of microchips, bits, and bytes. That is, remembered experience in QuickTime is often "bit-mapped" and "pixelated": boxed fragments of photorealist images are fragmented and compartmentalized further into smaller boxes yet, unresolving the personal meaning and contours of human memory and resolving them as the visible and controlled geometry that informs the computer's underlying memory and structuration.

There is, then, both without and within QuickTime and Cornell "memory boxes" the tension between two kinds of logic and order and between a desire for recollection and for remembering. Memory itself is thus generated and enacted by both "box" and "viewer" as a multistable phenomenon—one echoed in a *layered* and *palimpsestic* structure and imagery that together provoke a richly poetic ambivalence and ambiguity. On the one hand, the geometry of compartments and mattes and pixels recollect and contain the amorphous and ever-extensible material of experience; on the other, the composited and collaged accumulations and associations of this experiential material always also challenge the neatness of recollection by remembering it—and we are reminded there is a radical difference between a "pharmacy" and a "treasure box," between a computer's memory and our own. Thus, we could say, according to Bachelard, that the "two kinds of space"—"intimate" and "exterior"—that frame and are framed by Cornell and QuickTime "memory boxes" gain poetic power through their juxtaposition and layering: they "keep encouraging each other, as it were, in their growth."[24]

"Little Movies": Memory, Miniaturization, and Compression

Here the poet inhabits the cellular image.—GASTON BACHELARD, *The Poetics of Space*

Although he argues that "cinema" is a primary "cultural interface" in our engagement with the digital, Lev Manovich has used Quick-Time to make a series of what he calls "little movies" that use "classic" cinematic imagery as the "aw material" of a digital exploration that interrogates the differences between these media.[25] Furthermore, all six of his "little movies" privilege and foreground the limitations of computer memory and storage space under which they are constructed and by which they are constrained.[26] Appearing in only a small portion of the lower third of a black background (itself framed within the computer screen by the Web browser), each of the six pieces variously explore and emphasize their *miniature size* and *compressed nature*.[27] In this regard, one piece, titled *A Single Pixel Movie*, is particularly striking. To a quite literally "loopy" tune reminiscent of Laurel and Hardy's theme music, we watch the already small square of a primitive "movie" in which a strong man holding a pole does exercises and is intermittently interrupted by a "blip" and a digitized circle of "light," where both "movie" and "digital blip" become increasingly smaller (and less audible) at each interruption until both are reduced to a single pixel on the screen. The effect is more compelling and poignant than the mild comedic repetition of mechanical motion and the see-sawing music would seem to warrant: that is, we watch more and more intently as the already miniaturized image becomes smaller and smaller and we are aware throughout of the increasing fragility and impending disappearance not only of the oblivious optimism of the strong man and "early" cinema but also of the QuickTime "movie" presently being extinguished from our human sight.

It is no small thing that these "little movies" are "small" both spatially and temporally. As Bachelard tells us in *The Poetics of Space*: "It must be understood that *values become condensed and enriched in miniature*."[28] Susan Stewart also notes of the miniature in her *On Longing: Narratives of the Miniature, the Gigantic, the Souvenir, the Collection*: "A reduction in dimensions does not produce a corresponding reduction in significance."[29] Indeed, quite the opposite. Pointing out that "we should lose all sense of real values if we interpreted miniatures from the standpoint of the simple relativism of large and small," Bachelard writes: "A bit of moss may well be a pine, but a pine will never be a bit of moss. The imagination does not function with the same conviction in both directions."[30]

Thus, QuickTime "movies"—or, as I prefer, "memory boxes"— not only emerge from and allegorize the present objective necessities and constraints of data storage involving digital memory and compression, but they also accrue phenomenological and aesthetic value as an effect of these necessities and constraints. Objectively, the miniature is a compression and condensation of data in space, but phenomenologically and poetically the compression and condensation of the miniature in space *intensifies* the experience and value of the "data" and makes of it something "rare" and "precious," something spatially "condensed" yet temporally "interiorized" and thus "*vast* in its way."[31] Furthermore, the miniature exaggerates *interiority*: in the "little movies" or "memory boxes" of QuickTime, not only the interiority of the individual perceiving subject but also of the computer. As a digital version of *The Incredible Shrinking Man*, the strong man exercising in Manovich's *A Single Pixel Movie* is extinguished from human vision but not from the computer's: while "in the mind of God, there is no zero," in the memory of the computer there is always zero—and always also one.[32] Thus, as Stewart suggests, "that the world of things can open itself to reveal a secret life—indeed, to reveal a set of actions and hence a narrativity and history *outside the given field of perception*—is a constant daydream the miniature presents."[33] The miniature, then, is always to some degree secretive, pointing to hidden dimensions and unseen narratives. Its "nestedness" within a larger whole draws us not only *beyond* its frame, but also *into* and *beneath* it.

In this aspect, the miniature is transcendent, its "metaphoric world" making "everyday life absolutely anterior and exterior to itself."[34] One gets this sense of "transcendence and the interiority of history and narrative" viewing QuickTime's "little movies" and Cornell's small "boxes." For Stewart, however, these effects are most dominant in our encounter with what she considers "the most consummate of miniatures—the dollhouse." Nonetheless, her description also speaks to the phenomenology of QuickTime's and Cornell's miniaturization: "Occupying a space within an enclosed space, . . . the dollhouse is a materialized secret; what we look for is the dollhouse within the dollhouse and its promise of an infinitely profound interiority."[35] Thus, Cornell's miniaturized "memory boxes" (themselves constituted from compartments and spaces "within an enclosed space") become, as McShine puts it, not only "sanctifications of the small object," but also constitute "an infinity of atmospheres within a small space." And it is not merely a fortunate "coincidence" that McShine echoes Stewart when he writes: "Although Cornell's choice of intimate scale also reflects the world of childhood, of containment, of the architecture of dollhouses, it almost makes reference to Vermeer interiors—with tables, cupboards, maps, globes, light, glass—holding captive a moment in a transient, enclosed world."[36]

In sum, the spatial condensations of Cornell and QuickTime and their framings within the frame constitute an interiority that transcends quotidian spatial and temporal relations—and "as an object consumed," their miniaturization "finds its 'use value' transformed into the infinite time of *reverie*." [37] In the dollhouse spaces and interior chambers of the "memory box," now excluded by their physical size, both artist and viewer imaginatively prospect and inhabit the empty rooms, filling them with their own missing presence in fragments of autobiography, dream, memory, confession. (Speaking both to us and its maker, one QuickTime miniature superimposes over a vague, empty, and receding hallway the following textual reverie: "Here is the solitude from which you are absent.") [38] Thus, whether in my sight or not, the strong man of Manovich's "little movie" will exercise forever in the depths of my—and the computer's—memory: unlike my engagements with cinema, I never quite have the sense that QuickTime "movies" are ever really "over" (indeed, that their terminus is ever really "under"). Thus, Cornell, although he used slots, drawers, and compartments to contain and control the materials of overwhelming experience, he also used them to draw us inward into an ever-extensible reverie: the compartments, according to no "rational or logical sequence," further housing and condensing "private and nearly unfathomable associations, almost like a metaphor for the cells of the unconscious mind." [39] Here, in the space-time that is the miniature and the reverie it provokes, it can indeed be said that "the poet inhabits the cellular image." [40]

Mnemonics, Reverie, and Reliquaries

The casket contains the things that are *unforgettable*, unforgettable for us, but also unforgettable for those to whom we are going to give our treasures. Here the past, the present and a future are condensed.—GASTON BACHELARD, *The Poetics of Space*

The miniature "memory boxes" of QuickTime and Cornell memorialize fragments of past experience in all their secretive interiority and mystery. In framing and effect, they act as "reliquaries," preserving "under glass" remnants and souvenirs that gain power from partiality but also from the *precious nature* of the boxes' own small size: as discussed previously, to a great degree the "valorization of the contents" emerges through a "valorization of the container." [41]

Hence the fragment and the miniature "encourage" each other, evoking the "singular," the "rare," the "fragile," the "ephemeral," and the "compressed" as materially and poetically valuable.[42] Manovich makes "little movies" that his text suggests will disappear, as "the artifacts of the early days of digital media." Bachelard privileges treasure chests and caskets.[43] And Cornell creates "jewel cases" and places some of his compositions "under bell jars" as if "holding captive a moment in a transient, enclosed world."[44]

The preciousness articulated here also emerges from the particular kind of contingency that informs the artfully arranged but "found" objects of the "memory box." That is, we encounter these remembered objects as objective recollections that have been subjectively assembled according to ephemeral associations, the very slightness of the links among them making their present appearance seem singular, fragile, fleeting—and thus precious. Stewart, writing of the material fragments of the past gathered in photograph albums or collections of antiquarian relics or souvenirs, points out: "There is no continuous identity between these objects and their referents. Only the act of memory constitutes their resemblance. And it is in this gap between resemblance and identity that *nostalgic desire* arises."[45]

This sense of a "gap between resemblance and identity," of the tenuous and fleeting associations of memory, leads not only to nostalgic desire but also to a desire to *preserve* the associations, to *keep* them "in mind." Thus, these "memory boxes" tend to contain and enact what I would call a *mnemonic aesthetic*. This aesthetic both practices and privileges devices and operations that serve to fix and preserve the fleeting ephemera of memory, to "pin them down" and "put them under glass" as are the gloriously colored butterflies one sees "fixed" in the vitrines of natural history museums. Such mnemonic practices are all based on *repetition* and *rhythm* and in the "memory boxes" of both Cornell and QuickTime can be seen in a variety of forms and modes such as "rote quotation" and mnemonic clichés; "looping," duplication, and cyclical recurrence or repeated uses of images, objects, and sounds; rhythmic and repetitious patterning of images, objects, sounds, and music whose modes can be "ritualistic," "mantric," or "mechanical." All these devices and modes are mobilized in a "concentrated" effort—to keep hold of a memory that keeps threatening to slip away and vanish.

We certainly see this mnemonic aesthetic in Cornell and Quick-

Time "memory boxes." What Ratcliff observes in Cornell's work can be also observed in QuickTime. The artist, we are told, "is drawn to material facts—objects and images—whose preciousness is ratified by memory and he often calls on popular memory to reinforce his own. His image-chains often run along lines of well-worn cliché—butterfly, swan, ballerina."[46] His boxes also contain and, through repetition, make mysterious the most common of objects: a row of wine glasses, a field of thimbles, a series of cork balls or pharmacy vials. Nonetheless, although the seriality and the idea of repetition is "central to Cornell's *oeuvre*," this is "not the intellectualized notion of serialization, but more like the ritualized repetition of the alchemist."[47] Indeed, as Ratcliff says: "To duplicate an image endlessly is often to make its spell all the more binding."[48] The use of the term "binding" here in relation to duplication and repetition is telling, for it expresses the desire to preserve what escapes preservation, to tie the ephemeral down without undoing its ephemerality; it expresses the desire to remember. Both QuickTime and Cornell memory boxes are thus also highly citational: that is, they don't only attempt to fix personal memories through repetition but also quote and repeat previous artifacts of cultural memory—especially privileging those that speak mnemonically to technologies of reproduction and preservation. Hence, both QuickTime and Cornell memory boxes are deeply involved with the photograph, the postcard, the photocopy, and the printed reproduction of works of art.[49] In addition, the boxes are also marked with great frequency by repeated art historical images that reference the past: well-known paintings, old lithographs, classical statuary.

In QuickTime, to an extraordinary and remarkable degree, sound is also used mnemonically. That is, it marks time in repetitive patterns and, in musical form, is generally less melodic than it is insistently rhythmic. While often voiced (literally) in fragments, it is often also looped, repeating a partial thought, setting up a percussive rhythm of mechanical repetition, scratching or stuck in a temporal sonic groove as if in an old phonograph record, creating a mantra. Indeed, Middle Eastern and Indian music are used to a striking degree—particularly given the often unrelated cultural imagery being remembered.

The boxes, then, use repetition and rhythm in their attempts to grasp and preserve the ephemeral fragments and fragile relics of memory. They construct mnemonic rituals of remembering and, as

Ratcliff notes, ritual is mechanical, so any ritualizing aesthetic must have the power to mechanize the artist's meanings.[50] This mechanization is particularly compelling in QuickTime memory boxes — for along with the ritualized repetition of the alchemist that marks Cornell's work, the QuickTime boxes also convey the intellectualized notion of serialization. That is, duplication and repetition as ritualized in QuickTime "memory boxes" often seem much more "mechanical" than "alchemical." Indeed, duplication and repetition in QuickTime derive much of their poetic power from mimesis: the boxes duplicate and repeat their "memory fragments" as figural repetitions of the functional capacities of the computer itself to "duplicate," "copy," and "paste." Here, the mnemonic aesthetic emerges not only from a desire to preserve scarce and rare memory but also from the ritualized and routinized (or "mechanical") capacity of the computer to do the same. In *Two Marks Jump* (1993), for example, serial images are stutteringly animated, as duplicated and endlessly looped images of two "Marks" leap into and out of a scene accompanied by a similarly looped and endless yell; here the titular description of "two" Marks is belied by the rote duplication of an infinite series. Another example, *Hommage à Magritte* by Lisa Osta (1993), may "alchemically" duplicate and transform the artist's emblematic bowler hats, but also "mechanically" animate his famous painting *Golconde*, in which dozens of indistinguishable little bourgeois men in similar hats rain down on a sterile townscape. In QuickTime "memory boxes," mechanical serialization and mnemonic repetition often combine — each "encouraging" the other to keep in mind — to recollect and represent the ephemera of memory that would otherwise disappear from view.

Time, Movement, and the "Illusion of Life"

Thus we find that the disjunctions of temporality traced here create the space for nostalgia's eruption. — SUSAN STEWART, *On Longing*

The miniature encourages the phenomenological experience of intensity, interiority, and material preciousness by virtue of its compression and condensation of data in space. But the miniature also affects our sense of time. As Stewart points out, there is "a phenomenological correlation between *the experience of scale* and the *ex-*

perience of duration."[51] That is, time also compresses and condenses in the miniature: it "thickens" in significance and implodes. Constrained or "nested" in small spaces, time is reflexive: it falls back upon itself and "encrusts," building up into the "weight" of a generalized past, or it collapses under its own weight, diffusing the present into an ahistorical and "infinitely deep" state of reverie. Thus, as Stewart says, "the miniature does not attach itself to lived historical time. Unlike the metonymic world of realism, . . . the metaphoric world of the miniature makes everyday life absolute anterior and exterior to itself."[52] Furthermore, unlike in "real-time" and "live-action" cinema, our sense of temporality as we engage the miniature never "streams" toward the future (and this is so even when movement is involved). Temporal compression and condensation conflict with forward movement and "lifelike" animation. As a result, "the miniature always tends toward *tableau* rather than toward narrative, toward silence and spatial boundaries rather than towards expository closure."[53] Fragments and bits and traces of past experience exist "now" in our sight and reverie, not only evocative but also *emblematic* of irrecoverable "originary" moments of wholeness. These broken and poignant units of time are silent (or, put in motion, they stutter), but their static and tableaulike presence points both to the passage of everyday "life" from particularity into allegory and to the great temporal mysteries of matter's slow and inexorable emergence and extinction. (In this regard, we might remember the tendency of the "memory box" to figure and often make thematic cosmological imagery suggesting not human temporality but the imperceptible dynamics and perspective of *longue durée*: an "almost immobile history" written not in human events, but in the cosmic temporality of geologic or climatic transformation.)[54]

There is, then, an extraordinary obfuscation (and questionable utopianism) in the nomination "QuickTime." QuickTime is anything but quick: its animations are forestalled, its "illusion of life" incomplete. Compressing and condensing its imagery in a "miniature" number of bits of digital memory and display space, the material conditions that inform QuickTime's miniature "memory boxes" are literally dramatized in the "half-life" of its objects. Not only are these objects constituted as "fragments," in space they are also "fragmented" in temporality and motion. Thus, even when they take human form, the animated "subjects" of QuickTime are experienced as partially discontinuous and without agency. Phenomenologically, their movement is seen as imposed from "without" rather than as emerging intentionally from "within." At best, like the puppet Pinocchio, they struggle against their existence as mere "kinetic objects," in frustrated fits and starts stuttering out the desire to become a "real boy"—that is, fully alive in the temporal continuity and spatial coherence of intentional and realized action.

My evocation of Pinocchio here is hardly coincidental to the temporal and spatial qualities of both the miniature and the "memory box." The way in which both together transform time and space and thus question the nature of human animation and agency seems to call up both puppets and theater, "subjects" whose lives are directed from without and a space that miniaturizes, condenses, and foregrounds the "illusion" of life. Indeed, in both QuickTime and Cornell "memory boxes" the "theatrical stage is evoked," particularly "children's puppet theaters with cutout cardboard scenery."[55] Central also here is *intermittent motion*: time and action broken into fragments, foregrounding gaps and the laborious struggle to "become" really human or "real" cinema. In this regard, Pinocchio's bildungsroman of self-realization is countered with the oxymoronic miniaturization and intermittencies that undo cinema *within* cinema in the uncanny films of Svankmajer and the Brothers Quay. Indeed, Cornell's own forays into filmmaking were meant to undo "live-action" and "real-time": he insisted that his *Rose Hobart*—shot at sound speed (24 fps) and using fragments of a 1931 sound melodrama (*East of Borneo*)—be projected at silent speed (16 to 18 fps) to the accompaniment of scratchy phonograph recordings.[56] In Cornell and QuickTime "memory boxes," intermittent motion is always more than merely mechanical: it also articulates the temporal and existential conundrum of *discontinuity*. Thus, in Cornell's kinetic constructions such as his "sand fountains," Fenton tells us that "the sand was deliberately mixed with some larger impurities, so that the flow was supposed to be somewhat discontinuous rather than like an egg timer."[57] And a QuickTime work like Victoria Duckett's *Self Portrait*, which shows a naked little girl running—but not—over a background of repetitious forms, merely figures and foregrounds the discontinuity informing both QuickTime and the medium where the selected fragment and the digital bit are animated discretely, discontinuously, in "tableau" time.

In sum, movement in time in both Cornell and QuickTime "memory boxes" becomes emblematic as it condenses and compresses "momentum" into a series of reified and frozen "moments." The effortless and continuous animation of "life" becomes temporally solidified in what we might call a kinetic "souvenir": a memory of motion that is now merely its token. Connecting the souvenir with the disjuncture between the past and present, Stewart tells us that it "speaks to a context of origin through a language of longing" and arises "out of the necessarily insatiable demands of nostalgia." That is, "the souvenir generates a narrative which reaches only 'behind,' spiraling in a continually inward movement rather than outward toward the future."[58] Both QuickTime and Cornell boxes are, in the end, always engaged as souvenirs.

It is worth noting—even as we know that Pinocchio became a "real boy" and that QuickTime will eventually and seamlessly "stream" into "live-action"—that, as Stewart suggests, the "point of desire which the nostalgic seeks is in fact the absence that is the very generating mechanism of desire."[59] Both Cornell and QuickTime boxes mobilize memory and desire through an *aesthetics of absence*: a privileging of the poetically and philosophically charged gap between a present artifact and the past experience of which it is only a fragment. Call me retrograde: as the "gap" closes and QuickTime enlarges and quickens, I feel nostalgia at the impending loss of a unique historical experience and a rare and miniature digital object.

Notes

This essay first appeared in *Millennium Film Journal* 34 (fall 1999): 4–23.

1 For a sense of the strange contents and associational logic of the Museum of Jurassic Technology, see Lawrence Weschler, *Mr. Wilson's Cabinet of Wonder* (New York: Pantheon, 1995). On the *Wunderkammer* (and *Kunstkammer*), see Anthony Grafton, "Believe It or Not," *New York Review of Books* (5 November 1998): 14–18. In particular, the relation of the *Wunderkammer* to Joseph Cornell's work is illuminated in James Fenton, "Monuments to Every Moment," *New York Review of Books* (14 August 1997): 28–31.

2 Cornell, of course, made several "movies," although they aesthetically share more with his own assemblages and boxes than they do with cinema. In this regard, they also presage common aesthetic elements of QuickTime "movies." Annette Michelson, in her seminal essay, "*Rose Hobart* and *Monsieur Phot*: Early Films from Utopia Parkway," *Artforum* 11, no. 10 (June 1973): 47–57, lists twelve characteris-

tics of Cornell's work, ten of which are also characteristic of Quick-Time "movies," including affirmative use of the frame; use of found materials; assemblage or montage as the organizing principle; play with and variation on scale; the implication of temporal flow and its arrest; narrative tension; rhythmic use of compositional elements; repetition and variation; the use of color to make space ambient; and the use of other artworks as material (54).

3 While electronic depth can be figured on a horizontal plane as in cinema, I would argue that our basic experience of depth relative to the computer screen is vertical. Depth emerges in a sense of "layers": that is, as with collage or the "desktop," objects are generally perceived not "in front of" or "behind" each other as in cinema, but "on top of" or "under" each other.

4 Kynaston McShine, "Introducing Mr. Cornell," in *Joseph Cornell*, ed. Kynaston McShine (New York: Museum of Modern Art, 1980), 10–11.

5 Ibid., 9.

6 The phrase here, as well as thoughts about the animated film's struggle to achieve—and to *not* achieve—are derived from Alan Cholodenko, ed., *The Illusion of Life: Essays on Animation* (Sydney: Australian Film Commission/Power Publications, 1991).

7 This "rumor" was passed on to me by animation scholar Norman Klein. True or not, I thank him for it.

8 See Lev Manovich, *The Language of New Media* (Cambridge: MIT Press, 2001). For Manovich, the three "key cultural forms which are shaping cultural interfaces" are cinema, the printed word, and a "general-purpose human-computer interface" (the latter referring to principles and visualizations—like the "desk top"—that involve "direct manipulation of objects on the screen, overlapping windows, iconic representation, and dynamic menus" (69–93). It is important to note that despite his emphasis on the primary relation of cinema to digital media, Manovich's own "little [digital] movies" provide a gloss on and interrogate the cinema as a cultural interface for digital media. See his home page: http://jupiter.ucsd.edu/~manovich/home.html.

9 "Introduction to QuickTime," developer documentation for Quick-Time 3, Apple Computer, Inc., 1997, n.p. Web access to documentation is at http://developer.apple.com/techpubs/quicktime/qtdevdocs/RM/rmQToverview.htm.

10 André Bazin, "The Myth of Total Cinema," in *What Is Cinema?*, trans. Hugh Gray (Berkeley: University of California Press, 1964), 17 (emphasis mine), 20, 22.

11 Manovich describes the computer as "a universal media machine," an apt description insofar as it is able to translate various media

through digitization of those media. However, this very digitization constitutes another and a new *medium*: a metamedium, perhaps, but a medium nonetheless.

12 "QuickTime Concepts," developer documentation for QuickTime 3, Apple Computer, Inc., 1997, n.p. (emphasis mine).

13 Gaston Bachelard, *The Poetics of Space*, trans. Maria Jolas (Boston: Beacon Press, 1964), 77.

14 This said, there is certainly also a "phenomenology of discomfort" afforded by the "file cabinet" and the "database": a phenomenology that is associated with the inhuman "literal-mindedness" of the computer's techno-logic and the bureaucratic imperatives and constraints that go against the grain of the lived-experience of human work and communicative practices (in which I sometimes "file" things in an "illogical" way and then often can't find them).

15 Dawn Ades, "The Transcendental Surrealism of Joseph Cornell," in McShine, ed., *Joseph Cornell*, 33.

16 Carter Ratcliff, "Joseph Cornell: Mechanic to the Ineffable," in McShine, ed., *Joseph Cornell*, 43.

17 Ibid., 59. One might well read this production of nostalgia as tied to the bourgeois culture of consumerism and the antiquarianism that surrounds the collection and the souvenir; for such an argument, see Susan Stewart, *On Longing: Narratives of the Miniature, the Gigantic, the Souvenir, the Collection* (Baltimore: Johns Hopkins University Press, 1984).

18 Fenton, "Monuments to Every Moment," 30.

19 Ratcliff, "Joseph Cornell," 43.

20 Grafton, "Believe It or Not," 16.

21 Bachelard, *Poetics of Space*, 82.

22 Ratcliff, "Joseph Cornell," 60.

23 Ibid., 43.

24 Bachelard, *Poetics of Space*, 201.

25 *Little Movies: Prolegomena for Digital Cinema, 1994–1997* can be accessed on the Web at http://jupiter.ucsd.edu/~manovich/little-movies/. This "classic" cinematic imagery (and, in the last example, sound) includes material from the Lumiéres' *Train Arriving at Ciotat Station* and *Workers Leaving the Lumiére Factory*; Georges Méliès's *A Trip to the Moon*; and Alfred Hitchcock's *Psycho*.

26 "Introduction to QuickTime," explains: "Image data requires a large amount of storage space. Storing a single 640-by-480 pixel image in 32-bit color can require as much as 1.2 MB. . . . Consequently, minimizing the storage requirements for image data is an important consideration for any application that works with images and sequences of images. The Image Compression Manager provides your application with an interface for compressing and decompressing images

and sequences of images. . . . It takes a large file and makes it smaller, hence requiring less hard disk space to save it, less memory to run it, or less bandwidth to play it over the Internet" (n.p.).

27 The six are titled as follows (with file size in brackets): (1) "Binary Code" [2.2M]; (2) "On the Ephemeral Nature of Little Movies" [3.3M]; (3) "A Single Pixel Movie" [2.0M]; (4) "Classical Cinema I" [1.1M]; (5) "Classical Cinema II" [1.3M]; (6) "On the Transient Nature of an Elusive Image" [2.6M]. Affirming the pervasiveness of "cinema" as "cultural interface" to the computer, it is worth noting that Manovich is using a compressor sold under the name of "Cinepak."

28 Bachelard, *Poetics of Space*, 150 (emphasis mine).

29 Stewart, *On Longing*, 44.

30 Bachelard, *Poetics of Space*, 163.

31 Ibid., 215.

32 This refers to Jack Arnold's 1957 science fiction film that concerns a man, Scott Carey who literally is shrinking. By the film's end he is infinitesimally small but still exists and "matters" in the universe. At one point he narrates his realization that "in the mind of God, there is no zero."

33 Stewart, *On Longing*, 54.

34 Ibid., 65.

35 Ibid., 61.

36 McShine, "Introducing Mr. Cornell," 10–11.

37 Stewart, *On Longing*, 65 (emphasis mine).

38 This is from a work titled *Flight from Intention* by Victoria Duckett, made in the Laboratory for New Media in the Department of Film and Television at UCLA (for information, contact http://pixels.filmtv.ucla.edu/).

39 Ades, "Transcendental Surrealism," 26.

40 Bachelard, *Poetics of Space*, 228.

41 Ibid., 86.

42 This poetic connection of miniaturization with "uniqueness" and "fragility" has its material basis in the very hardware of digital technology. See Alexander Stille, "Overload," *New Yorker* (8 March 1999): 38–44. Stille quotes Charles Mayne, head of the laboratory for the Department of Special Media Preservation in the National Archives on the latest digital audiotape: "People love these things because they are so small, compact, and lightweight, and can store tons of data, but as larger and larger amounts of data are crammed into smaller and smaller spaces the technology gets more precise, more complex, and therefore more fragile. We have a lot of these tapes from the late nineteen-eighties that can't be played at all" (42). And, in relation to storage and "preservation," Stille points out, "the extreme precision of the new miniaturization technologies is such that

each machine produces tapes that are *unintentionally customized* to a particular alignment of the laser beams that encode and read information"; that is, as a specialist tells him, "a slight misalignment of the head is sufficient to guarantee that you will never read the tape except on a machine that has the same misalignment" (44; emphasis mine). Paradoxically, the process of miniaturizing technologies of reproduction and preservation leads to an opposite result: singularity, fragility, and loss.

43 See Bachelard, *Poetics of Space*, 84.
44 McShine, "Introducing Mr. Cornell," 10–11.
45 Stewart, *On Longing*, 145 (emphasis mine).
46 Ratcliff, "Joseph Cornell," 54.
47 Dore Ashton, quoted in Ratcliff, "Introducing Mr. Cornell," 57.
48 Ratcliff, "Joseph Cornell," 64.
49 McShine, "Introducing Mr. Cornell," 13.
50 Ratcliff, "Joseph Cornell," 58.
51 Stewart, *On Longing*, 66 (emphasis mine).
52 Ibid., 65.
53 Ibid., 66 (emphasis mine).
54 The concept and study of *longue durée* as a historical form is connected to Fernand Braudel, Emmanuel Le Roy Ladurie, and other historians of the *Annales* school. See Jacques LeGoff, *History and Memory*, trans. Steven Rendell and Elizabeth Claman (New York: Columbia University Press, 1992), xxi–xxiii.
55 Ades, "Transcendental Surrealism," 27.
56 For key discussions of Cornell's films, see Michelson, "*Rose Hobart* and *Monsieur Phot*," 47–57, and P. Adams Sitney, "The Cinematic Gaze of Joseph Cornell, in McShine, ed., *Joseph Cornell*, 69–89.
57 Fenton, "Monuments to Every Moment," 30.
58 Stewart, *On Longing*, 125.
59 Ibid., 24.

SELECTED BIBLIOGRAPHY

Aarseth, Espen J. *Cybertext: Perspectives on Ergodic Literature*. Baltimore: Johns Hopkins University Press, 1997.

Balsamo, Anne Marie. *Technologies of the Gendered Body: Reading Cyborg Women*. Durham: Duke University Press, 1996.

Barney, Darin. *Prometheus Wired: The Hope for Democracy in the Age of Network Technology*. Chicago: University of Chicago Press, 2000.

Barthes, Roland. *Camera Lucida: Reflections on Photography*. Trans. Richard Howard. New York: Hill and Wang, 1981.

Beniger, James R. *The Control Revolution: Technological and Economic Origins of the Information Society*. Cambridge: Harvard University Press, 1986.

Benjamin, Walter. "The Work of Art in the Age of Mechanical Reproduction." In *Illuminations*, ed. Hannah Arendt, trans. Harry Zohn. New York: Schocken Books, 1968.

Birkerts, Sven. *The Gutenberg Elegies: The Fate of Reading in an Electronic Culture*. Winchester, Mass.: Faber and Faber, 1994.

Bolter, J. David. *Writing Space: The Computer, Hypertext, and the History of Writing*. Hillsdale, N.J.: L. Erlbaum Associates, 1991.

Bolter, J. David, and Richard Grusin. *Remediation: Understanding New Media*. Cambridge: MIT Press, 1999.

Braun, Marta, and Etienne-Jules Marey. *Picturing Time: The Work of Etienne-Jules Marey (1830–1904)*. Chicago: University of Chicago Press, 1992.

Brown, John Seely, and Paul Duguid. *The Social Life of Information*. Boston: Harvard Business School Press, 2000.

Bukatman, Scott. *Terminal Identity: The Virtual Subject in Postmodern Science Fiction*. Durham: Duke University Press, 1993.

Burch, Noel. *Life to Those Shadows*. Trans. Ben Brewster. Berkeley: University of California Press, 1990.

Bush, Vannevar. "As We May Think." *Atlantic Monthly* (July 1945): 101–8.

Caldwell, John Thornton, ed. *Electronic Media and Technoculture*. New Brunswick: Rutgers University Press, 2000.

Carey, James W. *Communication as Culture: Essays on Media and Society, Media and Popular Culture*. Boston: Unwin Hyman, 1989.

Cartwright, Lisa. *Screening the Body: Tracing Medicine's Visual Culture*. Minneapolis: University of Minnesota Press, 1995.

Case, Sue-Ellen. *The Domain-Matrix: Performing Lesbian at the End of Print Culture*. Bloomington: Indiana University Press, 1997.

Casetti, Francesco. *Inside the Gaze: The Fiction Film and Its Spectator*. Trans. Nell Andrew and Charles O'Brien. Bloomington: Indiana University Press, 1998.

Crary, Jonathan. *Suspensions of Perception: Attention, Spectacle, and Modern Culture*. Cambridge: MIT Press, 1999.

———. *Techniques of the Observer: On Vision and Modernity in the Nineteenth Century*. Cambridge: MIT Press, 1990.

Crary, Jonathan, and Sanford Kwinter. *Incorporations*. New York: Zone Books, 1992.

Damasio, Antonio. *Descartes's Error: Emotion, Reason, and the Human Brain*. New York: G. P. Putnam, 1994.

Dreyfus, Hubert L. *On the Internet: Thinking in Action*. London: Routledge, 2001.

Druckrey, Timothy, ed. *Ars Electronica: Facing the Future: A Survey of Two Decades*. Cambridge: MIT Press, 1999.

———, ed. *Electronic Culture: Technology and Visual Representation*. New York: Aperture, 1996.

Edwards, Paul N. *The Closed World: Computers and the Politics of Discourse in Cold War America*. Cambridge: MIT Press, 1996.

Foster, Thomas, Carol Siegel, and Elle E. Berry, eds. *Bodies of Writing, Bodies in Performance*. New York: New York University Press, 1996.

Foucault, Michel. *The Birth of the Clinic: An Archaeology of Medical Perception*. Trans. A. M. Sheridan Smith. New York: Pantheon Books, 1973.

———. *Discipline and Punish: The Birth of the Prison*. Trans. Alan Sheridan. New York: Pantheon Books, 1977.

Gitelman, Lisa. *Scripts, Grooves, and Writing Machines: Representing Technology in the Edison Era*. Stanford: Stanford University Press, 1999.

Grosz, Elizabeth. *Volatile Bodies: Toward a Corporeal Feminism*. Baltimore: Johns Hopkins University Press, 1994.

Hague, Barry N., and Brian Loader, eds. *Digital Democracy: Discourse and Decision Making in the Information Age*. New York: Routledge, 1999.

Hayles, N. Katherine. *How We Became Posthuman: Virtual Bodies in Cybernetics, Literature, and Informatics*. Chicago: University of Chicago Press, 1999.

Heidegger, Martin. "The Question Concerning Technology." In *Basic

Writings, ed. David Farrell Krell. San Francisco: Harper Collins, 1977.

Herman, Andrew, and Thomas Swiss, eds. *The World Wide Web and Contemporary Cultural Theory*. New York: Routledge, 2000.

Joyce, Michael. *Of Two Minds: Hypertext Pedagogy and Poetics, Studies in Literature and Science*. Ann Arbor: University of Michigan Press, 1995.

———. *Othermindedness: The Emergence of Network Culture, Studies in Literature and Science*. Ann Arbor: University of Michigan Press, 2000.

Kevles, Bettyann. *Naked to the Bone: Medical Imaging in the Twentieth Century*. New Brunswick: Rutgers University Press, 1997.

Kirby, Lynn. *Parallel Tracks: The Railroad and Silent Cinema*. Durham: Duke University Press, 1997.

Kittler, Friedrich A. *Discourse Networks 1800/1900*. Stanford: Stanford University Press, 1990.

———. *Gramophone, Film, Typewriter: Writing Science*. Stanford: Stanford University Press, 1999.

Landow, George P. *Hyper/Text/Theory*. Baltimore: Johns Hopkins University Press, 1994.

———. *Hypertext 2.0*. Rev. ed. Baltimore: Johns Hopkins University Press, 1997.

Lenoir, Timothy, ed. *Inscribing Science: Scientific Texts and the Materiality of Communication*. Stanford: Stanford University Press, 1998.

Lunenfeld, Peter. *The Digital Dialectic: New Essays on New Media*. Cambridge: MIT Press, 1999.

Manovich, Lev. *The Language of New Media*. Cambridge: MIT Press, 2001.

McGann. Jerome. *The Textual Condition*. Princeton: Princeton University Press, 1991.

McKenzie. D. G. *Bibliography and the Sociology of Texts*. 1986. Cambridge: Cambridge University Press, 1999.

McLuhan, Marshall. *The Gutenberg Galaxy: The Making of Typographic Man*. Toronto: University of Toronto Press, 1962.

———. *The Medium Is the Massage*. New York: Random House, 1967.

———. *Understanding Media: The Extensions of Man*. New York: New American Library, 1964.

Mitchell, W. J. T. *Picture Theory: Essays on Verbal and Visual Representation*. Chicago: University of Chicago Press, 1994.

Moravec, Hans. *Mind Children: The Future of Robot and Human Intelligence*. Cambridge: Harvard University Press, 1988.

Ong, Walter J. *Orality and Literacy: The Technologizing of the Word*. London: Methuen, 1982.

Peters, John Durham. *Speaking into the Air: A History of the Idea of Communication*. Chicago: University of Chicago Press, 1999.

Plant, Sadie. *Zeros and Ones: Digital Women and the New Technoculture*. New York: Doubleday, 1997.

Poster, Mark. *What's the Matter with the Internet?* Minneapolis: University of Minnesota Press, 2001.

Ricour, Paul. *Freud and Philosophy: An Essay on Interpretation*. New Haven: Yale University Press, 1970.

Ronell, Avital. *The Telephone Book: Technology—Schizophrenia—Electric Speech*. Lincoln: University of Nebraska Press, 1989.

Rosenzweig, Roy. "Wizards, Bureaucrats, Warriors, and Hackers: Writing the History of the Internet." *American Historical Review* 103, no. 5 (December 1998): 1530–52.

Rydell, Robert W. *All the World's a Fair: Visions of Empire at American International Expositions, 1876–1916*. Chicago: University of Chicago Press, 1984.

Schivelbusch, Wolfgang. *The Railway Journey: Trains and Travel in the Nineteenth Century*. Trans. Anselm Hollo. New York: Urizen, 1977.

Smith, Crosbie, and M. Norton Wise. *Energy and Empire: A Biographical Study of Lord Kelvin*. Cambridge: Cambridge University Press, 1989.

Stafford, Barbara Maria. *Artful Science: Enlightenment, Entertainment, and the Eclipse of Visual Education*. Cambridge: MIT Press, 1994.

———. *Body Criticism: Imaging the Unseen in Enlightenment Art and Medicine*. Cambridge: MIT Press, 1991.

———. *Good Looking: Essays on the Virtue of Images*. Cambridge: MIT Press, 1996.

———. *Visual Analogy: Consciousness as the Art of Connecting*. Cambridge: MIT Press, 1999.

Stewart, Garrett. *Between Film and Screen: Modernism's Photo Synthesis*. Chicago: University of Chicago Press, 1999.

Stewart, Susan. *On Longing: Narratives of the Miniature, the Gigantic, the Souvenir, the Collection*. Baltimore: Johns Hopkins University Press, 1984.

Stone, Allucquère Roseanne. *The War of Technology and Desire at the Close of the Mechanical Age*. Cambridge: MIT Press, 1996.

Trend, David, ed. *Reading Digital Culture*. Malden, Eng.: Blackwell Publishers, 2001.

Turing, Alan M. "Computing Machinery and Intelligence." *Mind* 59 (1950): 433–60.

Virilio, Paul. *War and Cinema: The Logistics of Perception*. London: Verso, 1989.

Welch, Kathleen E. *Electric Rhetoric: Classical Rhetoric, Oralism, and a New Literacy*. Cambridge: MIT Press, 1999.

Wiener, Norbert. *Cybernetics; or, Control and Communication in the Animal and the Machine*. Cambridge, Mass.: Technology Press, 1948.

———. *The Human Use of Human Beings; Cybernetics and Society*. Boston: Houghton Mifflin, 1950.

CONTRIBUTORS

JUDITH BABBITTS teaches American and Asian history at the University of Maryland University College. She is completing a book on the emergence of visual culture in the United States in the early twentieth century.

SCOTT CURTIS is Assistant Professor of Radio/Television/Film at Northwestern University. He has published on a wide range of topics, including animation, Alfred Hitchcock, and early cinema. A former medical photographer, he is currently writing a book on the relation between science, medicine, and the moving image.

RONALD E. DAY is Assistant Professor at the Library and Information Science Program, Wayne State University. He is the author of *The Modern Invention of Information: Discourse, History, and Power* (2001) and numerous articles, many of which can be found in the *Journal of the American Society for Information Science*.

DAVID DEPEW is Professor of Communication Studies and Rhetoric of Inquiry at the University of Iowa. He is coauthor, with Bruce H. Weber, of *Darwinism Evolving: Systems Dynamics and the Genealogy of Natural Selection* (1996), as well as author of many papers in the history, philosophy, and rhetoric of the life sciences.

ABRAHAM GEIL is a Ph.D. student in the Department of American Studies at the University of Iowa.

SHARON GHAMARI-TABRIZI is an independent historian of science and technology with a special interest in military modeling and simulation.

She is working on a book titled "The Intuitive Science of the Unthinkable: Herman Kahn, RAND, and Thermonuclear War."

LISA GITELMAN is Assistant Professor of Media Studies at Catholic University. She is the author of *Scripts, Grooves, and Writing Machines: Representing Technology in the Edison Era* (1999) and coeditor of *New Media, 1740–1914* (2002).

N. KATHERINE HAYLES, Professor of English and Media Arts/Design at the University of California at Los Angeles, teaches and writes on relations of literature, science, and technology in the twentieth century. Her book *How We Became Posthuman: Virtual Bodies in Cybernetics, Literature, and Informatics* won the Rene Wellek Prize for the best book in literary theory for 1998–99. Her most recent book is *Writing Machines* (2002).

JOHN DURHAM PETERS is Wendell F. Miller Distinguished Professor of Communication Studies at the University of Iowa. Author of *Speaking into the Air: A History of the Idea of Communication* (1999), he has held fellowships from the NEH, Fulbright Foundation, and the Leverhulme Trust. He is currently working on books on the problem of public and private, and on the deep history of acoustic and optical media technologies.

LAUREN RABINOVITZ is Chair of the American Studies Department and Professor of American Studies and Cinema at the University of Iowa. Her most recent book is *For the Love of Pleasure: Women, Movie, and Culture in Turn-of-the-Century Chicago* (1998). She is currently completing "Yesteryear's Wonderlands: Introducing Modernism to America," an NEH-sponsored educational developmental project in multimedia software.

LAURA RIGAL is Associate Professor in English and American Studies at the University of Iowa. She is the author of *The American Manufactory: Art, Labor, and the World of Things in the Early Republic* (1998). She has published articles in *American Literary History*, *Theatre Journal*, *Huntington Quarterly*, and *Commonplace: An Interactive Journal of American History and Culture*. Her work on Franklin's electricity is part of a larger project titled *The Digital State: Republican Technology in the Age of Information*.

VIVIAN SOBCHACK is Associate Dean and Professor in the Department of Film, Television, and Digital Media at the UCLA School of Theater, Film, and Television. Her work focuses on film theory and its intersections with philosophy and cultural studies, genre studies of American film, and studies of electronic imaging. She is author of *Screening Space: The American Science Fiction Film* (1997) and *The Address of the Eye: A Phenomenology of Film Experience* (1992), and she has edited two anthologies: *Meta-Morphing: Visual Transformation and the Culture of Quick Change* (2000) and *The Persistence of History: Cinema, Television and the Modern Event* (1996). Currently, she is completing a volume of her own essays called, "Carnal Thoughts: Bodies, Texts, Scenes, and Screen."

THOMAS SWISS is Professor of English and Rhetoric of Inquiry at the University of Iowa. He is the author of two collections of poems: *Rough Cut* (1997) and *Measure* (1986). He is the coeditor of a number of books, including *Mapping the Beat: Cultural Theory and Pop Music* (1997) and *The World Wide Web and Contemporary Cultural Theory: Magic, Metaphor, and Power* (2000).

INDEX

Department of Defense, 10, 151, 156; "Operations Other than War," 154; simulation technology budget for, 153; University of Southern California and, 163. *See also* Pentagon

de Rimini, Francesca, 299

Dewey, John, 140

Dewey, Melvil, 81

Digital literature. *See* New Media

Disappearing Rain. See Larsen, Deena

Distributed cognition, 265

DNA, 49, 61, 63, 257

Droysen, Johann Gustav, 223, 239

Druckrey, Timothy, 5

Duchamp, Marcel, 284

Duckett, Victoria: *Self Portrait*, 324

DuMoncel, Théodore, 189

Eastgate Systems, 286, 288, 294, 298

Edison, Thomas Alva, 177, 180, 186, 187–93; hearing loss of, 191; Helmholtz compared to, 180; sound recording and, 187–90; "spot film" technique of, 239; tone tests of, 189

Electricity. *See* Franklin, Benjamin

Electronic Literature Organization, 297–98

Electronic Poetry Center, 297

Electronic writing. *See* New Media

Eliot, T. S., 234, 271; fictional film adaptation of *The Waste Land*, 271, 273, 274

Elmer, Greg, 298

Embodiment, 257, 258. *See also* Body

Enlightenment: digital culture and, 7–8; digital technology and, 40; information and, 36; print culture and, 34, 36; subjectivity and, 7–8, 103; world clock of, 35

Federalist political theory, 39

Feedback. *See* Cybernetics

Fielding, Raymond, 105

Figlio, Karl, 230

Final Flurry, 160, 161

Finitude, 178; media and, 194; of sense organs, 187

Fluoroscope, 239

Fortner, Hans, 244

Foster, Hal, 283–84

Foucault, Michel, 222, 226, 228–29; *Birth of the Clinic*, 222, 226, 229; on death, 230–32, 238; *Discipline and Punish*, 228; on "the medical gaze," 229–34

Franklin, Benjamin, 23–40; Peter Collinson and, 26, 29, 30, 38; electricity and, 23–40; experiments on bodies by, 24, 29–33; experiments on books by, 34–39; the erotic and, 31–32; J. C. Heilbron on, 39; Leyden jar and, 29, 32, 34, 36, 38; lightning rod and, 23; *New Experiments and Observations on Electricity*, 24–40; Thomas Penn and, 29; Joseph Priestly on, 33, 34–39; scientific print culture and, 34, 36; Seven Years' War and, 28; *Tatler* and, 31–32

Freud, Sigmund, 192, 223

Gadamer, Hans-Georg, 90

Gender, digital media and, 258

Gentleman's Magazine (London), 26, 30

Gesell, Arnold, 244

Gifford, Fred, 106, 108

Gilbert, Walter, 49–50

Ginzburg, Carlo, 224

Gitelman, Lisa, 287

Godard, Jean-Luc, 235

Graphic recording instruments, 178–79

Great Train Robbery, The, 109

Motion simulation rides, 116–121. See also *Hale's Tours and Scenes of the World*
Moulthrop, Stuart, 258, 265–78, 286, 293, 294, 295, 301 n.10; *Reagan Library*, 258, 260, 265–78, 279
MP3 files, 200, 214
Müller, Johannes, 181
Museum of Jurassic History, 306
Music rolls. *See* Piano rolls
Muybridge, Eadweard, 237, 307

National Institutes for Health, 11, 61
National Science Foundation, 8
New Media, 257–80, 283–300; electronic publishing, 285–86; electronic writing, 285, 286, 287, 296; literary community in, 293–98, 303 n.37; and literary culture, 285; literary prizes for, 298; *lume*, 296; synonyms for, 301 n.7; Web-based poetry, 283, 284. *See also* Eastgate Systems; Hypertext
Newton, Isaac, 24, 52, 232

Obermann Center for Advanced Studies, 13
Omnimax, 102, 105
Osta, Lisa: *Hommage á Magritte*, 322
Otlet, Paul, 76, 77, 79–83, 87, 90; *Monde*, 82; Répetoire Bioliographique Universal (world bibliography) and, 80; *Traité de documentation*, 79; universal decimal classification and, 81; World Congress on Universal Documentation and, 81; world peace and, 80

Paramount Digital Entertainment, 160, 169; and *StoryDrive*, 161, 162, 167

Patchwork Girl. See Jackson, Shelley
Pavlov, Ivan Petrovich, 243
Peirce, Charles Sanders, 193–94
Pentagon, 151, 156, 158; and Distributed Mission Training, 156; and field exercises, 154; Hollywood and, 150–69. *See also* Department of Defense
Perloff, Marjorie, 292
Perriault, Jacques, 194
Philadelphia, 27, 28, 31
Phonograph, 177–79, 185, 187–90, 191, 193, 194, 202; cultural consequences of, 188–90; philosophy of, 188; public demonstrations of, 189–90, 191–92. *See also* Edison, Thomas Alva
Phonograph records, 200–203
Photography, 221, 235, 236–38, 246
Physics, ballistics and, 48
Physiology, science of, 178–79, 182. *See also* Helmholtz, Hermann von
Piano rolls, 200, 201, 202, 205, 213; as analog vs. digital medium, 211; companies producing, 209; compared to sheet music, 203, 204, 210, 214; material meanings of, 203–4; as "word rolls," 209–10
Pianos, 205, 208, 215 n.11. *See also* Player piano
Plant, The, 285
Plato, 232; *Phaedrus*, 177–78, 193
Player piano, 201, 202, 204, 205–9
Player Piano, 207, 208
Pollack, Neal, 291–92
Positivism, 76–77, 79
Poster, Mark, 6
Postmodern Culture, 295
Priestly, Joseph, 33
Prigogine, Ilya, 58–59
Print culture, 34, 36, 277, 279–80

U.S. Copyright Act of 1909, 201, 213

U.S. Supreme Court, 201, 211

Vesalius, 225–26

Vico, Giambattista, 47

Virilio, Paul, 113–14

Virtual reality: in military training simulations, 150–69; and narrative, 159; National Research Council report on, 157, 158; player pianos and, 212

Visible Human Project, 226

Voge, Marc, 299

Vogel, Amos, 121

Walt Disney Company, 116, 159

Watson, James, 52, 63, 65; Francis Crick and, 60, 62

Watson, William, 24

Watt, James, 25

Weaver, Warren, 61, 62, 64

Web, the, 267, 287

Weinstein, Michael A., 6

Weisenbaum, Joseph, 268

Wells, H. G., 81

White, Hayden, 165–67, 173 n.53

White-Smith v. Apollo, 199, 201

Whittaker, Alan: on military simulation, 169

Wiener, Norbert, 58, 59, 62, 64; *Cybernetics: Control and Communication in the Animal and the Machine*, 58, 62, 63

World's fairs: Louisiana Purchase Exposition of St. Louis, 106; Expo 67, 101; Expo 70, 101

Wunderkammer, 306, 311, 313–14; Grafton on, 313

X rays, 239, 243, 244

Zeno of Elea, paradoxes of, 234

LIBRARY OF CONGRESS CATALOGING-IN-PUBLICATION DATA

Memory bytes : history, technology, and digital culture / editors, Lauren Rabinovitz and Abraham Geil.

p. cm.

Includes bibliographical references and index.

ISBN 0-8223-3228-0 (alk. paper) — ISBN 0-8223-3241-8 (pbk. : alk. paper)

1. Mass media—Technological innovations. 2. Communication—History. 3. Digital media. I. Rabinovitz, Lauren. II. Geil, Abraham.

P96.T42M45 2004

302.23—dc22 2003015045